RESTORATIVE JUSTICE
An Essential Guide for Research and Practice

Dr. Mark Umbreit is a Professor and founding Director of the Center for Restorative Justice & Peacemaking in the School of Social Work at the University of Minnesota. He is also a Visiting Professor at the Marquette University Law School in Milwaukee. Dr. Umbreit is an internationally recognized researcher, practitioner, and author, having trained thousands of individuals from more than forty countries. As a practitioner, Mark facilitates peacebuilding circles in the community and dialogues between family survivors of homicide and the offender.

Dr. Marilyn Peterson Armour is an Associate Professor and founding Director of the Institute for Restorative Justice and Restorative Dialogue in the School of Social Work at the University of Texas at Austin. Besides her noteworthy research and reputation as teacher and trainer, Dr. Armour has pioneered the use of restorative justice for a variety of social issues including offender re-entry and domestic violence. Dr. Armour is recognized for her outstanding work with family members of homicide victims.

Restorative Justice Dialogue

An Essential Guide for Research and Practice

MARK UMBREIT, PhD
MARILYN PETERSON ARMOUR, PhD

SPRINGER PUBLISHING COMPANY
NEW YORK

Copyright © 2011 Springer Publishing Company

All rights reserved.

No part of this publication may be reproduced, stored in a retrieval system, or transmitted in any form or by any means, electronic, mechanical, photocopying, recording, or otherwise, without the prior permission of Springer Publishing Company, LLC, or authorization through payment of the appropriate fees to the Copyright Clearance Center, Inc., 222 Rosewood Drive, Danvers, MA 01923, 978-750-8400, fax 978-646-8600, info@copyright.com or on the web at www.copyright.com.

Springer Publishing Company, LLC
11 West 42nd Street
New York, NY 10036
www.springerpub.com

Acquisitions Editor: Jennifer Perillo
Project Editor: Peter Rocheleau
Project Manager: Ragavia Ramakrishnan
Cover Design: David Levy
Composition: S4Carlisle Publishing Services

ISBN: 978-0-8261-2258-2
E-book ISBN: 978-0-8261-2259-9

12 13/ 5

The author and the publisher of this Work have made every effort to use sources believed to be reliable to provide information that is accurate and compatible with the standards generally accepted at the time of publication. Because medical science is continually advancing, our knowledge base continues to expand. Therefore, as new information becomes available, changes in procedures become necessary. We recommend that the reader always consult current research and specific institutional policies before performing any clinical procedure. The author and publisher shall not be liable for any special, consequential, or exemplary damages resulting, in whole or in part, from the readers' use of, or reliance on, the information contained in this book. The publisher has no responsibility for the persistence or accuracy of URLs for external or third-party Internet Web sites referred to in this publication and does not guarantee that any content on such Web sites is, or will remain, accurate or appropriate.

Library of Congress Cataloging-in-Publication Data

Umbreit, Mark S., 1949–
  Restorative justice dialogues: an essential guide for research and practice / Mark S. Umbreit, Marilyn Peterson Armour.
      p. cm.
   Includes index.
   ISBN 978-0-8261-2258-2
  1. Restorative justice. 2. Mediation. 3. Victims of crimes. I. Armour, Marilyn Peterson. II. Title.
    HV8688.U527 2010
    364.6—dc22
                                                                    2010021853

Printed in the United States of America by Gasch Printing.

Contents

Foreword by Howard Zehr   vii

Preface   ix

Chapter 1   Restorative Justice as a Social Movement   1

Chapter 2   A Movement Grounded in Core Social Work Values   35

Chapter 3   Spirituality   67

Chapter 4   Restorative Justice Dialogue as Intervention   81

Chapter 5   Victim-Offender Mediation   111

Chapter 6   Family Group Conferencing   143

Chapter 7   Peacemaking Circles   179

Chapter 8   Victim-Offender Dialogue in Crimes of Severe Violence   211

Chapter 9   The Facilitator's Role in Restorative Justice Dialogue   239

Chapter 10   Dimensions of Culture in Restorative Dialogue   265

Chapter 11   Emerging Areas of Practice   291

Index   327

Foreword

In their book *Restorative Justice Dialogue: An Essential Guide for Research and Practice,* Mark Umbreit and Marilyn Armour offer the equivalent of a state-of-the-union address for the restorative justice movement: a comprehensive overview and a stock-taking of the field as it has developed, as it currently exists, and what lies ahead. The timing is excellent.

Thirty years ago restorative justice consisted of a handful of victim-offender dialogue programs in North America and Europe handling primarily property offenses. In 1980, the field did not yet have its name. Today, in 2010, restorative approaches have expanded exponentially, with applications on every continent not only in criminal justice (including crimes of severe violence) but also in schools, the workplace, and in societal-level interventions after mass violence.

In the 1980s when I was writing my book *Changing Lenses: A New Focus for Crime and Justice,* which outlined the concept of and rationale for restorative justice, I expected it to be the object of derision. Instead, today restorative justice is in the mainstream of justice discourse.

Throughout the 1980s, and even much of the 90s, I knew many of the practitioners and advocates of restorative justice; I could identify what and where things were happening. I could provide a decent overview of the field and the issues it faced. That is no longer true. Although I attribute this inability in part to the reduced memory that comes with age, I console myself with the realization that it is almost impossible for one person to track the numerous applications and programs that exist, and the hundreds of practitioners and academics involved. Just last week, for example, I participated in the annual conference of the Academy of Criminal Justice Sciences that now has a restorative justice section and found dozens of academics engaged with it, many of whom I didn't know.

The global explosion of restorative justice is partly why this book is so important: it is the most comprehensive overview of the field available and is written in a highly accessible style. While the authors are restorative justice advocates, practitioners, and researchers, they are self-critical of the field, indicating areas of challenge and concern as well as success. The chapters include anecdotes that help the applications come alive, but their descriptions, analyses, and research of these approaches are not merely anecdotal. They wrestle with some difficult but highly relevant areas including the role of spirituality, the qualities of good facilitation, dynamics around culture and power, and, toward the end, explore newer and "frontier" areas of application.

In addition to the comprehensive overview of practices and practice issues, I especially appreciate the authors' attention to issues around values and principles. I have long warned that restorative justice, like all change efforts, is likely to go astray. All social interventions have unintended consequences, no matter how good our intentions. Change efforts are often first ignored, then resisted, then likely to be co-opted. Indeed, there are ample signs of the latter already in the field. An ongoing dialogue about principles and values, an openness to evaluation and feedback, and a self-reflective stance are crucial to help offset this tendency.

Umbreit and Armour offer Restorative Justice Dialogue: An Essential Guide for Research and Practice as an example of, as well as a contribution to, the commitment to practice what we preach—to live up to the values and vision of a justice that restores rather than destroys.

HOWARD ZEHR
Professor of Restorative Justice
Center for Justice & Peacebuilding
Eastern Mennonite University
Harrisonburg, VA

Preface

From its humble beginnings in the mid-1970s, the vision of restorative justice has truly grown into a social movement that is weaving increasing threads of hope, healing, and impact in the fabric of the global community. While influenced by the rich wisdom and practices of many indigenous cultures, restorative justice began as a largely white, North American and European vision to fundamentally change our juvenile and criminal justice systems. As a social movement with growing diversity within its ranks, the vision of restorative justice understands crime as a wound within the community and recognizes that justice requires not just accountability but also healing. It is healing that focuses on repairing harm and providing opportunities for those most directly affected by criminal behavior (the victim, offender, families, and communities) to engage each other in dialogue and problem solving. This focus on healing elevates the role of crime victims and the community in the process of responding to their needs and building safer communities. It also offers those who have harmed others the opportunity to repair the harm, as much as possible, directly to the people affected by their actions, and the chance to rebuild their lives and reenter their community in a good way with increased connections of support.

Much has changed over the past three decades. Today the vision of restorative justice is being embraced by many in other cultures and parts of the world. It is now endorsed by the United Nations and recommended for development in the global community. Most importantly, restorative justice principles and practices today are being applied in a growing number of settings entirely removed from the juvenile and criminal justice system. Some of the most hopeful signs of the impact of restorative practices are being seen in school systems, workplaces, faith communities, and in fostering reconciliation and healing in the wake of massive, violent conflicts within nations such as in Northern Ireland, South Africa, and Liberia. Even in current zones of deeply entrenched violent conflict, such as Israel and Palestine (the occupied territories), peacebuilding through restorative justice dialogue is beginning to appear.

Restorative justice provides an entirely different way of understanding and responding to conflict and violence within our communities. Neither a specific program nor a strategy, the values and principles that restorative justice is grounded in can challenge us to change the way each one of us treats others and how we respond to conflict, both in our professional and personal lives. At the deepest level, restorative justice provides a fundamentally different way of approaching life and the many conflicts we face in multiple roles and settings. Restorative justice, as a way of life, challenges us to continually engage the energy of compassion and humility within ourselves.

Precisely because restorative justice principles and practices are sprouting up in the form of so many different policies and programs, in this book we focus on the most widespread and empirically grounded expression of restorative justice, what we refer to as "restorative justice dialogue" in its many forms, most notably victim-offender mediation and dialogue, group conferencing, and peacemaking circles.

The first three chapters provide an overview of the restorative justice movement and its connection with core social work values and spirituality (not religion). Restorative justice dialogue and its most widespread applications are then presented in Chapters four through eight. Each chapter on a specific application of restorative justice dialogue includes a thorough description of the process, including case examples, followed by a review of empirical research that is available. The concluding three chapters, nine through eleven, focus on broader issues related to restorative justice dialogue. The crucial role of the facilitator in restorative justice dialogue is highlighted, followed by identifying the dimensions of culture in the restorative justice movement and the very real possibility of unintended negative consequences if we are not mindful of these dimensions. Finally, emerging areas of practice that go beyond the juvenile and criminal justice system are addressed.

This book benefitted from the tremendous help provided by several of our graduate student assistants. We want to acknowledge the valuable contributions offered by Joel Grostephan at the University of Minnesota School of Social Work and Daniel Pickhardt and Megan Schegel at the University of Texas School of Social Work.

Restorative Justice Dialogues: An Essential Guide for Research and Practice is offered as a guide to understanding core restorative justice values and practices and what we have learned from research on the impact of this emerging social movement in the global community. It is a movement that is deeply rooted in the values of social work and other human service fields. Individual social work practitioners and educators have provided leadership and support to the restorative justice movement from its beginning in the mid 1970s and throughout the past three decades. Restorative justice is neither a quick fix nor some sort of panacea that effectively addresses all of the issues of conflict confronting our society. Many lingering, if not troubling, questions remain and are addressed at different points in the book. Restorative justice is a movement loaded with complexity, if not ambiguity. Yet the underlying values and increasingly research-based interventions that drive the vision of restorative justice do provide a beacon of light and hope in areas of public policy and community life, which is so desperately needed in the midst of the conflict, violence, and fear that continue to be so widespread in the twenty-first century. In the final analysis, this book bears witness to the incredible strength, resilience, and compassion of the many thousands of people who have had the courage to either initiate or engage in restorative justice dialogue and achieve a greater sense of peace within their lives.

Mark Umbreit, PhD
Marilyn Armour, PhD

1. Restorative Justice as a Social Movement

> *"For me, as a victim of home burglary, restorative justice did something very different than the traditional justice system which focuses on punishing the offender and leaving the victim on the outside looking in. In the restorative justice system, I was part of the process. I saw the offender face-to-face and we talked about the impact of the burglary on my life and his. From a victim's perspective, voluntarily choosing to meet with the offender was crucial to my healing process, and crucial to the accountability and healing of the offender."*

*T*he past four decades have seen an unprecedented rise in violence, a drastic deterioration of community fabric, and a growing sense of personal danger, which breeds fear, isolation, and estrangement from those who are different from us. As spectators to this vast social change, we watch more and more people get incarcerated for longer periods of time. We watch as crime victims retreat from their former full involvement in meaningful activities. We watch impoverished neighborhoods become home to feuding gangs and drug dealing.

These conditions leave us feeling overwhelmed and powerless, eventually promoting an apathetic attitude. It seems that there is little we can do to change things. Indeed, we are encouraged to rely heavily on external systems of control such as the police or to live in more secluded and protected communities. However, our predominant dependency on external systems has resulted in an overreliance on punishment to deter crime, physical separation to ensure safety, and surveillance to monitor danger and seems to have made little progress, if any, in solving the levels of crime and violence. Yet we persist in doing more of the same, fearful that if we stopped, circumstances might get worse.

While the increase in socially toxic conditions creates a generalized fear mentality, reactionary policies of protection, and broadly based punitive responses, there is a philosophically different and demonstrably effective approach to crime and violence that is becoming a groundswell. In contrast to current negative trends, this approach generates hope, meaning, and healing through processes of seeking justice and personal accountability.

Restorative justice is a fast-growing state, national, and international social movement that seeks to bring people together to address the harm caused by crime, through empowerment of those involved. This important social reform has been developing alongside mounting social problems, escalating rates of incarceration, and the evidence that punishment-oriented policies are not very effective. Restorative justice views violence, community decline, and fear-based responses as indicators of broken relationships. It offers a different response, namely the use of restorative solutions to repair the harm related to conflict, crime, and victimization. In a very short time, restorative justice has grown from a relatively beginning ideology into a generative force that impacts the way we understand and respond to crime and conflict in diverse communities throughout the world. For example, it has spawned hundreds of individual programs in many countries, leading to a rising number of system-wide policies across various components of many justice systems.

Restorative justice is also gaining the increased attention of scholars throughout the world. It has established a rapidly expanding database from studies both in the United States and abroad that examine the processes and outcomes of restorative justice policies and practices. Restorative justice has also been increasingly applied to individual, community, and national healing in response to massive human rights violations, including countries in South America, Africa, the United Kingdom, and the Middle East.

This chapter provides an overview of the restorative justice movement in the twenty-first century. It describes the movement's accelerated growth over the past 30 years as it has moved from small outposts of activity to being an international presence with legislative support from countries like Canada and New Zealand and mandates from the United Nations for its use by member nations. As the movement's geographical scope has widened so has its range of practices both in addressing an ever-increasing range of social issues as well as its efforts to advance system-level changes. The rapid growth provides evidence that the use of restorative dialogue has been effective. The areas of its effectiveness include healing victim's pain, reducing offender recidivism, and increasing participants' satisfaction with the outcomes of meeting face-to-face. Another area of effectiveness is providing communities with a new direction for their citizenry to be meaningfully invested in the social health and well-being of their neighborhoods. Doing restorative justice work has a sleeper effect; in the aftermath of crime and other wrongdoing, participants discover its potential for healing but also realize that it has the power to renew and instill the kind of hope that can treat the toxicity of indifference that today's cynicism breeds.

The first section of this chapter contains a summary of the distinguishing characteristics of the restorative justice movement, its history and development, and the areas where it has been practiced with effectiveness. The chapter's second section focuses on restorative justice dialogue, which is the most widely practiced and extensively researched process of the restorative justice movement. The section covers the public policy support for such dialogue in settings across the United States. In the third section, opportunities for expanding the vision and questions for the future are discussed.

OVERVIEW OF RESTORATIVE JUSTICE

In a groundbreaking study, Norwegian criminologist Nels Christie examined the circumstances that led to the deaths of 70% of prisoners incarcerated in a Norwegian prison camp during World War II (Rutherford, 1984). After interviewing 50 Norwegian guards convicted of killing or severely maltreating a group of captured Yugoslavian prisoners, he determined that those who had abused their prisoners were much more distant from them than those guards who had treated the prisoners as human and with consideration. He subsequently proposed that social distance was a necessary precursor to moral indifference based on his finding that those who had mistreated the prisoners experienced their "sickness, dirtiness, and incontinence . . . in a completely different way than had the guards who had gotten closer to the prisoners" (Cayley, 1998, p. 17).

This research suggests that if we move up close to the harm created by crime or other injustices, we experience it differently than if we remain distant from the offender and apply only cruelty and pain. Similarly, restorative justice is built on the significance of relationship and the belief that bringing together those most directly affected by crime or wrongdoing will produce a different outcome for all involved than would occur through maintaining the social distance, a nonrestorative focus toward the offender, and the primary use of punishment to achieve justice.

Restorative justice, on the other hand, offers a very different way of understanding and responding to crime. Instead of viewing the state as the primary victim of criminal acts and placing victims, offenders, and the community in passive roles, restorative justice recognizes crime as being directed against individual people. It is grounded in the belief that those most impacted by crime should have the opportunity to become actively involved in resolving the conflict. Repairing harm and restoring losses, allowing offenders to take direct responsibility for their actions, and assisting victims to move beyond vulnerability and move toward some degree of closure stand in sharp contrast to the values and practices of the conventional criminal justice system with its focus on law violation, past criminal behavior, the need to hold offenders accountable through ever-increasing levels of punishment, and other state interests.

Moreover, actual crime victims and the harm done to them play little or no role in the traditional process. As one crime victim remarked about her family's experience within the contemporary criminal justice system, "[W]e were bystanders. While we could be a presence at [the trial] so the judge could see someone cared about the man who was killed, . . . we had nothing to do with this. I was just a spectator in a show. Completely left out" (Peterson, 2000). This statement reflects the marginalization that crime victims often experience because the crime is deemed an offense to the state rather than to the real victim. Crime victims, therefore, have generally no legal standing in the proceedings. Many crime victims experience the offender-driven nature of this process and the secondary concern of the criminal justice system for their distress as a subsequent injustice that victimizes them still further (Armour & Umbreit, 2007; Goodrum & Stafford, 2001; Miller, 2001; Tontodonato & Erez, 1994). In contrast, restorative justice is a victim-centered process that places the harm experienced by crime victims at the center of a restorative justice and elevates their position in determining what they need for their own restoration.

Antecedents to Restorative Justice

Although the restorative justice movement is often portrayed as either on the fringe of legal practice or as setting a new direction, the principles and practices of restorative justice, although not named as such, were the dominant model of criminal justice in Western countries before the eleventh century and embedded in numerous indigenous cultures from throughout the world (see Figure 1.1).

Within the English-speaking world, roots of the prevailing focus on crime as a violation to the state can be traced back to eleventh century England when crime was viewed as a violation of one person by another with a focus on harmful consequences and liability to repair damage. Following the Norman invasion of Britain, a major paradigm shift occurred in which there was a turning away from the well-established understanding of crime as a victim-offender conflict within the context of community. William the Conqueror's son, Henry I, issued a decree securing royal jurisdiction over certain offenses (robbery, arson, murder, theft, and other violent crimes)

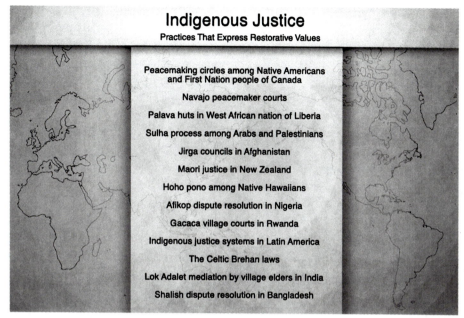

FIGURE 1.1

against the King's peace. This decree established that the fines that had been paid by offenders to their victims would now be paid to the state in the person of the king. These fines served a useful purpose because they became a revenue-generating system that supplemented unpopular taxes (Johnstone, 2002). The shift from the victim's right to restitution also pulled away the community's controls, including its ability to give offenders a sense of the magnitude of the harm and the opportunity to redeem themselves by repairing that harm.

Restorative justice values, principles, and practices also hearken back to numerous indigenous cultures from throughout the world. Many of these cultures are built on a deep understanding that all things are interconnected through relationships. When a violation occurs, it breaks the connections, thereby throwing the entire community into disharmony with itself. The first priority is the restoration of relationships between community members.

Navajo peacemaker courts use a respected community leader to bring together interested parties to resolve the dispute (Yazzie & Zion, 1996). The process is guided, in part, by a tradition that disallows the imposition of a decision on another. Consequently, the offender must voluntarily agree to participate and make things right in order for justice to proceed. Aboriginal/First Nations peoples of Canada employ elements of customary law and traditional practices in response to wrongdoing. Peacemaking and sentencing circles are used in Canada and among Native Americans and others in numerous communities in the United States. The Hollow Water First Nation community used a 13-step community-based process to address the harm from longstanding sexual abuse (Griffiths & Hamilton, 1996). This initiative included rituals reflecting traditional culture, involved community elders, and maintained a focus on healing, spirituality, and responding to offenders holistically by considering many issues beyond the specific criminal behavior.

The Maori in New Zealand built their system of justice on the idea that we are all part of one another (Considine, 1999). The aim of the Maori justice process is to restore the *mana* or personal standing of the victim, the victim's family, and the family of the offender and to reestablish the social order of the wider community. A public hearing is used, subsequent to determining guilt, to hold the offender and his or her family accountable, followed by consultation with a volunteer panel to determine the measures necessary to heal hurts and restore things to normal again.

Other indigenous groups that use restorative practices include, among others, Native Hawaiians and various African tribal councils. The practices include the Afghani tradition of jirga, the Arab/Palestinian tradition of Sulha, and many of the ancient Celtic practices found in the Brehon laws.

The values of restorative justice are also deeply rooted in the ancient principles of Judeo-Christian culture (Zehr, 1990). Zehr notes that the unifying concept of shalom in the Old and New Testaments is particularly noteworthy because, among other things, it refers to the need to live in right relationship with one another and with God as well as the need for honesty or the absence of deceit in dealing with one another. The biblical concept of covenant also has application to restorative justice because it implies mutual responsibilities and commitments between people and with God and, as such, provides both the basis and a model for shalom. When wrongdoing occurs, therefore, both the Old and New Testaments set forth the obligation of offenders to directly repair the harm they caused to individuals, harm that has created a breach in the "Shalom community."

Defining Restorative Justice

From disparate practices arrived at from different cultures over the centuries, a social movement applying a cohesive set of principles and practice has emerged. The most succinct and accepted definition of restorative justice is offered by Howard Zehr (2002), whom many consider to be the leading visionary and architect of the restorative justice movement. His seminal book *Changing Lenses* (Zehr, 1990) provided the conceptual framework for the movement and has influenced policy makers and practitioners throughout the world. According to Zehr,

> Restorative justice is a process to involve, to the extent possible, those who have a stake in a specific offense and to collectively identify and address harms, needs, and obligations, in order to heal and put things as right as possible. (2002, p. 37)

Core to restorative justice principles is the understanding that it is a victim-centered process. This means that the harm done to the victim takes precedence and serves to organize the essence of the interaction between the key players. Although victim centered, the process is not victim controlled. This allows the process to address the needs of all the various stakeholders. For offenders, therefore, this means that restorative justice, while denouncing criminal behavior, yet emphasizes the need to treat offenders with respect and to reintegrate them into the larger community in ways that can lead to their lawful behavior. Restorative justice, in this regard, views accountability as central to the rehabilitation of offenders. Indeed, restorative justice attempts to draw upon the strengths of offenders and crime victims and their capacity to openly address the need to repair the harm caused instead of focusing on the offender's weaknesses or deficits. Similarly, restorative justice believes communities, by pulling on their strengths, can be rebuilt despite crime.

From a restorative perspective, the primary stakeholders are individual victims and their families, affected communities, and offenders and their families. The state and its legal justice system also have an interest as a stakeholder, but in restorative justice, proceedings are removed from the direct impact of the crime and their focus instead is at the macro- rather than micro-level of engagement. Thus, the needs of those most directly affected by the crime come first. State institutions, however, are frequently called upon to provide support and space for forms of restorative justice dialogue between victims and offenders.

In its early years, the restorative justice movement, like many reform movements, focused on contrasting its values and principles with those of the status quo. Restorative justice was seen as an alternative paradigm to the dominant paradigm used by the criminal justice system. That paradigm was "retributive justice." It meant that offenders should get what they deserved or their "just deserts." In practice, retributive justice resulted in offenders receiving punishments that were commensurate with the seriousness of their crimes. The pain the offender felt was justified as an effective deterrent to future lawbreaking (Umbreit, 1994; Van Ness, 1999; Wright, 1996; Zehr, 1985, 1990).

After more than 25 years of practice, research, and continuing analysis, Zehr (2002) has come to a different understanding: that a sharp polarization between retributive and restorative justice is somewhat misleading. Zehr's thinking is shared by the philosopher of law Conrad Brunk (2001) who argues that on a theoretical level, retribution and restoration are not the polar opposites that many assume. He notes that both actually have much in common: specifically, a desire to vindicate by some type of reciprocal action and some type of proportional relationship between the criminal act and the response to it. Retributive theory and restorative theory, however, differ significantly in how to "even the score," how to make things right. Retributive theory holds that the imposition of some form of pain will vindicate, most frequently through deprivation of liberty and, in some cases, even through loss of life. Restorative theory argues that "what truly vindicates is acknowledgement of victims' harms and needs, combined with an active effort to encourage offenders to take responsibility, make right the wrongs, and address the cause of their behavior" (Zehr, 2002, p. 59).

Even so, Zehr (2002) notes that restorative justice can be contrasted with conventional criminal justice along at least four key principles (see Table 1.1).

These two approaches also differ in the fundamental questions they pose in the search for justice. The conventional criminal justice system wants answers to three questions. What laws have been broken? Who did it? What do they deserve? From a restorative justice perspective, an entirely different set of questions are asked. Who has been hurt? What are their needs? Whose obligations are these? (Zehr, 2002)

TABLE 1.1 Two different views of justice

Criminal Justice	Restorative Justice
• Crime is a violation of the law and the state.	• Crime is a violation of people and relationships.
• Violations create guilt.	• Violations create obligations.
• Justice requires the state to determine blame (guilt) and impose pain (punishment).	• Justice involves victims, offenders, and community members in an effort to put things right.
• **Central focus:** *Offenders getting what they deserve.*	• **Central focus:** *Victim needs and offender responsibility for repairing harm.*

These questions suggest that restorative justice requires a radically different way of viewing, understanding, and responding to the presence of crime within our communities. As the movement has grown so has the interest in addressing broader, system-level applications of restorative justice principles. Among others, Braithwaite (2002) speaks of restorative justice in these larger dimensions:

> Restorative justice is not simply a way of reforming the criminal justice system, it is a way of transforming the entire legal system, our family lives, our conduct in the workplace, our practice of politics. Its vision is of a holistic change in the way we do justice in the world. (p. 1)

Sullivan and Tifft (2004) similarly speak of restorative justice in broad macroterms, noting that it requires a commitment to "create patterns of interaction among us all that take into account the needs of all from the very outset, structurally" (p. 117). These visions are nothing less than changing the way we do justice in the world.

Whether at the level of system-wide interventions or in individual programs, we are working toward restorative justice when our work meets the following criteria:

1. Focus on the harms of wrongdoing more than the rules that have been broken.
2. Show equal concern and commitment to victims and offenders, involving both in the process of justice.
3. Work toward the restoration of victims, empowering them, and responding to their needs as they see them.
4. Support offenders while encouraging them to understand, accept, and carry out their obligations.
5. Recognize that while obligations may be difficult for offenders, they should not be intended as harms and they must be achievable.
6. Provide opportunities for dialogue, direct or indirect, between victims and offenders as appropriate.
7. Involve and empower the affected community through the justice process, and increase their capacity to recognize and respond to community bases of crime.
8. Encourage collaboration and reintegration rather than coercion and isolation.
9. Give attention to the unintended consequences of our actions and programs.
10. Show respect to all parties including victims, offenders, and justice colleagues (Mika & Zehr, 1998).

The second section of this chapter focuses on restorative justice dialogue, the most widely practiced and extensively researched modality of the restorative justice movement, as well as the public policy support for such dialogue across the United States.

History and Development of the Restorative Justice Movement

A small and scattered group of community activists, justice system personnel, and a few scholars began to advocate, often independently of each other, for the implementation of restorative justice principles and a practice called victim-offender reconciliation during the mid to late 1970s. These advocates in both the United States and Europe began establishing connections with one another, but they remained largely on the margins of the criminal justice system as a whole and were not initially connected with efforts to reform the system. Few of those involved in these early years would have ever thought that their modest yet passionate efforts to promote restorative justice would trigger a widespread social reform movement with international impact. These early thrusts, however, coalesced into what has become known as the restorative justice movement.

The first "child" of this birthing process was the Victim Offender Reconciliation Program (VORP) in Kitchener, Ontario, in 1974. This experiment involved two teenagers who pleaded guilty to 22 counts of property damage following a vandalism spree. After meeting individually with all the people they had victimized, the youth agreed to make restitution and within three months, handed each victim a check for the amount of his or her loss. From the late 1970s to the early 1980s, a number of experimental programs, modeled after the Kitchener program and built on restorative justice principles, were initiated in several jurisdictions in North America and Europe, with the first U.S. VORP started in Elkhart, Indiana, in 1978. VORP programs were rooted in the Mennonite experience and staffed, in part, by the Mennonite Central Committee (Cordella, 1991; Merry & Milner, 1995).

Through the mid-1980s, though introduced in many jurisdictions, restorative justice initiatives remained small in size and number. Consequently, they had little impact on the larger system. Indeed, few criminal justice officials viewed restorative justice programs as a credible component of their system. From the mid-1980s to the mid-1990s, however, the movement slowly began to be recognized in many communities as a viable option for interested crime victims and offenders, though still impacting a small number of participants. Indeed, England initiated the first state-supported Victim Offender Mediation Programs (VOM) during this period. VOM was similar to VORP but used language to describe the restorative justice process that was secular and closer to conflict resolution or civil dispute resolution, rather than faith-based, for example, shalom, atonement, and forgiveness (McCold, 1999).

In 1994, restorative justice took a giant step forward to becoming mainstream when the American Bar Association (ABA) endorsed VOM. Although this recognition followed a year-long study and considerable skepticism, the ABA ultimately recommended the use of VOM and restorative dialogue in courts throughout the country and provided guidelines for its use and development. These guidelines included that participation by both offenders and victims be entirely voluntary, that offenders not incur adverse repercussions, and that statements and information shared are inadmissible in criminal or civil court proceedings (American Bar Association, 1994).

Victim organizations were initially skeptical about victim-offender mediation and other restorative justice initiatives, in part because they felt that the movement, in its early history, was not sufficiently victim driven. However, in 1995, the National Organization for Victim Assistance (NOVA) endorsed the principles of restorative justice through publishing a monograph entitled *Restorative Community Justice: A Call to Action*. NOVA's approval helped elevate the victim centeredness of the approach, and as dialogue programs and other restorative initiatives have continued to demonstrate a strong commitment to the needs and wishes of crime victims, victim organizations have become increasingly supportive.

The movement began to enter the mainstream in some local and state jurisdictions beginning in the mid-1990s, a development that has led to mixed consequences. On the one hand, recognition by and active collaboration with the formal justice system are vital to implementing the underlying vision of restorative justice. On the other hand, such widespread growth and impact have made the movement increasingly vulnerable to being subsumed and diluted by the very justice systems that were initially so critical of its existence. This issue is discussed in more detail in our concluding section.

Today, restorative justice policies and programs are developing in nearly every state, and they range from small, individual, and marginal programs in many communities to a growing number of state and county justice systems that are undergoing major systemic change. Examples of such systemic change initiatives are occurring in the states of Arizona, California, Colorado, Illinois, Iowa, Minnesota, New York, Ohio, Oregon, Pennsylvania, Texas, Vermont, and Wisconsin.

Restorative justice programs are being developed in many other parts of the world, including Australia, Canada, numerous European countries, Japan,

China, New Zealand, South Africa, several South American countries, South Korea, Russia, and Ukraine. The United Nations, the Council of Europe, and the European Union have been addressing restorative justice issues for a number of years. Meeting in 2000, the United Nations Congress on Crime Prevention considered restorative justice in its plenary sessions and developed a draft proposal for "UN Basic Principles on the Use of Restorative Justice Programs in Criminal Matters" (United Nations, 2000). The proposed principles encourage the use of restorative justice programming by member states at all stages of the criminal justice process, underscore the voluntary nature of participation in restorative justice procedures, and recommend beginning to establish standards and safeguards for the practice of restorative justice. This proposal was adopted by the United Nations in 2002.

The Council of Europe was more specifically focused on the restorative use of mediation procedures in criminal matters and adopted a set of recommendations in 1999 to guide member states in using mediation in criminal cases. In 2001, the European Union adopted a victim-centered policy in support of "penal mediation," otherwise known as VOM. This policy stated that member states (nations) of the European Union should promote mediation in criminal cases and integrate this practice into their laws (Commission of the European Communities, 2001).

European nations have clearly outpaced American policy development and implementation in support of restorative justice practices, with Austria having established the first national policy commitment in the world to broad implementation of VOM in 1988. Numerous other European countries have now made strong policy commitments to restorative justice and, particularly, VOM. Germany, for example, has an exceptionally broad and large commitment to VOM, with more than 468 programs and 20,000 cases referred annually. Other European countries that have developed local VOM programs or national initiatives include Denmark, Finland, Sweden, Ireland, the Netherlands, Luxembourg, Switzerland, Albania, Slovenia, Romania, Poland, Bulgaria, Italy, Spain, and Ukraine. England has gone far beyond a focus just on VOM, with a national policy recommendation to implement restorative justice policies and practices throughout the country (Home Office, 2003).

In contrast to many previous criminal justice reform movements that have primarily dealt with fine-tuning the existing structure, the restorative justice movement has major implications for system-wide change in how justice is done in democratic societies. While initiating restorative justice interventions, such as victim-offender mediation, family group conferencing, peacemaking and sentencing circles, restorative community service, victim panels, and other forms of victim-offender dialogue or neighborhood dispute resolution, is important, restorative justice, as a movement, places heavy emphasis upon changing the current system. Already, there are

19 states in America that have introduced and/or passed legislation promoting a more balanced and restorative juvenile justice system. Thirty other states have restorative justice principles in their mission statements or policy plans. There are individual restorative justice programs in virtually every state of America, and a growing number of states and local jurisdictions are dramatically changing their criminal and juvenile justice systems to adopt the principles and practices of restorative justice (O'Brien, 2000). This institutionalization of restorative justice is further buttressed by the ABA who, in 2006, began a national survey of restorative justice programs and, in 2008, offered grants to its members to develop restorative justice initiatives in criminal law settings.

RESTORATIVE JUSTICE IN PRACTICE

A wide range of restorative justice practices, programs, and policies are developing in communities throughout the United States and abroad. In this section, several different examples are briefly described, followed by a more detailed presentation of a system-wide change effort.

Program Examples

In Orange County, California, a victim-offender mediation and conferencing program receives nearly a thousand referrals of juvenile offenders and their victims annually (Niemeyer & Shichor, 1996). This program is supported by a large government grant and provides needed support, assistance, and restoration for victims of crime, while also holding young people accountable to the victims and their communities for their misdeeds. By diverting these juveniles from further penetration into the justice system, if the victim's needs are met, the County also benefits from a significant cost reduction in the already overcrowded court system. The program in Orange County is part of a much larger network of more than 1,500 victim-offender mediation and conferencing programs in 17 countries, working with both juvenile and adult courts.

In several U.S. cities, prosecuting attorney offices routinely offer choices to victims of crime to actively participate in the justice system, including participation in restorative dialogue with the offender and others affected by the crime, and to meet other needs that victims are facing. A program in Indianapolis works closely with the police department in offering family group conferencing services where young offenders and their families meet the individuals they have victimized and work through dialogue with each other toward repairing the harm, resulting in a significant reduction in recidivism among these offenders (McGarrell, Olivares, Crawford, & Kroovand, 2000).

Restorative justice principles and practices are increasingly being used in additional juvenile and criminal justice settings as well as in addressing larger issues of human rights violations and deeply entrenched national conflict and political violence. A dialogue-based format was creatively used in Eugene, Oregon, following a hate crime against the local Muslim community that occurred within hours of the September 11 attacks (Umbreit, Lewis, & Burns, 2003). The prosecutor's office gave the victimized representatives of the Muslim community a choice of either following the conventional path of prosecution and severe punishment or the restorative justice path of participating in a neighborhood accountability board, including face-to-face conversations with the offender and others in the community who were affected by this crime. The victims elected to meet in dialogue; together they were able to talk openly about the full impact of this hate crime and to develop a specific plan to repair the harm and promote a greater sense of tolerance and peace within the community.

In several jurisdictions, restorative justice procedures are being used to enable ethnic communities to access elements of their traditional means of handling infractions and breaches of trust among themselves. The Hmong peacemaking circles in St. Paul, Minnesota, receive referrals from local judges in cases involving Hmong participants so that the offense is handled in a more culturally appropriate way that fosters peacemaking and accountability (Allam, 2002, March 2). In Canada, aboriginal groups are using the circle-sentencing format of restorative justice dialogue to handle a wide range of offenses within the community (Lajeunesse, 1996).

Restorative justice dialogue responses are increasingly being offered to victims of severe and violent crime, driven by requests from victims for such opportunities. Departments of Corrections in Texas, Ohio, Pennsylvania, and more than 20 other states have initiated statewide victim-offender mediation and dialogue programs through their victim services units (Umbreit, Vos, Coates, & Brown, 2003). In such programs and in the wake of trauma caused by extreme violence, including homicide, victims meet in facilitated dialogue with the offenders who have harmed them as part of their search for meaning and some measure of closure. Extensive preparation of all involved parties is required in these cases. In a related program, a retired Wisconsin Supreme Court Justice facilitates dialogue groups in a state prison among prisoners and with several victims of severe violence in an effort to ingrain the full human impact of the prisoners' behavior upon victims and their communities.

Most recently, restorative practices are emerging as part of the healing process for victims of political violence. The Truth and Reconciliation Commission hearings in South Africa were established to foster national healing in the wake of severe violent political conflict as the apartheid system of racial segregation and oppression was dismantled (Dissel, 2000). The West African nation of Liberia has initiated a Truth and Reconciliation Commission to hold hearings in both Africa and Minnesota where the largest population of Liberian refugees reside and to incorporate restorative justice practices in the hearing process (The Advocates for Human Rights, 2008).

A victim-offender mediation was held in Israel between two Israeli-Palestinian youths and a young Israeli mother who had been assaulted and robbed; families of both the offenders and the victim were involved. Both the Jewish and the Palestinian communities actively participated and forged a path toward greater understanding, accountability, and mutual respect. Again within Israel, a restorative justice conference allowed the Arab victims of a Jewish hate crime and assault to meet face-to-face, talk about the full impact of the crime, and to develop a plan to repair the harm. In another case, a former prisoner who was an icon of the Irish Republican Army (IRA) movement in Northern Ireland met face-to-face with the daughter of one of the men he killed in their mutual search for greater understanding, meaning, and peace in their lives.

These are a sample of the increasing number of cases in which restorative justice dialogue is being used. These examples demonstrate the flexibility of using restorative justice in multiple settings from local to international to foster accountability and healing in the midst of severe criminal and political violence.

Systemic Change Examples

As many advocates point out, restorative justice is a process not a program. Therefore, some proponents are hopeful that a restorative justice framework can be used to foster systemic change. Such changes are beginning to occur. For example, within Minnesota, the state Department of Corrections established a policy to handle letters of apology by prisoners to their victims in a highly restorative and victim-centered manner. First, the state agency encouraged and assisted prisoners who wanted to write such letters. Instead of sending the letters directly to victims, an act that could revictimize them, the letters were deposited in a victim apology letter bank in the central office for later viewing by victims should they choose to want to do this (Minnesota Department of Corrections, nd).

Broad systemic change initiatives have been undertaken in a number of other countries. In 1988, Austria adopted federal legislation that promoted the use of victim-offender mediation throughout the country (Van Ness & Heetderks, 2002). In 1989, legislation was adopted in New Zealand that totally restructured their youth justice system based on the traditional practices of their indigenous people, the Maori, and principles consistent with restorative justice (Daly, 2001). The largest volume of youth justice cases now go to family group conferences, rather than court. This has resulted in a significant reduction in both court cases and incarceration, with no evidence of increased recidivism. Finally, a nation-wide systemic change effort has been undertaken in the United Kingdom through its policy commitment to adopt restorative justice principles and practices throughout the country (Van Ness & Heetderks, 2002). These changes are focused on increased participation by crime victims, youth accountability boards, and different forms of victim-offender mediation and dialogue.

Washington County Court Services near St. Paul, Minnesota, is one of few jurisdictions in the United States that has explicitly undertaken system-wide change through adopting policies informed by restorative justice principles. Here is a summary of data gathered from a more extensive study from interviews with key system and community decision makers to document the change process and gather participant assessments regarding significant changes made (Coates, Umbreit, & Vos, 2004).

Often reform efforts in criminal justice are prompted by a crisis, for example, a jail riot or an offender suicide. This was not the case in Washington County. Instead, key leaders built upon long established relationships among criminal justice professionals and with community groups that started when the Community Corrections Act passed in 1973, giving counties more administrative control and resources for developing community-based programs for offenders. Washington County took advantage of the Act and chose to participate by providing services that were as community based as possible. It established a Community Corrections Advisory Board comprising citizens, judges, the County Attorney, the County Sheriff, and representatives from Probation, Community Services, Public Defenders, and Law Enforcement plus ex officio members, for example, County Board Commissioner. Growing out of a long tradition of providing prevention and early intervention services to youth, Court Services wrote a grant to develop and strengthen restitution programs, community service, and VOM. When VOM was cut, the staff for the program pushed for broad systemic change and a more open endorsement of movement toward a restorative justice philosophy. A variety of change strategies were adopted. The department staff began learning about restorative justice and became committed to a victim focus and using restorative practices for their internal relationship issues. Criminal justice decision makers gradually signed on as they were more exposed to restorative justice principles and because of concerns for the unmet needs of victims. Community members and groups became involved as they were invited to participate on ad hoc committees, which increased communication, relationship building, and trust with Court Services.

There were also expected tensions around conflicting ideas or use of resources. Some community advocates felt, for example, that Court Services was not moving fast enough, while others felt that the staff was moving too fast or was directly or indirectly critical of what community-based providers had been doing for years. Some resisted the focus on offender's needing to understand the impact of their actions on victims and the community claiming that this added more to their workload. Still others felt that a restorative justice approach was not punitive enough.

However, Court Services also recognized that a restorative justice teamwork increased options available to staff. For example, more consideration was given to the nature of reparations and how services provided by offenders could more meaningfully give back to the victim and community rather than just hours of work because the system ordered it. Peacemaking Circles as well became an additional option that builds on community partnerships and collaboration.

After a time of experience with some restorative practices, Washington County Court Services decided to revise its mission statement to incorporate the changes. This was accomplished by getting staff together to hash out a thoughtful vision, mission, and values statement along with reviewing policy and procedures with the restorative mission in mind. Attention was given as well to how best to measure the impact of their restorative justice programs. Each one of these developments has brought waves of reaction to possible change. For example, tensions arose among staff members as debate was carried out regarding next steps in a proposed idea, accountability measures, and the role of Court Services in the community and other justice system components. However, as one community participant said, "It takes time to establish an effective process. It takes a lot of time to establish relationships because the most effective restorative justice is a partnership and doesn't come from the top down. Nor does it come from the bottom up. It kind of grows together between community members and court services and everyone else."

The collective focus on offenders, victims, and community has provided a new foundation for thinking and action that applied to everything from writing case reports, to assessment, to new program development. In reviewing the change that occurred both in mindset and strategy, the director of court services often used a "seed planting" metaphor. To that end, it took considerable time to provide the education and training necessary to switch gears. Likewise, seeds were planted through one-on-one conversations and through relationship building. When workers were asked about the development of restorative justice in the county system, most of the individuals interviewed identified mutual respect and relationship building as pivotal for this effort at reform to succeed.

The restorative justice frame, however, brought victim issues into focus, which resulted in an explicit broadening of the mission of the county to include victims along with offenders and community.

Indeed, community support was central in providing the impetus for change, a change that was not always appreciated. "It is the community piece that has some in the system reacting to restorative justice with resistance," the director said. He believed that systems changed primarily because of outside forces. In this instance, that was the community, including victim groups, as well as service providers. Community members participated on ad hoc department committees, as volunteers in victim-offender conferencing and peacekeeping circles, and as developers of private community-based services. This involvement was not without tension. Some community participants wanted the system to move further and faster than many key decision makers were prepared to do. A few long established community service providers were skeptical of some restorative practices. Yet it was this partnership among community participants, criminal justice decision makers, and court service personnel that formed the foundation for the reform and upon which the ongoing process depends.

Reform proponents point to specific changes reflecting a restorative justice lens as responsible for the county's success. These include the use of victim-offender conferencing and peacekeeping circles, case planning focused on victim and community needs as well as those of offenders, and assessment tools considering the impact on all three groups. Much work is left to be done to make these changes system wide and to help systems remain open to new restorative possibilities. Participants acknowledge that continuation of the reform will require risk taking and that this restorative process "is a marathon not a sprint."

RESTORATIVE JUSTICE DIALOGUE

As a means of providing an in-depth examination of restorative justice practices, the focus turns to restorative justice dialogue. In so doing, we do not mean to imply that it is the best practice in all situations or the only practice worth examining. It is discussed here because it is the oldest, most widely

Restorative Justice as a Social Movement   19

practiced, and most thoroughly researched of the various processes that fall under the broad umbrella of restorative justice.

Description

Four general types of restorative justice dialogue are examined in this review. These include victim-offender mediation, group conferencing, circles, and "other." All have in common the inclusion of victims and offenders in direct dialogue, nearly always face-to-face, about a specific offense or infraction; the presence of at least a third person who serves as mediator, facilitator, convener, or circle keeper; and usually, advance preparation of the parties so they will know what to expect. The focus of the encounter nearly always involves naming what happened, identifying its impact, and coming to some common understanding, often including reaching agreement as to how any resultant harm will be repaired. Use of these processes can take place at any point in the criminal justice process, including prearrest, precourt referral, presentencing, or postsentencing, and even during incarceration.

Victim-offender mediation (often called "victim-offender conferencing," "victim-offender reconciliation [VORP]," or "victim-offender dialogue") usually involves a victim and an offender in direct mediation facilitated by one or sometime two mediators/facilitators; occasionally the dialogue takes place through a third party who carries information back and forth, a process known as "shuttle" mediation. In face-to-face meetings between the victim and offender, support persons (such as parents or friends) for victims and/or offenders are often present; a 1999 survey of victim-offender mediation programs in the United States found that support persons, including parents in juvenile cases, were present in nearly nine out of ten cases (Umbreit & Greenwood, 1999).

Group conferencing (usually known as "family group conferencing" or "community group conferencing" or "restorative group conferencing") routinely involves support persons for both victims and offenders as well as additional participants from the community. Many group conferencing programs rely on a script, though some are more open ended. The number of support persons present can often range from 6 to 10 to only a few, much like victim-offender mediation. Some group conferences can have well over 10 people.

Circles are variously called "peacemaking circles," "restorative justice circles," "repair of harm circles," and "sentencing circles." The numbers and types of participants gathered for circles are similar to those gathered for conferences, though sometimes there is even wider community member participation, either as interested persons, representatives of the criminal justice system, or as additional circle keepers or facilitators. The process involves the use of a "talking piece" that is passed around the circle to designate who may speak.

"Other" refers to programs such as reparative boards and other community-based programs that invite victims and offenders to participate together in crafting an appropriate response to the offense.

Increasingly over time, distinctions across these categories have begun to blur, in particular between "mediation" and "group conferencing." Thus there are programs that refer to their process as "family group conferencing" or "restorative group conferencing" but in fact convene only offenders and victims with few if any support persons and no outside community representatives. Similarly, many "victim-offender mediation" or "victim-offender conferencing" programs have moved towards more routinely including support persons and occasional additional affected community members.

Despite the overlap, there are differences in the relative importance of various stakeholders in each type of restorative dialogue. (See Figure 1.2.) For example, victim-offender mediation highlights the victim and offender as the primary parties in the offense and gives greater emphasis to storytelling and problem solving through dyadic dialogue (Bazemore & Schiff, 2005). Group conferencing puts a central focus on the role of the family and other support persons because those people have the best chance of

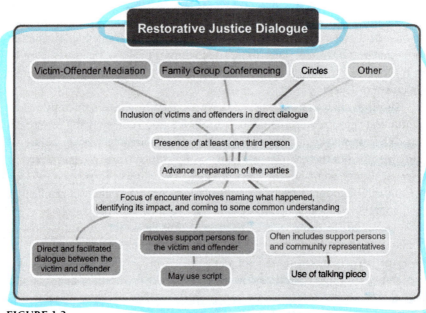

FIGURE 1.2

influencing the offender through the importance of their prior or ongoing relationship and the use of empathy, support, and respectful disapproval. Circles feature shared leadership and consensus-based decision making as core to the functioning of the group and the development of the group's process. Although the purpose of the circle may be to address the offender's behavior, circles also tend to place more attention philosophically on stakeholder and community needs. Boards operate under a small decision-making body of community volunteers that gives primary consideration to the offender and reparation. Boards underscore the citizenry's ownership of the criminal justice system because of the member's direct involvement in the justice process (Bazemore & Umbreit, 2003).

The present review attempts to maintain the distinction between these four types of restorative dialogue especially between victim-offender mediation (or victim-offender conferencing) and group conferencing (family group conferencing). However, it seems likely that knowledge building may be better served in the future by collapsing the categories. So doing would allow for participant responses and outcomes to be analyzed across actual variations in structure and format, rather than according to what the intervention is called. Zehr has also called for a reconsideration of the conventional typology, suggesting that restorative justice programs can be placed on a continuum from fully restorative to not restorative based on not dialogue type but the meeting of specific criteria including, among others, the involvement of the relevant stakeholders, the victim-centered nature of the process, and the adequacy of the restorative justice dialogue to deal with harms, needs, and causes (2002).

Humanistic Mediation

Facilitation of restorative justice dialogues rests on the use of humanistic mediation. Contemporary mediation practice has been heavily undergirded by the legal profession, concerns about procedural fairness, and the need for settlement agreements. In contrast, humanistic mediation rests on client empowerment, recognition of each other's humanity despite the conflict, and the building of a deeper, mutually respectful relationship. It acknowledges that most conflicts develop within a larger emotional and relational context characterized by powerful feelings of disrespect, betrayal, and abuse. When these feelings about the past and current state of the relationship are suppressed or not aired in a healthy manner, an agreement might be reached, but the underlying emotional conflict remains. Little healing of the emotional wound is likely to occur without an opening of the heart through genuine dialogue, empowerment, and recognition of each other's humanity despite the conflict. Instead of being directive, therefore, humanistic mediation is nondirective and dialogue driven. It prepares the parties, through separate premediation sessions with the mediator, so that they feel safe enough to have an opportunity to engage in a genuine conversation about the conflict, to experience their own sense of empowerment, and to express "compassionate strength," including empathy for the other party in the conflict (Bush and Folger, 1994). It allows the parties to discuss the full impact of the conflict and to assist each other in determining the most suitable resolution. The art of mediation is found in connecting with people at a human level through the expression of empathy, warmth, and authenticity.

Evidence-Based Practice

Restorative justice is more a process than a product. Consequently, the measurement of its success requires an evaluation of the factors that influence the process as much as its outcomes. Restorative justice research, therefore, has concentrated on participation rates and reasons, participant satisfaction, and participant perception of fairness as indicators of the health of the process as well as restitution and repair of harm, diversion, recidivism, and cost. Moreover, evaluations of restorative justice dialogue are extensive and, in relationship to youth, indicate a closer examination over a longer period of time than most other programs in the juvenile offender service, including cognitive behavioral treatment, juvenile drug courts, and family-based therapy programs (Aos, Miller, & Drake, 2006).

For example, over 85 studies have been conducted of various types of restorative justice dialogue including 4 meta-analyses, one of which was based on a sample of over 12,000 youth (Bradshaw & Roseborough, 2005). This research that has been generated over the past 30 years suggests that the restorative justice paradigm can make a substantial contribution to increased victim involvement and healing, offender responsibility for behavior change and learning from experience, and community participation in shaping a just response to law violations and destructive behavior.

Participant satisfaction has remained the most commonly studied outcome variable across all restorative justice approaches. Expression of satisfaction with victim-offender mediation is consistently high across sites, cultures, and offense severity for both victims and offenders. Indeed, those offenders who find the process satisfying also tend to display lower recidivism rates and are more likely to adhere to restitution agreements (Latimer, Dowden, & Muise, 2005). Typically, eight out of ten participants report being satisfied with the process and resulting agreement (Carr, 1998; Evje & Cushman, 2000; L. Roberts, 1998; T. Roberts, 1995; Umbreit, Coates, & Vos, 2001).

Restitution is regarded by many as an important by-product of bringing victim and offender together. Restitution or what is called reparation can be quite varied and include direct compensation to the victim, community service, work for the victim, and sometimes unique paybacks devised between victim and offender. Apologies are also often included in program reports as a component of repairing the harm. In some settings, restitution amounts are established before cases are referred for a restorative justice intervention; in others, deciding whether the victim should receive restitution, the type, and how much are seen as important domains for the dialogue session.

Victim participation seems to contribute to the nature and willingness to meet the conditions of the agreement. For example, one study found that reparation occurred 42% of the time when victims were present compared to 29% across all cases that harmed victims (Maxwell & Morris, 1993). Moreover, when victims are present, work performed by offenders is more likely to be done for the victim than when victims are not present. There are no known studies of restitution for peacemaking circles. The Vermont Reparation Board program, however, reported that restitution was ordered in 69% of cases where material harm was identified. Of the victims surveyed, 66% indicated that their losses were addressed. Victim participation appears to be an important determinant as demonstrated by the fact that the percentage of apologies rose from 18% for all cases to 67% in cases where victims attended (Karp, Sprayregen, and Drakulick, 2002).

Recidivism studies are important indicators of restorativeness because a major objective in all restorative justice approaches is to change offending behavior. Moreover, desistance from crime indicates both individual and social well-being (Presser & Van Voorhis, 2001). Although studies indicate that victim-offender mediation and group conferencing have significant impact on reoffending, little is known, as yet, about the contribution peacemaking circles and reparation boards make to reducing recidivism or the durability of their imprint. Because peacemaking circles involve community members and therefore have a potentially wider effect, there is some evidence that this practice could also serve as a community control mechanism to prevent crime. For example, a study of the impact of "healing circles" on the Hollow Water First Nation community located in the Canadian Province of Manitoba suggests that the effect might be substantial. Hollow Water has had a recidivism rate of approximately 2% over a 10-year period (Native Counseling Services of Alberta, 2001).

Indeed, there is little research on the systemic impact of restorative justice. Those countries, however, that legislate the use of restorative justice provide opportunities to measure its influence more broadly. In Australia, for example, group conferencing reduced the total number of policy interventions involving youth and increased the proportion of cases handled through cautioning rather than in court (Moore & Forsythe, 1995). In New Zealand, systemic changes made through the Children, Young Persons and Families Act of 1989 have dramatically reduced the court load from up to 13,000 cases per year to as little as 2,587 in 1990 (Maxwell & Morris, 1993).

Although the viability of restorative justice is dependent on the findings of evaluation research, the nature of its goals calls for future studies of process and outcome that are built, with greater precision, on a restorative justice base. These goals include considerations such as systemic social change; complexity of interactional processes that involve encounters between victims, offenders, and communities; and diversity of implementations. Presser and Van Voorhis (2001) identify three core restorative justice processes, namely dialogue, relationship building, and communication of societal values, and two overarching restorative justice outcomes, namely reparation and social well-being, as useful points of departure. Likewise, Bazemore and Schiff (2005) propose that future practice and research be tied to restorative justice principles that encompass both micro- and macrolevel objectives, for example, making amends, but they go further in suggesting that studies also examine more nuanced relationships between restorative justice and intervention theories such as social support and social exchange in order to understand the impact of short-term outcomes on long-term results. Both suggestions indicate that restorative justice research needs to be guided by a restorative justice framework in order to illuminate the full potential of what restorative justice can offer to victims, offenders, and the community.

OPPORTUNITIES FOR EXPANDING THE VISION

The restorative justice movement is built on a foundational vision of an entirely different way of understanding and responding to crime and conflict. In some instances, restorative justice is seen as a replacement for the criminal justice system. In some instances, restorative justice is seen as an option to use when the current situation has failed to bring about its intended purpose. In other instances, restorative justice is viewed as complementary to the criminal justice system because it attends to issues that the traditional system neglects. Regardless of the position taken, the vision of restorative justice is grounded in values that are resonating with an increasingly broad range of individuals and communities throughout the world, presenting many opportunities for new and widened impact. A number of these opportunities are listed below; many others continue to emerge.

1. Initiating a system-wide commitment to providing local citizens who are victimized by all but the most serious violent crime the opportunity

to first choose a local community-based restorative justice response. Both parties would retain the legal right to go before the formal criminal or juvenile justice system if either felt that they were not treated fairly or were dissatisfied with the outcome of the restorative justice intervention. Such a policy would place restorative justice in the forefront of our collective response to crime, rather than consigning it to a marginal position as an option for only a select number of individuals. This policy would also result in huge cost savings.
2. Developing an increasing number of hybrids that integrate the strengths and limitations of each individual restorative justice intervention. For example, in more serious cases the use of victim-offender mediation on a small or intimate level could first be offered to the specific victim and offender. This could be later followed by a session involving a number of family members and support people, and then even this phase could be followed at a later time with a much larger community intervention involving a peacemaking circle of perhaps 20–30 individuals. Case examples of such combinations go all the way back to the experience of Genesee County, New York, in responding to a sniper shooting case in the early 1980s (Latimar, Dowden, & Muise, 2001). Examples also include a case in Dakota County, Minnesota, in which the response to a pipe bomb incident by students in a high school resulted in combining elements of victim-offender mediation, family group conferencing, and a community peacemaking circle (Adams, 1998).
3. Increasing the use of surrogate victim-offender community dialogue. Encounters with surrogates can be a partial response to the large volume of crime victims whose offenders are never caught. Such victims are equally in need of gaining a greater understanding of why people commit such crimes and letting others in the community know about the impact on their lives. Often they also find it beneficial to help hold other similar offenders accountable for their actions even though their own offender was never caught. Dialogue groups in prisons and other correctional facilities that include offenders, victims of similar crimes, and community members have been shown to benefit all who are involved at a relatively low cost. Examples of these practices exist in the states of Minnesota, Texas, Washington, and Wisconsin (Armour, Sage, Rubin, & Windsor, 2008; Burns, 2002; Helfgott, Lovell, & Lawrence, 1999).
4. Applying restorative justice principles and practices in school settings from elementary level through college. Examples of this possibility include the use of peacemaking circles to deal with student conflicts

in an entire school district in Minnesota and other schools throughout the country that use various forms of victim-offender mediation, peer mediation, family group conferencing, circles, or other types of restorative dialogue. Skidmore College (Karp & Conrad, 2003) and The University of Colorado at Boulder (Warters, Sebok, & Goldblum, 2000) are two institutions of higher learning that have developed and implemented a formal restorative justice program on campus.
5. Expanding the use of restorative justice principles and practices in work place settings among coworkers.
6. Increasing the use of restorative justice principles and practices to foster healing in the wake of severe political violence and in the context of national healing.
7. Building increased coalitions among unlikely allies within communities that focus on the real human impact of crime, the need for direct and understandable accountability of law violators, and the need to foster healing within the community.
8. Offering more support for victims of severe violence. This prospect would include greatly expanding the opportunities for victim-offender dialogue for those victims who seek to meet. It would also involve much wider use of victim intervention projects that respond to the needs of victims immediately after the crime, whether or not there ever is any direct engagement with the offender. Defense-Initiated Victim Outreach (DIVO) is an emerging restorative justice program that offers victim survivors in capital murder cases the chance to have their judicial needs met, especially those that can be addressed by the defense and the defendant (Redfield, 2006).
9. Developing strong legislative support for public resources being appropriated to support the restorative justice movement, based on evidence of its effectiveness in reducing recidivism, cutting costs, and increasing victim and citizen satisfaction with the justice process. Such initiatives would also involve building stronger alliances with the crime victim advocacy community through focusing on joint interests between restorative justice advocates and crime victim advocates.
10. Building ever-increasing bridges between the dominant culture and the many ethnic groups and communities of color within our society. One approach already being used is that of tapping into the ancient wisdom among many indigenous people who have for centuries practiced elements of what today is called restorative justice. Tribal Justice Exchange in Syracuse, New York, seeks to promote the sharing of information between state and tribal courts, assist tribal communities in enhancing their justice systems, and explore ways in which state courts can benefit from traditional tribal justice practices (Center for Court Innovation, 2008).

11. Using the principles of restorative justice to engage in a new framework for research on the public policy and human impact of the death penalty.
12. Strengthening the very fabric of community and civic responsibility through increasing involvement of neighbors and citizens in restorative community-based justice initiatives that provide opportunities for more frequent and meaningful contact with each other in activities that benefit all of society. A project in a poverty-ridden neighborhood in San Antonio, Texas, is using the underpinnings of restorative justice to improve the quality of life for area residents by addressing institutional and social structure problems (Gilbert and Settles, 2007).

QUESTIONS FOR THE FUTURE

Restorative justice has made vast strides in the past quarter century. With growth, however, come new dilemmas that, despite the wide and increasing international acceptance of restorative justice principles and practices and despite the many opportunities facing the movement in the twenty-first century, present numerous unresolved and often troubling issues. Many of these speak to the core integrity of the movement, while others pose concerns about fair and effective implementation. We present the most salient of these questions in the following list:

1. The growth in restorative justice makes the concept increasingly ambiguous.
    - Is restorative justice in fact about developing an entirely new paradigm of how our criminal justice systems operate at a systemic level, or is it a set of processes, specific principles, and practices that can operate within our conventional criminal justice systems (Robinson, 2003)?
2. Restorative justice needs to influence the social injustice that permeates our society.
    - How does the restorative justice movement avoid becoming only a microlevel intervention serving victims, offenders, and communities?
3. Society is overwhelmingly focused on retribution.
    - Can restorative justice really be a victim-centered approach when the overwhelming emphasis and resources in the system are so heavily focused upon identifying, apprehending, processing and punishing, or even treating the offender?
4. As Susan Sharpe (2004) points out, there are at least two camps: the "purist" who would severely limit who is really in "the movement" and

the "maximalist" who would be so inclusive that it becomes hard to distinguish what makes the policy and practice uniquely restorative.
- How big is the tent under which policies and practices are considered to be part of the restorative movement?

5. Zehr argues that restorative and retributive justice are not in competition but rather need to work in concert with each other.
   - How can the restorative justice movement avoid the predictable co-opting of its philosophy as it seeks to mainstream itself within the criminal justice system?

6. The vast majority of crime victims never have their offenders apprehended and processed in the system. These victims are largely ignored by the justice system—restorative or conventional.
   - How can restorative justice address the multitude of needs facing victims of crime whose offenders are never caught and who are never given the opportunity therefore to enter a mediation session or conference or peacemaking circle or other related interventions?

7. Restorative justice has the potential for a broad reach in its ability to address harms related to a variety of social issues.
   - Will restorative justice be marginalized through being required to deal, in effect, with only the most minor types of criminal and delinquent offences, many of which would self-correct on their own?

8. A variety of restorative practices are emerging.
   - Will restorative justice as a movement gravitate toward a "one size fits all" approach in which a specific intervention or approach will be viewed as appropriate for nearly all cases or all cases of a given type?

9. A major pillar of the restorative justice approach is its emphasis upon the involvement of communities and respecting the needs of the community.
   - How will the restorative justice movement deal with the reality that many communities express a wish for policies and practices that are far from being restorative in nature? Will the movement be able to integrate respect for those positions while still advocating more restorative approaches?

10. Some believe that domestic violence cases can be routinely referred to such programs as victim-offender mediation, while others are more cautious. In theory, restorative justice may have a great deal to offer to the field of domestic violence. In practice, however, it holds the potential for doing irrevocable harm, despite good intentions.
    - How will the restorative justice movement effectively deal with cases involving domestic violence?

- How can the dangerous territory of domestic violence be reconciled with the good intent of those involved with the restorative justice movement?
- What changes are needed programmatically to assure the victim's safety?
11. Within the United States, the criminal justice system has a vastly disproportionate number of persons of color caught in its policies and practices.
    - How does the restorative justice movement avoid mirroring this same reality?
    - How many restorative justice policies and programs affect communities of color?
    - How many of these programs and policies actively engage people of color in leadership roles and service delivery roles?
12. Concerns continue to be raised about the relationship between restorative justice and the current legal system that rests on an adversarial model of justice.
    - How can the informal nature of community-based justice that characterizes the restorative justice movement be reconciled with the protection of rights offered by our formal criminal and juvenile justice systems?
    - How can extensive and unfair disparity in sanctions and outcomes be avoided as individual victims and communities are given a wide range of options for holding the offender accountable?

CONCLUSION

The restorative justice movement has an increasing impact upon criminal justice system policy makers and practitioners throughout the world. As a relatively young reform effort, the restorative justice movement holds a great deal of promise as we enter the twenty-first century. By drawing upon many traditional values of the past, from many different cultures, we have the opportunity to build a far more accountable, understandable, and healing system of justice and law that can lead to a greater sense of community through active victim and citizen involvement in restorative initiatives.

REFERENCES

Adams, J. (1998, August 20). Hastings tends, city finally comes full circle. *Minneapolis Star Tribune*, p. B1.

Allam, H. (2002, March 2). Sentencing circle aims to rebuild lives. *St. Paul Pioneer Press*, p. 12A.

American Bar Association. (1994, Approved August 1994). Policy on legislative and national issues. In American Bar Association (Ed.), *Policies and procedures handbook* (p. 730). Chicago, IL: Author.

Aos, S., Miller, M., & Drake, E. (2006). *Evidence-based public policy options to reduce future prison construction, criminal justice costs, and crime rates*. Olympia: Washington State Institute for Public Policy.

Armour, M., Sage, J., Rubin, A., & Windsor, L. (2008). Bridges to life: The impact of an in-prison restorative justice intervention. *International Community Corrections Association Journal, 18*(1), 19–27.

Armour, M., & Umbreit, M. S. (2007). The ultimate penal sanction and "closure" for survivors of homicide victims. *Marquette Law Review, 91*(1), 101–141.

Bazemore, G., & Schiff, M. (2005). *Juvenile justice reform and restorative justice: Building theory and policy from practice*. Portland, Oregon: Willan Publishing.

Bazemore, G., & Umbreit, M. S. (2003). A comparison of four restorative conferencing models. In G. Johnston (Ed.), *A restorative justice reader* (pp. 225–244). Portland, Oregon: Willan Publishing.

Bradshaw, W., & Roseborough, D. (2005). Restorative justice dialogue: The impact of mediation and conferencing on juvenile recidivism. *Federal Probation, 69*(22), 15–21.

Braithwaite, J. (2002). *Restorative justice and responsive regulation*. New York: Oxford Publishing.

Brunk, C. (2001). Restorative justice and the philosophical theories of punishment. In M. Hadley (Ed.), *Spiritual roots of restorative justice* (pp. 31–56). New York: SUNY Press.

Burns, H. (2002). *Citizens, victims and offenders restoring justice project: Minnesota Correctional Facility Lino Lakes*. St. Paul, MN: University of Minnesota, School of Social Work, Center for Restorative Justice & Peacemaking.

Carr, C. (1998). *VORS program evaluation report*. Inglewood, CA: Centenela Valley Juvenile Diversion Project.

Cayley, D. (1998). *The expanding prison: The crisis in crime and punishment and search for alternatives*. Cleveland, OH: Pilgrim Press.

Center for Court Innovation. (2008). *Annual report, Center for Court Innovation*. Retrieved January 5, 2010, from http://www.courtinnovation.org/_uploads/documents/2008_Annual_Report1.pdf

Coates, R., Umbreit, M. S., & Vos, B. (2004). Restorative justice systemic change: Washington County, Minnesota. *Federal Probation, 68*(3), 16–23.

Commission of the European Communities. (2001). *Report from the Commission on the basis of Article 18 of the Council Framework Decision of 15 March 2001 on the standing of victims in criminal proceedings*, COM (2004) 54 final/2, 16.02.04. Retrieved January 7, 2010, from http://europa.eu/bulletin/en/200012/p104015.htm

Considine, J. (1999). *Restorative justice: Healing the effects of crime*. Lyttleton, NZ: Ploughshares.

Cordella, J. (1991). Reconciliation and the mutualist model of community. In H. Pepinsky & R. Quinney (Eds.), *Criminology as peacemaking* (pp. 30–46). Bloomington, IN: Indiana University Press.

Daly, K. (2001). Restorative justice in Australia and New Zealand: Variations, research findings, and prospects. In A. Morris & G. Maxwell (Eds.), *Restoring justice for juveniles: Conferencing, mediation and circles* (pp. 59–84). Oxford: Hart Publishing.

Dissel, A. (2000). *Restoring the harmony: A report on a victim offender conferencing pilot project.* Johannesburg: Centre for the Study of Violence and Reconciliation.

Evje, A., & Cushman, R. (2000). *A summary of the evaluations of six California victim offender rehabilitation programs.* San Francisco: Administrative Office of the Courts.

Gilbert, M. J., & Settles, T. L. (2007). The next step: Indigenous development of neighborhood-restorative community justice. *Criminal Justice Review, 32*(1), 5–25.

Goodrum, S. D., & Stafford, M. C. (2001). *Homicide, bereavement, and the criminal justice system.* Doctoral dissertation, The University of Texas at Austin, Austin, 2001.

Griffiths, C. T., & Hamilton, R. (1996). Sanctioning and healing: Restorative justice in Canadian aboriginal communities. In B. Galaway & J. Hudson (Eds.), *Restorative justice: International perspectives* (pp. 175–192). Monsey, NY: Criminal Justice Press.

Helfgott, J., Lovell, M., & Lawrence, C. (1999). Results from the pilot study of the citizens, victims, and offender restoring justice program at the Washington State Reformatory. *Journal of Contemporary Criminal Justice, 16*(1), 5–31.

Home Office. (2003). *Restorative justice: The government's strategy. A consultation document on the government's strategy on restorative justice.* London: Home Office.

Johnstone, G. (2002). *Restorative justice: Ideas, values and debates.* Devon, UK: Willan Publishing.

Karp. D., Sprayregen, M., & Drakulick, K. (2002). *Vermont Reparative Probation Year 2000 Outcome Evaluation Final Report.* Waterbury, VT: Vermont Department of Corrections.

Karp, D. R., & Conrad, S. (2003). Restorative justice and college student misconduct. *Public Organization Review: A Global Journal, 5,* 315–333.

Lajeunesse, T. (1996). *Community holistic circle healing, in Hollow Water, Manitoba: An evaluation.* Ottawa, Canada: Solicitor General Canada, Ministry Secretariat.

Latimar, J., Dowden, D., & Muise, D. (2001). *The effectiveness of restorative practices: A meta-analyis.* Ottawa, Canada: Department of Justice, Research and Statistics Division Methodological Series.

Latimer, J., Dowden, C., & Muise, D. (2005). The effectiveness of restorative practices: A meta-analysis. *Prison Journal, 85,* 127–145.

Maxwell, G., & Morris, A. (1993). *Family, victims, and culture: Youth justice in New Zealand.* Wellington: Social Policy Agency (Ropu Here Kaupapa), and Institute of Criminology, Victoria University of Wellington.

McCold, P. (1999, August 5–7). *Restorative justice practice: State of the field.* Paper presented at Building Strong Partnerships for Restorative Practices, Burlington, VT.

McGarrell, E., Olivares, K., Crawford, K., Kroovand, N. (2000). *Returning justice to the community: The Indianapolis Juvenile Restorative Justice Experiment.* Indianapolis, IN: Hudson Institute Crime Control Policy Center.

Merry, S., & Milner, N. (1995). *The possibility of popular justice. A case study of community mediation in the United States.* Ann Arbor, MI: University of Michigan Press.

Mika, H., & Zehr, H. (1998). Fundamental principles of restorative justice. *Contemporary Justice Review, 1*(1), 47–55.

Miller, D. (2001). Disrespect and the experience of injustice. *Annual Review of Psychology*, 52, 527–552.

Minnesota Department of Corrections. (n.d.). *Victim assistance program: Apology letters*. Retrieved January 5, 2010, from http://www.doc.state.mn.us/crimevictim/apology.htm

Moore, D., & Forsythe, L. (1995). *A new approach to juvenile justice: An evaluation of family conferencing in Wagga Wagga*. Wagga Wagga, AU: Centre for Rural Social Research.

Native Counseling Services of Alberta. (2001). *Cost-benefit analysis of Hollow Water's community holistic circle healing process*. Alberta, Canada: Aboriginal Corrections Policy Unit, Solicitor General Canada.

Niemeyer, M., & Shichor, D. (1996). A preliminary study of a large victim/offender reconciliation program. *Federal Probation*, 60(3), 30–34.

O'Brien, S. (2000). *Restorative juvenile justice in the States: A national assessment of policy development and implementation*. Washington, DC: U.S. Department of Justice Office of Juvenile Justice and Delinquency Prevention.

Peterson, M. (2000). *The search for meaning in the aftermath of homicide*. Doctoral dissertation, University of Minnesota, St. Paul, 2000.

Presser, L., & Van Voorhis, P. (2001). Values and evaluation: Assessing processes and outcomes of restorative justice programs. Crime & Delinquency, 48(1), 162–188.

Redfield, T. L. (2006). The role of victim outreach. Champion Magazine, 49.

Roberts, L. (1998). *Victim offender mediation: An evaluation of the Pima County Juvenile Court Center's Victim Offender Mediation Program (VOMP)*. Masters thesis, University of Arizona, Tucson, AZ.

Roberts, T. (1995). *Evaluation of the Victim Offender Mediation Project, Langley, BC: Final report*. Victoria, BC, Canada: Focus Consultants.

Robinson, P. H. (2003). The virtues of restorative processes, the vices of "restorative justice". *Utah Law Review*, 1, 375–388.

Rutherford, A. (1984). *Prisons and the process of justice: The reductionist challenge*. London: William Heinemann.

Sharpe, S. (Ed.). (2004). *How large should the restorative justice "tent" be?* Monsey, NY: Criminal Justice Press.

Sullivan, D., & Tifft, L. (2004). *Restorative justice: Healing the foundations of our everyday lives*. Monsey, NY: Criminal Justice Press.

The Advocates for Human Rights. (2008). *U.S. Public Hearings*. Retrieved January 5, 2010, from http://liberiatrc.mnadvocates.org/Public_Hearings.html

Tontodonato, P., & Erez, E. (1994). Crime, punishment, and victim distress. *International Review of Victimology*, 33, 49–51.

Umbreit, M. S. (1994). *Victim meets offender*. Monsey, NY: Criminal Justice Press.

Umbreit, M. S., Coates, R., & Vos, B. (2001). *Juvenile victim offender mediation in six Oregon counties*. Salem, OR: Oregon Dispute Resolution Commission.

Umbreit, M. S., & Greenwood, J. (1999). National survey of victim offender mediation programs in the U.S. *Mediation Quarterly*, 16, 235–251.

Umbreit, M. S., Lewis, T., & Burns, H. (2003). A community response to a 9/11 hate crime: Restorative justice through dialogue. *Contemporary Justice Review, 6*(4), 383–391.

Umbreit, M. S., Vos, B., Coates, R., & Brown, K. (2003). *Facing violence: The path of restorative justice & dialogue.* Monsey, NY: Criminal Justice Press.

United Nations. (2000). *Basic principles on the use of restorative justice programmes in criminal matters.* (ECOSOC Res. 2000/14). New York: Author.

Van Ness, D. (1999). Legal issues of restorative justice. In G. Bazemore & L. Walgrave (Eds.), *Restorative juvenile justice: Repairing the harm of youth crime* (pp. 263–284). Monsey, NY: Criminal Justice Press.

Van Ness, D., & Heetderks, K. (2002). *Restoring justice* (2nd ed.). Cincinnati, OH: Anderson Publishing Company.

Warters, B., Sebok, T., & Goldblum, A. (2000). Making things right: Restorative justice comes to campuses. *Conflict Management in Higher Education Report, 1*(1).

Wright, M. (1996). *Justice for victims and offenders: A restorative response to crime* (2nd ed.). Winchester, UK: Waterside Press.

Yazzie, R., & Zion, J. (1996). Navajo restorative justice: The law of equality and justice. In B. Galaway & J. Hudson (Eds.), *Restorative justice: International perspectives* (pp. 157–174). Monsey, NY: Criminal Justice Press.

Zehr, H. (1985). *Retributive justice, restorative justice.* Elkhart, IN: Mennonite Central Committee, U.S. Office of Criminal Justice.

Zehr, H. (1990). *Changing lenses: A new focus for crime and justice.* Scottsdale, PA: Herald Press.

Zehr, H. (2002). *The little book of restorative justice.* Intercourse, PA: Good Books.

2. A Movement Grounded in Core Social Work Values

> *It is doubtless that only during a time of war that the men and women of Chicago could tolerate whipping for children in our city prison, and it is only during such a time that the introduction in the legislature of a bill for the re-establishment of the whipping post could be possible. National events determine our ideals, as much as our ideals determine national events.*
>
> Jane Addams

*F*rom its very beginning, social work practitioners, policy makers, and academicians have been actively involved in the restorative justice movement. In fact, restorative justice and social work are natural bedfellows in that they share the similarities in values and practice principles critical to restorative justice's efforts to redress harm and the conditions that contribute to criminal behavior.

For example, restorative justice elevates the status of crime victims and makes the harm they suffered more important than the law that was broken. In addition, social work and restorative justice serve the same vulnerable and disadvantaged groups, for example, incarcerated youth, students in troubled schools, victims of family violence, and residents of poverty-ridden neighborhoods. Social work, for decades, has disaffiliated itself from the traditional criminal justice system due, in part to the mismatch between social work values and the retributive philosophy that mostly guides current criminal justice practice.

The recent emergence of selective applications of restorative justice within criminal justice practices throughout the world as well as the United States offers the profession of social work a way to meaningfully reengage with criminal justice in ways compatible with social work values and ethics. In this chapter, we review the historic relationship between social work and the criminal justice system and the significance of restorative justice to the social work profession and demonstrate the strong implicit relationship between social work and restorative justice by reviewing the core social work values and how those values are manifest in restorative justice philosophy and practices.

SOCIAL WORK AND THE CRIMINAL JUSTICE SYSTEM

Social work boasts a proud legacy for the role it played in corrections during the early part of the twentieth century. Its concern with the adverse effects of urbanization, industrialization, and immigration on children resulted, for example, in the establishment in 1899 of the first juvenile court in Cook County, Chicago (Gumz, 2004). This bold and pioneering step launched policy specific to youth instituting separate hearings for children's cases, separate detention from adult offenders, and a juvenile probation system staffed by social workers. Indeed, until the mid-1920s, social work practice focused principally on people confined to institutions, including prisons, reform schools, state mental hospitals, and state schools for the feebleminded. Social work continued a strong affiliation with corrections through the National Conference of Charities and Corrections, providing services such as presentence investigations and supervision, helping prisoners while incarcerated, and helping plan for their reentry (Chaiklin, 2008).

As long as rehabilitation was the guiding philosophy, there was a natural affinity between social work and criminal justice. By the 1970s, though, there was a rising crime rate and increased recidivism, which resulted in the public's demand for more effective measures (Stinchcomb & Fox, 1999). In addition, the credibility of the rehabilitative model was challenged by the 1974 Martinson report, which questioned whether psychotherapy or any treatment program, educational or vocational, could reduce recidivism. The report concluded that rehabilitation could not impact the powerful tendency of offenders to continue in criminal behavior (Lewis, 2006). As long as rehabilitation was the dominant model, social workers played leadership roles in the dialogue, debate, research, and practice related to criminal justice (Reamer, 2004). By the mid-1970s, a punitive philosophy of criminal justice had set in, giving way to a more conservative doctrine of retribution (Gumz, 2004). This trend was accompanied by assigning a more marginal status to social services throughout the criminal justice system, making social workers, their values, and practices less relevant to the field of corrections (Orzech, 2006). Social workers themselves also began leaving agency-based practice in the mid-1970s, opting instead for greater autonomy and more career options than just to work with the poor and disenfranchised.

As the philosophical base of the criminal justice system changed, so did its goals and the increasing emphasis, to the present time, on punishment of offenders, societal retribution for criminal acts, and protection of the community and society (Gumz, 2004). The priority given to order, control, and punishment clashed with the basic tenets of social work practice, namely the innate dignity of the individual, self-determination of the client, confidentiality, moral neutrality, and social justice. Van Wormer notes the vast distance that emerged between social work and corrections: "Contrast the terminology of criminal justice, punishment, zero tolerance, criminal personality with that of social work—empowerment, social justice, cultural competence—and the fields come across as worlds apart" (2002, p. 216). As a consequence of this philosophical shift, social work largely abandoned the criminal justice field (Reamer, 2004). Although many social workers continued to work in probation and as parole officers, or in halfway houses or correctional institutions, there was a significant decline in social work's presence and leadership in the field (Gibelman & Schervish, 1993).

Social work's disaffiliation has had continuing consequences. Few social workers elect criminal justice as a specialty (Reamer, 2004). Faculty in schools of social work show little interest in corrections, and few courses are offered through continuing education (Knox & Roberts, 2002; McNeece & Roberts, 1997). A comparison of two studies found that the specialization area that lost the most ground in social work between 1982 and 1995 was corrections (Vinton & White, 1995). There is no section on corrections or criminal justice in NASW's eight specialty practice sections. The consequence of this shrinking investment in corrections is revealed in a survey that found that only 0.07% of graduate students list corrections or criminal justice as their primary specialty (Lennon, 2001).

At the same time that social work was redrawing its endorsement of the criminal justice system and its punitive practices, restorative justice was emerging, in large part, because of the efforts of individual social workers. Mark Umbreit, other social work practitioners, student interns and faculty at the University of Minnesota, a local judge, and several probation staff worked closely with Howard Zehr of the Mennonite Central Committee in providing support for the development of the first Victim-Offender Reconciliation Program (VORP) in the United States in 1978 (Umbreit, 2001). Umbreit founded the Center for Restorative Justice & Peacemaking in the School of Social Work at the University of Minnesota in 1994 and along with a team of social work scholars and practitioners prepared and distributed internationally a wide range of training materials, manuals, and video tapes on victim-offender mediation and other restorative justice interventions. Much of this work is highlighted in Umbreit's book, *The Handbook of Victim-Offender Mediation: An Essential Guide for Practice and Research* (Umbreit, 2001). The School of Social Work at the University of Minnesota not only established the first academic-based restorative justice website and Center but also founded the National Restorative Justice Training Institute, which has trained thousands of practitioners and policy makers throughout North America and at least 21 other countries.

Two Canadian social work educators, Burt Galaway and Joe Hudson, edited the volume, *Restorative Justice: International Perspectives* (1998), which provided information on First Nations' indigenous practices such as circle sentencing. Hudson, along with Gail Buford, later edited the definitive study on family group conferencing, *Family Group Conferencing: New Directions in Community-Centered Child and Family Practice* (2000).

Van Wormer is a strong advocate for the inclusion of restorative justice in social work education and practice. Besides her articles aimed directly at social work educators, she has used her books to persuasively advance her argument for the linkages between restorative and social justice and between restorative justice and the strengths perspective. Primary sources include *Confronting Oppression, Restoring Justice* (2003), *Counseling Female Offenders and Victims: A Strengths-Restorative Approach* (2001), and *Restorative Justice Across the East and the West* (2008).

Elizabeth Beck is the Director of *Defense-Initiated Victim Outreach* (DIVO), a semirestorative justice initiative out of the School of Social Work at Georgia State University. DIVO seeks to bridge the historic and antagonistic tension between victim survivors and defense attorneys to reduce victim trauma and better meet survivors' needs while opening the possibility that the defense team's expressions of civility and sympathy toward the victim's family members may paradoxically be reciprocated.

Although these social work educators and practitioners have been influential in the professional restorative justice community, the social work profession has been slow to see the natural affinity between the two. Restorative justice advocate van Wormer found only five articles on restorative justice from 1977 to 2004 in *Social Work Abstracts* (2006). She also reports that when she submitted a proposal on restorative justice for the annual CSWE conference in 2002, it was rejected as "not relevant to social work education" (2006, p. 58). Until recently, this reticence has stood in marked contrast to the rapid development of practices that overlap social work and restorative justice. Victim-offender mediation is relevant to victim advocacy. Family group conferencing is employed in child welfare work as well as with extended family structures. Peacemaking circles are appropriate to school social work, community organizing, and addictions treatment.

In 2005, the *NASW (National Association of Social Workers) News,* which is the newsletter of the dominant professional association, published a lead article titled "Restorative Justice: A Model of Healing." The subtitle read "Philosophy Consistent with Social Work Values" (Fred, 2005, p. 1). This publication marked social work's recognition of restorative justice as allied with social work practice. Besides interviews with spokespersons for restorative justice, it included endorsements from NASW members and personnel.

Social work is starting to acknowledge the potential of restorative justice, as a major social work domain, because of its focus on truth, accountability, and healing, to fill voids not addressed by the criminal justice system. Buford and Adams (2004) challenge social work further. Instead of the ethical but purist position that social work tends to take against coercion and manipulative practice with clients, they remind us that social workers have long functioned as agents of social control and have had to deal with the dichotomy at the heart of the profession between care and control and empowerment and coercion. They suggest that one way to reconceptualize the relation between these two aspects of social work is to apply the regulatory pyramid of John Braithwaite (2002). Braithwaite's schema combines the possibilities of restorative, dialogue-based, and empowering approaches at the base of the pyramid where regulation starts, with movement up the pyramid to more coercive, deterrent, and restrictive responses, if the responsible regulatory group is not effective.

The recent attention given to restorative justice in the professional newsletter and the effort by social work practitioners to integrate social control with restorative justice are indicative that social work is moving closer to fully embracing restorative justice and according it significant status in the profession. Moreover, restorative justice offers social work a path for reentry and an exciting opportunity to return to its roots in corrections.

RESTORATIVE VALUES AND SOCIAL WORK PRACTICE

Social work is unique among the mental health professions because it is the only one built on a fundamental set of values. This values base ultimately shapes the field's mission and priorities. Similarly, restorative justice rests on a set of guiding principles:

1. Crime is a violation of people and of interpersonal relationships.
2. Violations create obligations.
3. The central obligation is to put right the wrongs.

The high degree of consistency between restorative justice and social work values is best illustrated by some of the early values-based concepts that were proposed as the foundation for social work practice (Gordon, 1965). When you read them, think about the beliefs that undergird restorative justice:

1. The individual is the primary concern for this society.
2. There is interdependence between individuals in this society.
3. They have social responsibility for one another.

40 RESTORATIVE JUSTICE DIALOGUE

   4. There are human needs common to each person, yet each person is essentially unique and different from others.
   5. An essential attribute of a democratic society is the realization of the full potential of each individual and the assumption of his social responsibility through active participation in the society.
   6. Society has a responsibility to find ways in which obstacles to this self-realization can be overcome or prevented.

Although the core values of social work have shifted somewhat over the years reflecting the profession's different priorities, the list has remained fairly constant including, among others, individual dignity and worth, client self-determination, seeking to meet common human needs, nondiscrimination, confidentiality and privacy, and client empowerment (Reamer, 2004). In 1999, the NASW included for the first time a list of core values for the profession in the NASW Code of Ethics. Each value was named followed by a value-based ethical principle. The next section lists each social work core value and associated ethical principle named in the NASW Code of Ethics followed by a commentary on how that value is evident in restorative justice philosophy and practice. (See Figure 2.1.)

1. Service

Ethical Principle: Social workers' primary goal is to help people in need and to address social problems.

Social workers elevate service to others above self-interest. Social workers draw on their knowledge, values, and skills to help people in need and to address social problems. Social workers are encouraged to volunteer some portion of their professional skills with no expectation of significant financial return.

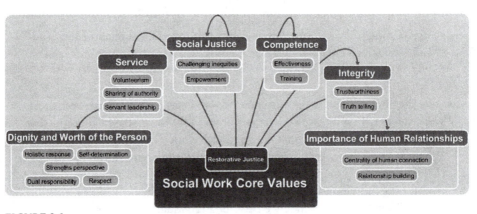

FIGURE 2.1

Voluntarism

Restorative justice rests on voluntarism and the spirit of giving that undergird bringing people together for dialogue. Participants in peacemaking circles, facilitators of victim-offender mediation or larger group conferences, and members of neighborhood reparation boards are most often volunteers who generously contribute their time because they want to help and make a difference.

Within the restorative justice framework, these individuals represent the "community," a critical part of the restorative justice process. They therefore have a personal investment in being part of the dialogue both because they are part of the community and because they too, as community members, will be affected by the outcome of the dialogue. Restorative justice advocates contend that members of the community erroneously turned over their responsibility for their neighborhoods to social institutions that include the criminal justice system thereby weakening the community's fabric (Christie, 1977; Sullivan & Tifft, 2006). Increased citizen participation in restorative justice initiatives is one way of strengthening the community because it returns both the responsibility and power back to those who in reality own them. Voluntary community service associated with restorative justice practices provides an additional bonus for the community because community members are exposed to nonviolent conflict resolution and may learn skills that can be applied to other potentially volatile situations (Dzur, 2003). Voluntarism in restorative justice is essential because it reduces the costs that might otherwise make restorative practices prohibitive (van Wormer, 2002).

The South Saint Paul Restorative Justice Council uses peacemaking circles to deal with conflict in both the community and the schools (Coates, Umbreit, & Vos, 2003). They draw on community residents to be part of the process. When asked about recruitment of community volunteers, leaders of the program indicated that volunteers were identified through word of mouth, or "I knew him/her and thought they would be a good circle member" (2003, p. 274). In the final analysis, circle participants felt that the most reliable mechanism for recruiting was "inviting people you know and trust" (2003, p. 273).

Much of the success attributed to restorative justice practices occurs because the people who come together engage in authentic and trustworthy ways for the community's common good. Offenders frequently remark that they can trust the process because it uses volunteers whose care is more trustworthy than the caring of paid professionals. Indeed, in many countries (including many parts of the United States) where restorative justice has not been incorporated into the legal system, many restorative justice programs operate on a shoe string and are maintained only because of the dedication and enthusiasm of volunteers. When professionals participate as facilitators, they reconstruct their roles so that they share common authority with the other participants (Ames, 2007; Pranis, Stuart, & Wedge, 2003). In family group conferencing, for example, private family deliberations occur so that family members can develop their own plan. The coordinator takes a back seat and joins the family only at their request (MacRae & Zehr, 2004).

Sharing of Authority

This illustration of democratic professionalism speaks to another aspect of service in restorative justice, which is the idea that when professionals participate, they strive to reduce the hierarchy and detachment that, in effect, distances or removes them from others and "professionalizes" their care so that they tend to engage in more formal or stilted ways. This demystification of the professional as expert requires the social worker to be more transparent about his or her motivation. It has to be more than a job for the professional's involvement to count in restorative justice. Rather the service element or sense of gifting by virtue of giving beyond oneself is often weighed by the sense of personal commitment others feel from a participating professional. For professionals, therefore, restorative justice is not just a response to harm but a way of relating to others whenever we enter into human interactions (Sullivan & Tifft, 2004).

Servant Leadership

Service in restorative justice also refers to the discipline necessary to suspend or delay one's own needs for gratification. Whether as facilitator or as circle participant, this reduction of ego involvement permits them to focus on what the victim and offender need from each other (Umbreit, 1997; Umbreit & Burns, 2006). In practices like victim-offender mediation, the facilitator's silence or minimal involvement during the dialogue allows the meeting to belong to the victim and to the offender. This ability to recede into the background requires restraint and humility, qualities that call for inner reflection and inner work. Even for circle members, the taking of turns and use of a talking piece become signals to postpone themselves when it is someone else's turn and elevate the speaker above oneself in order to foster the deep listening that connects and heals (Pranis et al., 2003). Indeed, the willingness to become a servant to the process opens the door to experiencing empathy or sensitivity to the expressed needs of others—an ability that requires awareness and the setting aside of one's own biases or work habits. This level of giving while remaining connected to the governing beliefs of restorative justice furthers the congruence in thinking, feeling, and doing that helps make a facilitator or participant believable and opens the way to connect with the humanity of others (Gold, 1993).

2. Social Justice

Ethical Principle: Social workers challenge social injustice.

Social workers pursue social change, particularly with and on behalf of vulnerable and oppressed individuals and groups of people. Social workers' social change efforts are focused primarily on issues of poverty, unemployment, discrimination, and other forms of social injustice. These activities seek to promote sensitivity to and knowledge about oppression and cultural and ethnic diversity. Social workers strive to ensure access to needed information, services, and resources; equality of opportunity; and meaningful participation in decision making for all people.

As a social reform movement, restorative justice is social justice in action. It is concerned with the harm people suffer, not just from individual acts of criminality but also harm caused by insensitivities and inequities in the criminal justice system and other institutions. Restorative justice responds to these injustices by empowering others to make change on both personal and community levels. The wisdom and values of indigenous people in various parts of the world, most of whom have been deeply harmed and marginalized by the dominant society, have had a great deal of influence upon many restorative justice practitioners, both in humbling those of European background and providing a path to promote deep levels of accountability and healing, most notably through the circle process. For example, practices among many Native American communities that are inherently restorative have been adapted in a culturally appropriate manner for use in the dominant society, often with leadership from within Native American communities or First Nation communities in Canada. Restorative justice attempts to include all stakeholders in its practices and, consequently, gives voice to those who, otherwise, have no recognized place in criminal justice proceedings. Restorative justice elevates the role of an affected community so that solutions come from the community rather than imposed by officials of the state. Finally, restorative justice champions advocacy for just policies and systems reform. These examples illustrate how central social justice is to the purpose of restorative justice, with its emphasis on righting wrongs and employing attitudes and practices that create a sense of fairness for all concerned.

Challenging Inequities

The value of social justice in social work is undergirded by the mandate to challenge social injustice. Restorative justice fulfills that mandate by seeking to rectify the inequities created by the criminal justice system, namely the lack of attention given to victims and the harm they have suffered and the lack of opportunity for offenders to take responsibility and make restitution for the harm they caused.

Because under state statutes the state considers itself to be the injured party in a crime (e.g., the state is the victim of a broken law), it creates conditions that, inadvertently, silence and diminish the actual victims. Victims have no official role in criminal justice proceedings other than to be called as possible witnesses. When the state argues that it is acting on behalf of the victims, such a position is both paternalistic and disempowering (King, 2004). Victims frequently comment on the unfairness of their marginalized status, noting that offenders have all the rights because of their constitutional due process protections and they, in contrast, have none. Information about their case, including the smallest of details, may be withheld pending trial, which leaves them suspended and without the tools to understand what happened to them (Umbreit, Lewis, & Burns, 2003). They often feel further traumatized by the system fearing that their emotional response during the trial could result in a mistrial or finding that they are excluded from being in the court room until it's time for them to give their testimony (Armour, 2002).

Restorative justice corrects the social injustice done to victims. Opportunities for restorative justice dialogue gives them back their voice both through the telling of what happened to them as a result of the crime and through their having influence over what they need from the offender. It also gives them control over whether or not they want to participate, the questions they pose to the offender, and what will help them heal. If the dialogue occurs in the context of their support system, it reduces the sense of isolation that may further alienate them from the community.

Just as restorative justice challenges the injustice of the system by instituting a socially just process for victims, it also establishes a process for offenders that rectifies some of the inequities they may suffer. In the conventional system, many offenders are punished through imprisonment for having broken the law. The United States has the highest per capita rate of incarceration in the world. This form of remediation removes and isolates them from the prosocial relationships of communities and provides them access only to other prisoners who then teach them skills to reoffend more effectively (South & Wood, 2006). When offenders reenter society, they find that they are stigmatized as criminals, excluded from most employment, and have limited abilities to manage the complexities of navigating a world that has significantly changed since they were imprisoned. Moreover, while in prison, they received no help in understanding the harm they caused, the need for self-examination, remorse, and apology. The result is that they focus on the injustices they have received in their life and while in prison and the anger they feel as victims of the system.

Restorative justice, on the other hand, gives offenders the opportunity to take responsibility for their actions through making things right, or as right as possible, with the victim (Umbreit et al., 2003; van Wormer, 2002, 2003). Restorative justice guides and supports them to examine themselves, their motivation for committing the crime, and the feelings they have as they realize the impact of their behavior on others' lives, including the lives of their own family members. Instead of feeling diminished, offenders find that holding themselves accountable, making amends, and meaningful attitudinal and behavioral changes orient them toward the present and future state of affairs and toward membership in the community (van Wormer, 2004). Their accountability with support directed to the victim, thereby, becomes the path to their own recovery. Instead of the stigma associated with serving time, offenders discover self-pride and a variety of options that they control.

Besides making the victim tangential to the process and separating the offender from sources of help, the criminal justice system creates an additional sense of injustice for secondary victims, for example, family and neighbors in the local community, who also have no voice at all, no matter how great the impact of the crime on their own lives (van Wormer, 2004). These stakeholders, however, may be vitally important to the lives of victims and offenders. The injustice associated with not being recognized is particularly evident when a hate crime occurs (Umbreit et al., 2003). It can terrorize an entire community, but without evidence that they have been directly harmed, community members have no legal standing in the court.

Restorative justice lessens the disparity between those who have been directly and indirectly affected by keeping the dialogue process flexible and encouraging all those who have been affected by the crime to participate. The inclusiveness of this process sends the message that everyone's experiences and feelings are valued as are the interrelationships between people.

Empowerment

In social work, empowering others becomes the way to achieve social justice (Gutierrez & Suarez, 1999). In restorative justice, the victim, offender, and community are empowered through the process to take action themselves to improve their situations. This change happens for the victim because their sense of helplessness is countered by being an active participant in the process (Koss, 2000). The ability of restorative justice to intervene on the helplessness of victims is supported by research, which found that victims of battering who had a say in formal or informal proceedings felt more empowered to get help, even to terminate the relationship (Presser & Gaarder, 2004). Offenders feel empowered when they have a voice in determining and accepting the consequences for the harm they caused and hold the power to make things right for the victim by following through on making amends. Moreover, they have an increased appreciation for the choices they made when they committed the crime, the choices they can make in the future, and the changes that are possible to make, including helping others.

Empowerment in both social work and restorative justice also applies to specific groups who have been oppressed, economically disadvantaged, and fragmented by the dominant society. Some of these groups are overrepresented in the criminal justice system, notably African-American and Hispanic offenders. This disparity is supported by statistics that show that about 10.4% of all black males in the United States between the ages of 25 and 29 years are sentenced and in prison, compared to 2.4% of Hispanic males and 1.3% of white males (Harrison & Beck, 2003). Restorative justice serves to meet these groups in that its recognition of the importance of spirituality for many groups, nonbureaucratic processes, and reliance on mutual aid are compatible with the cultural values and traditions of the Latino community (Gutierrez & Suarez, 1999) as well as with African-centered principles (Carter, 1997).

Restorative justice directly challenges the disregard given to indigenous cultures by tapping into their natural resources and making its practices culturally specific. In Hawaii, for example, there has been a revitalization of the use of *ho'oponopono*, an ancient Hawaiian conflict resolution process embedded in the value of extended family, respective elders, need for harmonious relationships, and the restoration of goodwill or aloha. The process is ritualistic and follows a definite protocol with an opening prayer, open discussion of the problem, and confession of wrongdoing in the seeking of forgiveness (Hurdle, 2002).

In some instances, the practices of indigenous groups have even been given priority over the practices of the conventional justice system. In New Zealand, for example, family group decision making emerged only after the Maori found that they were disproportionately affected by the Western system of justice and pushed for implementation of their traditional practices, which included involvement of the whole community in the punishment process, a focus on finding the cause of the crime, and a concern with healing and problem solving (MacRae & Zehr, 2004).

Restorative justice actively pursues social change and meaningful participation in decision-making by identifying community representation as its central premise (Schatz, 2008). Indeed, it elevates the low status accorded poverty-ridden neighborhoods by giving preference to the community's informal social control over the formal control of the state (Dzur, 2003). Moreover, inclusivity of representation in restorative justice practices and the value placed on agreement by consensus support the collectivity of the group, a practice that is consistent with the collective social structure that characterizes many culturally diverse groups. The consensus model also helps community members find a balance between participants who have varying degrees of power (van Wormer, in press). Involving community members in the process of doing justice is significant because by taking responsibility for the social conditions that contribute to problems, including criminal behavior, and building stronger, more connected, and caring communities, the community can better challenge the social injustices it endures from the dominant society.

Besides empowering individuals and communities, proponents of restorative justice engage in policy advocacy and systems reform. Through their efforts, over 29 states in the United States have Victim-Offender Mediation or Dialogue-related statutory authority to implement programs. Outside this county, the Youth Justice Board for England and Wales set a target for restorative justice processes to comprise 80% of each Youth Offending Team's interventions by 2004. By 2002, over half the interventions were already in place and identified as restorative or reparative (Davey, 2005). In 1989, the Children, Young Persons and Their Families' Act legally mandated family group conferencing in New Zealand for juvenile offenders, with court intervention only as a last resort (MacRae & Zehr, 2004). The 2002 Sentencing Act extended the law to include adult offenders as well (Bowen & Boyack, 2003). Besides policy specific to restorative justice, advocates also promote a variety of reforms, including proposals to allow ex-inmates with felonies to qualify for some occupations that require state licensure or to include persons who lived in nonlegal union with a homicide victim to qualify for crime victim compensation.

Restorative justice is a form of social justice that originates at both the grassroots and macrolevels, exposes and responds to the inequities in the criminal justice system that oppress both victims and offenders, and promotes conditions that encourage respect for social and cultural diversity. Similar to social work, it operates from an empowerment perspective that puts energy into the future, not into what is past.

3. Dignity and Worth of the Person

Ethical Principle: Social workers respect the inherent dignity and worth of the person.

Social workers treat each person in a caring and respectful fashion, mindful of individual differences and cultural and ethnic diversity. Social workers promote clients' socially responsible self-determination. Social workers seek to enhance clients' capacity and opportunity to change and to address their own needs. Social workers are cognizant of their dual responsibility to clients and to the broader society. They seek to resolve conflicts between clients' interests and the broader society's interests in a socially responsible manner consistent with the values, ethical principles, and ethical standards of the profession.

In restorative justice, supreme importance is given to respect as an inherent human right and to creating a respectful process between victim and offender plus additional stakeholders. Instead of cursory attention to the acts that caused the harm, restorative justice is concerned with the whole person and what victims and offenders need in order to move forward. As such, restorative justice builds on the good in people, helping them to carve out their own future paths.

Respect

Restorative justice emerged as a social movement, in part, because the judicial system was concerned only with the offender and responded from a deserts-based system of justice, which made punishment the central feature of what an offender deserved and its severity a measure of an offender's just deserts (Sullivan & Tifft, 2001). The conventional system therefore barely recognized the victim and paid little or no attention to what would help victims heal or offenders to right their wrongs. In contrast, restorative justice maintains the dignity of participants by using a process that is fair but more importantly, requires victim, offender, and related others to present and listen to each other and remain open to each other's desires, pain and suffering, needs, and feelings so that they can experience each other as fellow human beings, while understanding and respecting their differences (Umbreit & Burns, 2002). Its expectation that offenders learn about the human consequences of their criminal behavior—that people are harmed by what they have done and that victims are people, not just objects or targets—challenges them to learn respect, even reverence, for the needs of others. Moreover, the opportunity given offenders to apologize or own up to their wrongdoing potentially enhances their own self-respect because they can walk away with their self-esteem intact due to the active role they have played in the process (Holtquist, 1999).

Holistic Response

The value given to the dignity and worth of the individual is particularly evident in the restorative justice principle that references the need to examine the social conditions that impact the offender's behavior. Rather than limiting itself to the acts that have caused harm, restorative justice addresses the offenders' whole personality. This person-in-environment perspective is equivalent to the ecological model in social work and understanding the significance of social context on human behavior. In restorative justice, this means recognizing the effect of relationships and structures on people's capacities and decisions. In a conference with three youth who had vandalized a construction site, the daughter of the old man who owned the property asked the oldest boy why he was hanging around with younger kids rather than boys his own age. This question sparked comments that gave a much fuller picture of what had contributed to his behavior and what he needed. He talked about the fact that his mother had left the city with another man—abandoning her son. He described how angry he was and how he had gotten in trouble at school for beating up some other students. Therefore, he had few friends at the moment.

Although these additional stressors do not excuse the vandalism, they would likely inform the agreement drawn up between the daughter and the youth at the end of a victim-offender mediation and the actions that this particular boy would need to take in making amends. He might be asked to get some grief counseling or attend an anger management class, help on a Habitat for Humanity project with the daughter of the construction owner, and talk to other kids his age to discourage them from destroying other people's property. These assignments are expressions of care and personal worth because they are derived from the boy's needs and convey that he is deserving of getting help and is of value to others. This holistic response to the offender's behavior and its antecedents further meets the goal of restoring the boy to the community.

Strengths Perspective

The strengths perspective in social work subscribes to the notion that people have a natural power within themselves, and when this source of strength is supported, it enhances the probability for positive growth (Weick & Chamberlain, 2002). Restorative justice pulls on the inherent power of victims and offenders to transform their own lives. With victims, it encourages them to directly deal with rather than avoid the impact of the crime so that it can be resolved. With offenders, it encourages active behavior change, not passive acceptance, as an indicator that they are taking responsibility. Oftentimes, they are surprised by what they were able to do, particularly when they are allowed to come up with their own solutions.

A mother whose son was killed when a drunk driver hit his motorcycle described how difficult it was to meet with the young woman. "I really didn't know what I was going to say. I just thought I'd bawl through the whole thing. I really wanted her to know Tony and so I took pictures of him so she could see who he was." Besides drawing on the victim's or offender's own reservoirs of strength to overcome adversity, restorative justice focuses on solutions and working toward the future instead of going to the past. The question for victims is what they need from the offender to help them move forward. The question for the offender is what they owe to the victims, the community, and even themselves.

In addition to tapping into, supporting, and enhancing people's strengths, restorative justice employs the strengths of community resources. The outcome of a peacemaking circle might be a healing circle for the victim. The practice of family group decision making works with the family or the resource itself and uses the strengths of the family in developing a workable plan. Whether the concentration is on the strengths of the individual or the community resource, restorative justice promotes development of the potential in others which, again, is a commentary on the worth of the individual. The facilitator demonstrates this belief in each person's capacity by listening and not dictating because "just" listening promotes personal power in the lives of those who have been affected by crime (van Wormer, 2004, 2001).

Self-Determination

Self-determination is an extension of human worth and holds that individuals ought to take part in the decisions that affect their lives. Self-determination gives men and women choice, which gives them control and a sense of mastery over their fate. Moreover, because it makes them instrumental, it ultimately makes them responsible for the options they select and their impact on others. Honoring the expressed needs of the individual, therefore, is tied directly with a belief in social responsibility.

The decision to participate in a restorative justice dialogue is an exercise in self-determination that includes both choice and social obligation to attend to the damage. Victim and offender are presented with the option for a meeting, but each chooses whether or not to participate. Even before meeting, they may elect whether or not to invite additional family members, a clergyperson, neighbor, or friend and what ritual, if any, will help establish a climate for deep and respectful listening. Victims commonly select who will speak first and in some forms of dialogue, like victim-offender dialogue in crimes of severe violence, victims may even determine the width of the table to put between themselves and the offender. Victim and offender develop their own agendas based on their questions or what they want to say to each other and again exercise choice about what they will express verbally and emotionally in the meeting. Ultimately, the victim or community, in concert with the offender, decides on what they need to restore losses and repair the harm to the extent possible. The offender, in response, decides whether or not to comply with the agreement that he or she helped to develop. This entire process must be planned fully and carefully done through joint decision making with the victim.

Offenders and victims frequently comment on the gains they have made after they realize or act on their power to make their own choices. A victim described her sense of freedom, "The reoccurring nightmare that haunted me for decades, no longer visits me. The songs, smells, tastes, and other things that I avoided for long, no longer hold me hostage." An offender commented on his sense of social obligation. Participating in the circle ". . . taught me how to treat and respect people. I now know that I have victims. I promise that I will be a man and a father."

Dual Responsibility

Restorative justice functions in a state of in-betweenness. It may be simultaneously concerned with the needs of victims and offenders or offenders and the community or all three groups. Rather than mediating between diverse groups whose interests conflict, restorative justice works with the collective energy and emotional intensity associated with the crime and seeks to transform the harm caused by an act that cannot be undone into a less entrenched, angry, and bitter standoff with a constructive, negotiated, and future-oriented resolution for all concerned. Because it operates from a nondichotomous paradigm that involves multiple and diverse stakeholders, restorative justice moves fluidly between practice and policy and micro- and macrosystems depending on the work to be done. For restorative justice, therefore, dignity and worth refer to being inclusive based on the assertion that, as humans, we are dependent on one another and the belief that all voices have value.

4. Importance of Human Relationships

Ethical Principle: Social workers recognize the central importance of human relationships.

Social workers understand that relationships between and among people are an important vehicle for change. Social workers engage people as partners in the helping process. Social workers seek to strengthen relationships among people in a purposeful effort to promote, restore, maintain, and enhance the well-being of individuals, families, social groups, organizations, and communities.

Centrality of Human Connection

Much of the criminal behavior and the harm victims suffer develop within an emotional and human relationship that may be characterized by powerful feelings of disrespect, betrayal, and abuse. Even if no prior relationship existed between victim and offender, the actual violation creates an involuntary relationship that affects the key players and their families on both sides and, without intervention, may remain volatile but frozen in time. Human connection, therefore, has the potential to wreak tremendous damage. Although relationships have the potential to be destructive, human connection is also fundamental to activating the change processes that can bring healing. Indeed, victims and offenders are more likely to experience emotional benefits from a restorative justice dialogue because the healing occurs in the relationship encounter in the present (Umbreit, 1997).

Besides using the relationship between victim and offender for healing and accountability, restorative justice joins with others who have relationships with the victim and offender. The facilitator of a family group conference or a peacemaking circle may call on those relationships, when appropriate, to teach the offender about his or her responsibilities, to attest to the impact of the violation on the victim's life, to provide additional support for the victim's healing or the implementation of the restitution plan, and to remind the victim and offender that they are not alone. Indeed, proponents of restorative justice frequently remark that comments from a trusted friend, teacher, or grandparents have more lasting influence than anything a facilitator could say because what is said grows out of a preexisting, powerful relationship. Moreover, the offenders' amends in the form of restitution or reparative acts assist to restore relationships with the community through community service and psychologically with crime victims through the contrition and remorse shown them (van Wormer, 2003).

Although the significance of the facilitator varies by type of dialogue (i.e., neighborhood reparation board vs. victim-offender mediation vs. circle processes), the nature of the relationship between the facilitator and participants is essential to the success of the dialogue. For many of the restorative justice practices, the facilitator needs to do significant preparatory work so that victim and offender are ready to meet together. Much of the initial preparation work involves deeply listening to the story of the involved participant and the impact of the event on their lives as well as clarifying expectations and describing how the process will unfold. This may at times include coaching the victim on the expression of intense and potentially hurtful feelings so that the victim can be heard by the offender. It may include role playing with the offender so that the offender's defensiveness does not get in the way of what the offender wants to say to the victim. The facilitator may not speak much at the actual meeting because that meeting belongs to the victim and offender. The relationships the facilitator has built with the key players, however, are present at the dialogue meeting and provide the foundation of respect, genuineness, and truth telling for how people will engage. Indeed, the ability of participants to feel safe and stay open to each other rests on the trust and rapport the facilitator has built with each person.

Relationship Building

The structure of the restorative justice dialogue contributes to the building of relationship between victim and offender. In face-to-face victim-offender mediations, victim and offender sit directly across from each other at a table, a practice that assists in maintaining the focus on the other as well as eye contact. The focus of the dialogue is on fully relating and hearing the impact of the violation as well as taking responsibility for the harm. Consequently, participants are urged to open their hearts to the expression of feelings, the telling of story, the willingness to disclose and share, the owning of responsibility, the readiness to set aside biases, and the making of "I" statements rather than attacks on the other participant(s). These conditions foster the potential for mutual recognition of each other's humanity, empathy, and authentic human connection.

The foundation for meaningful engagement is also built on the victim's and offender's need for each other. Victims may have questions about the crime and how it happened. What is the offender's background? What was the person's motivation? Offenders may need the opportunity to show remorse or apologize. They may also need the victim to know that the crime they committed is not the full measure of their character. These concerns shape the agenda and the interaction during the dialogue. The give and take between victim and offender in victim-offender mediation, or between offender and community in peacemaking circles, however, both builds the relationship and furthers its significance as the channel for healing.

This focus on the relationship is congruent with the goal of restorative justice, which is helping people to be in "right" relationship with one another (Zehr, 1990). Indeed, restorative justice measures justice or restoration for the victim, offender, and community by the extent to which responsibility is taken, needs are met, and the healing of individuals and relationships is advanced (Holtquist, 1999). As a result, "right" relationship is the outcome of respect for the connectedness of all things and our common humanity. When victim, offender, and community are restored, as much as possible, to their original or desired state, they regain a sense of strength and expand their perspective to include an appreciation for the circumstances the other person is faced with (Umbreit & Burns, 2002). The close ties between restorative justice and social work is particularly evident here because the state of being in "right" relationship to others promotes individual and communal well-being as prescribed by social work.

5. Integrity

Ethical Principle: Social workers behave in a trustworthy manner.

Social workers are continually aware of the profession's mission, values, ethical principles, and ethical standards and practice in a manner consistent with them. Social workers act honestly and responsibly and promote ethical practices on the part of the organizations with which they are affiliated.

In restorative justice, integrity refers both to the trustworthiness of the process and to the emphasis placed on truth and frank disclosure. In contrast to a retributive system where offenders fight against disclosures of guilt, restorative justice promotes open sharing. This sharing is expected to include actions from offenders that convey honesty, moral purpose, and uprightness, actions that are difficult to promote in a system that espouses punishment and exclusion from the social relationships of the community, thereby preventing offenders from understanding the full consequences of their behavior and making amends. The significance of integrity to restorative justice is represented by Skidmore College, which fashioned a restorative justice student-led judicial process to address student misconduct called the Integrity Board (Karp, 2004).

Trustworthiness

Restorative justice is guided by a set of principles and precepts, which, if followed, ensure that the dialogue process will be fair, respectful, transparent, honest, and nonoppressive. The core principles include giving priority to the victim's harm, assessing what is owed to the victim and from whom, and direct dialogue between the involved parties to right the wrong. In addition, restorative justice is voluntary for victim and offender, concerned with restoration rather than punishment, encouraging of community involvement, focused on amends making rather than severity of punishment, and inclusive of the community's responsibility for the social conditions that contribute to the offender's behavior. This process is trustworthy because it is built on a non-manipulative, noncoercive, and nonadversarial paradigm and set of practices.

An additional indicator of integrity is the trustworthiness of the individuals involved, especially the facilitator or mediator. How this person is congruent in conveying care and concern, respect, honesty, and reliability influences the level of trust given by others. Congruence, according to noted family therapist Virginia Satir, is a condition of being emotionally honest with yourself and having consistency in your words, feelings, body and facial expressions, and your actions (Umbreit & Burns, 2002). This alignment transmits clarity and a sense of safety to others while also providing them with a basis for assessing how trustworthy another person is.

Truth Telling

In contrast to court adjudication, restorative justice encourages truth telling and the making of amends. For offenders, telling the truth about what happened, answering the victim's or community's questions truthfully, expressing genuine remorse, and making restitution are significant because instead of being done as part of being answerable to the state, these acts are done as expressions of self-accountability made directly to the person and representatives of the community they victimized. Indeed, it is the offenders holding themselves accountable to those they have harmed that allows the victim see their "human" face. Accountability through the person's taking responsibility for how his or her behavior affected others can be freeing and empowering to offenders and victims. Offenders who have been through Bridges to Life, an in-prison program in Texas, stated, "If I want to live and not cause harm to others, I have to give up all old ways and habits." This different perspective makes them more conscientious. "No longer is a store just a store. It is a place where a person is . . . someone who could become a victim." Their ability to feel empathy fortifies them because they feel warmth toward others. "For the first time in my life I feel other's feelings. I've spent 26 years of my life in prison and lived a very cold existence." Because offenders can see options, they recognize more fully that they are in charge of their choices and the direction of their futures.

Truth telling in restorative dialogues is particularly potent because the informal meeting between victim and offender is often part of a public process. Although the interaction between parties may be confidential, the gathering of neighbors for a peacemaking circle, the assembling of key players for a sentencing circle, and the getting together of family members and child protection officials for a family group decision making take the transgression into the public realm where others witness what takes place between victim and offender. In that context, the integrity of the offender's apology or response to the victim is judged by others to whom the offender is accountable for his or her future behavior including the completion of what needs to be done to make amends to the victim or community. In the Asian nation of Timor Leste, the victims who participated in the Truth and Reconciliation Commission to establish the truth about politically motivated violence during Portuguese decolonization and the Indonesian occupation rated the perpetrator's *public admission of responsibility and apology* as the most important to reconciliation (Androff, 2008).

The making of a voluntary and public profession is fast becoming a gauge of the offender's integrity. In the Bridges to Life program, offenders read aloud to other offenders and crime victims unsent letters they have written to their own victims and family members expressing remorse about the harm they have caused and their plans for redressing the damage (Armour, Sage, Rubin, & Windsor, 2009). The Minnesota Department of Corrections offers offenders the option of writing letters of apology to their victims, which are stored in an apology bank to be accessed at will by victims who may someday want to read them.

Truth telling also refers to the victims' story, which often challenges offenders to be more forthcoming when, heretofore, they had little awareness of the harm they caused. Indeed, when victims tell their story directly to the person responsible for their suffering, they, in effect, hold up a mirror that makes the impact of the crime real, tangible, and unforgettable. As one offender remarked, "It's hard not to feel or acknowledge what you have done. Seeing the pain in the victim's eyes made me feel the pain I caused and woke me up".

6. Competence

Ethical Principle: Social workers practice within their areas of competence and develop and enhance their professional expertise.

Social workers continually strive to increase their professional knowledge and skills and to apply them in practice. Social workers should aspire to contribute to the knowledge base of the profession.

Competence, in restorative justice dialogue, refers to the skills of facilitators or mediators who serve in leadership roles. The system of checks and balances on competence is maintained, in part, through evaluating the effectiveness of restorative dialogues, which also contributes to the field's base of knowledge.

Training

Restorative justice seeks to return responsibility to the community for responding to the people and conditions that create victim harm. It is the absence of community involvement that some maintain has contributed to the poor outcomes of the current formal justice system. Consequently, restorative justice maintains that having community members involved in restorative practices fortifies and promotes the community's strength and influence on its members.

The voice of the community is heard through representatives that volunteer to be facilitators or mediators or members of sentencing circles or reparation boards. It is also heard through those who volunteer to participate in peacemaking circles, larger group conferences, or neighborhood accountability boards. People who perform these roles are diverse and include lawyers, tribal leaders, clergy, mental health professionals, and lay persons. These individuals receive training in restorative practices through skill-building workshops, seminars, and apprenticeships and increasingly through academic coursework. Indeed, the Center for Restorative Justice and Peacemaking in the School of Social Work at the University of Minnesota conducts basic training in restorative justice dialogue through mediation, conferencing, or circles in property crimes and minor assaults and advanced training for restorative justice dialogues in cases of severely violent crime, hate crimes, and political violence. The International Institute for Restorative Practices in Bethlehem, Pennsylvania, offers a summer training institute; specialized trainings for teachers, social workers, and law enforcement; and two graduate degrees in education and youth counseling. The Center for Justice and Peacebuilding at Eastern Mennonite University in Pennsylvania houses the summer peacebuilding institute with specific courses in restorative justice. As more counties incorporate restorative justice into their systems, they also offer ongoing training for facilitators and volunteers. Barron County, Wisconsin, for example, provides training in victim-offender conferencing, victim impact panels, and restorative practices for school communities.

Along with their support for training as a way to reduce further harm, restorative justice proponents promote voluntarism because of the need to keep practices grounded in a grassroots and community base. Indeed, when community members join community conferences as participants, they are identifying themselves as members of the same community the offender has harmed. The concentration on voluntarism, however, is different in New Zealand and the United Kingdom. In New Zealand, family group conferences are conducted by child welfare workers, which is a practice that is now followed by many in the United States. In the United Kingdom, youth conferences are led by law enforcement personnel, a practice begun in Australia. These individuals, however, receive specialized training in restorative justice, which helps keep them mindful that the goal is not to take over but rather to turn the power and responsibility back to the people most affected by crime.

Effectiveness

It is assumed that the effectiveness of restorative justice is enhanced when facilitators or mediators are educated about restorative justice principles and competently trained in a humanistic approach to restorative dialogue, which will be covered in Chapter 8.

Many studies show that restorative justice has a positive impact on participant satisfaction, perceptions of fairness, completion of restitution agreements, and so on. (Armour & Umbreit, in press). The Jerry Lee Program on Randomized Controlled Experiments in Restorative Justice is conducting rigorous long-term, life-course follow-up of crime victims and offenders who have been randomly assigned to restorative justice (victim-offender mediation and family group conferencing) or control groups. Thus far, the research shows that restorative justice substantially reduces repeat offending at least for some offenders, reduces crime victim's posttraumatic stress symptoms, provides more satisfaction with justice than criminal justice, reduces victim's desire for violent revenge against their offenders, and reduces recidivism more than prison (adults) or as well as prison (youth) (Sherman & Strang, 2007). Several meta-analyses of the (Sherman & Strang, 2007) impact of victim-offender mediation on juvenile offenders have found significant reductions in recidivism (Nugent, Umbreit, Wiinamaki, & Paddock, 2001; Nugent, Williams, & Umbreit, 2003).

A recent report on reoffending by adult and juvenile offenders found a significant difference for those who participated in a restorative justice conference (Hapland et al., 2008). In an attempt to explain the reasons for the difference, researchers found no relationships between frequency of reconviction and offender demographics such as age, gender, education, and so on. They also found no relationship between frequency of reconviction and whether the offender gave a verbal apology to the victim, promised to stay out of trouble, agreed to pay compensation or whether progress letters or other forms of subsequent contact with the victim occurred.

Using an observational measure, they further examined frequency of reconviction and degree of remorse, whether the victim forgave the offender, how much discussion of reparation to the victim occurred, how much consensus there was on the outcome agreement, the discomfort of the offender during the meeting, the extent of involvement in the meeting by offenders and victims, the level of offender shaming, and how much disapproval of the offender was expressed by the victim. The only significant relationship found was between offenders' views about the meeting and decreased subsequent offending. In particular, all results related to the extent to which the conference had made the offender realize the harm done, whether the offender wanted to meet the victim, the extent to which the offender was observed to be actively involved in the meeting, and how useful the offender felt the meeting had been.

Although this finding shows that offender motivation is critical in reducing the possibility of reconviction, it is also apparent that the competence of the facilitators or mediators affects offenders' motivation because they use their skills to increase participants' openness to the process, help victims more fully and poignantly describe to the offender the harm done, heighten the offender's desire to meet the victim, increase offender involvement in the meeting itself, and strengthen the conclusion that the meeting was useful.

Competence in restorative justice is an evolving value. The leaders in the field fear the overprofessionalization of restorative justice because that defeats the purpose of community engagement. Neither does it want to cause harm because of practices that do not adhere to core restorative justice principles. There is increased demand for education and training commensurate with the growth in programs and general interest in doing restorative justice work. As the research ferrets out the critical factors that influence change processes, the knowledge base builds and restorative justice educators can tailor training to specific change processes.

EXPRESSION OF SOCIAL WORK VALUES AND RESTORATIVE JUSTICE PRINCIPLES IN PRACTICE

The interface of social work values and restorative justice values, principles, and foundational concepts will be further illustrated in further chapters. The significance of human relationships is fundamental to both social work and restorative justice. The importance of social interaction is particularly evident in Family Group Conferencing (FGC) and Victim-Offender Dialogue (VOD) involving crimes of severe violence. Among other relationships, FGC more fully, as described in Chapter 6, focuses on strengthening the family unit of an offender by giving it needed support if the youth's wrongdoing is connected to the family's dysfunction or by looking to the family as an additional resource to reinforce what the youth may need to do in making reparations. Because the nature of the harm is so profound in crimes of severe violence, the relationship independently built by the facilitator with each of the two parties during preparation for VOD is instrumental to establishing the trust necessary for the dialogue meeting itself. The essential quality of these relationships is described more fully in Chapter 8 followed by Chapter 9, containing a description of the necessary characteristics and skills needed by a facilitator for effective restorative practice.

In addition to the shared value of human relationships, social work and restorative justice share a deep concern for social justice. This is illustrated in Chapter 6 with descriptions of how Circles are used in a community agency in Boston, Roca, that assists disadvantaged youth with their transition to adulthood and also used in Canada and parts of the United States with sex offenders to provide long-term support for not reoffending. Restorative justice's concern with "righting" social inequities is exemplified in Chapter 10, which focuses on hate crimes and interethnic conflict. Its attention to empowerment of the individual is demonstrated by an emerging program to address elder abuse (described in Chapter 6) and by a program called Domestic Violence Surrogate Dialogue (described in Chapter 11), which empowers victims of domestic violence to speak openly to unrelated or surrogate batterers about the abuse they have endured.

The significance of service is particularly noteworthy in Circles of Support and Sentencing Circles both of which draw on the voluntarism of community members. Their contributions, as described in Chapter 7, are often pivotal. Because Circles are nonhierarchical and require a sharing of authority, offenders are better able to listen and receive what is offered with less reactivity to issues of power and control. Moreover, the intent of members' contributions are often more credible because they are offered without an agenda other than care and concern for the parties or the well-being of the community that is mutually shared. The importance of service is also shown through the attitude of facilitators who set the tone for dialogue through being servant leaders. The characteristics and qualities of being a servant leader are detailed both in Chapter 4, which delineates the essence of restorativeness found in all restorative approaches and in Chapter 9, which defines the attitudes a facilitator needs to cultivate to establish safety and set the tone for healing and meaningful accountability.

The manifestation of the social work value of dignity and worth is best shown in the principle of respect, which Zehr refers to as synonymous with restorative justice. "Restorative justice, in a word, is respect for everyone involved, offenders as well as victims" (Zehr, 2009, pp. 5–6). Respect in restorative justice is shown through efforts to approach offenders from a holistic perspective. The practice of bringing together key stakeholders for a Sentencing Circle allows the full story to emerge so that the recommended outcome for the offender targets the core issues rather than just the symptomatic behavior or wrongdoing. The supreme importance of preparation as detailed in Chapter 4 as well as the practice-based chapters on VOM, FGC, Circles, and VOD allows for setting the climate and the planning necessary for significant issues related to the context of the wrongdoing to emerge.

The value of individual dignity and worth is also found in creating or utilizing the strengths inherent in the concept of community. Chapter 6 describes the intricacy that goes into constructing Circles so that a community's strengths are maximized. Chapter 10 describes the newfound strengths that have emerged for members of the Parents Circle-Families Forum, a peacemaking initiative comprising hundreds of Israeli and Palestinian parents whose children have been killed in the ongoing interethnic conflict. The cultivation of self-determination is another expression of dignity and worth that is found in restorative practices. Defense-Initiated Victim Outreach is an emerging program described in Chapter 11 that serves to provide victims with the opportunity to engage with the defense in capital cases, in order to address some of their unmet needs for information. By providing access to this historically blocked resource, crime victims are given additional control over what they need for healing.

The current recognition accorded competence as a social work value is mirrored in restorative justice in two ways. First, the field is concerned that facilitators receive special training regardless of whether they volunteer or are paid staff. The skills necessary for each type of practice are outlined in the chapters on VOM, FGC, Circles, and VOD as well as Chapter 9 on the facilitator's role. The skills for VOD, in particular, require knowledge of trauma, mental health, and complicated bereavement.

Second, competence is highlighted in restorative justice through the attention given to the results of research for each of the core approaches. The chapters on VOM, FGC, Circles, and VOD include special sections on what the evidence shows for the effectiveness of the different approaches. VOM in particular is steeped in research that shows reductions in recidivism across time, studies, and geography. In contrast, circles, which are used extensively in schools, have limited and variable findings regarding their effectiveness. Part of this contrast reflects the fact that VOM is used to address a specific wrongdoing often between parties who are strangers to each other. Success is more easily measured specific to recidivism, completion of reparation agreements, and participant satisfaction. Circles, on the other hand, bring together people who are often in ongoing relationships with each other, may involve multiple meetings, and exist, among other agendas, for the purpose of building community. The measurement of success, in this approach, may be more complicated than that in VOM.

Finally, the social work value of integrity is infused throughout restorative justice because of its emphasis on trustworthiness. This jointly held value is part of the essence of what makes practices "restorative" as noted in Chapter 4. The numerous stories in upcoming chapters provide countless illustrations of the trustworthiness that develops between parties as a result of their authentic engagement. Chapter 9 describes interactions between the Director of a Muslim center and would-be terrorist in a hate crime. Chapter 5 describes what happens when a youth has to give his car to a mother after he has stolen her vehicle. Chapter 7 describes how an elder guides other Circle members by telling the story of making beautiful the ragged and torn feather that he holds. These stories demonstrate that in restorative justice a person's truth and the courage to speak it from the heart comprise the integrity necessary for change.

CONCLUSION

Until the 1980s, social workers held key positions in corrections and juvenile justice (van Wormer & Jenkins, 2007). With the advent of zero tolerance policies and resurgence of a punitive response to lawbreaking, social work largely abandoned the criminal justice field (Reamer, 2004). Restorative justice offers a paradigm shift to the conventional model and a response to crime that is compatible with social work values. Indeed, restorative justice has already surfaced in child welfare agencies in response to child abuse and neglect, namely through family group decision-making programs (Buford & Hudson, 2000; van Wormer, 2003). These programs are usually coordinated by social workers and work well in close knit minority communities with extended family ties. They mesh easily with social work values because they give voice to those who are traditionally disadvantaged and place high value on mutual aid and empowerment through KinCare, close friends, and other social supports.

Although restorative justice is compatible with other fields as well, for example, religious ministries, law, criminal justice, and international studies, it shares an especially broad commonality with social work, specifically its values, concern with populations at risk, apprehension about the impact of a retributive model on human worth and dignity, and the requirement to address both individual need and systemic change. Most important, however, is the fact that the values espoused by both social work and restorative justice humanize all participants in their quest for justice. Humanizing the "other" is grounded in the belief that human beings are redeemable (van Wormer, 2008) and the compelling recognition that the current system denigrates both victim and offender through its lack of empathy for victim's needs and its punitive response to wrongdoers.

The priority given to the humanity of both makes restorative justice particularly appealing to social workers, who are uniquely trained to use a humanistic model of engagement. Umbreit (2000) cautions, for example, that the use of probation officers or school officials as facilitators or mediators in restorative face-to-face processes may be counterindicated because of their tendency to use shaming or blaming practices. Indeed, a statistically significant relationship has been found between the reconviction of adults and the experience of being shamed when they participated in family group conferences as youth. In contrast, social workers who are trained in conflict resolution skills and guided by a strong code of ethics may be better equipped to attend to the emotional needs of diverse participants.

Regardless of a person's specialty, however, it is important to recognize the significance of social work values embedded in the field of restorative justice. Not only is there a strong overlap philosophically and in practice, but social work's focus on cultural sensitivity and the strengths-empowerment approach can help restorative justice become more aware of the need for developing culturally specific approaches, responding to the unique concerns of female offenders and training that intentionally focuses on building skills in the strengths-based approach. In return, restorative justice offers an avenue for social work to reclaim part of its place and early birthright in criminal justice by providing competencies for principled practice in corrections and other systems that deal with harm and wrongdoing.

REFERENCES

Ames, J. C. (2007). *Restorative justice: Including victims, offenders and communities in criminal justice dialogue.* Masters thesis, Smith College, Northampton.

Andoff, D. (2008). Working in the mud: Community reconciliation and restorative justice in Timor Leste. In K. van Wormer (Ed.), *Restorative justice across the East and the West* (pp.123–144). Hong Kong: Casa Verde Publishing.

Armour, M. (2002). Journey of family members of homicide victims: A qualitative study of their posthomicide experience. *American Journal of Orthopsychiatry*, 72(3), 372–382.

Armour, M., Sage, J., Rubin, A., & Windsor, L. (2008). Bridges to Life: The impact of an in-prison restorative justice intervention. *International Community Corrections Association Journal*, 18(1), 19–27.

Armour, M., & Umbreit, M. S. (2011). Restorative justice and juvenile offenders. In D. W. Springer & A. R. Roberts (Eds.), *Juvenile justice and juvenile delinquency* (391–414). Sudbury, MA: Jones and Bartlett.

Bowen, H., & Boyack, J. (2003). *From youth justice to adult restorative justice in New Zealand/Aotearoa* (pp. 1–10). New South Wales: University of Sydney, Institute of Criminology.

Braithwaite, J. (2002). *Restorative justice and responsive regulation.* New York: Oxford Publishing.

Buford, G., & Adams, P. (2004). Restorative justice, responsive regulation and social work. *Journal of Sociology and Social Welfare*, 31, 7–27.

Buford, G., & Hudson, J. (Eds.). (2000). *Family group conferencing: new directions in community-centered child and family practice.* New York: Aldine de Gruyter.

Carter, C. (1997). Using African-centered principles in family preservation services. *Families in Society, 78*, 531–538.

Chaiklin, H. (2008). Epilogue: Social work and criminal justice. In D. W. Springer & A. R. Roberts (Eds.), *Handbook of forensic mental health: Assessment, treatment and research* (pp. 573–595). New York: Springer.

Christie, M. (1977). Conflicts as property. *British Journal of Criminology, 1*, 104–118.

Coates, R., Umbreit, M. S., & Vos, B. (2003). Restorative justice circles: An exploratory study. *Contemporary Justice Review, 6*(3), 265–278.

Davey, L. (2005). *The development of restorative justice in the United Kingdom: A personal perspective*. Paper presented at 'Building a Global Alliance for Restorative Practices and Family Empowerment, Part 3', the IIRP's Sixth International Conference on Conferencing, Circles and other Restorative Practices, March 3–5, Penrith, New South Wales, Australia.

Dzur, A. W. (2003). Civic implications of restorative justice theory: Citizen participation and criminal justice policy. *Policy Sciences, 36*, 279–306.

Fred, S. (2005). Restorative justice: A model of healing. *NASW News, 2*, 1–4.

Galaway, B., & Hudson, J. (Eds.). (1998). *Restorative justice: International perspectives*. Monsey, NY: Criminal Justice Press.

Gibelman, M., & Schervish, P. (1993). *Who we are: The social work labor force as reflected in NASW membership*. Washington, DC: NASW Press.

Gold, L. (1993). Influencing unconscious influences: The healing dimension of mediation. *Mediation Quarterly, 11*(1), 55–66.

Gordon, W. E. (1965). Knowledge and value: Their distinction and relationship in clarifying social work practice. *Social Work, 10*(3), 32–35.

Gumz, E. (2004). American social work, corrections and restorative justice: An appraisal. *International Journal of Offender Therapy and Comparative Criminology, 48*(4), 449–460.

Gutierrez, L. M., & Suarez, A. (1999). Empowerment with Latinas. In L. M. Gutierrez & E. A. Lewis (Eds.), *Empowering women of color* (pp. 167–186). New York: Columbia University Press.

Hapland, J., Atkinson, A., Atkinson, H., Dignan, J., Edwards, L., Hibbert, J., et al. (2008). *Does restorative justice affect reconviction?: The fourth report from the evaluation of three schemes* (pp. 1–76). London: Ministry of Justice.

Harrison, P. M., & Beck, A. J. (2003). Prisoners in 2002. *Bureau of Justice Statistics Bulletin*. U.S. Department of Justice, Office of Justice Programs.

Holtquist, S. (1999). Nurturing the seeds of restorative justice. *Journal of Community Practice, 6*(2), 63–77.

Hurdle, E. (2002). Native Hawaiian traditional healing: Culturally based interventions for social work practice. *Social Work, 47*(2), 183–192.

Karp, D. R. (2004). Integrity boards. In D. R. Karp & T. Allena (Eds.), *Restorative justice on the college campus: Promoting student growth and responsibility and reawakening the spirit of the campus community* (pp. 29–41). Springfield, IL: Charles C Thomas.

King, S. (2004). *Social work and restorative justice*. Paper presented at the Global Social Work Conference, October 2004, Adelaide, Australia.

Knox, K., & Roberts, A. R. (2002). Police social work. In A. R. Roberts & G. J. Greene (Eds.), *Social worker's desk reference* (pp. 668–672). New York: Oxford University Press.

Koss, M. (2000). Blame, shame and community: Justice responses to violence against women. *American Psychologist, 55*(11), 1332–1343.

Lennon, T. (2001). *Statistics on social work education, 1998–2000*. Alexandria, VA: Council on Social Work Education.

Lewis, J. (2006). Correctional education: Why it is only promising? *Journal of Correctional Education, 57*(4), 286–296.

MacRae, A., & Zehr, H. (2004). *The little book of family group conferencing: New Zealand style*. Intercourse, PA: Good Books.

McNeece, A., & Roberts, A. R. (1997). *Policy and practice in the justice system*. Chicago: Nelson-Hall.

Nugent, W., Umbreit, M. S., Wiinamaki, L., & Paddock, J. (2001). Participation in victim-offender mediation and severity of subsequent delinquent behavior: Successful replications? *Journal of Research in Social Work Practice, 11*(1), 5–23.

Nugent, W., Williams, R. M., & Umbreit, M. S. (2003). Participation in victim-offender mediation and the prevalence and severity of subsequent delinquent behavior: A meta-analysis. *Utah Law Review, 2003*(1), 137–165.

Orzech, D. (2006). Criminal justice social work—New models, new opportunities. *Social Work Today, 6*(6), 34–37.

Pranis, K., Stuart, B., & Wedge, M. (2003). *Peacemaking circles: From crime to community*. St. Paul, MN: Living Justice Press.

Presser, L., & Gaarder, E. (2004). Can restorative justice reduce battering? In B. Price & N. Sokoloff (Eds.), *The criminal justice system and women: Offenders, prisoners, victims, and workers* (3rd ed., pp. 403–418). New York: McGraw Hill.

Reamer, F. G. (2004). Social work and criminal justice: The uneasy alliance. *Journal of Religion and Spirituality in Social Work, 23*(1/2), 213–231.

Schatz, M. (2008). Vital voice for restorative justice: The community members. In K. van Wormer (Ed.), *Restorative justice East and West* (pp. 77–92). Hong Kong: Casa Verde.

Sherman, L., & Strang, H. (2007). *Restorative justice: The evidence*. London: Smith Institute.

South, C. R., & Wood, J. (2006). Bullying in prisons: The importance of perceived social status, prisonization and moral disengagement. *Aggressive Behavior, 32*, 490–501.

Stinchcomb, J. B., & Fox, V. B. (1999). *Introduction to corrections* (5th ed.). Upper Saddle River, NJ: Prentice Hall.

Sullivan, D., & Tifft, D. (2006). *Handbook of restorative justice: A global perspective*. New York: Routledge.

Sullivan, D., & Tifft, L. (2001). *Restorative justice: Healing the foundations of our everyday lives*. Monsey, NY: Willow Tree Press.

Sullivan, D., & Tifft, L. (2004). *Restorative justice: Healing the foundations of our everyday lives*. Monsey, NY: Criminal Justice Press.

Umbreit, M. S. (1997). Humanistic mediation: A transformative journey of peacemaking. *Mediation Quarterly, 14*, 201–213.

Umbreit, M. S. (2000). *Family group conferencing: Implications for crime victims.* Washington, DC: U.S. Department of Justice, Office for Victims of Crime.

Umbreit, M. S. (2001). *The handbook of victim offender mediation: An essential guide to practice and research.* San Francisco, CA: Jossey-Bass.

Umbreit, M. S., & Burns, H. (2002). *Humanistic mediation: Peacemaking grounded in core social work values.* St. Paul, MN: University of Minnesota.

Umbreit, M. S., & Burns, H. (2006). Humanistic mediation: Peacemaking grounded in core social work values. *Italian Journal of Sociology and Political Science, 9,* 93–104.

Umbreit, M. S., Lewis, T., & Burns, H. (2003). A community response to a 9/11 hate crime: Restorative justice through dialogue. *Contemporary Justice Review, 6*(4), 383–391.

van Wormer, K. (2002). Restorative justice and social work. *Social Work Today, 2*(1), 16–19.

van Wormer, K. (2004). *Confronting oppression, restoring justice: From policy analysis to social action.* Alexandria, VA: Council on Social Work Education.

van Wormer, K. (2006). The case for restorative justice: A crucial adjunct to the social work curriculum. *Journal of Teaching in Social Work, 26*(3/4), 57–69.

van Wormer, K. (2009). Restorative justice as social justice for victims of gendered violence: A standpoint feminist perspective. *Social Work, 54*(2), 107–116.

van Wormer, K. (Ed.). (2001). *Counseling female offenders and victims: A strengths-restorative approach.* New York: Springer.

van Wormer, K. (Ed.). (2003). *Confronting oppression, restoring justice from policy analysis to social action.* Alexandria, VA: Council on Social Work Education.

van Wormer, K. (Ed.). (2008). *Restoring justice across the East and the West.* Hong Kong, China: Casa Verde.

van Wormer, K., & Jenkins, M. (2007). Restorative justice: Cultural and gender considerations. In D. W. Springer & A. R. Roberts (Eds.), *Handbook of forensic mental health for victims and offenders: Assessment, treatment and research* (pp. 541–562). New York: Springer.

Vinton, L., & White, B. (1995). The "Boutique Effect" in graduate social work education. *Journal of Teaching in Social Work, 11*(1/2), 3–13.

Weick, A., & Chamberlain, R. (2002). Putting problems in their place: Further explorations in the strengths perspective. In D. Saleeby (Ed.), *The strengths perspective in social work practice* (pp. 95–105). Boston: Allyn & Bacon.

Zehr, H. (1990). *Changing lenses: A new focus for crime and justice.* Scottsdale, PA: Herald Press.

Zehr, H. (2009). Speaking notes. Paper presented at Colorado Springs Restorative Justice Conference. Retrieved April 15, 2010, from http://www.youthtransformationcenter.org/PPRJC/2009Conference/Zehr-ColSprings-for-web.pdf

3. Spirituality

> *The more I study physics, the more I am drawn to metaphysics. . . . Our task must be to free ourselves . . . . by widening our circle of compassion to embrace all living creatures and the whole of nature in its beauty.*
>
> Albert Einstein

> *Humankind has not woven the web of life. We are but one thread within it. Whatever we do to the web, we do to ourselves. All things are bound together. All things connect.*
>
> Chief Seattle, 1854

*T*he criminal justice system in the United States has evolved through many paradigms, moving from being a moralistic system, where crime was regarded as a sin, to a punitive-deterrence system to a rehabilitative system, in its effort to provide justice and protect society (Brunk, 2001). Underlying each paradigm is a philosophy about what will ultimately deter people from committing crimes. The current retributive paradigm, for example, maintains that offenders are guilty of committing violations of the law against the state, that those offenders should be punished and get what they deserve, and that the severity of their punishment sends a warning that serves to prevent future crime (Zehr, 2002).

The roots of restorative justice can be traced to Aboriginal traditions that use the principles of healing and living in harmony with all beings and with nature as the basis for mending damaged personal and communal relationships (Johnstone, 2002; Melton, 1995). Other peacemaking roots of restorative justice can be found in the nonretaliatory responses to violence endorsed by many faith communities, for example, Quakers (Williams & Williams, 1994). Moreover, in the United States, restorative justice has received some of its strongest support from Christian-affiliated organizations whose teachings are rooted in forgiveness, for example, United Methodist Church (Wray, 2002).

THE CHALLENGE

In the last chapter, we discussed the values, principles, and core concepts of restorative justice that are allied with social work. These broad and noble ideas enable the diversity and complexity that undergird the conceptual framework for understanding what restorative justice stands for and how the processes of restorative dialogue work. Although restorative justice principles were stated in secular terms, these principles contain spiritual overtones, for example, the humility involved in being a servant leader. This reality, when voiced, in spiritual terms often generates negative reactivity because spirituality inevitably becomes fused with religiosity, raising concern that restorative justice might be used for purposes of conversion and evokes the need, therefore, to maintain the necessary separation between church and state. This chapter distinguishes between spirituality and religiosity. It reports on a study that begins to deconstruct the elements in restorative justice that might be considered spiritual. Some of the elements are descriptive of what participants say happens to them as a result of engaging in a restorative dialogue process. Other elements are built into the process in order to create a sacred space or time away from the distractions of everyday life.

The findings from the study invite proponents in the field to consider holding both the secular and spiritual dimensions of restorative justice as part of its overarching values-based framework while still respecting and listening well to the ongoing concerns about church and state. This challenge for a "both/and" response is made throughout the book. The challenge is core to restorative justice, which seeks to move beyond the kind of dichotomous thinking that polarizes positions and narrows options. The basic challenge, therefore, is to work to develop a critical consciousness about dichotomous thinking and to learn to hold seemingly opposing positions at the same time. When that happens, it makes room so that something new can emerge.

IS RESTORATIVE JUSTICE SPIRITUAL?

As it has evolved, restorative justice has been described as having a spiritual component. Zehr (1990) draws a parallel between the principles underlying restorative justice and spirituality. He defines spirituality as involving universal principles or natural laws that are beyond the individual's control, for example, our interconnectedness as human beings. These principles represent an objective reality that we cannot change or a set of rules that are beyond us that ultimately govern our behaviors. Zehr argues that restorative justice similarly relies on clear guiding principles that are not related to any one particular ideology or religion but instead represent universal principles about human interactions. This parallel between the guiding principles of restorative justice and those of spirituality has led to the conclusion that restorative justice is inherently spiritual and that restorative justice and the phenomenon of spirituality are intimately intertwined (Zehr, 1990).

WHAT IS SPIRITUALITY AND HOW IS IT DIFFERENT FROM RELIGIOSITY?

Spirituality has different meanings, definitions, and connotations, which reflect the elusiveness of the concept (Batley, 2004). Many of the definitions presume a belief in the supernatural. For the purpose of this chapter, spirituality is defined as a reverence for life. Reverence is defined as being in awe of and deep regard or veneration (Brown, 1993). This definition is compatible with other definitions of spirituality but is simpler and embodies the intent of restorative justice, which is a life-giving act. Spirituality defined as "reverence for life" also recognizes the universality of life—the life we connect to in ourselves and in each other so that we can give ourselves more fully to what life asks of us (Peterson, 1992).

It can be difficult but important to separate the spiritual components of restorative justice from religiosity, which may be associated with some practices of restorative justice. Restorative justice may be reinforced and justified, for example, by teachings from different religions or denominations (Hadley, 2001). Moreover, religious leaders are often strong promoters at the forefront of many rehabilitative justice practices including restorative justice (Wuthrow, 1997). This connection is not surprising considering that Christianity and other religions and restorative justice share many common values, including the goals of creating healing, empowering victims, offering compassion, and advocating for forgiveness (Anderson, 2000). Some authors make an even more explicit connection by claiming that restorative justice has its roots in the Judeo-Christian Bible (Aitken, 2003) and uses specific examples from the Bible to demonstrate restorative justice principles (Kerber, 2003). This emphasis tends to merge religiosity and spirituality.

To the extent that restorative justice is aligned with spirituality, it has had universal appeal. However, to the extent that restorative justice is considered a religious endeavor, it becomes more problematic, more controversial, and less useful as a generally acceptable tool to promote justice in our society. A nonexclusionary distinction is made in this chapter, therefore, between the spiritual components inherent to restorative justice and religiosity. Whereas spirituality is defined as a reverence for life, religiosity is defined as a set of beliefs, values, and practices based on the teachings of a spiritual leader (American Heritage Publishing Company, 2000) that are formally structured or institutionally grounded (Zinnbauer et al., 1997). For the purposes of this chapter, religious components are incorporated under the umbrella of spirituality, thus including religious ideas without being constrained by them.

Little has been written that clarifies the relationship between spirituality and restorative justice practices. This chapter draws on a study done to identify the specific spiritual components of restorative justice by examining how spirituality is treated in the restorative justice literature (Bender & Armour, 2007). By delineating these components, the concept of spirituality is made clearer and more usable by social workers and other mediators of restorative justice practice.

STUDY METHODOLOGY

Bender and Armour (2007) examined texts about restorative justice using a hermeneutic phenomenological approach. Hermeneutic phenomenology attempts to find, describe, and understand experience by systematically determining the invariant components of a particular phenomenon, for example, spirituality in restorative justice (Giorgi, 1997; Van Manen, 1990). The goal is to delineate the essence of the phenomenon or experience; however, there is a realization that the interpretation of that experience is socially constructed by the authors of the texts and the researchers who interpret the authors' interpretations. The essential themes found in this research are therefore tentative and related to the contexts in which they are found.

A thorough search of restorative justice and spirituality texts was conducted using search engines PsycINFO and Academic Search Premier. Texts selected for this study were any restorative justice literature that attended to spirituality, values, the supernatural, morals, or higher beings. Texts included empirical articles, books, informational guidebooks, published newsletters, editorial comments, and interviews with leaders in the field of restorative justice. After conducting a holistic reading of all sources, texts most relevant to an examination of spiritual principles were selected for closer examination and relevant passages were isolated. A thematic analysis of these passages specific to spirituality was done within and across the texts. Passages were clustered into categorical themes. Some passages fit into more than one category, resulting in some overlap among the themes.

COMPONENTS OF SPIRITUALITY IN RESTORATIVE JUSTICE

Nine components of spirituality emerged from the research on the restorative justice literature (see Figure 3.1). Although connections exist between these themes, each was determined to be a unique component that adds new information about the intersection of restorative justice and spirituality. Most restorative justice literature to date has focused on offenders. This imbalance in the current literature is partially reflected in the findings. When possible, themes were interpreted in relation to the experience for both offenders and victims.

Transformation

Perhaps the most widely mentioned theme in restorative justice literature is the notion of experiencing a radical or profound change that is magical or deeply spiritual (Hadley, 2001). That metamorphosis may consist of developing a new outlook on life and/or changing emotionally, psychologically, and ultimately spiritually into someone different. This transformation of will, mind, and emotions can occur for both offenders and victims and can be an individual or collective experience (Zehr, 1990). As both offender and victim experience the restorative justice process, they may pass through a time of ordeal in which they undergo pain and sorrow but eventually find a healing breakthrough once restoration occurs (Hadley, 2001). Miller and C'De Baca

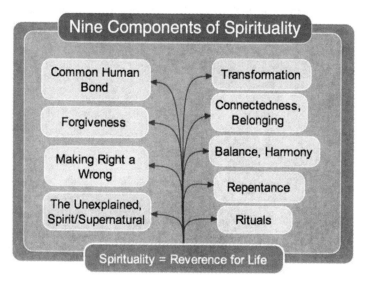

FIGURE 3.1

(2001) describe what they term quantum change, which involves "a new way of making sense out of life" (p. 7). Such change is vivid and surprising, often triggered by the actions of other people or referred to as an act of God. The experience of transformation has been described as a surprising feeling of "peace, calm, tranquility, self-assurance, and release" (Hadley, 2001, p. 10) that involves "coming to grips with who we are, what we have done, [and] what we can become in the fullness of our humanity" (Hadley, 2001, p. 9).

For offenders, this internal transformation can cause behavioral change based on the premise that offenders come to terms with the pain that they have caused to their victims. Transformation, therefore, decreases the chance that they will commit further crimes. For victims and their families, transformation comes from healing as a result of the offender's repentance and their own ability to forgive (Hadley, 2001). Transformations from feeling isolated to feeling connected or from feeling anger to finding forgiveness are described as "a stirring movement of the spirit" (Greenwood, 2001, p. 5).

As a result of this transformation, a new reality is generated for participants. Imagining oneself differently in relationship to others and to the universe can transform an offender into a member of society and transform a victim into a survivor. Sometimes, the literature implies that a spirit leads people to this new reality (Aitken, 2003; Miller, 2001).

Connectedness or Belonging

Restorative justice encounters create empathy and mutual understanding. For offenders who often feel isolated and withdrawn from mainstream society, connectedness can be a spiritual experience even allowing for the transformation described above. Such connectedness can give offenders a sense of reattaching or belonging to the community in which they committed the crime. It may allow for the reintegration that could decrease the likelihood of their reoffending.

Furthermore, feeling connected to one's community offers offenders a supportive environment in which they can acknowledge their shame. Through reintegrative shaming, offenders can break through their own denial, fully experience the shame involved in committing their crime, and finally open themselves up to a way out of that shame, for example, truth telling (Ahmed, Braithwaite, & Braithwaite, 2001). Shaming in the context of acceptance can create a spiritual transformation for the offender from isolated criminal to becoming a contributing member of the society.

The experience of connectedness can be spiritual for victims as well. When victims feel heard or attended to by their offenders, the connection can feel spiritual because it may lessen shame or personal diminishment related to the crime and transform their negative reactions toward offenders into feelings of care and concern.

Similarly, the experience of feeling cared about by the person least likely to care helps offenders recognize that they are not alone in the world and helps both parties recognize the common space they share. The inexplicable irony in this situation often leads offenders and victims to feel a part of something larger than them. Moreover, both parties may recognize that, in some core way, they cannot make it out of this experience without each other. For victims, they are acknowledging that they cannot recover fully from this experience without offenders taking on the shame that they otherwise carry. For offenders, they are acknowledging that they cannot reintegrate fully without gaining, at some level, a feeling that victims accept them even after what they've done.

Common Human Bond

Restorative justice practices encourage a sense of inclusion and recognition of the humanness in all people that culminates in a common human bond (Greenwood, 2001). Experiencing this bond can be a spiritual occurrence because it connects people under a power bigger than themselves (Zehr, 1990).

From a slightly different perspective, Kerber (2003) explains that people share a common bond of responsibility in that people are at once victims and sinners. Even if they do not overtly commit a crime, people are guilty of implicitly creating communities filled with conditions of oppression, inequality, and discrimination that may lead to others' more explicit crimes (Mackey, 2000). Because all people have the capacity to harm and to heal, the community has an obligation to promote compassion and healing for offenders, resulting in a sense of inclusion (Greenwood, 2001). This common human bond is responsible for replacing the "us vs. them" adversarial mentality that fuels a retributive system with a "oneness" that necessitates restoration of a community. In this way, offender, victim, and community members are joined. Greenwood (2001) relates this common human bond to the duty to love thy neighbor and love thy enemy. Having faith in a higher power involves a call to have compassion for all people.

Repentance

Repentance is a crucial principle of restorative justice (Hadley, 2001) that is vital to rehabilitating offenders and affirming common values of the group (Wuthrow, 1997). Repentance involves genuinely regretting one's deeds, feeling sorrow, authentically expressing remorse for harm caused to others, and having a strong desire to avoid repeating the crime (Etzioni, 1997). Although repentance is associated with Christian beliefs, other religions have similar concepts, for example, atonement in Judaism.

Expressing repentance can be a deeply spiritual experience. Offenders are often viewed as sinners (Etzioni, 1997). Such a belief creates the ultimate barrier between a person and God because it damages or destroys the life God has given. By repenting, offenders acknowledge what they took and accept the burden of responsibility for the harm they inflicted. In so doing, they become closer to God or more complete spiritual beings (Brown, 1997) and gain redemption from sin (Wuthrow, 1997). Thus, repenting in restorative justice is more than something offenders do for victims; it is also something that they do to get back into right relationship with God or a higher power.

Many of the rituals in restorative justice provide opportunities for offenders to repent and for their community to witness that repentance. It is hoped that repentance can have long-term effects (Wuthrow, 1997), causing offenders to restructure their lives and themselves as a means of behaviorally expressing sorrow for their sins (Etzioni, 1997). During these rituals, the show of real repentance can be deeply relieving, moving, and healing for the victim as well, particularly if an unremorseful offender in the courtroom took no responsibility for the crime. Repentance, therefore, reestablishes right relationship and gives victims a sense of putting the universe back into balance. What was once lost or taken from them, for example, safety, begins to be repaired.

Forgiveness

In restorative justice, forgiveness is multifaceted because it involves crime victims, offenders, and the affected communities. This tripartite representation suggests that the place, definition, and significance of forgiveness will vary depending on the needs of people in each group and the relationships they have with one another. For example, healing or salvation for the offender requires forgiveness from the community (Zehr, 1990), which may be symbolic, referring to the willingness of the community to reinstate the offender after he or she atones for the crime (Armour & Umbreit, 2006; Dickey, 1998; Van Biema, 1999).

From the victim's perspective, in restorative justice practices forgiveness is never an expectation or goal (Armour & Umbreit, 2006). Instead, restorative justice fosters the possibility for forgiveness if the victim voluntarily chooses that path. Restorative justice does recognize, however, that forgiveness can be healing for victims. Zehr (1990) claims that victims' ability to forgive allows them to regain the power taken from them as a result of the violation. This process can be transformational for victims who shift from being objects of crimes to being group members improving society through crime reduction.

In addition, forgiveness, in the sense of letting go of anger and control over the outcome, also allows the victim to be whole again. This turning over is spiritual in nature because victims release the conditions that hold them prisoner, for example, anger, to something larger than themselves. This exercise of forgiveness relieves victims of the responsibility for their own anger, the crime, and the offender and replaces it with the trust that something else will prevent further crimes toward themselves and others.

Making Right a Wrong

The goal for offenders who participate in restorative justice is to "make things right" (Zehr, 2002) and, in so doing, to reform themselves into the sort of person who is unlikely to repeat the offense. Righting a wrong involves a variety of behaviors, including apologizing, expressing remorse, promising to reform their behavior, or offering restitution or another gesture of good will (Radzik, 2004). The repairing gesture may involve ordeal, penance, and expression of moral obligation that requires offenders to recognize the harm they have caused, acknowledge their wrongdoing, and make efforts to follow a more spiritual path.

By making things right, the offender rebalances the ledger of wrongdoing. The offender places the victim's needs before his own, leading to positive consequences for both. For victims, having their needs recognized and prioritized by the offender elevates them from being diminished by the crime to feeling valued and respected. Helping the victim also gives to the offender, leading to a restoration of his or her relationship with the community and a larger universal power. Although the responsibility is ultimately in the hands of the offender to make amends, there is mutuality in the endeavor. The offender gives to the victim, which, simultaneously, is rewarding to the offender himself who can then begin the path to self-forgiveness.

Balance or Harmony

In concordance with indigenous traditions, restorative justice maintains the ideal that the earth must be in balance or harmony for peaceful coexistence. Committing crimes against others disturbs that balance for the community (Boyes-Watson, 2005). Harmony and balance are often symbolized by a circle used to emphasize the interconnectedness of each element. A circle, symbolically and practically, serves to restore the balance and harmony lost when a crime is committed. Peacemaking circles, one form of restorative justice practice, bring together community members to solve problems and resolve conflicts. In Navajo tradition, these peacemaking circles are described as "a gift from the creator to keep us in harmony" (Meyer, 2002, p. 1379). Similarly, sentencing circles, used to determine a consequence for wrongdoings, also have the primary goal of restoring harmony in the effected community. Thought to come from the earth, sentencing circles are considered a spiritual practice of conflict resolution (Blue & Rogers Blue, 2001).

Although peacekeeping circles and sentencing circles, in form and practice, explicitly use the symbol of the circle, all restorative justice dialogues use the concept of a circle implicitly. The circle represents the idea that the process of restoring the harmony and balance is never ending. The circle also represents a sense of completeness or wholeness that is regained. Thus, although some restorative justice practices embody the circle more explicitly than others, the conceptual idea of a circle and what it represents is core to restorative justice across settings.

Rituals

In restorative justice, rituals are used to transform the space into an environment like no other place in participants' lives, setting the stage for an elevated level of intimacy and understanding rarely experienced (Boyes-Watson, 2005). For example, some practices involve passing around a talking piece that is said to have mystical powers that connect members in the circle while allowing each of the members the power of their own voice (Coates, Umbreit, & Vos, 2000).

Although certain restorative justice practices are noticeably more ritualistic, such as using talking pieces or doing group meditations, more subtle forms of ritual exist as well. In fact, almost everything connected to restorative justice uses rituals to convey to participants that they are entering into a metaphysical or spiritual space. For example, many restorative justice encounters are often not time limited; a single session may last up to 8 hours, enforcing the idea that this practice has nothing to do with chronological time. These rituals symbolically signify the stopping of the physical world and suspension of time, as it exists in the outside. Deep listening is expected, and it is not uncommon for participants to take a number of minutes to reflect on what others have said before responding. Inherent in this concept of time is the idea that participants have transitioned into a different space where there is room for everyone to talk as long as is needed.

Other rituals, which on the surface may seem to be logistical, are also used to intentionally create a sacred space conducive to restorative justice work. Thoughtful consideration is given to who will speak first in the session, who may accompany the victim and offender for support, where people will sit in relation to one another, and how far apart they may sit. For example, the victim and offender often sit facing each other with the facilitator off to the side to symbolically represent the relationship under repair and the peripheral role of the facilitator. Although the facilitator is often responsible for creating this space, all participants must agree to adhere to these norms and in doing so become part of the whole. The result of this ritualistic practice is the creation of a space in which there is ample room for everyone's voice and the acknowledgement by all participants that they are making room for one another. The creation of this space is an acknowledgement of a sacred reverence for life that is innately spiritual.

The Unexplained—The Spirit or Supernatural

In a study of restorative justice circles in Minnesota, Coates et al. (2000) found that many participants described a mysterious component. Unable to put a name on it, circle participants described that they felt cared about at a new level. Participants came to "aha moments" that were created, in part, by group facilitators (or circle keepers), but also by being touched by the Spirit. One facilitator stated, "Participants speak often of unexpected changes of the heart, a profound sense of connection, the freeing experience of honesty and humility, unanticipated outbreaks of generosity—as an awareness of a power greater than the individuals present moving through them" (Coates et al., 2000, p. 19). Described as epiphanies, these mystical experiences are qualitatively different from insight-oriented change and often leave the person in awe, knowing that something major yet indescribable has happened to them. The spiritual atmosphere and purposely ritualistic context created in many restorative justice settings may advance the opportunity for such forms of mystical change to occur.

CONCLUSION

The study by Bender and Armour (2007) explicated nine spiritual components of restorative justice. Although each component is discrete, they intersect with and reinforce each other. For example, the feeling of connectedness may be enhanced by the recognition of the common human bond that unites victim, offender, and community members as one. The need to restore connectedness or belonging is made salient by the recognition that ongoing brokenness throws off the harmony or balance with nature that is necessary for human survival.

Also related are the components of repentance and forgiveness. Although not dependent on one another, these components are commonly discussed in relationship to one another. For example, a community may be spiritually or morally responsible to forgive after an offender truly repents and attempts to change his or her behavior.

Rituals such as opening and closing meditations or moments of silence create atmospheres in which other spiritual components can be actualized.

Transformations, for example, may take place only after rituals have been used to make the place, time, and space open for such experiences. Ineffable experiences of the supernatural may occur, in part, because chronological time has been suspended.

Whether secular, faith-based, or indigenous groups offer restorative justice practices, the practices themselves are inherently spiritual because restorative justice, in philosophy and practice, embodies a reverence for life. Indeed, restorative justice is built on the premise that crime is a violation of that life by virtue of the fact that it causes harm to others. Moreover, each of the components embraces life-giving properties. As such, they instill, restore, or affirm the regard for life that is necessary for peaceful coexistence.

Within restorative justice practice, the concept of spirituality is recognized as important but is often elusive and vaguely understood by practitioners and participants. Bender and Armour (2007) unpack the concept of spirituality by explicitly showing its discrete but connected dimensions.

The delineation of nine components of spirituality has implications for restorative justice dialogues. First, the definition of spirituality as a reverence for life embodies all practices whether they are religious or not. Second, these components offer a foundation for the principles of spirituality to be used universally, without evoking the confusion, suspicion, or defensiveness that arises when spirituality is viewed as the exclusive territory of religious expression or merged with the missions of formal religious organizations. Third, the components that comprise spirituality in restorative justice give facilitators more tools to use to deepen their interactions with victims, offenders, and community members. This is particularly important for training mediators with less experience, who may have skill in dealing with the people involved and the crime that has taken place but may need help to recognize and intentionally incorporate the underlying spiritual nature of restorative justice practice.

There has been little research on the influence of spirituality on restorative justice practices. Although the study done by Bender and Armour (2007) advanced a framework for assessing components of spirituality in restorative justice work, empirical evidence is needed to confirm their existence as well as their role in the restorative justice process. One approach would be to conduct a meta-analysis of existing empirical restorative justice studies that address one or more of the spiritual components identified in this study. The Office of Juvenile Justice and Delinquency Prevention (OJJDP) of the Department of Justice has emphasized the importance of restorative justice research in recent years by creating the BARJ (Balance and Restorative Justice Program). This has resulted in several empirical evaluations of restorative justice programs across the United States. Conducting a meta-analysis that reviews these studies may yield insight into the effect sizes and, thus, the relevance of spirituality in restorative justice practices.

Besides reviewing existing work, study of the spiritual elements of restorative justice should be incorporated into future empirical evaluations. The nine components of spirituality, for example, could be developed into an assessment tool of spirituality to empirically examine the presence or absence of spiritual components in specific practices. Furthermore, the purposeful inclusion of questions regarding spiritual components is one way to ascertain both the role and significance of spiritual components in influencing recidivism and/or satisfaction.

REFERENCES

Ahmed, E. H., N., Braithwaite, J., & Braithwaite, V. (2001). *Shame management through reintegration*. Melbourne: Cambridge University Press.

Aitken, J. (2003). Divine justice. *American Spectator, 36*(5), 42–44.

American Heritage Publishing Company. (2000) *American Heritage® Dictionary of the English Language* (4th ed.). Boston: Houghton Mifflin.

Anderson, G. M. (2000). Restorative justice: Interview with Jim Consedine. *America, 182*(6), 7–11.

Armour, M., & Umbreit, M. S. (2006). Victim forgiveness in restorative justice dialogue. *Victim and Offender, 1*(2), 123–140.

Batley, M. (2004). What is the appropriate role of spirituality in restorative justice? In H. Zehr & B. Toews (Eds.), *Critical issues in restorative justice* (pp. 361–374). Monsey, NY: Criminal Justice Press.

Bender, K., & Armour, M. (2007). The spiritual components of restorative justice. *Victim and Offender, 2*(3), 251–267.

Blue, A. W., & Rogers Blue, M. A. (2001). The case for aboriginal justice and healing: The self perceived through a broken mirror. In M. L. Hadley (Ed.), *The spiritual roots of restorative justice* (pp. 57–79). New York: State University of New York Press.

Boyes-Watson, C. (2005). Seeds of change: Using peacemaking circles to build a village for every child. *Child Welfare League of America, 84*(2), 191–208.

Brown, H. (1997). Godly sorrow, sorrow of the world: Some Christian thoughts on repentance. In A. Etzioni & D. E. Carney (Eds.), *Repentance: A comparative perspective* (pp. 31–42). New York: Rowman & Littlefield Publishers, Inc.

Brown, L. (Ed.). (1993). *The new shorter Oxford English dictionary* (Vol. 2). New York: Oxford University Press.

Brunk, C. (2001). Restorative justice and the philosophical theories of punishment. In M. Hadley (Ed.), *Spiritual roots of restorative justice*. New York: SUNY Press.

Coates, R., Umbreit, M. S., & Vos, B. (2000). *Obstacles and opportunities for developing victim offender mediation for juveniles: The experience of six Oregon counties*. St. Paul: Center for Restorative Justice and Peacemaking, University of Minnesota.

Dickey, W. J. (1998). Forgiveness and crime: The possibilities of restorative justice. In R. D. Enright & J. North (Eds.), *Exploring forgiveness* (pp. 106–120). Madison, WI: University of Wisconsin Press.

Etzioni, A. (1997). Introduction. In A. Etzioni & D. E. Carney (Eds.), *Repentance: A comparative perspective* (pp. 1–20). New York: Rowman & Littlefield Publishers, Inc.

Giorgi, A. (1997). The theory, practice, and evaluation of the phenomenological method as a qualitative research procedure. *Journal of Phenomenological Psychology, 28*(2), 235–226.

Greenwood, J. (2001). Restorative justice and the dynamics of faith. *The Clergy Journal*, April, 3–5.

Hadley, M. L. (2001). Introduction: Multifaith reflection on criminal justice. In M. L. Hadley (Ed.), *The spiritual roots of restorative justice* (pp. 1–29). New York: State University of New York Press.

Johnstone, G. (2002). *Restorative justice: Ideas, values and debates*. Devon, UK: Willan Publishing.

Kerber, G. (2003). Overcoming violence and pursuing justice. *Ecumenical Review, 55*(2), 151–158.

Mackey, V. (2000). Holistic restorative justice: A response to McCold. *Contemporary Justice Review, 3*(4), 451–458.

Melton, A. P. (1995). Indigenous justice systems: Tribal society is a way of life. *Judicature, 79*, 126–133.

Meyer, J. (2002). It is a gift from the Creator to keep us in harmony: Original (verses alternative) dispute resolution on the Navajo Nation. *International Journal of Public Administration, 25*, 1379–1401.

Miller, D. (2001). Renewed hearts: Transforming power of restorative justice. *The Clergy Journal*, April, 10–11.

Miller, W. R., & C'De Baca, J. (2001). *Quantum change: When epiphanies and sudden insights transform ordinary lives*. New York: Guilford Press.

Peterson, M. (1992). *At personal risk: Boundary violations in professional-client relationships*. New York: W. W. Norton & Company.

Radzik, L. (2004). Making amends. *American Philosophical Quarterly, 41*, 141–154.

Van Biema, D. (1999). Should all be forgiven? *Time, 153*, 55.

Van Manen, M. (1990). *Researching lived experience: Human science for an action sensitive pedagogy*. London, Ontario: State University of New York Press.

Williams, S., & Williams, S. (1994). *Being in the middle by being at the edge: Quaker experience of non-official political mediation*. London: Quaker Peace & Service.

Wray, H. (2002). *Restorative justice: Moving beyond punishment*. Cinncinati, OH: General Board of Global Ministries, The United Methodist Church.

Wuthrow, R. (1997). Repentance in criminal justice procedure: The ritual affirmation of community. In A. Etzioni & D. E. Carney (Eds.), *Repentance: A comparative perspective* (pp. 171–186). New York: Rowman & Littlefield Publishers, Inc.

Zehr, H. (1990). *Changing lenses: A new focus for crime and justice*. Scottsdale, PA: Herald Press.

Zehr, H. (2002). *The little book of restorative justice*. Intercourse, PA: Good Books.

Zinnbauer, B. J., Pargament, K. I., Cole, B., Rye, M. S., Butter, E. M., Belavich, T. G., et al. (1997). Religion and spirituality: Unfuzzying the fuzzy. *Journal for the Scientific Study of Religion, 36*(4), 549–564.

4. Restorative Justice Dialogue as Intervention

> *"I wanted to look him in the face and ask him why he broke into my home. As a victim, I realized what the terms mean—'it takes a village to raise a child'—because meeting the offender made me realize that I can make a difference. I think I became a real human being to him."*

A burglary victim comes face-to-face with the young offender and his father. She is able to express the full impact of the crime, get answers to many questions, and help develop a plan to repair the harm. Her involvement in this community-based victim-offender mediation program leads to a deep sense of satisfaction, fairness, and ability to move on with her life. Meeting his victim has a huge impact on the young offender and leads to his getting his life in order and staying out of further criminal activity.

The term *restorative justice* refers to policies and practices that embody restorative justice principles and values. In contrast to the first three chapters that provided a historical backdrop and conceptual framework for restorative justice practice, the next chapters describe the most widely used applications, namely Victim-Offender Mediation (VOM) (Chapter 5), Family Group Conferencing (FGC), (Chapter 6), Circles (Chapter 7), and Victim-Offender Dialogue (VOD) (Chapter 8) in crimes of severe violence. We distinguish between restorative justice as a reform movement and restorative justice as an intervention by using the phrase *restorative justice dialogue* when referring to core approaches and research-based restorative justice practices. This separation distinguishes the idea of restorative justice from its implementation. The separation also allows for highlighting the different restorative dialogue approaches, all of which have the same primary purpose: to bring people together for a face-to-face dialogue about the harm caused by a person(s) who committed a crime. It is significant to note that "doing" VOM, FGC, or Peacemaking Circles at the same time advances restorative justice as a social movement.

This chapter serves as an introduction to the three basic dialogue practices and the expansion of VOM to include severely violent crime. The first part of the chapter reviews the three most used practices (VOM, FGC, and Circles) and evaluates their strengths and weaknesses. VOM, for example, due its restriction of participation to core parties inherently evokes emotional intensity as it fosters the necessary emotional intimacy for change. Family group conferencing, on the other hand, provides additional support to the offender by using his or her family as a vital resource for buttressing what the offender must do to "make right the wrong." When Circles are used, they place greater emphasis on community responsibility by widening membership to ensure that all stakeholders and key members of the community are included. Besides the advantages associated with each approach, there are also costs based on their structure, that is, less attention can be given to the interaction between the key players as the number of participants is increased.

The second part of the chapter answers the question, "What delineates a restorative dialogue? How would we know it if we saw it?" It describes the components of a restorative dialogue that are a part of all approaches. Many of these components reflect the restorative justice values, principles, and core concepts described in Chapter 2. The decision by parties to participate in a dialogue, for example, is a voluntary endeavor that rests on and enhances self-determination. The role of the facilitator as nondirective and nonjudgmental during the dialogue meeting is a measure of the respect accorded the parties and the fact that the dialogue and its outcome belong to them. The facilitator's nondirectiveness also empowers the participants to engage directly with each other.

The third part of the chapter delineates the stages in developing a dialogue including referral, preparation, dialogue meeting, and follow-up. Again these stages demonstrate how restorative justice values, principles, and core concepts are actualized in the process. For example, the stories shared by victims, offenders, and community members in the dialogue meeting are empowering. Similarly, preparation for the meeting requires the facilitator to educate parties about restorative justice so that they understand the differences between restorative justice and criminal justice. The education of the parties also empowers them because they are invited to participate in a process very different from their experience with the criminal justice system and a process that allows, even requires, greater involvement, control over the outcome, and open discussion.

The fourth part of the chapter describes the conditions necessary for creating the context that enables change during the dialogue. Those conditions include a process orientation, establishment of safety, respectful interaction, and the flow of positive energy. Besides embodying restorative justice values, these conditions also represent spiritual components discussed in Chapter 3. Some of the components include a sense of transformation as a result of positive energy weakening the toxicity of the violation, the experience of a common human bond because of feeling safe enough to express deep emotions, a sense of connectedness or belonging because of feeling listened to, and being part of a process that disconnects the parties from the chaos of the everyday world.

THE MEANING OF DIALOGUE

The concept of a dialogue has special meaning because it frames conversation as more than communication and suggests that people will be influenced or even changed as a result of how they engage. Indeed, the roots of the term *dialogue* are the Greek *dia* and *logos*, which translate to *through meaning*. Furthermore, the most ancient meaning of the word *logos* is to gather together suggesting that "dialogue is a conversation in which people think together in relationship" (Isaccs, 1999, p. 19). In this context, the word *think* is inclusive of emotions, intentions, and desires (Bohm, Factor, & Garrett, 1991). William Issacs, the director of the MIT dialogue program, argues that "thinking together implies that you no longer take your own position as final" (Isaccs, 1999, p. 19). Consequently, a dialogue is a conversation with a center, not sides as in a polarized debate. In order to move toward the center, there must be (1) the suspension of opinion and the certainty that lies behind it, which allows us to step back and see things differently, (2) the capacity to listen to ourselves and others including listening for and receiving meanings that come from deep inside, (3) the ability to see the whole person, which implies coming to a place of respect both for others and ourselves, and (4) speaking our authentic voice independent of other influences (Isaccs, 1999). Dialogue, therefore, is a relational framework that has the potential to transform difficult conversations into profound experiences of connectedness with ourselves, each other, and the larger ecology in which we live.

Dialogue in the context of restorative justice has additional meaning because it emerges out of the recognition that we live in a relational universe. The harm done as the result of criminal acts threatens and damages those relationships. It also diminishes the social worth of both victims and offenders because the crime disconnects them both from the rest of the community. Restorative justice, therefore, is grounded in a relational conception of justice, which has as its aim the restoration of victims and offenders to their full potential as relational beings (Archibald & Llewellyn, 2006). Dialogue is the medium used to create relational justice because it provides the structure for safe and respectful engagement and offers the possibility for healing, meaningful accountability, authentic engagement, and life-generating outcomes.

DIALOGUE AND RESTORATIVE JUSTICE PRACTICES

The three most common restorative justice practices are victim-offender mediation, family group conferencing, and peacemaking circles. Although there is variation in the number and category of participants, for example, family group conferencing usually has more participants than victim-offender mediation and is built on engaging the offender's community of care, these practices all rest on the construction of a dialogue or encounter between the key stakeholders, namely victim, offender, and community.

Victim-Offender Mediation

Victim-offender mediation (VOM), also called victim-offender conferencing or victim-offender reconciliation, was the first formal approach developed for restorative justice dialogue, initially developed in the 1970s. It is typically used with victims of property crimes or minor assaults but may be requested by victims of serious crimes as well. Depending upon the jurisdiction, participants may be referred by judges, probation officers, or attorneys. Occasionally, individuals have heard of the programs on their own and seek assistance. Once an offender and victim have agreed to participate in mediation or conferencing, typically a trained mediator or facilitator will meet with each separately one or more times before the actual meeting. Separate preparatory meetings are done to listen to each individual's story, to educate them about the process, to help participants shape realistic expectations, and to screen out those few individuals who are not appropriate for mediation. These trained mediators or facilitators are most frequently volunteers and as such represent the community in the process. Their task is to facilitate a discussion between victim and offender so that their questions and issues may be dealt with. If a restitution plan emerges, the mediator will often write up the details in the form of a contract for the participants. In some jurisdictions, the mediator reports the results of the mediation to the courts and may have responsibilities for follow-up.

Because the face-to-face meeting is centrally focused on the victim and offender accompanied by a small number of possible support persons (such as parents or friends), it increases the likelihood of deepening the emotional intensity that may make it easier for each person to speak from the heart (Sharpe, 1998). Some of the strengths of VOM include greater directness between the participants, more intimate engagement, and information to the primary people affected. A challenge posed by this approach is that the impact of the offense on others is not shared nor are their needs included in the dialogue because of their absence. Given the small size of the forum, it also may be somewhat more likely for participants, at times, to polarize and for power imbalances to be exaggerated (Sharpe, 1998).

Family Group Conferencing

Family group conferencing (FGC), also called community conferencing, originated in New Zealand as a means of diverting young offenders from formal adjudication. Family group conferencing was based largely on the ancient tradition of indigenous people of New Zealand, the Maori. It later evolved in Australia into police-based conferencing that allowed police to bring together juvenile offenders, their families, and supporters and the crime victim and their family and supporters. Referrals for family group conferencing come from the police as part of an early warning system for juveniles or from the courts. Family group conferencing involves support persons for both victims and offenders as well as additional participants from the community, such as a teacher or police officer. The number of support persons present can often range from—six to ten to only a few. Some group conferences, however, can be considerably large. This approach emphasizes supporting offenders in taking responsibility for their actions and in changing their behaviors. Thus, the involvement of the offender's family is critical and expected because the members play a key role in addressing the harms already done and minimizing future harm. Supporters can be both a support for the offender and offer resources to help the offender succeed at making things right. The victim and victim's family are also invited but may not participate or participate directly. In the New Zealand model of FGC, conferences frequently take breaks for families to caucus to discuss what is happening in the larger conference and steps they may desire to be taken next.

This approach recognizes that others have been affected by the conflict, and family members and other support persons are a major part of the dialogue process. The involvement of the offender's community of care helps build understanding because these people know the offender well. Their participation also helps the offender shift back from the role of offender to community member. Some of the challenges of the approach include difficulties in bringing together the right people for the conference particularly if the offender is disconnected from his or her family, the extensive time needed for preconference preparation, and how much input from community members has to be packed into the time allotted for the dialogue, which may reduce the time to hear fully from the primary people affected, and most importantly, ensuring more consistent participation of victims in the process so that their voice is not lost.

Peacemaking Circles

Peacemaking circles are based on the process of dialogue, relationship building, and the communication of moral values in order to promote accountability, healing, and compassion through community participation in resolving conflicts (Presser & Van Voorhis, 2001). Circles are much more focused on the harm done to community and community responsibility for supporting and holding accountable its members than the two approaches described above (Pranis, 2005). Circles also serve to build community. Peacemaking circles are rooted in North American indigenous cultures and have been used in Canada to empower Native peoples and to transfer some aspects of the judges' role to Aboriginal communities (Jaccoud & Walgrave, 1999).

The circle process may be requested by offenders, victims, community members, or justice officials (Coates, Umbreit, & Vos, 2003). Participation is voluntary. Sitting around the circle may include the offender and his or her family members and support persons, the victim and his or her family members and support persons, any number of community members, and perhaps a justice official as well as the circle keeper who facilitates the process (Pranis, Stuart, & Wedge, 2003). In complex cases, smaller circles, perhaps one with the victims and their support persons and another with offenders and their support persons may take place before the larger circle meets to give persons more opportunities to share their stories of what happened and to clarify what they would like to have happen now.

The circle uses a talking piece for managing the circle interactions because it is believed that using a talking piece encourages respectful listening and respectful dialogue. The talking piece is passed around the circle and participants may speak only when holding the talking piece. As part of the circle process, offenders are expected to make reparation to the community as well as to the victims. Decisions rendered by the circle are made by consensus (Pranis, 2005). The circle process can be very time consuming and labor intensive, but of the approaches described here, it typically involves the broadest cross-section of persons touched by the conflict.

Circles can be part of a comprehensive response to harm and its damaging effects (Sharpe, 1998). It can facilitate offender accountability, strengthen the offender's sense of responsibility to the victim and community, provide positive role models, and find ways to support and reward the offender's changes while also building community. One of the challenges to this practice includes the need for resources to provide for the interventions established by the circle. Another difficulty may be the circle's limited effectiveness particularly in small and closed communities where families are highly interconnected and fighting and where leadership positions are undermined by political infighting.

Assessing Restorativeness by Type of Practice

Zehr (2002) places restorative justice practices on a continuum that ranges from fully restorative to not restorative. The extent of restorativeness in each practice rests on answers to six key questions (see Figure 4.1):

1. Does the model address harms, needs, and causes?
2. Is it adequately victim oriented?
3. Are offenders encouraged to take responsibility?
4. Are all relevant stakeholders involved?
5. Is there an opportunity for dialogue and participatory decision making?
6. Is the model respectful to all parties? (p. 55)

Zehr (2002) calls victim-offender mediation, family group conferencing, and peacemaking circles "encounter models" and makes the claim that all three are "fully restorative" because, among other factors, they involve a dialogue, with a preference for face-to-face meetings. Other practices, such as victim assistance, victim impact panels, and offender treatment or rehabilitation programs, religious teaching in prison, and letters of apology, may play an important role in a restorative system or be mostly partially or potentially restorative. These other practices, however, do not include direct dialogue or other criteria that

FIGURE 4.1

Zehr (2002) outlines. Others besides Zehr, for example, McCold and Watchel (2003), have also noted the significance of dialogue or emotional engagement in assessing the different practices but base the degree of their restorativeness on singular factors such as the representation of victim, offender, and community in the meeting.

COMPONENTS OF RESTORATIVE JUSTICE DIALOGUE

What is restorative justice dialogue? How would we know it if we saw it? What are the indicators that identify the interaction between key stakeholders as "restorative?" Restorative justice dialogue is often distinguished by its "primary" approaches, namely VOM, FGC, and peacemaking circles. Grouping restorative justice dialogue programs by type is useful. It facilitates discourse among policy makers, practitioners, theoreticians, and advocates. Resources can be directed toward a given type of programs. People can be trained to work within and across program types. Common data can be gathered for assessment and accountability purposes across these practices. At a deeper level, however, the three core practices share certain components that cut across their individual boundaries and provide a different way to identify restorative practices. Indeed, because these components are delineated, it is possible to assess the restorativeness of existing programs, explain some of the reasons some programs falter, and establish parameters for the creation of innovative programs to address emerging social issues, for example, domestic violence, offender reentry, and student misconduct in higher education. Many of the practice components reflect restorative justice principles and values.

The components include (1) harm as an organizing principle, (2) personal accountability in response to the harm, (3) inclusivity, (4) voluntarism, (5) nondirective facilitation, (6) preparation for the dialogue, (7) the telling of story as personal truth, (8) reparation and/or symbolic restitution, (9) consensus-based agreements, (10) process rather than outcome orientation, (11) safety, (12) respectful interaction, and (13) positive energy. (See Figure 4.2.)

Foundational Framework

Restorative justice dialogue is undergirded by principles that structure the content, who participates, the nature of the interaction, and the management of the process. These principles impact the organization and direction of the dialogue.

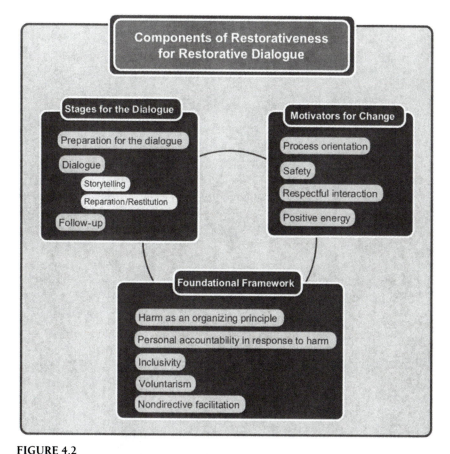

FIGURE 4.2

Harm as an Organizing Principle

In contrast to the criminal justice system and its focus on law breaking, restorative justice dialogue is predicated on the fact that emotionally or physically violent acts must be viewed first and foremost on personal terms; that is, in terms of the suffering and misery they create for those affected by the violence (Zehr, 1990; Zehr & Mika, 1998). Most often that harm was created by crime and wrongdoing. The harm may be seemingly insignificant: Someone broke into a car to steal a tape deck. A student attacked another boy with scissors at school. A young boy threw a lit paper into a house. But there is usually more to the story.

The tape deck was stolen from a handicap vehicle that belonged to a man who was a paraplegic. Because his vehicle could be easily recognized, he feared that the original thieves could again target him. He decided to break the lease on his apartment and move to a new place out of concern for his protection.

The student who started the fight at school actually had been the victim of verbal taunts of a personal nature inside and outside of school. Reports to the school had been unsuccessful in stopping the bullying. Finally he "snapped" and came at the boy who had bullied him, with scissors, narrowly missing the boy's shoulder. Terrified at his own reactions, he ran away unsure of what to do next and eventually returning home at night to frantic parents who had reported him missing.

The victim of the lit paper had been away when it was thrown into her home but returned the day before Christmas with her three children to find nothing left, other than the floors dripping with water from the firefighters' work. The two school-aged children had to move to different schools. One of them continued to be traumatized because the school's requirement that students take showers after doing sport activities triggered memories of seeing all the water dripping through the ceiling in the house that was burnt down.

Although these portrayals flush out some of the human costs and needs that are made visible when focus is on the harm, there are additional wounds because of having been a crime victim. Crime is itself a violation of the self, a desecration of who we are and what we believe (Zehr, 1990). The following contrast between the experience of victimization and the experience of bereavement shows the disequilibrium felt by victims who may experience both.

> The victim is deliberately, unjustly harmed or coerced by another human being. The bereaved feels loss. The victim feels like a loser. The bereaved feels sad. The victim feels humiliated. The bereaved may feel as though a part of himself or herself has been ripped away. The victim often feels diminished. (Ochberg, 1988, p. 110)

Indeed many if not most crime victims suffer because their fundamental beliefs about the world and how it operates have been shattered. For example, the world becomes malevolent because their injuries are the result of a conscious, malicious intention of another person. The world is no longer an orderly, meaningful place because there is no explanation for the question "Why?" or "Why me?" Indeed, crime victims often make up answers or evaluate themselves as weak or responsible in order to regain a sense of control through their formulating logical but often inaccurate explanations. All of these injuries at a concrete, emotional, and spiritual level are a part of the harm the victim carries. This harm creates the reason to come together with the offender. The crime victim needs reassurance that he or she is safe again and the person responsible will not do it again. The crime victim needs support and needs to understand why he or she became the victim, why the crime occurred, and why it specifically happened to him or her. The crime victim also needs to tell his or her own story about the effects of the crime and to have that story accepted and affirmed by other people (Zehr, 1990). The harm also creates the need for personal accountability and the obligation to make right, to the extent possible, the wrong that was done. For all these reasons, the harm, in effect, organizes the dialogue between stakeholders.

Personal Accountability in Response to the Harm

Indeed, the dialogue, at a deeper level, is really about the victim's need for vindication because in addition to the harm suffered, the victim was also wronged by another person who deliberately treated them as if they did not matter (Bennett, 2007). This secondary level of violation creates a moral injury, a degradation that sends the message, "You don't count" (Murphy, 1988). It is this injury of fundamental disrespect that carries lasting damage. It is this injury that gives rise to the need to be vindicated in such a way that the fact that the victim was wronged is undone (Bennett, 2007). Only the victim can really confront the offender at this level of violation with the profound meaning and impact of what he or she did. Likewise, only the offender can address the injury at the level it was experienced by the victim by accepting that what he or she did was wrong, that it came from him or her, and that he or she repudiates that aspect of self—weakness or failing—that caused the harm to occur (Swinburne, 1989). Consequently, a core component of restorative justice dialogue is for the offender to retract the attitude sent out in his or her actions by holding himself or herself personally accountable for the harm done. This reparative act is particularly powerful because it comes from the wrongdoer and is performed voluntarily.

> To have the one responsible for the harms acknowledge that you are a truth-teller . . . that was the beginning of my healing and return to normalcy. Of course, therapists, my psychiatrist, loved ones, tell you, "You're not responsible, it wasn't your fault". But you never really internalize that . . . I began to feel innocent the moment he declared himself "guilty," despite what the courts had said. He declared himself guilty and me "innocent" and I felt the shame I had carried drop away . . . I felt innocent for the very first time since the rape . . . That was the beginning . . . Since then, the nightmares have ended . . . the fear in gone . . . I can't even conjure up the terrifying images any longer . . . I'm finally free . . . . (Gustafson, 2005, p. 218)

Paradoxically, the offender's ability to help restore status to the victim through his or her genuine expression of deep regret begins to give the offender a way back because his or her actions attract respect and begins to move forward the offender's reinstatement as a moral citizen.

All three of the core approaches ask offenders to respond actively to their own crimes and to communicate directly with victims and members of their communities. They are expected to explain what they did and why they did it and to listen to what others have to say to them including how they have impacted, even changed, the direction of people's lives. In this process, they are treated both as capable of understanding and feeling, through the victim's experience, the effects of their actions and capable of acting morally in response to the victim's need and what they owe back.

The expectation in restorative justice dialogues of being answerable for the harm done to another is not limited to offenders. Indeed, a family group conference may include family members taking responsibility for problems in the family that contributed to the offender's wrongdoing. A peacemaking circle may focus on the needs of youth in the community who, like the offender, are vulnerable to the influence from gangs. Community members may need to hold themselves personally accountable for their noninvolvement and indirect contribution to gang activity as part of a renewed commitment to taking action. Likewise, offenders may need to express remorse to others besides the victim. In a family group conference, the mother of an offender read some prepared statements about how she felt about the damage her son did to a fence, which had resulted in the loss to a local farmer of his cattle which escaped. What she read was powerful and shocked everyone, including her son, who fought hard not to cry. He later apologized to his mother during the meeting, something which he admitted later was harder than doing so to the victim.

Inclusivity

Restorative justice rests on the principle of engagement, which implies involvement and active participation of an enlarged circle of stakeholders. This principle stands in marked contrast to the criminal justice system that typically limits the victim's role to being a witness for the prosecution and places the offender in a passive role, whose voice is represented only by his or her lawyers. Indeed, the attorneys decide who will and won't testify. Consequently, the primary players in a criminal act often feel excluded rather than included.

Inclusivity in restorative justice dialogues has several meanings. It refers to the need to hear from all sides in order to get a full picture of what happened and its impact. In a circle sentencing that took place in Yukon Territory, the victim, offender, community members, and representatives of the crown discuss the offender's history of domestic violence and substance abuse. Although his problems are longstanding, members of the community also describe that he hunts and catches fish for the elderly in the community during the cold winters and helps care for some of the children. They question what will happen to the older people without the offender's help. What good will come from imprisoning him? These comments from community members provide a more comprehensive account because of their inclusion. As the Quakers say, "Everyone has a piece of the truth."

Inclusivity also refers to the procedures followed that give everyone who attends the dialogue the chance to speak and be heard and the opportunity to give input for the decision-making and the outcome. All three restorative justice practices follow different protocols about who speaks and in what order, but each person is accorded equal concern, respect, and dignity. The space given to each person and regard shown for their opinion are reflected in the research that shows that over 80%–90% of VOM participants (Umbreit, Vos, & Coates, 2005a) and 73%–95% of FGC participants were satisfied with the process and outcome (Fercello & Umbreit, 1997; McCold & Wachtel, 1998; McGarrell, Olivares, Crawford, & Kroovand, 2000).

The concept of inclusivity in restorative justice dialogue, however, means more than numbers or having the chance to speak. It connotes as well that there will be opportunity for direct and full involvement based on the fact that part of the agenda in a dialogue is getting others to work together to solve problems related to the crime. Those that attend have full freedom of expression and are empowered to define and meet their own needs, roles, and responsibilities and to speak "from the heart." Inclusivity in the sense of full and open expression is vital to making the dialogue a meaningful experience. Indeed, it is the fullness of an individual's contribution that often shifts the dialogue to a deeper level or a more positive outcome. Consequently, each dialogue is individualized and custom designed to include different stakeholders depending on the parameters of the approach (for example, VOM, FGC, or peacemaking circles), the affected community, and the persons best able to help.

VOM, FGC, and peacemaking circles have in common the inclusion of victims and offenders in direct face-to-face or indirect dialogue and the presence of one or more parties who serves as mediator, facilitator, convener, or circle keeper. Victim-Offender Mediation dialogues may be limited just to the victim, offender, and facilitator or may include a few people who attend as a support to the key players. In cases of severe violence, for example, the victim and offender often choose to limit who attends to themselves because of the personal nature of the offense and the need for an intimate and intense engagement in order to address the wrongdoing. FGC brings criminal justice officials together with offenders, their families, and supporters on the one hand and on the other the crime victim and their family and supporters. This approach emphasizes supporting offenders in taking responsibility for their actions and in changing their behaviors. Thus, the involvement of the offender's family is critical and expected. Peacemaking circles are more focused on harm done to community and the community's responsibility for supporting and holding accountable its members. Consequently, the circle's membership might include community representatives or leaders. When VOM, FGC, and peacemaking circles are viewed as three different restorative justice processes, it becomes clearer that restorative justice invites all stakeholders to participate but adjusts its processes to meet their needs and interests.

Voluntarism

Restorative justice dialogue is a voluntary and consensual process. Indeed, restorative justice mandates that people must choose of their own free will to engage in a dialogue. This position stands in marked contrast to the criminal justice system, which demands attendance at proceedings, compels or disallows speech, and requires behavioral adherence to prescribed rules.

Participants' willingness to participate sets a tone of cooperation but, more important, the voluntariness of their engagement lends power to the trustworthiness of what they have to say because they were not coerced into participating. Rather, their contribution was freely given. For victims, voluntarism is manifested by their freedom to choose whether or not to participate in the dialogue and how much to share. Their ability to make choices is particularly important for victims who, because of the crime, were robbed of their options. Voluntarism also describes as well the spirit behind the role of mediator, facilitator, or circle keeper, which is frequently performed by community volunteers. In addition, community volunteers may attend FGC or peacemaking circles just as members of the process. Indeed, community volunteers often serve as mediators, facilitators, or circle keepers. As volunteers, what they bring of themselves and donate of their time is a gift because it is generated by their care for others and is done without remuneration. Their selflessness and willingness to give makes what they contribute more genuine because it is not paid work.

Although restorative justice prescribes that offenders' participation be voluntary, offenders are often ordered to VOM, FGC, or a sentencing circle or experience the option as a limited choice over going through the court system. They therefore do not always perceive the process as "voluntary." Care must be taken to engage with offenders in the least coercive manner possible and to allow offenders to "choose out" of the program if necessary. Attention to the voluntary nature of participation is important because the experience of choice, along with other factors, for example, opportunity to speak during the dialogue, influences the participants' sense of empowerment and willingness to move beyond blaming and defending (Umbreit et al., 2005a). It also may play a role in offenders deciding what they need to do to right the wrong and agree to make reparation including whether to follow through. Voluntary action is a prerequisite for any apology made to victims because this allows offenders' remorse or amends to be spontaneous and real.

Nondirective Facilitation

Much of the work of skilled mediators or facilitators and circle keepers will go unnoticed. Indeed, if facilitation is done well, victims and offenders will have difficulty identifying specifically what their facilitators did because the dialogue was between the key stakeholders. The goal of facilitation in restorative justice dialogue is to play in the background so that participants are free to communicate as fully as they wish by sharing experiences, perceptions, emotions, and perspectives.

The facilitator, however, is not passive. Dialogue does not come easily, especially when people are hurt and feeling angry (Sharpe, 1998). The facilitator therefore readies participants to talk to each other as persons, to clarify beforehand what each person wants, what needs to be said, and how to hear what needs to be understood. He or she carefully sets the stage for what will happen in the dialogue by preparing the victim and offender, his or her family members, or support people in a VOM or FGC and community members in a peacekeeping circle. The facilitator may also provide follow-up or monitor agreements made.

During the dialogue, however, the facilitator ensures the safety of the environment while staying out of the way as much as possible in order to empower participants to work out their own entanglements. He or she pays close attention to nonverbal behavior as well as to what is being said. He or she respects and does not interrupt long periods of silence, which may be necessary for reflection or for participants who need time to garner their next thoughts and feelings before speaking. He or she pays attention to how well the dialogue is facilitating a deeper level of communication, helping participants speak from the heart and hear what lies beyond each other's behavior (Sharpe, 1998). There may be rare moments when participants are stuck and need assistance. There may be occasions when the facilitator must intervene because of safety concerns. Most of the time, the facilitator is an active presence who starts the dialogue, explains the process, introduces procedures such as an opening or closing ritual, provides for breaks, and formalizes whatever agreement comes out of the session. As one facilitator stated, "It's like having all your sensors in overdrive while trusting the process."

Facilitation could be rated on a continuum from direct to nondirect depending on the practice. The Wagga Wagga model of FGC from Australia has the facilitator use a script to conduct the dialogue. Circle keepers may initially hold tight to a structure in order to ensure that the necessary groundwork is laid for the quality of the interaction that needs to occur for healing. Family Group Decision Making (FGDM) in child welfare cases follows a sequential format that is guided by the facilitator. The intent of any facilitation in a restorative justice dialogue, however, is for the interaction to take place between participants, not between the facilitator and the participants.

The components that comprise the foundational framework for VOM, FGC, and peacemaking circles work together to generate an open and unrestricted dialogue that has the potential to move people past their defenses and into a here-and-now realm where they can encounter each other anew and actually make a difference in each other's lives. Paradoxically, the foundational framework prescribes the lack of control and voluntariness of their engagement that allows for a central focus on harm and personal accountability, the two features that are shared by all restorative justice approaches.

Stages of the Dialogue Process

Although there are variations within and between the different practices, the dialogue process for VOM, FGC, and peacekeeping circles follows a similar order. The process has three distinct phases: (1) preparation, (2) dialogue meeting, which includes (a) storytelling and (b) the reparation agreement, and (3) follow-up.

Given the variation within practices, the following statistics indicate the average attendance for the different dialogue types. About 7 people attend a typical dialogue including volunteer facilitators and staff persons. In VOM, the average is 5.4 persons; for FGC programs, the average is 9.5; for circles, the average is 11.8. Across all three approaches, victims are present, on average, 83.8% of the time and the victim's family is present in 51.7% of cases (Bazemore & Schiff, 2005). Offenders' families are present at about two-thirds of the meetings. Other support persons participate about one-third of the time, with the highest concentrations found in FGC and peacemaking circles. Programs also use surrogate victims 17.7% of the time if there is no identifiable victim or the actual victim is not able or willing to participate (Bazemore & Schiff, 2005; Umbreit, Vos, & Coates, 2005b). They may also provide for indirect dialogues by having the facilitator shuttle back and forth between victims and offenders to get questions answered and work out agreements regarding restitution, community service, counseling plans, and other things that the victim and offender decide the offender can do to make things right. A national inventory of restorative dialogue programs for youth found that dialogues are held without a clear victim in 25% of cases (Bazemore & Schiff, 2005).

Preparation

The process begins with a referral, most often but not exclusively, from the court. For example, 62% of juvenile referrals for the three types of dialogue occur during precourt diversion, 13% are accepted after adjudication, and 23% are made after sentencing (Bazemore & Schiff, 2005). Criteria for referral include type and severity of crime, admission of guilt, identifiable loss and need for restitution, prior convictions, and assessment of major mental health problems and substance abuse. In contrast, Victim-Offender Dialogue (VOD) in crimes of severe violence occurs after the offender is incarcerated and the referral is generated by a request from the victim. At Roca, a community-based youth organization that serves an impoverished Boston neighborhood, peacemaking circles are internally generated by staff and youth for a variety of concerns including talking about a particular issue, addressing difficulties in a relationship, or dealing with the conflict between rival gang members (Boyes-Watson, 2008).

Once the referral is made, the dialogue, in effect, begins. The decision by different stakeholders about whether or not to participate is a part of the unspoken conversation. Victims, for example, may not be immediately enthusiastic about meeting with the offender and may need time to consider whether they will agree to meet. These considered choices are part of the preparation, which is, without question, the most critical factor for the success of the dialogue process (Armour & Umbreit, 2007). Indeed, the final decision to continue may not occur until after the first meeting with the facilitator. Preparation consists of one or more separate meetings conducted by the facilitator with victims, offenders, and other prospective participants that focus on an orientation to the dialogue, discussion of expectations and objectives, setting of ground rules, and review of specific concerns and alleviation of fears. Preparation varies based on the approach used. It is more likely to be used in VOM and FGC than in peacemaking circles (Bazemore & Schiff, 2005).

Preparation consists of bringing each party to the other, establishing safety, and assessing readiness. During orientation meetings, the facilitator clarifies the purpose of the dialogue; helps the victim and offender as well as family and community members discern why they want to meet with the other and what they want from the experience; assists participants to disclose their fears about what the process may involve and allays them where possible; explores the wrongdoer's ability to make restitution, do work for the victim, or do community work; and supports each party to make an informed decision about whether to participate. Each party is asked to describe the wrongdoing, what it means from their perspective, and how they see the other person. With this information, the facilitator brings each to the other, pointing out language that may in the dialogue meeting provoke the other, commenting on unrealistic expectations they may have about what is possible from the other, or providing information to encourage greater openness to each other. Part of the preparation process is tending to the safety of all participants. There must not be huge surprises that could harm participants or jeopardize the dialogue (Armour & Umbreit, 2007).

The facilitator must be sure that everyone understands the purpose of the meeting, the role of everyone present, and how the process will work. Because most participants are not familiar with restorative justice or the particular dialogue type, they are apt to interpret the intervention in the context of the criminal justice system (Gerkin, 2009). The facilitator may be seen as an authority figure, similar to a judge, able to make decisions and handout judgments. Participants may not realize that they are supposed to be actively involved in creating the outcome of the meeting and instead become subjects of the process rather than participants. Consequently, the facilitator needs to increase safety by educating participants so that they can see the purpose and intent of the dialogue through a restorative rather than a retributive lens. Safety is also increased when the facilitator recognizes out loud the factors that may impact the potential for dialogue such as power differentials or dynamics related to domestic violence or sexual abuse (Sharpe, 1998). Respect for whatever boundaries victims need for their own protection also boosts their sense of safety. In some cases, for example, victims may elect to participate only indirectly through sending a support person in their place or giving information through a video or audio message. Finally, safety is strengthened by encouraging participants to express their truths.

Preparation includes knowing when a case is ready to go forward. This assessment is based on a variety of factors including the readiness of the victim to hear the offender and the offender to hear the victim, the readiness of the offender to take responsibility, and the level of commitment to and understanding of a restorative approach (Sharpe, 1998). Sharpe wisely comments that "... such readiness, understanding, and commitment are rarely in place before victim and offender sit down together. These qualities develop largely through the experience itself" (1998, p. 22). The facilitator's assessment of readiness, therefore, is based on whether it is deep enough to carry participants through the hard work that can be required while remaining mindful that if participants are not ready, their anger and defensiveness could cause more harm.

Dialogue Meeting

The dialogue meeting consists of two parts, the telling of the story as personal truth and the reparation agreement. Not all of the dialogue types result in an agreement. A peacemaking circle that focuses singularly on victim healing or a victim-offender dialogue requested by a victim of severe violence with an incarcerated offender who will be in prison the rest of his life may not conclude with a formal plan.

Storytelling as personal truth. Narrative or storytelling is a means to communicate thoughts and feelings. Participants are encouraged to speak from the heart as well as the head to express the full impact of what happened as a result of the wrongdoing. This type of interaction reduces the avoidance or protective distance from the offense that otherwise blocks the full experience of what happened. It draws participants into the conversation and increases the likelihood that they will be fully present—physically, emotionally, intellectually, and even spiritually. Pranis says, "Listening to someone's story is a way of empowering them, of validating their intrinsic worth as a human being" (Pranis, as cited in Sawin & Zehr, 2007, p. 23). It also helps arouse offenders' empathy.

The dialogue meeting focuses upon a discussion of the facts and feelings related to the crime. If present, the victim tells the story of discovering the crime and the impact it had on his or her life. The offender tells the story of having committed the crime. Victims or others affected by the crime are given the rare opportunity to express their feelings directly to the person(s) who violated them as well as to receive answers to many lingering questions such as "Why me?" or "How did you get into our house?" or "Were you stalking us and planning on coming back?" During the meeting, the offenders are put in the uncomfortable position of having to face those whom they violated or impacted. They are given the equally rare opportunity to display a more human dimension to their character and to even express remorse in a very personal fashion.

In family group conferencing or peacemaking circles, family and community members also have the chance to ask questions or express their feelings toward the victim and/or offender and about the harm that was done. Indeed, their lives may also be disrupted, their security threatened, or their trust betrayed (Sharpe, 1998). Family members of both the victim and offender may share what happened to them as they learned of the violation including the guilt or anger it aroused, the terror they observed in the victim, or the misplaced pride siblings now feel toward their older brother for his aberrant behavior. Community members may tell stories to offenders from their own lives to model what else can happen or the decisions they made to no longer offend. These accounts help offenders become able and willing to acknowledge to victims the pain their actions have caused them. Moreover, through open discussion of their feelings, both victim and offender and other participants have the opportunity to deal with one another as people, often from the same neighborhood, rather than as stereotypes and objects (Armour & Umbreit, 2007).

Reparation and symbolic restitution. Telling the story builds a larger perspective so that everyone present can see more than they did before (Sharpe, 1998). Indeed, giving the full context provides an increased understanding of the offense and all that surrounds it so that participants can better see what needs to be done, by whom, and when. One of the hallmarks of restorative justice dialogue is that what a victim should receive to acknowledge their loss and what an offender should do to atone are uniquely tailored to each case and depend on the individual circumstances of who they are, what they need, and what they are able to give. Moreover, decisions must be based on consensus and feel fair to everyone involved.

The second part of the dialogue therefore focuses upon a discussion of the losses and negotiation of a mutually acceptable restitution agreement. The agreement may include monetary recompense but may also consist of steps offenders will take to change whatever behavior caused the harm, for example, participation in drug or alcohol counseling, mechanisms to ensure community safety, or relationship-building arrangements. They may also include some sort of community service or a genuine apology. A recent study found that most agreements specified multiple conditions including verbal and/or written apologies (71% of cases), a written report or presentation (13%), service work (33%), and financial restitution (48%) (Bergseth & Bouffard, 2007). From the victims' perspective, restitution does not mean that situations are restored to where they were before the crime. Rather the focus is on meaningful accountability and what offenders can do to take responsibility for the harm they caused and to offer some form of recompense (Armour & Umbreit, 2007). The agreement is a tangible product of the making of amends and may hold symbolic significance in the eyes of participants. Its completion demonstrates to others the offender's commitment not to reoffend (Clear & Karp, 1999).

Research on factors highly predictive of postconference offending found that reoffending was lower for offenders who expressed remorse and whose outcome decisions were consensual (Hayes & Daly, 2003). The need for consensus on the terms of the reparative agreements underscores the democratic nature of the process. It supports healing because the victim has a say in the outcome. It increases the likelihood that the offender will honor the agreement because it feels fair; it is built around the offender as well as the victim needs, assists the offender in finding ways to make amends, and gives the offender a voice in constructing it. Indeed, consensus-based agreements are an expression of people's ability to work together to solve problems related to crime.

Follow-Up

Because there can be considerable slippage between what was agreed and what actually happens, many restorative practices incorporate mechanisms of support and monitoring to strengthen the process of personal accountability. Programs do agreement follow-up in 80% of all cases. Circles have the highest rates, followed by FGC programs and then VOM (Bazemore & Schiff, 2005). In some instances, key participants may come together again to discuss why an agreement is not being met or to celebrate its completion (Armour & Umbreit, 2007). Studies indicate that 80%–93% of agreements are completed after participation in VOM. This finding is consistent across sites, cultures, and severity of offense (Bergseth & Bouffard, 2007; Umbreit & Coates, 1993; Umbreit et al., 2005b).

The three types of restorative justice practices allow an opportunity for participants to tell their stories, discuss issues, and come to a common understanding or agreement. Each has its own format for how the dialogue is structured, who is included, and how agreements are reached. What matters most, according to research, is whether harm gets addressed in meaningful ways. Specifically, the critical variables for a successful conference are (1) whether the conference was a memorable event, (2) if it evoked remorse, and (3) if this led to the offender meeting the victim, apologizing, and attempting to make amends. These factors remained significant after controlling for the demographics of reoffending (Maxwell, Kingi, Roberson, & Morris, 2004).

Creating the Context for Change

Regardless of particular dialogue type or the structure and stages of the process, the primary test of the restorativeness of an outcome is the extent to which it results from a restorative process. Three conditions must be met for a process to be restorative, namely safety of the environment, respectful interaction, and the creation of positive energy.

Process Orientation

The way that justice is done rather than its outcome is the subject matter of restorative justice dialogue (Presser & Van Voorhis, 2001). Indeed, because the dialogue is built on the exercise of restorative justice values, for example, humility, respect, equality, truth telling, compassion, mutual care, and so on, the facilitator must pay primary attention to those values that nurture relationships and ensure that participants are held by the process in a good way. Restorative processes are designed, in fact, to encourage participants to act on those values and to move in the direction of health and healing. Pranis

(2007) maintains that these values are universal and embedded in human nature because humans are communal. The ability to act on these better values becomes blocked when the world is not safe. Consequently, safety must be paramount in the dialogue in order to bring these deeply buried values to the surface (Pranis, 2007). A process orientation also requires acceptance that there is no right way to express these values but instead cultivates the awareness that the values are consistent across a variety of ways of expressing them. Instead of a focus on technique, therefore, the focus is on the values-based actions that allow movement and creating the conditions that encourage that movement.

Safety

The goal of the restorative process is to create a safe place for the victim and offender to discuss the wrongdoing and its aftermath (Raye & Roberts, 2007). Creating a safe context allows participants to access and communicate their thoughts and feelings without having to defend or protect themselves. It also allows them to listen nondefensively to what others are saying. When people are able to communicate more congruently about what they are feeling, both their sense of self-worth and sense of self-determination grow. Establishing a safe climate, therefore, furthers participants' abilities to connect.

Safety is especially critical because of the sense of endangerment victims feel as a result of the crime. They take significant risks when they share their experiences and the hurt and emotions connected to them (Raye & Roberts, 2007). Likewise, offenders need protection from abuse so that they can effectively communicate their compassion and regret and receive assistance as they start to make amends. Consequently, facilitators have to pay close attention to the circumstances of bringing people together. It should be expected, for example, that safety will be a point of real anxiety for potential dialogue participants (Coates & Gehm, 1985). Indeed, it has been cited by some as giving them reason to hesitate about agreeing to participate in the first place (Coates & Gehm, 1985; Coates, Umbreit, & Burns, 2004).

Facilitators, therefore, carefully consider questions such as the following: Who comes into the room where the dialogue is held first? Who speaks first? Who sits where? How wide should the table be? Are there pictures or symbols in the room that could be triggering? Are there topics that could inflame participants? Could the clothes a male offender wears be a possible reminder to a female victim of violence? These questions require close facilitator scrutiny whether the case involves vandalism, burglary, sexual assault, or murder (Umbreit, Vos, Coates, & Brown, 2003).

Attention to safety concerns continues throughout the dialogue and may last beyond, for example, cases where the victim and offender had a prior relationship that included some level of domestic violence. Indeed, part of a safety assessment is whether a face-to-face encounter could cause harm to a participant. This assessment continues during the face-to-face dialogue. Although exceptionally rare in practice, facilitators need to be prepared to intervene if the dialogue environment sours and if it becomes unsafe for any participant. Such intervention may be mild such as reminding participants what they have agreed to not talk about or how they agreed to behave toward one another. In rare instances, the facilitator must be prepared to halt the dialogue. This willingness and ability to act sets a tone that serves to establish and maintain a safe environment in which dialogue can occur. Regardless of actual or potential safety considerations, the facilitator strives to convey a sense of safety during the dialogue through his or her involvement. To the extent that the facilitator, therefore, remains a calm and unobtrusive presence, and he or she conveys, even in the midst of strong emotions, that what is happening is productive and can be trusted.

Respectful Interaction

Howard Zehr says, "If I had to put restorative justice into one word, I would choose respect . . ." (2002, p. 36). He goes on to note that issues of respect and disrespect are at the heart of offending and are at the heart of trauma. Moreover, negative experiences with the criminal justice system often have to do with the issue of respect. Consequently, part of addressing the harm is to show respect and engage in respectful interaction, which is the cornerstone of restorative justice dialogue.

Respectful interaction refers both to respect for the participants and respect for the process. In their preparatory meeting and at the dialogue session, facilitators remind participants to be respectful listeners. They convey the idea that without the bedrock of respect, participants are not yet ready to meet, the likelihood of positive outcomes is slim, and safety will be an issue throughout the process. Facilitators must remain mindful of the fact that even though they may evaluate the level of respect shown in a particular dialogue, the final disposition rests with the participants. Did they feel respected by others in the process? By some or all? What actions made them feel respected or disrespected?

Respect comes from acknowledging the worth inherent in others (Pranis et al., 2003). Having respect, therefore, means seeing past the offense and the wrongdoer to discover a person's humanity. The ability to see past these restrictions may rest on developing empathy. Indeed, research shows that the ability of victims to feel empathetic helps reduce the injustice gap both because it helps victims to see themselves as less innocent as human beings and their offenders as less evil (Exline, Worthington, Hill, & McCullough, 2003; Worthington, 2003).

Empathy has a better chance of developing if participants hear each other fully and can establish common ground. That means not interrupting, showing disinterest, or whispering to others when someone is speaking and instead expressing respect by focusing their minds, bodies, and hearts on receiving what another is saying so that it is possible to hear the spoken words to their essence and the intent and feelings behind them. Some of the procedures used to facilitate deep listening include quieting the mind; not analyzing or judging what is being said; the passing of a talking piece, which gives each person the chance to share without interruption; following a sequential order as to who talks first, second, or third; and slowing time down so that participants have the chance to listen well, consider what is being said, reflect on its meaning, and respond from a deep and authentic place within the self. These practices increase the likelihood that each person will leave the dialogue with a renewed sense of respect for themselves and others as well as feeling respect for who they are.

Positive Energy

Restorative justice dialogue works with the energy of the conflict. The goal is to transform the negative or toxic energy associated with the offense and the trauma suffered into a power that can heal. This path is best understood through bearing witness to the healing power of story in people's lives.

> Sarah contacted me shortly after the parole hearing and expressed her strong inner sense of needing to meet Jeff, the very man who killed her father so many years ago. From the very beginning it was clear that she was on an intense spiritual journey to reclaim her soul and her sense of meaning, balance, and wholeness in life. Jeff felt tremendous remorse for what he had done and was willing, though scared, to meet with Sarah.
>
> After months of preparation, the mediated dialogue was scheduled and held in a maximum-security prison. My co-mediator and I practiced mindfulness through centering and breath work both during the preparation and in the dialogue so that our egos and voices stay out of the way, to allow Sarah and Jeff's strength and wisdom to emerge and flow as it needed to. After very brief opening comments by the mediators, we entered an extended period of silence as Sarah sobbed and tried to find her voice to tell her story. As mediators, we did not intervene to move the process along. Instead, we remained silent. We knew she had the strength and our mindfulness practice allowed us to stay out of the way. Sarah and Jeff told us later that the energy of our presence, the nonverbal language of our spirit, was vital to the process being safe and respectful of their needs and abilities. After nearly four minutes, Sarah found her voice and her story of trauma, loss, and yearning for healing flowed out with strength and clarity. Jeff then offered his story of what happened, how it has affected his life, and the enormous shame he felt.

They continued to share deeper layers of their stories, interspersed with lingering questions both had. After five hours and shortly before the session ended, following another moment of extended silence, perhaps a minute, Sarah looked directly at Jeff and told him she forgave him for killing her father. She made it clear that this forgiveness was about freeing herself from the pain she has carried with her for more than twenty years. She hoped this forgiveness might help him as well, but Sarah said she could not set her spirit free without forgiving him. Sarah had never indicated in our many months of preparation that forgiveness was an issue she was struggling with, nor did we raise the issue. When she and her husband came to the prison for the dialogue with Jeff, she had no plan whatsoever to offer forgiveness. Yet in the powerful moment of confronting her greatest fear Sarah speaks of how she felt within her soul that "this is the moment to free myself." In post-dialogue interviews with Sarah and Jeff they both indicated the enormous affect this encounter had on their lives. Sarah spoke of how meeting Jeff was like going through a fire that burned away her pain and allowed the seeds of healing to take root in her life. She spoke of how before meeting Jeff she carried the pain of her father's death like an ever-present large backpack. After meeting Jeff, the pain is more like a small fanny-pack, still present but very manageable and in no way claiming her life energy and spirit, as before. Jeff reported a sense of release and cleansing, as if his spirit was set free as well. (Umbreit et al., 2005a, p. 3)

The creation of a safe, if not sacred, place for people in painful conflict to tell their story and to listen deeply and compassionately to the stories of others require careful preparation and the presence of certain conditions. Specifically, positive energy can flow freely only if people feel safe, because they otherwise speak from the head or from the notion of what ought to be said. In addition, there must be a pervasive sense of respect for others and the process, which allows people to bare their soul without interruption or interference or at most, gentle verbal prompting. Finally, there must be an understanding that the purpose of the dialogue is to deal with the past but to do so in a future-oriented way. Indeed, the whole purpose of accountability and truth telling is to bring people into a process that contributes to the future.

When there is safety, respect, and the desire to move things, it opens the door for emotional expression, which, whether conveyed verbally or nonverbally, is the language of human energy. It allows participants to talk fully about what happened, thereby releasing the toxic emotional energy associated with the traumatic event. It also opens the door so participants can experience a harmonic resonance between what is said by one and what is heard by the other whose response serves as an echo back. This phenomenon allows all those present in the dialogue to feel more open and to enter a special dimension of time that disconnects them from the everyday world. This space is different from participants' normal state of consciousness and transcends the normal flow of communication between people. In this space, participants find the strength to say things and interact in ways they may not have known before. The energy cultivated and unfettered by this process is positive and moves things forward. For victims, the movement can be from feeling powerless and vulnerable to feeling in control and personally victorious. For offenders, the movement can be redemption not because they have been forgiven but because of what they do with themselves that generates self-respect and deservedness.

Creating the context for the dialogue requires giving primary and ongoing attention to the process because it helps clear the path so participants feel safe enough to find their voice. The establishment of a safe space and conditions that prompt respectful engagement contains the energy of the conflict so that its negative hold can surface and be released in ways that garner healing. These factors both influence the dialogue and are influenced, in turn, by the dialogue.

CONCLUSION

Although this chapter has focused on the three primary dialogue types and the restorative components they share and that cut across VOM, FGC, and peacemaking circles, there are significant differences in structure and focus within as well as across the practices. For example, a study of VOM programs in Oregon found vast differences (Coates, Umbreit, & Vos, 2000; Umbreit, Coates, & Vos, 2001). Some were operated privately while others were administered by departments of corrections. Some prepared participants with face-to-face meetings, others did not. Some included restitution as part of every contract, others did not. Nine out of ten cases resulting in face-to-face mediation included support persons; these were typically family members, friends, or significant others such as teachers or counselors. Among the staff and volunteers from the different programs, there were certainly those that believed that their way of doing things was "purer," "more restorative," and "had more potential for impact" than those of their counterparts (Umbreit & Coates, 2004).

Within the family group conferencing type, there are those that rely on scripts to shape the dialogue among participants and those who do not. Some of these programs function within police departments, whereas others operate outside any public system. In some programs, there is an effort taken to balance the number of supporters for the victim and the offender, whereas in others there is no such attempt.

To some advocates of peacemaking circles, the only "pure form" would exist within the community, yet peacemaking circles fostering dialogue among those impacted by crime are taking place within institutions and service providing programs. These are being used at points of prevention, diversion, incarceration, and reentry.

Because of the large number of variations within each dialogue type, it may be more important to assess restorativeness by indicators such as voluntariness, preparation, and sense of safety rather than dialogue type and the "purity" of the model. Indeed, these dialogue types will need to be altered based on a special social issue, for example, domestic violence, to ensure safety. The variations may do an even better job of ensuring the restorativeness of the encounter than the traditional practices. Consequently, it is important to bear in mind that the ultimate goal of any restorative justice practice is to redress harm and advance healing. Program development and the delineation of restorativeness may be better advanced by ensuring that the qualities of all components are present in whatever restorative dialogue process is used rather than focusing on a specific program type with its distinctive design, number of participants, and numerous techniques of facilitating dialogue.

REFERENCES

Archibald, B., & Llewellyn, J. (2006). The challenges of institutionalizing comprehensive restorative justice: Theory and practice in Nova Scotia. *Dalhousie Law Journal, 29*, 297–343.

Armour, M., & Umbreit, M. S. (2007). Victim-offender mediation and forensic practice. In D. W. Springer & A. R. Roberts (Eds.), *Handbook of forensic mental health with victims and offenders: Assessment, treatment and research* (pp. 519–540). New York: Springer.

Bazemore, G., & Schiff, M. (2005). *Juvenile justice reform and restorative justice: Building theory and policy from practice.* Portland, OR: Willan Publishing.

Bennett, C. (2007). Satisfying the needs and interests of victims. In G. Johnstone & D. Van Ness (Eds.), *Handbook of restorative justice* (pp. 247–264). Portland, OR: Willan Publishing.

Bergseth, K. J., & Bouffard, J. A. (2007). The long-term impact of restorative justice programming for juvenile offenders. *Journal of Criminal Justice, 35*, 433–451.

Bohm, D., Factor, D., & Garrett, P. (1991). Dialogue: A proposal. Retrieved August 6, 2009, from http://www.infed.org/archives/e-texts/bohm_dialogue.htm

Boyes-Watson, C. (2008). *Peacemaking circles and urban youth.* St. Paul, MN: Living Justice Press.

Clear, R. R., & Karp, D. R. (1999). *The community justice ideal: Preventing crime and achieving justice.* Boulder, CO: Westview.

Coates, R., & Gehm, J. (1985). *Victim meets offender: An evaluation of Victim-Offender Reconciliation Programs.* Valparaiso, IN: PACT Institute of Justice.

Coates, R., Umbreit, M. S., & Burns, H. (2004). Why victims choose to meet with offenders. *Offender Programs Report, 8*(4), 55–57.

Coates, R., Umbreit, M. S., & Vos, B. (2000). *Restorative justice circles in South Saint Paul, Minnesota.* St. Paul, MN: Center for Restorative Justice & Peacemaking.

Coates, R., Umbreit, M. S., & Vos, B. (2003). Restorative justice circles: An exploratory study. *Contemporary Justice Review, 6*(3), 265–278.

Exline, J. J., Worthington, E. L., Jr., Hill, P., & McCullough, M. E. (2003). Forgiveness and justice: A research agenda for social and personality psychology. *Personality and Social Psychology Review, 7,* 337–348.

Fercello, C., & Umbreit, M. S. (1997). *Client evaluation of family group conferencing in 12 Sites in First Judicial District of Minnesota.* St. Paul, MN: Center for Restorative Justice & Peacemaking, University of Minnesota.

Gerkin, P. (2009). Participation in victim-offender mediation: Lessons learned from observations. *Criminal Justice Review, 344*(2), 226–247.

Gustafson, D. (2005). Exploring treatment and trauma recovery implications of facilitating victim-offender encounters in crimes of severe violence: Lessons from the Canadian experience. In E. Elliott & R. M. Gordon (Eds.), *New directions in restorative justice: Issues, practice, evaluation* (pp. 193–227). Portland, OR: Willan Publishing.

Hayes, H., & Daly, K. (2003). Youth justice conferencing and re-offending. *Justice Quarterly, 20*(4), 725–764.

Isaccs, W. (1999). *Dialogue and the art of thinking together.* New York: Doubleday.

Jaccoud, M., & Walgrave, L. (1999). Restorative justice. *Criminologie, 3,* 3–160.

Maxwell, G., Kingi, V., Roberson, J., & Morris, A. (2004). *Achieving effective outcomes in youth justice research: Final report.* Wellington, New Zealand: Ministry of Social Development.

McCold, P., & Wachtel, B. (1998). *Restorative policing experiment: The Bethlehem Pennsylvania police family group conferencing project.* Pipersville, PA: Community Service Foundation.

McCold, P., & Wachtel, T. (2003). In *pursuit of paradigm: A theory of restorative justice.* XIII World Congress of Criminology. Rio De Janeiro, Brazil.

McGarrell, E., Olivares, K., Crawford, K., & Kroovand, N. (2000). *Returning justice to the community: The Indianapolis Juvenile Restorative Justice Experiment.* Indianapolis, IN: Hudson Institute Crime Control Policy Center.

Murphy, J. G. (1988). Forgiveness and resentment. In J. G. Murphy & J. Hampton (Eds.), *Forgiveness and mercy* (pp. 14–34). Cambridge: Cambridge University Press.

Ochberg, F. M. (1988). Post-traumatic therapy and victims of violence. In F. M. Ochberg (Ed.), *Post-traumatic therapy and victims of violence* (pp. 3–19). New York: Brunner/Mazel.

Pranis, K. (2005). *The little book of circle processes: A new/old approach to peacemaking.* Intercourse, PA: Good Books.

Pranis, K. (2007). Restorative values. In G. Johnstone & D. Van Ness (Eds.), *Handbook of restorative justice* (pp. 59–74). Portland, OR: Willan Publishing.

Pranis, K., Stuart, B., & Wedge, M. (2003). *Peacemaking circles: From crime to community.* St. Paul, MN: Living Justice Press.

Presser, L., & Van Voorhis, P. (2001). Values and evaluation: Assessing processes and outcomes of restorative justice programs. *Crime & Delinquency, 48*(1), 162–188.

Raye, B. E., & Roberts, A. W. (2007). Restorative processes. In G. Johnstone & D. W. Van Ness (Eds.), *Handbook of restorative justice* (pp. 211–227). Portland, OR: Willan Publishing.

Sawin, J. L., & Zehr, H. (2007). The ideas of engagement and empowerment. In G. Johnstone & D.W. Van Ness (Eds.), *Handbook of restorative justice* (pp. 41–58). Portland, OR: Willan Publishing.

Sharpe, S. (1998). *Restorative justice: A vision for healing and change.* Edmonton, Alberta: Edmonton Victim Offender Mediation Society.

Swinburne, R. (1989). *Responsibility and atonement.* Oxford: Clarendon Press.

Umbreit, M. S., & Coates, R. (1993). Cross site analysis of victim offender mediation in four states. *Crime & Delinquency, 39*(1), 565–585.

Umbreit, M. S., & Coates, R. (2004). *Restorative justice mediated dialogue* (pp. 1–28). St. Paul: Center for Restorative Justice and Peacemaking.

Umbreit, M. S., Coates, R., & Vos, B. (2001). *Juvenile victim offender mediation in six Oregon counties.* Salem, OR: Oregon Dispute Resolution Commission.

Umbreit, M. S., Vos, B., & Coates, R. (2005a). *Restorative justice dialogue: Evidence-based practice.* St. Paul, MN: Center for Restorative Justice and Peacemaking, School of Social Work, University of Minnesota.

Umbreit, M. S., Vos, B., & Coates, R. (2005b). Restorative justice in the 21st century: A social movement full of opportunities and pitfalls. *Marquette University Law Review, 89*(2), 251–304.

Umbreit, M. S., Vos, B., Coates, R., & Brown, K. (2003). *Facing violence: The path of restorative justice & dialogue.* Monsey, NY: Criminal Justice Press.

Worthington Jr., E. L. (2003). *Forgiving and reconciling: Bridges to wholeness and hope.* Downers Grove, IL: InterVarsity Press.

Zehr, H. (1990). *Changing lenses: A new focus for crime and justice.* Scottsdale, PA: Herald Press.

Zehr, H. (2002). *The little book of restorative justice.* Intercourse, PA: Good Books.

Zehr, H., & Mika, H. (1998). Fundamental concepts of restorative justice. *Contemporary Justice Review, 1*, 47–55.

5. Victim-Offender Mediation

> *"I used to be afraid to go out at night, but after having met the young man who broke into my house I'm really not afraid any more . . . From a victim's point of view, seeing the offender face to face is crucial to the healing process, but not only for the victim, the offender too."*

> *"I realized that the victim really got hurt by my actions and that made me feel really bad. To understand how the victim feels about what I did to them makes me different . . . I was able to understand a lot about what I did and the real impact on their family."*

Shane quickly accepted responsibility for the offence and apologized. But at this meeting, the victim refused to let him off so lightly. She interceded: 'No, you're going to hear how this affected me', and went on to explain how she couldn't take her asthmatic daughter to 'emergency', how she couldn't take her son to soccer training, and she couldn't do her shopping. Shane at that stage became a blubbering mess . . . He started to own the offence in its entirety. The action plan agreed to by both Shane and the victim involved Shane giving his car to the victim. Shane, apparently, would have preferred to go to prison. Giving up his car was deeply embarrassing, because he had to explain to his friends, who saw his car being driven by the victim, the circumstances about what had happened. This humiliating experience had a much more constructive affect on his behavior than a prison sentence would have had. (Cayley, 1998; Johnstone, 2002)

A youth got drunk, broke into a school along with his friends, and accidentally set fire to the school causing enormous damage. At a meeting with some of the teachers and parents, a young girl showed the youth the scrapbook that she had kept in her classroom. About one-half was just burned to a crisp, and the other half was charred. She said, 'This is all I've got as a remembrance of my brother, because this scrapbook is photos of my family and a photo of my brother, and he died not so long ago, about a year ago, and that's all I've got now.' Then you saw the tears trickling down the face of the youth. This was the start of a process in which the youth eventually took 'ownership' of the offense, apologized to all affected by it, and gave up his weekends to help build a new playground. He did not come to the attention of the police again. (Cayley, 1998; Johnstone, 2002)

Victim-offender mediation (VOM) is the oldest, most widely developed, and empirically grounded expression of restorative justice dialogue (Bazemore &

Umbreit, 1995; Umbreit, 2001; Van Ness & Heetderks, 2002; Zehr, 1990, 2002). It provides interested victims the opportunity to meet with the juvenile or adult offender, in a safe and structured setting, with the goal of holding the offender directly accountable for their behavior while providing important assistance and compensation to the victim (Umbreit, 2001). VOM usually involves a victim and an offender in direct mediation facilitated by one or sometimes two mediators or facilitators. Occasionally, the dialogue takes place through a third party who carries information back and forth, a process known as "shuttle" mediation.

Family group conferencing (FGC) is a closely related cousin to VOM and routinely includes support persons and outside community representatives. Increasingly over time, distinctions between VOM and FGC have begun to blur. A 1999 survey of VOM programs in the United States found that support persons, including parents in juvenile cases, were present in nearly nine out of ten cases (Umbreit & Greenwood, 1999). Although the increase in numbers of participants and diverse representation brings VOM closer to both FGC and some peacemaking circles, VOM stands apart because its primary emphasis is on the victim–offender interaction over the family or community. Specifically, in the New Zealand model of FGC (see Chapter 6), the family caucus for decision making does not include the victim and, in fact, that victim's voice may only be represented in the conference indirectly or through a victim design. Likewise, peacemaking circles (see Chapter 7) place major emphasis on the impact of the crime on the community as a secondary victim and the community's involvement in repairing the harm. Again the victim may not be present or may be represented by a third party.

VOM has been widely implemented in North America and abroad. Many thousands of cases are dealt with annually through more than 300 programs throughout the United States and more than 1,200 programs abroad, including in Europe, Canada, Israel, Japan, Russia, South Korea, South Africa, South America, and the South Pacific (Umbreit, Vos, & Coates, 2005). In addition to programmatic implementation, VOM has maintained a fairly constant commitment to documentation and assessment of its efforts. Indeed, it is probably more documented and assessed than many, if not most, justice reform initiatives over the years (Umbreit, Coates, & Vos, 2006). For this reason, it is appropriate to refer to this approach as an "evidence-based" practice.

This chapter covering VOM is the first of four chapters that focuses on specific restorative approaches. It covers the history and development of the practice, the issues involved in implementation of a VOM program, an outline of the stages a case goes through, and a review of the research that evaluates its effectiveness on a number of dimensions, for example, satisfaction, cost, recidivism. Because of its extensive history, it is possible to follow the development of VOM in both the United States and other countries where it has been employed. Its current status varies considerably depending on whether it receives state support.

Indeed, state support may be essential because without it VOM programs tend to falter if the original grassroots effort cannot be maintained. In addition, the ability to sustain a VOM program is controlled by the necessity for adequate referrals requesting VOM services. A diverse communication network is needed, therefore, both to ensure funding and a steady flow of cases.

The effectiveness of VOM is well documented by over 56 studies and 4 meta-analyses. Current research is beginning to examine what actually occurs in the dialogue between victim and offender. Results indicate that VOM participants are not adequately prepared for the dialogue. They tend to interpret it in the context of the criminal justice system and engage in the process, therefore, in more limited ways. As agencies try to find more efficient ways to deliver VOM, they too give less attention to preparation. Consequently, many VOM sessions are handled in a more business-like manner. Attention to these microlevel aspects is essential to ensure that the power of the approach, which rests on full and personal engagement between victim and offender, can be realized.

HISTORY AND DEVELOPMENT

Experimentation in bringing together victims and offenders with a trained mediator or facilitator to talk through what happened and to decide together what to do about what happened began in the early 1970s and 1980s. These first efforts to humanize the justice process through holding young offenders directly accountable to the victim of their crime were called Victim-Offender Reconciliation Programs (VORPs). The first VORP program was established in Kitchener, Ontario, in 1974, and the first VORP in the United States was initiated in Elkhart, Indiana, in 1978. The need to put a more human face on punishment for wrongdoing was promoted by practitioners working in community-based programs, churches, and even some within the justice system. As with any innovation that continues as long as 40 years, the initial experiments have gone through numerous iterations including the structure of the encounter, its focus, and even its name. VOM evolved somewhat differently in the United States compared to the European community. The growth in the United States through state legislative mandates and policies for VOM reflects its growing influence and acceptance for addressing both youth and adult crime, including misdemeanors and felonies.

Changes Over Time

VORP was initially established with leadership from the Mennonite community in both Canada and the United States. Its purpose was reconciliation involving the healing of injuries and restoring of right relationships (McCold, 2006). Some practitioners and criminal justice personnel were uncomfortable with the word *reconciliation*, feeling that it was too religious sounding and that it did little to describe a process (Umbreit et al., 2006). Furthermore, victims often balked at the notion of seeking reconciliation with the persons who offended them.

Many practitioners shifted how they referenced the process by calling it Victim-Offender Mediation. This name was considered more representative of the fact that many crimes involve victims and offenders who were strangers to each other before the offense, and these persons have no basis for "reconciling" (Van Ness & Heetderks, 2002). Although VOM was more descriptive of the interaction between victim and offender, critics worried that VOM would be regarded as simply one more form of mediation, or worse, that VOM would shift its emphasis from a victim-offender dialogue to following the negotiation settlement guidelines of other mediation services. Concerns were also raised about the likelihood of replacing trained community volunteers with the requirement for professional mediators.

The name "Victim-Offender Conferencing" (VOC) has emerged as an alternative based on the assertion that "conferencing" blunts the potential threat posed by professional mediators and the imposition of externally derived standards. Moreover, conferencing may be a more accurate nomenclature because it keeps the emphasis on the process of interaction rather than potential outcomes, which is the focus of a mediated settlement. Interestingly, victim-offender programs today continue to use different names for the same process including VORP, VOM, and VOC.

Changes over the years have occurred, as well, in the requisite participants for a face-to-face encounter. The early experiments with VORP and VOM brought together an offender and victim or victims with a trained community volunteer (Umbreit et al., 2006). If multiple offenders or victims were involved, each offender was expected to meet with each victim. Soon this became unwieldy and notions about who should be present began to shift. Besides the frequent practice of all offenders meeting as a group with a victim, the process began to include a support person each for the victim and offender, respectively. Although typically such support persons did not participate in the actual conversation, support persons came to include parents of involved youth, and they often gained a voice in the process. Today, face-to-face encounters often consist of still more persons, including persons from the community or neighborhood who are impacted by the crime or may be drawn upon for resources to help meet the ongoing needs of victims and/or offenders.

The role of community in VOM has gradually increased. Originally, the community's voice was represented by the mediator (Umbreit et al., 2006). As support persons were added, they too came to represent the community, at least in part. More recently, the community has become more visible through the inclusion of designated community representatives such as neighbors or other concerned citizens. Not all programs have expanded the community role. Rather, it appears that who is invited to participate is largely determined by the nature of the case.

Finally, there have been changes in the types of cases referred for VOM. With rare exceptions, cases in the early days focused on youth and on misdemeanors. Today, VORP, VOM, and VOC programs have expanded who they cover and what they cover. They are working with adults as well as youth and are increasingly relied upon in serious and violent cases and at different stages in the criminal justice system (Umbreit, Vos, Coates, & Brown, 2003). This trend toward broader application is occurring both in the United States and European nations.

Development of VOM in Europe

At the same time as the VORP experiment began in Kitchener, Ontario, in 1974, debate about bringing together crime victims and offenders had started in Europe. Pilot projects began in Norway in 1981 and in Finland in 1983 (Pelikan & Trencz, 2006). The Home Office in England funded four projects between 1985 and 1987. Germany started VOM in 1985 with a rapid expansion to more than 400 programs serving both juvenile and adult crime cases. Much of the development was influenced by Nils Christie, a Norwegian criminologist who, in 1977, challenged the state claiming that conflicts were like property and had been taken away from the people (Christie, 1977).

The current adoption of VOM in Europe has been guided, in part, by "Mediation in Penal Matters" (henceforth: CoE-R 99-19) set forth by the European Committee of Ministers (Pelikan & Trencz, 2006). This legislation and its explanatory memorandum address the general principles of VOM as well as training and practice standards. Although its provisions are not binding and its influence is variable depending on the country, the European Forum for Mediation and Restorative Justice founded in 2000 regards the CoE-R 99-19 as an important set of guidelines and an instrument for achieving its goals.

The development of VOM in Europe has not been uniform but consists of a wide variety of practices. In Norway, for example, VOM is part of a community-based conflict resolution approach, and volunteer mediators are recruited from each municipality and given 4 days of basic mediation training. In contrast, the Czech Republic VOM is offered as a professional service requiring extensive training organized by the Ministry of Justice in close cooperation with the Probation and Mediation Service (Pelikan & Trencz, 2006). In England, VOM is part of the national restorative justice strategy being developed by the United Kingdom (Pelikan & Trencz, 2006). The vast majority of the programs use indirect or shuttle mediation, where the mediator talks to the offender and victim individually and carries information, suggestions, and offers between the parties. This practice is justified by the fact that in cases where there is no ongoing relationship, where damage to property has been minor, and the emotional problems caused negligible, proceedings involving face-to-face contact are too time consuming and unnecessary for settling financial compensation.

Legislative Statutes in the United States

The growth in legislation for VOM on a state-by-state basis attests to its durability over time and the strength of its foothold in the criminal justice system. Indeed, without statutory provisions, there is little legal authority or protections for those involved in VOM, nor are there specific funding mechanisms (Lightfoot & Umbreit, 2004; Umbreit, Lightfoot, & Fier, 2001).

There currently exists a continuum of statutory authority related to VOM in the states, ranging from "little or no mention of VOM" to a "comprehensive VOM legislative framework" (Umbreit, Lightfoot et al., 2001, p. 3) (see Table 5.1). This continuum reflects the range of actions of 30 states that have VOM or VOM-type statutory authority. Twenty-three of those states have a specific statutory provision for VOM, and six more states have VOM-type programs that may entail dialogue between victims and offenders (see Table 5.2).

TABLE 5.1 Variations in statutory authority for victim-offender mediation

General "Referral" Language	State Program	Grants to Nonprofits	County Program	Specific Program	Grants to Counties or Nonprofits	Referrals to Individuals
Alabama	Colorado	Delaware	Arizona	Arkansas	Ohio	Louisiana
Alaska	Florida	Minnesota	Indiana			
North Carolina	Illinois	Montana	Kansas			
Washington	Iowa	Nebraska		Virginia		
Wisconsin	Maine	New York				
	Missouri	Oregon				
	Oklahoma	Tennessee				
	Texas	Vermont				

TABLE 5.2 Statutory authority for victim-offender mediation

Little/No Mention of VOM	Codes Detail Programs That May Involve Victim-Offender Dialogue	Basic Statutory Provision for VOM	Specific Statutory Provision for VOM	Comprehensive VOM Program
Connecticut	Alaska	Alabama	Arkansas	Delaware
DC	Florida	Arizona	Louisiana	Indiana
Georgia	Illinois	California	Minnesota	Kansas
Hawaii	Maine	Colorado	Ohio	Montana
Idaho	New York	Iowa	Oklahoma	Nebraska
Kentucky	Vermont	Missouri	Texas	Oregon
Maryland		North Carolina	Virginia	Tennessee
Massachusetts		Washington		
Michigan		Wisconsin		
Mississippi				
Nevada				
New Hampshire				
New Jersey				
New Mexico				
North Dakota				
Pennsylvania				
Rhode Island				
South Carolina				
South Dakota				
Utah				
West Virginia				
Wyoming				
21 States & DC	6 States	9 States	7 States	7 States

Just because a state does not have a state statute or code mentioning VOM or restorative justice, it does not mean that such programs cannot exist. For example, Pennsylvania's state statutes currently do not mention VOM. However, there is a general commitment to restorative justice within the Pennsylvania code, and indeed there are VOM programs in the state. In the 29 states with statutory authority, the VOM provisions extend from a simple reference to VOM within a long list of sentencing alternatives to comprehensive stipulations, including details on training requirements, costs, evaluation, confidentiality, and liability. Although the growth in legislative statutes is noteworthy, there are still 21 states and the District of Columbia that do not have any specific reference to VOM within their state statutes or codes. Formal state recognition benefits recipients in a number of ways, including the ability of restorative justice programs to withstand challenges from the criminal justice system. Most recently, the Minnesota Supreme Court overruled the appeals court, citing the VOM statute allowing the assignment of sanctions as the reason for allowing a sentencing circle's sanction to stand in *Minnesota v. Pearson*, 2002 (Minnesota Supreme Court, 2002). If Minnesota did not have this clause regarding VOM in its statute, it is quite possible that the Supreme Court would not have upheld the acceptance of recommendations by a sentencing circle.

Throughout the world, VOM is the bedrock tool of restorative justice. Its longevity and influence are evident in the ongoing debate over its name—a reflection of political shifts over time, the movement from lesser to more major crimes, the varied growth and development in most European nations, and the increasing emergence of statutes and case law specific to VOM. VOM stands as an important pioneering effort in refocusing how criminal justice is implemented. When compared to other restorative justice approaches, for example, neighborhood accountability boards and family group conferencing, VOM remains stalwart in its primary commitment to the victim. Indeed, there can be no VOM without the direct or indirect presence of the victim.

IMPLEMENTATION OF A VOM PROGRAM

More than 300 VOM programs exist in the United States (Umbreit, Greenwood, Schug, Umbreit, & Fercello, 2000). They are most often offered by private, not-for-profit agencies (43%). Various elements of the justice system are responsible for another 33%, including probation (16%), correctional facilities (8%), prosecuting attorney offices (4%), victim services (3%), and police departments (2%). The remaining 23% are offered by churches or church-related agencies. Although these programs are diverse, they share similarities by virtue of the fact that they all had to address similar issues when they first began. Those issues include identification of primary and secondary goals, development of community support, procuring funding, delineating sources of referral, designing the program, and training mediators or facilitators (Umbreit, 1994, 2001). Many of these issues need ongoing attention.

Primary and Secondary Goals

By definition, the mediation process is grounded in the primary goal of providing a conflict resolution process that is perceived as fair to both the victim and offender. Goals for victims might include their direct involvement, letting the offender know the impact of the crime on their lives, receiving answers to lingering questions, and influencing the manner in which the offender is held accountable. Goals for offenders might include the opportunity to repair the damage, to accept responsibility for their behavior, to portray a more human dimension to their character, and to apologize directly to the person they harmed. Secondary goals might be offender rehabilitation, prevention, or victim empowerment.

Development of Community Support

A broad base of support is necessary to counter the predictable initial skepticism that accompanies the start of a new program that allows the victim to meet with the person who victimized them. All possible stakeholders, for example, judges, directors of victim service agencies, civic and corporate leaders, and attorneys, should be considered as part of an analysis about the degree to which each individual could either offer resistance or significantly influence the development of the new program, including strategies for gaining support or neutralizing active opposition. Building local support requires the development of a plan to present the concept and program to the public in a clear and understandable fashion.

Procuring Funding

Securing sufficient funds is one of the most difficult jobs. Fortunately, VOM programs do not require huge budgets. Many begin with relatively small amounts of money, often from public foundations and churches, and later have secured amounts of public funding if the program develops. A brief concept paper can be distributed to potential funding sources. Multiple sources of funding provide safety nets in case one or more funders can no longer participate.

Sources of Referrals

Before deciding which agencies to approach for referrals, an emerging program must determine whether or not to focus on juvenile or adult cases and which types of cases, for example, property offenses, to accept. Depending on the choices made, a program can quickly gain a reputation for "light" cases, many of which would have been ignored by the system. Victims and offenders involved in more serious cases may have greater emotional and material needs than can be resolved through mediation. Identifying an appropriate target population for case referrals ultimately involves a balance between the desires of the program advocates and the willingness of the criminal justice system to support the new program as an experiment by taking some risks. By keeping the express goals of the program in the forefront of negotiations with the referral source, there is less chance that the program leaders will be pressured into taking cases that have little relationship to their ultimate objectives.

Program Design

Clarification of goals and identification of the target population can easily become an abstraction if there are not clear strategies for how a program will actually operate. Effective program design is also part of replicating the program in other communities. Identification of the appropriate agency to sponsor the VOM program is a first step. In some communities, an entirely new nonprofit organization may be appropriate. Collaborative efforts may be considered, such as a partnership between public and private agencies. In Austin, Texas, the juvenile probation department directly sponsors the program and relies on the local dispute resolution center to provide volunteer mediators to handle cases.

The number of staff can vary greatly based on the projected caseload, the level of funding, and the sponsoring organization. Having at least 1½ full-time equivalent staff members to initiate the program and coordinate volunteers is desirable. More staff are needed if the sponsoring agency cannot provide free office space, telephone, and secretarial support. The use of trained community volunteers needs to be addressed early since this issue has direct impact on the budget. The benefits of using volunteers include increases in participation in the justice process, broader community exposure to nonviolent conflict resolution skills, and reduced cost. Volunteers often bring a level of enthusiasm and commitment that is a valuable asset. The use of volunteers, however, requires planning and effort in recruitment, training, and ongoing monitoring, along with various events to provide recognition and support. Most VOM programs in the United States have chosen to use community volunteers as mediators. Programs must also determine if they will use a single or co-mediator model because this decision impacts the size of the requisite volunteer pool. Co-mediation allows for more flexibility in addressing cross-cultural issues (assuming one of the co-mediators is a person of color), provides opportunities for sharing responsibilities, and promotes broader citizen or volunteer involvement.

Programs also need to determine the point of referral (1) directly from the police before formal charges are filed; (2) after the police have filed a report but prior to trial as a diversion from prosecution; (3) after an admission or finding of guilt but before sentencing; or (4) after the sentencing hearing.

Established VOM programs report that slightly over one-third (34%) of referrals are true diversion, occurring after an offender has been apprehended but prior to any formal finding of guilt. Just under a third (28% each) occur postadjudication but predisposition and postdisposition. A small number of programs (7%) report that their mediations could occur at any point in the process, and the remaining 3% report working with cases prior to any court involvement (Umbreit & Greenwood, 1999). There are benefits and limitations to using any of these referral points. For example, if cases are received at a pretrial level, it is more likely that only relatively minor offenses will be referred. If more serious cases are referred, it is more likely that the referral will be at postconviction or postadjudication. There must be clear referral criteria and procedures. For example, immediately following conviction, probation staff temporarily place all burglary and theft case files in the VOM in-basket at the probation office. Programs contact the probation office daily to review all burglary and theft cases within 24 hours of conviction.

Programs need a management information system for collecting, storing, and retrieving important information. The management information system is used not only for delivery and documentation of services but also for presenting the program to potential users, funders, and other interested groups. Sample forms might include VOM case record form, case referral form, letter to victim, letter to offender, mediator log, and monthly statistical summary form.

Finally, programs must address the recruitment and training of volunteer mediators. Basic characteristics include good communication skills, particularly reflective listening and assertions; problem-solving and negotiation skills; ability to exercise appropriate leadership; good organizational skills; and the ability to understand and work within the criminal justice system. The length of training can vary from 24 to 40 hours. Training should introduce volunteers to VOM, how it operates within the local justice system, and procedures of the local program. It should also include a focus on the various elements of the process including calling the victim or offender, meeting with them separately, and then conducting a joint mediation session. Special units should focus on the victimization experience and the criminal justice process.

Although ideologically attractive, VOM programs struggle to survive. Two primary reasons for program failure are inadequate finances and/or the lack of case referrals (Goering, 2009). Goering hypothesized that a communication network was necessary to ensure ongoing sustainable funding and a steady flow of cases. She examined six successful and six struggling VOM programs to ascertain the impact of the organization's communication practices and patterns on its survival. She found that the networks of the successful VOMs tended to be more diverse and densely interconnected, that is, have numerous interconnections. Successful VOMs also had more links with prominent, key individuals as well as more coalitions. Links in the network were more equitable and had more overlap in relationships. Goering also found that successful, newly emerging programs had established an ongoing mentoring relationship with a well-known and respected individual within the restorative justice community or with a well-established VOM program in their area.

OUTLINE OF THE VOM PROCEDURE AND STAGES

The primary goal of VOM is to provide a safe place for dialogue among the involved parties that fosters both victim empowerment and assistance, as well as offender accountability and growth. The VOM process has four distinct phases: (1) referral or intake; (2) preparation for mediation; (3) mediation; and (4) follow-up. (See Figure 5.1.)

Referral or Intake Phase

Most programs accept referrals after a formal admission of guilt has been entered with the court. Some programs accept cases that are referred prior to formal admission of guilt, as part of a deferred prosecution effort. Each case is assigned to either a staff or volunteer mediator. Approximately two-thirds of the cases referred to VOM are misdemeanors; the remaining third are felony cases (Umbreit, 2004). The four most common offenses referred, in order of frequency, are vandalism, minor assaults, theft, and burglary (Umbreit & Greenwood, 1999). The primary referral sources are probation officers, judges, and prosecutors. Juvenile offenders are more likely to be the primary focus of VOM referrals in the United States, with 45% of programs offering services solely to juveniles and an additional 46% serving both juveniles and adults.

The referral or intake phase begins when the referral of a case (usually from probation) is received and ends with assignment of the case to a staff or volunteer case manager who will serve as the mediator. Most programs use the following criteria to make referrals:

- Type of crime, that is, property offense such as residential burglary, commercial burglary, theft, or vandalism; property offense that involves individuals or small businesses; and simple assault
- Admission of guilt by the offender
- Identifiable loss and need for restitution
- No more than two prior convictions
- No major mental health problems
- No major active substance abuse problem

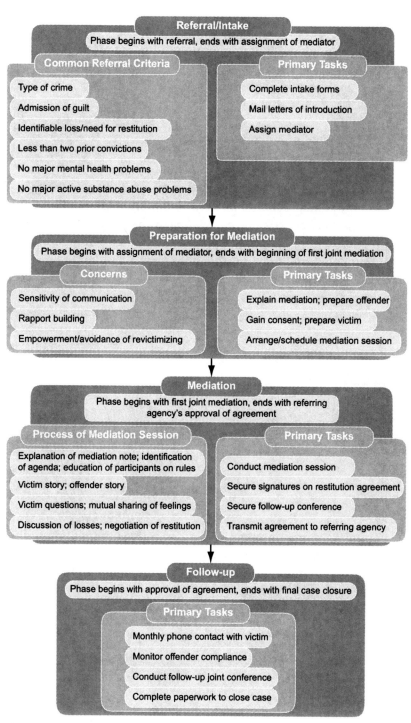

FIGURE 5.1

After the referral is made, there are three tasks that need to be accomplished. These include (1) accurately recording information about the victim and offender on intake forms; (2) mailing letters of introduction to the victim and offender; and (3) assigning the case to a staff or volunteer case manager (mediator).

Preparation Phase

Preparation begins with the assignment of the case to a case manager (mediator) and ends with the beginning of the first joint mediation session. There are three primary tasks to be completed during the preparation for mediation phase. They include (1) explaining the mediation and preparing the offender to participate in the process; (2) securing the victim's consent to participate and preparing the victim for the mediation process; and (3) arranging and scheduling the mediation session. The quality of work done during this phase will have a great deal of impact on the actual mediation session. In fact, unless rapport and trust are effectively established with both the victim and offender, there will be no mediation session. Problems that may occur later in the mediation session often originate during this phase of the process and are the result of incomplete preparation.

To prepare the offender, the mediator first asks for and listens to the offender's story about the crime. Then the mediator explains the program and potential benefits thus encouraging the offender's participation. The mediator also assesses the offender's ability to pay restitution, do work for the victim, or do community service. In some instances, the offender's family members or other support persons may attend and participate in the preparation meeting with the offender as well.

The rhetoric of much of the literature in the field would imply that offender participation in the mediation process is "voluntary." Actual practice in the field would suggest something quite different. When offenders are ordered to mediation by the court, via probation, or are diverted from prosecution if they complete the program, a rather significant amount of state coercion is exercised. Research has also indicated that offenders certainly do not perceive the process as "voluntary." Some programs attempt to temper this by trying to get referrals in the least coercive manner possible and to allow those offenders who are strongly opposed to participating or who the program staff has determined are inappropriate for mediation to "choose out" of the program.

To prepare the victim, the mediator first calls and invites the victim to a meeting to learn about mediation and its possible benefits. Every effort is made to avoid having to "sell" the program to the victim over the phone during this initial call. Rather, the mediator attempts to obtain a commitment from the victim to meet at a mutually convenient place in order, first, to listen to the impact of the crime on the victim's life and the concerns he or she may have, and, second, to invite the victim's participation in the victim-offender mediation process. Although the mediator encourages the victim's participation, the mediator also makes clear that participation in the program is absolutely voluntary. Many programs have the first meeting with the offender so that his or her perspective and attitude about the offense can be determined. It can often be helpful for a mediator to share some of what was learned about the offender when the initial meeting with the victim occurs.

It is not uncommon for victims to need time to consider participating, rather than making a quick decision on the spot. Few victims are immediately enthusiastic about such a confrontation with the offender. While the mediator will attempt to persuade the victim to participate by pointing out a number of potential benefits, the victim, during this preliminary meeting and throughout the victim-offender mediation process, has total voluntary choice. For example, the victim can initially agree to participate and later withdraw. A great deal of sensitivity must be exercised in communicating with victims during the entire process. Because of this, flexibility is required in selecting locations and scheduling meetings, as well as in the overall time frame in which the process will occur. The process is meant to be empowering for victims, presenting them with choices.

The importance of a delicate communication process being involved in these preliminary meetings cannot be overstated. Victim participation can easily be lost at the first phone call. The initial process of building rapport and trust with both the victim and offender is essential for the later joint meeting with both individuals. This is closely linked to listening deeply to the stories of how the crime impacted both of their lives. The strongest ethical principle that pervades the mediation process is that the mediation program must not be the cause of victimizing victims again, however unintentionally.

Mediation Phase

The mediation phase begins with the first face-to-face conference between the victim and offender and ends with the referring agency's approval of the agreement, either as part of a deferred prosecution program or as a condition of probation. There are four primary tasks to complete during the mediation phase: (1) conducting the mediation session; (2) securing signatures on the restitution agreement; (3) securing a follow-up conference, if appropriate; and (4) transmitting the agreement to the referral source.

It is only after the separate preparation sessions with the victim and offender are finished and there is an expression of willingness by both the victim and offender to proceed that the mediator schedules a face-to-face meeting. The meeting begins with the mediator explaining his or her role, identifying the agenda, and educating the participants on any communication ground rules. The first part of the meeting focuses on a discussion of the facts and feelings related to the crime. Initially, the victim tells the story of discovering the crime. Subsequently, the offender tells the story of having committed the crime. Victims are given the rare opportunity to express their feelings directly to the person who violated them as well as to receive answers to their lingering questions such as "Why me?" or "How did you get into our house?" or "Were you stalking us and planning on coming back?"

Victims are often relieved to actually see and interact with the offender finally, who usually bears little resemblance to the frightening character they may have conjured up in their minds. Contrary to what many might assume, the expression of feelings by the victim typically does not take the form of highly emotional, verbal violence. In fact, some of the initial anger is dissipated through the preliminary meeting with the mediator. It is often important, however, that some of the initial intensity of feelings be recalled and expressed directly to the offender during the joint meeting.

The meeting with the victim puts the offender in the very uncomfortable position of having to face the person they violated. They are given the equally rare opportunity to display a more human dimension to their character and to even express remorse in a very personal fashion. Through open discussion of their feelings, both victim and offender have the opportunity to deal with each other as people, often from the same neighborhood, rather than as stereotypes and objects.

Following this essential sharing of facts and feelings, the second part of the meeting focuses upon a discussion of losses and a negotiation of a mutually acceptable restitution agreement, which serves as a tangible symbol of conflict resolution and a focal point for accountability. Actions taken by offenders to repair the harm caused can take as many forms as creative minds can devise and agree upon. And what one victim will accept as adequate reparation another victim may reject for failing to meet their need for a just outcome. Some victims will be pleased only if they receive monetary recompense. Others will want the offenders to take steps to change their behavior reducing the likelihood that new crimes will be committed. Perhaps, these victims will encourage the offender to participate in alcohol or drug counseling. Some victims will want the offenders to personally repair damage caused by careless vandalism. Others will want the offenders to perform some sort of service to the community—whether it is carried out through a formally recognized community service program or not. Some victims only want to hear a genuine apology. And there will be some victims who will feel that simply having the opportunity to tell the story of the pain the offenders caused them and to see the impact that has on the offenders is enough to "repair the harm."

"Repairing the harm" and "making things right" does not mean that situations are restored to where they were before the crime. Some stolen items are irreplaceable. The feeling of having one's life and space invaded and violated may be lessened, but that experience remains part of one's life journey. Yet victims frequently point out that the attitude of the offenders is as important as any tangible action. Do they believe they see genuine remorse? Do they believe the offenders are really accepting responsibility for what they did? Do they regard the offenders as cocky or is there a kind of humility expressed as the offenders attempt to repair the harm caused? Was there a genuine apology? Was a plan for repairing harm agreed upon? Did participants believe that they had a role in developing the agreement? These questions and their answers suggest that although restitution is an important additional goal, it is, for many programs, secondary to the importance of allowing the parties to talk with each other about the real emotional and practical impact the crime has had on their lives.

Follow-Up Phase

The follow-up phase begins with the approval of the restitution agreement by the referring agency and ends with the final closure of the case. There are four primary tasks to complete during this phase: (1) maintaining monthly phone contact with the victim to monitor fulfillment of the restitution agreement; (2) if the offender is out of compliance, working with the offender and probation officer to secure compliance; (3) conducting the prescheduled follow-up joint conference with the victim and offender; and (4) completing the final paperwork related to closing the case.

In order to strengthen the process of personal accountability of the offender to the victim, one or more follow-up meetings between the victim and offender can play a significant role. Although these follow-up meetings are briefer and less structured than the initial victim-offender mediation session, they provide an informal opportunity to review the implementation of the restitution agreement as well as discuss any problems that may have arisen related to the payment schedule and simply share "small talk" if the victim and offender feel so inclined.

The need for and willingness to have follow-up meetings is certainly tempered by the actual amount of restitution to be paid. If only a very small amount of restitution is owed, a follow-up meeting might not be appropriate. On the other hand, if a larger amount is due, brief follow-up sessions, including mid-contract and "close out" meetings, can be quite helpful. As with the initial victim-offender mediation session, victims must not be coerced into follow-up meetings. To date, only a relatively small proportion of victim-offender mediation cases include follow-up victim-offender meetings.

VOM is often used with juveniles who may lack the ability to make full material reparation to the victim. In Germany, offenders without sufficient financial means may borrow without interest from so-called victim funds in order to compensate the victim. Offenders can pay off the loan in installments or perform community or charity work. The rate of back repayments is over 90% (Pelikan & Trencz, 2006).

THE MEDIATOR'S ROLE

Although many other types of mediation are largely "settlement driven," victim-offender mediation is primarily "dialogue driven," with the emphasis upon victim healing, offender accountability, and restoration of losses. The mediator is often most active in preparing the parties for the mediation session. During this phase, the mediator listens to their stories about what happened, outlines the program, reviews the participant's goals and expectations for getting together, explores their fears and other reactions to the upcoming encounter, and may help them reflect on what a reparation agreement might include. If the preparation is done well, the victim and offender and their support people, if included, will see the mediation as an opportunity to deal directly with each other, and the mediator will fade into the background appearing only to facilitate the dialogue and ensure participants' safety. The mediator, however, remains extremely attentive to the dialogue including the nonverbal communication. When the time comes for negotiating a reparation agreement, the mediator becomes more active to ensure participation from both victim and offender and to work out the details to everyone's satisfaction.

EFFECTIVENESS OF VOM

Considerable empirical work has been done over the past 25 years to document the impact of VOM programs. A total of 56 studies were examined for this chapter, including 53 mediation studies and three meta-analyses. The following review summarizes the results on participation rates and reasons for participation, participant satisfaction, participant perception of fairness, restitution and repair of harm, diversion, recidivism, and cost. Figure 5.2 illustrates some of the dimensions of VOM effectiveness.

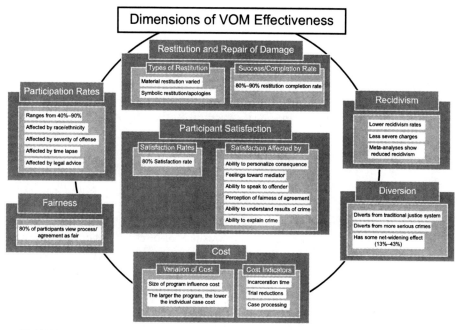

FIGURE 5.2

Participation Rates and Reasons

Approximately 40%–60% of crime victims participate in VOM programs, though rates as high as 90% have been reported. A multistate study found that, of 280 victim participants, 91% felt that their participation was voluntary (Umbreit, 1994). Coates, Burns, and Umbreit (2004) found that victim reasons for choosing to participate were rank ordered as follows: to possibly help the offender, to hear why the offender did the crime, to communicate to the offender the impact of the crime, and to be sure the offender would not return to commit a repeat offense. The most frequent reason for not participating was that it was not worth the time and trouble. Two studies examined offender race or ethnicity as a potential factor in the likelihood of a case coming to mediation. Gehm (1990) found that victims were more likely to mediate if the offender was white. Wyrick and Costanzo (1999), however, found in California that white offenders were no more likely to do mediation than Hispanic offenders, although the Hispanic offenders were significantly more likely to do so than offenders of other minority groups. Victims are also more likely to participate if the offense was a misdemeanor rather than a felony (Gehm, 1990). However, longer time lapses for property cases resulted in fewer mediations, whereas longer time lapses for hearing personal offenses resulted in more mediations (Wyrick & Costanzo, 1999).

Offenders choosing to participate often want to pay back the victim, to get the whole experience behind them, to impress the court, or to apologize to the victim (Abrams & Umbreit, 2002; Coates & Gehm, 1985). Offenders do not participate because their lawyers told them not to (Schneider, 1986) or they simply did not want "to be bothered" (Coates & Gehm, 1985). Offenders are more likely than victims to report that they do not see their participation as voluntary. In studying juvenile VOM programs in six Oregon counties, nearly half of the juvenile offenders felt that they had no choice (Umbreit, Coates, & Vos, 2001).

Participant Satisfaction

Expression of satisfaction with VOM is consistently high for both victims and offenders across sites, cultures, and seriousness of offenses. Eight out of ten participants report being satisfied with the process and the resulting agreement. Moreover, when comparison groups are studied, VOM participants indicate being more satisfied with the criminal justice system than those victims and offenders who go through traditional court prosecution.

It is hypothesized that personalizing the consequences of crime enhances satisfaction levels with the entire justice process. Indeed, victims report being satisfied with being able to share their stories and the pain resulting from the crime event. Interestingly, victims frequently report that while restitution was the primary motivator for them to participate in VOM, what they appreciated most about the program was the opportunity to talk with the offender (Coates & Gehm, 1985; Umbreit & Coates, 1992). A victim stated that she had wanted to "let the kid know he hurt me personally, not just the money . . . I felt raped" (Umbreit, 1989). Another female victim indicated, "I felt a little better that I've [had a] stake in punishment" (Coates & Gehm, 1985). Offenders report surprises about having positive experiences. One youth said, "He understood the mistake I made, and I really did appreciate him for it" (Umbreit, 1991). Some reported changes: "After meeting the victim I now realize that I hurt them a lot . . . to understand how the victim feels makes me different" (Umbreit & Coates, 1992).

A secondary analysis of satisfaction data from a U.S. and Canadian study yielded remarkably similar results (Bradshaw & Umbreit, 1998; Umbreit & Bradshaw, 2003). Three variables emerged to explain over 40% of the variance: (1) the victim felt good about the mediator; (2) the victim perceived the resulting restitution agreement as fair; and (3) the victim, for whatever reason, had a strong initial desire to meet the offender. Satisfaction with VOM also results in greater satisfaction with the criminal justice system than that with traditional court prosecution (Umbreit, 1995).

Fairness

Studies have found that over 80% of VOM participants across settings, cultures, and types of offenses report believing that the process was fair to both sides and that the resulting agreement was fair (Evje & Cushman, 2000; Umbreit & Roberts, 1996). Again, these experiences led to feelings that the overall criminal justice system was fair. Where comparison groups were employed, those individuals exposed to mediation came away more likely feeling that they had been treated fairly than those going through the traditional court proceedings. In a study of burglary victims in Minneapolis, Umbreit (1989) found that 80% who went through VOM indicated that they experienced the criminal justice system as fair compared with only 37% of burglary victims who did not participate in VOM.

Restitution and Repair of Damage

About half the studies under review addressed the issue of restitution or repair of harm (Umbreit & Coates, 1992; Umbreit, Coates et al., 2001). The form of restitution is quite varied and can include direct compensation to the victim, community service, work for the victim, and sometimes unusual paybacks devised between victim and offender. Apologies are also often included in program reports as a component of repairing the harm. Of those cases that reached a meeting, typically 90% or more generated agreements. Approximately 80%–90% of the contracts are reported as completed.

Results from comparative studies have been somewhat mixed, with some studies reporting higher amounts of restitution and/or greater completion rates for VOM participants than comparison groups (Evje & Cushman, 2000; Umbreit & Coates, 1992) while another reported no difference (Roy, 1993). The meta-analysis covering both mediation and family group conferencing found that offenders participating in these programs had substantially higher completion rates than offenders processed in other ways (Latimer, Dowden, & Muise, 2005).

Among other reasons, many restorative programs are nominally established to divert offenders from the traditional justice system processes. Although such diversion was a goal lauded by many, others expressed concern about the unintended consequence of widening the net, that is, sanctioning offenders who otherwise would not have received sanctions through traditional procedures. Only a handful of the studies reviewed here address this question.

Two mediation studies, both in the United Kingdom, have reported a netwidening impact for the intervention. One concluded that at least 60% of the offenders participating in mediation were true diversion from court prosecution and that overall there was a 13% net-widening effect, much less than expected (Dignan, 1990). In the other, 43% of the comparison group cases were not prosecuted and received no sanction, a fairly broad net-widening result (Warner, 1992). Two studies done in the United States found that the mediation programs successfully diverted offenders from court. A North Carolina program apparently reduced court trials by as much as two-thirds (Latimer et al., 2005). An Indiana-Ohio study compared consequences for 73 youth and adults going through VOM programs with those for a matched sample of individuals who were processed in the traditional manner (Coates & Gehm, 1985). VOM offenders spent less time incarcerated than did their counterparts, and when incarcerated, they did county jail time rather than state time.

Recidivism

Preventing recidivism is often used as a long-term measure of the "effectiveness" of VOM programs; clearly, such prevention benefits offenders directly, and more broadly, benefits communities. The following studies used some type of comparison group. Studies simply reporting overall reoffending rates with no comparison data are not included.

Results from studies examining the impact of mediation on recidivism have been mixed overall. Several studies found lower rates for mediation participants than for offenders processed through traditional means (Katz, 2000; Schneider, 1986). In addition, five of the six programs examined by Evje and Cushman (2000) also found reduced recidivism. Two studies also found that youths who did reoffend tended to incur less serious charges than their counterparts (Nugent & Paddock, 1995; Umbreit & Coates, 1992). Others reported little or no difference (Roy, 1993; Stone, Helms, & Edgeworth, 1998) as did one of the six programs studied by Evje and Cushman (2000). A study of a county-wide restorative program that included VOM as one component found virtually equal recidivism rates between the sample and the control group (Bradbury, 2002).

Four meta-analyses have addressed recidivism issues. Nugent, Umbreit, Wiinamaki, and Paddock (2001) conducted a rigorous reanalysis of recidivism data reported in four previous studies involving a total sample of 1,298 juvenile offenders, 619 who participated in VOM and 679 who did not. Using ordinal logistical regression procedures, the authors determined that VOM youth recidivated at a statistically significant 32% lower rate than non-VOM youth, and when they did reoffend, they committed less serious offenses than the non-VOM youth.

In a subsequent report, Nugent, Williams, and Umbreit (2003) expanded their database to include 14 studies. This analysis relied on a combined sample of 9,037 juveniles and similarly found that the mediated adolescents committed fewer and less serious offenses than their counterparts.

The third meta-analysis included both mediation and group conferencing and found that the two types of programs together yielded reductions in recidivism compared to other, nonrestorative approaches and that offenders in the two program types were significantly more successful during the follow-up periods (Bradshaw & Roseborough, 2005; Latimer et al., 2005).

Most recently, Bradshaw and Roseborough (2005) did a meta-analysis of 11,950 juveniles from VOM and FGC programs at 25 different service sites and 4 countries. Together, the programs contributed to a 26% reduction in recidivism. However, VOM had a statistically significant higher effect size (M = 0.34, SD = 0.46) than FGC (M = 0.11, SD = 0.12). Bradshaw and Roseborough also found that effect size was influenced by type of control group. Studies that used a control group consisting of juveniles referred to a restorative justice intervention but who refused participation had significantly higher effect sizes than those control groups that were made up of juveniles participating in an alternative treatment such as diversion programs, that is, juveniles referred to but refusing participation in a restorative justice intervention versus participation in an alternative treatment. Bradshaw and Roseborough (2005) note that there is now sufficient data to support VOM as a well-established, empirically supported intervention for reducing juvenile recidivism.

Cost

Cost per unit case is obviously influenced by the number of cases handled and the amount of time devoted to each case. Evaluation of a large-scale VOM program in California led the authors to conclude that the cost per case was reduced dramatically as the program went from being a fledgling to being a viable option (Niemeyer & Shichor, 1996). Cost per case was $250. A Missouri program reported total cost per case that ranged from $232 to $338 but did not provide comparison data (Katz, 2000).

As noted earlier, some programs have impacted either total incarceration time (Coates & Gehm, 1985), place or cost of incarceration, or reduction of trials (Clarke, Valente, & Mace, 1992). Additionally, time spent to process a case has implications for overall cost. Stone et al. (1998) found that the total time required to process mediated cases was only a third of that needed for nonmediated cases.

In an evaluation of a large-scale restorative program (of which VOM was one component) for youths who would have been referred to state custody, Bradbury (2002) found that the yearly cost per case was less than that for the state custody program ($48,396 vs. $65,866). Since recidivism was virtually the same between the two groups, the restorative program was less costly on the surface. However, the author concluded that because the restorative youths spent more days in the community, they posed more risk to community residents, so neither program could be designated as "clearly superior."

Developments in VOM Research

VOM has been more thoroughly examined than most other interventions for youth justice. Accurate comparisons between programs are difficult, however, because of a lack of standardized measures. Moreover, existing studies have focused primarily on outcomes, such as recidivism and restitution rates, neglecting the fact that restorative justice is also the process. The development of the Victim Satisfaction with Offender Dialogue Scale (VSODS) (Bradshaw & Umbreit, 2003) provides greater assurance of the reliability and validity of findings. The emergence of several qualitative studies of the VOM process allows a first-hand examination of the interactions that take place in VOMs.

Victim Satisfaction With Offender Dialogue Scale

Victim satisfaction is one of the most essential components of evaluation in restorative justice programs. It can provide feedback about program services; identify problems and needs from the victim's perspective; and provide data that increase knowledge about the process of mediated dialogue. In many areas, there are now legislative mandates to include victim input. Historically, victim satisfaction was measured by a single global question, making it difficult to assess the multidimensional aspect of satisfaction, for example, satisfaction with mediator compared to satisfaction with restitution compared to satisfaction with the offender's emotional response.

The Victim Satisfaction With Offender Dialogue Scale (VSODS) is a short 11-item scale that takes 3–5 minutes to complete. It can differentiate between victim satisfaction along multiple dimensions. The dimensions include mediator skills, preparation for mediation, restitution, meeting the offender, experience of the criminal justice system, experience of the mediation family conferencing session, and the subjective experience of the victim. The alpha coefficient is 0.87. Open-ended questions can be added to the measure if programs want specific information on other topics.

Studies of the VOM Process

Zehr (1990) asserts, "Justice may be a state of affairs, but it is also an experience" (p. 28). Four studies have examined the experience that begins to provide information about the "black box" or what actually happens in the VOM process.

Four of the studies have responded to critiques about the power dynamics in restorative practices, (Arrigo, Milonvanovic, & Schehr, 2005; Arrigo & Schehr, 1998; Levrant, Cullen, Fulton, & Wozniak, 1999; Pavlich, 2005). Presser and Hamilton (2006) observed 14 VOM sessions with offenders to answer questions about coercion, the reproduction of social hierarchies, and challenges to pro-crime attitudes. They noted the disempowerment of youth by adult victims who lectured to them and the limited attention to confronting attitudes and causes of the crime. Presser and Hamilton (2006) call for more studies on restorative processes and the desirable and undesirable uses of control.

Gerkin (2009) observed 14 mediations including the premeditation sessions. Gerkin concluded the following: (1) offender needs were not acknowledged or addressed; (2) victims often created stipulations in the agreement that grew out of the victims' personal feelings about what the offender needed and far exceeded the scope of the harm they experienced; and (3) barriers to participation exist because VOM participants do not understand and are not prepared to participate in restorative processes. Consequently, they interpret the restorative justice intervention in the context of the criminal justice system, that is, authority, compliance, rather than through a restorative filter, for example, empowerment, meaningful participation. Gerkin (2009) calls for educating individuals during preparation to help develop a restorative lens so that restorative outcomes make sense to the participants. She also warns that unless offenders' needs and participation are encouraged, VOM will continue to be plagued by uneven participation and victim dominance.

Abrams, Umbreit, and Gordon (2006) examined the mediation experiences of VOM offender participants and their family members. Reasons for participating ranged from wanting to impress the court to believing VOM would help heal personal relationships with victims. The mediation itself was "business like" and offenders experienced the telling of their stories to the victims as a bit surreal. "I was really used to telling the story, but it was a bit odd to be telling to the people it meant the most to . . . I had to take it much more seriously." Offenders reported feeling bad, guilty, and ashamed as they told their stories to the victims and as they heard victims' accounts. Offenders reported that they felt victims' perceptions of them change during the session and experienced changes themselves in how they viewed victims. Offenders indicated that the VOM session was helpful in reinforcing and incentivizing the process of change in their lives.

Choi and Severson (2009) examine the multiple perspectives of VOM participants to the genuineness of apology letters read to victims during the session. Victims accepted the letters but felt that the apologies were not sincere and heartfelt enough. Offenders and their parents, however, believed that their apologies were genuine and were under the impression that the victims felt the same way. Choi and Severson (2009) suggest that teaching offenders and victims about the nature of the letter and the process of composing, delivering, and receiving an apology will increase the likelihood that apologies will better exemplify the principles of restorative justice.

These qualitative studies open the door to evaluating the quality of the VOM experience through an in-depth examination of the process. By placing the interaction between participants and participants' perceptions of each other at the center of inquiry, these studies expand the research focus beyond satisfaction and recidivism and provide crucial feedback to mediators and program administrators.

CONCERNS AND ONGOING ISSUES

Because VOM has an extensive history, more is known about some of its pitfalls and potential problems. Ongoing concerns include compromising the separate preparation of the victim and offender prior to the mediation session, pressuring participation and controlling the dialogue, applying VOM in cross-cultural contexts, and cultivating a referral base.

VOM is often seen as a time-intensive program both because of the total hours it takes per case and the time needed to create a climate that fosters trust, thoughtful engagement, and the sharing of feelings. In addition, VOM programs struggle with a lack of financial and staff resources. Consequently, it is almost predictable that administrators who do not understand the important role of separate premediation preparation in the overall outcome will try to make the process more cost effective by reducing preparation to a phone call or eliminating it all together. A recent study of three VOM programs in Texas found that these programs did not reduce recidivism and that the programs had compromised its practices and procedures, which included a lack of preparation in addition to problems with (1) voluntary participation; (2) the offender's admission of guilt; and (3) the employment of a neutral, trained volunteer mediator. Instead of closing the programs, efforts are underway to incorporate these practices to ensure the future success of the programs.

Because VOM is most often used as part of an effort to divert offenders away from the criminal justice system, there is a natural tendency to focus attention on the offender over the victim's needs or to use the victim in the service of the offender's rehabilitation. For example, the practice of allowing victims to lecture offenders can result in victim dominance but, ironically, bypass the victim's pain and the potential for a more engaged, satisfying, and meaningful dialogue between victim and offender. Victims have felt pressured into participating and controlled by the nature of the role they are allowed to play. In response to the reading of apology letters, for example, victims may feel that they cannot question the authenticity of the offender or may feel compelled to forgive.

Studies indicate that victims and offenders of color are less likely to participate in VOM (Abrams et al., 2006; Armour & Umbreit, 2007; Choi, 2009; Williams-Hayes, 2002). In reviewing 39 studies of VOM, Bonta, Jesseman, Rugge, and Cormier (2006) found that most offenders were Caucasian youth (79.2%). African–American youth were only 6.3%. Given the overrepresentation of persons of color in the criminal justice system, these statistics suggest that VOM programs may require more sensitivity and proactivity in providing services to culturally diverse groups. Choi (2009) suggests following the suggestions made by the New Zealand Ministry of Justice that include working with mediators of the same ethnicity as the participants, recruiting volunteer mediators from all segments of the community (with appropriate gender, cultural, and ethnic balance), holding sessions at locations of the culturally significant group, using cultural advisors, providing adequate translators, and so on.

Many programs falter because of difficulties in obtaining adequate numbers of referrals. Goering's (2009) comparison of successful and struggling VOM programs found that decentralizing referral sources, with cases coming from a variety of courses (i.e., parole officers, judges, county attorneys, and community corrections officers) and at various stages of the justice process (i.e., diversionary, predisposition, postadjudication, etc.) furthered a more steady supply of case referrals. The need to diversify is vital to VOM programs because of the tendency to associate VOM with minor offenses, many of which may never get referred because they are essentially ignored by the system in the first place (Umbreit, 1994). Using VOM for more serious cases, however, requires greater risk taking by referral sources who may see VOM as inappropriate for more major crimes.

CONCLUSION

VOM is a strong evidence-based practice. None of the other approaches, for example, family group conferencing, peacemaking circles, neighborhood accountability boards, are supported as fully by research that attests to victims' and offenders' satisfaction, perceptions of fairness, completion of reparation agreements, and a reduced recidivism rate. VOM remains central to the restorative justice movement because it serves to remind us of the centrality of the victim and the victim's harm and the power of the victim's voice and story to advance the dialogue, creating the context for offender's accountability and deep learning.

REFERENCES

Abrams, L., & Umbreit, M. S. (2002). *Youthful offenders response to Victim Offender Conferencing in Washington County.* St. Paul, MN: Center for Restorative Justice & Peacemaking.

Abrams, L., Umbreit, M. S., & Gordon, A. (2006). Young offenders speak about meeting their victims: Implications for future programs. *Contemporary Justice Review, 9*(3).

Armour, M., & Umbreit, M. S. (2007). Victim-offender mediation and forensic practice. In D. W. Springer & A. R. Roberts (Eds.), *Handbook of forensic mental health with victims and offenders: Assessment, treatment and research* (pp. 519–540). New York: Springer.

Arrigo, B. A., Milonvanovic, D., & Schehr, R. C. (2005). *The French connection at criminology: Rediscovering crime, law, and social change.* Albany: SUNY Press.

Arrigo, B. A., & Schehr, S. C. (1998). Restoring justice for juveniles: A critical analysis of victim-offender mediation. *Justice Quarterly, 15*(4), 629–666.

Bazemore, G., & Umbreit, M. S. (1995). Rethinking the sanctioning function in juvenile court: Retributive or restorative responses to youth crime. *Crime and Delinquency, 41*(3), 296–316.

Bonta, J., Jesseman, R., Rugge, T., & Cormier, R. (2006). Restorative justice and recidivism: Promises made, promises kept? In D. Sullivan & L. Tifft (Eds.), *Handbook of restorative justice* (pp. 108–120). New York: Routledge.

Bradbury, B. (2002). *Deschutes County delinquent youth demonstration project.* Salem, OR: Secretary of State Audit Report # 2002-29, Office of the Secretary of State.

Bradshaw, W., & Roseborough, D. (2005). Restorative justice dialogue: The impact of mediation and conferencing on juvenile recidivism. *Federal Probation, 69*(2), 15–21.

Bradshaw, W., & Umbreit, M. S. (1998). Crime victims meet juvenile offenders: Contributing factors to victim satisfaction with mediated dialogue. *Juvenile and Family Court Journal, 49*(3), 17–25.

Bradshaw, W., & Umbreit, M. S. (2003). Assessing satisfaction with victim services: The development and use of the victim satisfaction with offender dialogue scale (VSODS). *International Review of Victimology, 9,* 71–83.

Cayley, D. (1998). *The expanding prison: The crisis in crime and punishment and search for alternatives.* Cleveland, OH: Pilgrim Press.

Choi, J. J. (2009). Best practices for achieving restorative justice outcomes for crime victims and offenders in the United States. In C. G. Petr (Ed.), *Multidimensional evidence-based practice* (pp. 154–178). New York: Routledge.

Choi, J. J., & Severson, M. (2009). "What! What kind of apology is this?": The nature of apology in victim offender mediation. *Children and Youth Services Review, 31,* 813–820.

Christie, M. (1977). Conflicts as property. *British Journal of Criminology, 1,* 104–118.

Clarke, S., Valente, E., & Mace, R. (1992). *Mediation of interpersonal disputes: An evaluation of North Carolina's programs.* Chapel Hill, NC: Institute of Government, University of North Carolina.

Coates, R., Burns, H., & Umbreit, M. S. (2004). Why victims choose to meet with offenders. *Offender Programs Report, 8*(4), 55–57.

Coates, R., & Gehm, J. (1985). *Victim meets offender: An evaluation of victim-offender reconciliation programs*. Valparaiso, IN: PACT Institute of Justice.

Dignan, J. (1990). *Repairing the damage: An evaluation of an experimental adult reparation scheme in Kettering, Northamptonshire*. Sheffield, UK: Centre for Criminological Legal Research, Faculty of Law, University of Sheffield.

Evje, A., & Cushman, R. (2000). *A summary of the evaluations of six California victim offender rehabilitation programs*. San Francisco: Administrative Office of the Courts.

Gehm, J. (1990). Mediated victim-offender restitution agreements: An exploratory analysis of factors related to victim participation. In B. Galaway & J. Hudson (Eds.), *Criminal justice, restitution, and reconciliation* (pp. 177–182). London: Sage.

Gerkin, P. (2009). Participation in victim-offender mediation: Lessons learned from observations. *Criminal Justice Review, 344*(2), 226–247.

Goering, E. (2009). *From retribution to restitution: A network analysis of victim offender mediation program success*. Paper presented at the Annual Meeting of the International Communication Association, Dresden, Germany. May 25, 2009.

Johnstone, G. (2002). *Restorative justice: Ideas, values and debates*. Devon, UK: Willan Publishing.

Katz, J. (2000). *Victim offender mediation in Missouri's juvenile courts: Accountability, restitution, and transformation*. Jefferson City, MO: Missouri Department of Public Safety.

Latimer, J., Dowden, C., & Muise, D. (2005). The effectiveness of restorative practices: A meta-analysis. *Prison Journal, 85*, 127–145.

Levrant, S., Cullen, F. T., Fulton, B., & Wozniak, J. F. (1999). Reconsidering restorative justice: The corruption of benevolence revisited. *Crime & Delinquency, 45*, 3–27.

Lightfoot, E., & Umbreit, M. S. (2004). An analysis of state statutory provisions for victim-offender mediation. *Criminal Justice Policy Review, 15*(4), 418–436.

McCold, P. (2006). The recent history of restorative justice. In D. Sullivan & L. Tift (Eds.), *Handbook of restorative justice* (pp. 23–51). New York: Routledge.

Minnesota Supreme Court. (2002). *State of Minnesota v. Signe Elissee Pearson, C9-99-2021*. Retrieved January 5, 2010, from http://www.lawlibrary.state.mn.us/archive/supct/0201/c9992021.htm

Niemeyer, M., & Shichor, D. (1996). A preliminary study of a large victim/offender reconciliation program. *Federal Probation, 60*(3), 30–34.

Nugent, W., & Paddock, M. (1995). The effect of victim-offender mediation on severity of reoffense. *Mediation Quarterly, 12*, 353–367.

Nugent, W., Umbreit, M. S., Wiinamaki, L., & Paddock, J. (2001). Participation in victim-offender mediation and severity of subsequent delinquent behavior: Successful replications? *Journal of Research in Social Work Practice, 11*(1), 5–23.

Nugent, W., Williams, R. M., & Umbreit, M. S. (2003). Participation in victim-offender mediation and the prevalence and severity of subsequent delinquent behavior: A meta-analysis. *Utah Law Review, 2003*(1), 137–165.

Pavlich, G. (2005). *Governing paradoxes of restorative justice*. Portland, OR: Cavendish.

Pelikan, C., & Trencz, T. (2006). Victim offender mediation and restorative justice: The European landscape. In D. Sullivan & L. Tifft (Eds.), *Handbook of restorative justice: A global perspective* (pp. 63–90). New York: Routledge.

Presser, L., & Hamilton, C. A. (2006). The micropolitics of victim-offender mediation. *Sociological Inquiry*, 76(3), 316–342.

Roy, S. (1993). Two types of juvenile restitution programs in two midwestern counties: A comparative study. *Federal Probation*, 57(4), 48–53.

Schneider, A. (1986). Restitution and recidivism rates of juvenile offenders: Results from four experimental studies. *Criminology*, 24, 533–552.

Stone, S., Helms, W., & Edgeworth, P. (1998). *Cobb County juvenile court mediation program evaluation.* Carrolton, GA: State University of West Georgia.

Umbreit, M. S. (1989). Violent offenders and their victims. In M. Wright & B. Galaway (Eds.), *Mediation and criminal justice* (pp. 337–352). London: Sage.

Umbreit, M. S. (1991). Minnesota Mediation Center produces positive results. *Corrections Today*, 194–197.

Umbreit, M. S. (1994). *Victim meets offender.* Monsey, NY: Criminal Justice Press.

Umbreit, M. S. (1995). Restorative justice through mediation: The impact of offenders facing their victims in Oakland. *Journal of Law and Social Work*, 5, 1–13.

Umbreit, M. S. (2001). *The handbook of victim offender mediation: An essential guide to practice and research.* San Francisco: Jossey-Bass.

Umbreit, M. S. (2004). Victim offender mediation in juvenile or criminal courts. *Alternative dispute resolution handbook for judges.* American Bar Association.

Umbreit, M. S., & Bradshaw, W. (2003). Factors that contribute to victim satisfaction with mediated offender dialogue in Winnipeg: An emerging area of social work practice. *Journal of Law and Social Work*, 9(2), 35–51.

Umbreit, M. S., & Coates, R. (1992). *Victim offender mediation: An analysis of programs in four states of the U.S.* Minneapolis, MN: Minnesota Citizens Council on Crime and Justice.

Umbreit, M. S., Coates, R., & Vos, B. (2001). *Juvenile victim offender mediation in six Oregon counties.* Salem, OR: Oregon Dispute Resolution Commission.

Umbreit, M. S., Coates, R., & Vos, B. (2006). Victim offender mediation: An evolving evidence-based practice. In D. Sullivan & L. Tifft (Eds.), *Handbook of restorative justice: A global perspective* (pp. 52–62). New York: Routledge.

Umbreit, M. S., & Greenwood, J. (1999). National survey of victim offender mediation programs in the U.S. *Mediation Quarterly*, 16, 235–251.

Umbreit, M. S., Greenwood, J., Schug, R., Umbreit, J., & Fercello, C. (2000). *Directory of victim-offender mediation programs in the United States.* Washington, DC: U.S. Department of Justice, Office of Justice Programs, Office for Victims of Crime.

Umbreit, M. S., Lightfoot, E., & Fier, J. (2001). *Legislative statutes on victim offender mediation: A national review.* St. Paul, MN: Center for Restorative Justice and Peacemaking.

Umbreit, M. S., & Roberts, A. W. (1996). *Mediation of criminal conflict in England: An assessment of services in Coventry and Leeds.* St. Paul, MN: Center for Restorative Justice and Mediation.

Umbreit, M. S., Vos, B., & Coates, R. (2005). *Restorative justice dialogue: Evidence-based practice*. St. Paul, MN: Center for Restorative Justice and Peacemaking, School of Social Work, University of Minnesota:.

Umbreit, M. S., Vos, B., Coates, R., & Brown, K. (2003). *Facing violence: The path of restorative justice and dialogue*. Monsey, NY: Criminal Justice Press.

Van Ness, D., & Heetderks, K. (2002). *Restoring justice* (2nd ed.). Cincinnati, OH: Anderson Publishing Company.

Warner, S. (1992). *Making amends: Justice for victims and offenders*. Aldershot, UK: Avebury.

Williams-Hayes, D. D. (2002). *The effectiveness of victim-offender mediation and family group conferencing: A meta analysis*. Knoxville, TN: University of Tennessee.

Wyrick, P., & Costanzo, M. (1999). Predictors of client participation in victim-offender mediation. *Mediation Quarterly, 16*, 253–267.

Zehr, H. (1990). *Changing lenses: A new focus for crime and justice*. Scottsdale, PA: Herald Press.

Zehr, H. (2002). *The little book of restorative justice*. Intercourse, PA: Good Books.

6. Family Group Conferencing

> *"We really came to understand each other and how we could work together. It meant so much to me that it felt that people were finally really listening to my concerns."*
>
> *"I liked the way people talked about me. They didn't make me seem like an angel or a bad guy at the conference, people were neutral. They told the story the way it is but also talked about what I do well."*

A family group conference is convened to allow the parents of the young offender who vandalized a home in the neighborhood to meet the victim's family. Several other support people are present as well. Together, along with the young offender, they talk about the impact of the crime on their lives and the community, followed by the development of a plan to repair the harm. All involved feel good about the process, believing it to be a very practical way of holding this young person accountable.

Family group conferences (FGCs) are an approach to planning and decision making about youth crime and youth care that involves the wider family network in partnership with representatives of governmental institutions and other community agencies. FGCs are used by the police for reprimanding or cautioning youth about their misconduct, by youth justice officials for determining what youth should do to make material and symbolic reparations, by schools for addressing with youth their serious behavior problems, and by child welfare programs with families for determining placement and other services for the well-being of neglected or abused children.

FGCs are likely the strongest restorative justice approach in their potential for educating offenders about the harm their behavior causes victims and others because FGCs draw on a group of persons who play meaningful roles in the lives of youth to both challenge and support them (Bazemore & Griffiths, 2003). Consider the following case that involved the theft by Troy, age 14, of clothes from a backyard clothesline. A family group conference is held and the attendees are Troy's father, uncle, mother, three victims, and the coordinator. As the conference starts, Troy's uncle enters the room (Moore & Forsythe, 1994).

> Troy begins the story of how he came to be at the scene of the crime. Troy's father then appears at the door of the conference room. He is greeted and seated. The story continues with some pauses as Troy stops to confirm that the coordinator and victims know exactly what corner, what fence, what

shop he is talked about. Troy is asked how things have been at home since the incident, whether he has talked to friends about it, and what he had thought about since. The answers, respectively, are not good, not much and not at all. So one of the three victims, Jenny, is asked what she felt about the whole affair. Jenny explains, "We had only been broken into about a month before at another place, and we moved so we could feel safe again." Jenny's flatmate, Sam, is asked about his involvement in the incident. He had actually chased Troy when he saw him jump the back fence with the clothes from the line. He describes the chase, being sworn at by Troy's friends, finding the police as they apprehended Troy. Andrea, who wasn't there at the time, has also been affected by the compounding effect of one burglary and two thefts, of which this was the first. Then the coordinator asks Troy's mother about how she has been affected by the incident and its aftermath. She says, "I don't trust him like I did before. He knows that. He has betrayed my trust." Troy's mother explains that she's trying to deal with some of the attitude she feels he's picked up from "rough boys." She also talks about the victims. "I can imagine how they feel, having their property taken. It's happened to me. I mean brand new jeans that I hadn't worn, things they had taken, so I can understand how they feel, how bitter they are. "The coordinator turns to Troy's sister who says, "I can't believe he would steal from anyone. I can't face anyone." The coordinator then asks Troy's father for his response. "I was a bit upset. I wanted to flog him." Troy's uncle is just simply shocked because Troy's behavior is so out of character. (pp. 12–15)

After everyone has spoken, the coordinator suggests that no one escapes having done something silly in their lives and asks Troy what he has learned. After some discussion, Troy extends apologies to everyone. He has returned the clothes. However, he also hears his parents extend their apologies to the three victims. Troy's father says, "I'm sorry for what my son put you through" (p. 15). His mother again references how she felt when her jeans were taken as an expression of empathy for what this must have been like for the victims.

This chapter examines three different models of family group conferencing (FGC): the New Zealand style model, the Wagga Wagga model from Australia, or the New Zealand Family Group Decision Making model. (See Figure 6.1 for a summary overview of these models.) The New Zealand and Wagga Wagga models are used primarily for young offenders. The Family Group Decision Making model is specific to Child Welfare cases where parents are under stress, and it concerns the care and support of children and other family members.

All three models are built on the philosophy that (1) families and their immediate community, such as extended family and friends, should have a say in how the offense or child protection issue should be resolved, (2) processes should be used that address the offending or issue in meaningful ways and reconcile the affected parties through consensus-based agreements, and (3) efforts should be made to reintegrate or reconnect victims and offenders at the local

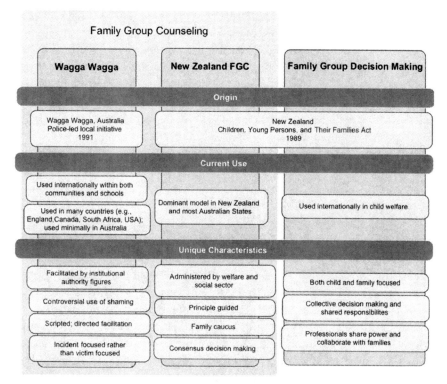

FIGURE 6.1

community level through healing the hurt and harm caused by the offending (Maxwell, Morris, & Hayes, 2006).

Besides its focus on youthful offenders, FGC is being applied with increasing frequency to juvenile and adult offenders as part of their reentry process. Project Greenlight in New York City as well as state correctional services in Oregon, Kansas, Minnesota, Washington, and Maryland have initiatives that use family conferences for offender reentry planning within 6 months of release (Bobitt & Nelson, 2004). A manual that details the victim's role in offender reentry has been written as well (Seymour, 2006).

Besides its focus on youthful offenders, FGC is being applied with increasing frequency to juvenile and adult offenders as part of their reentry process. Kansas Department of Corrections, for example, brings together the offender, family, Community Reentry Facilitator, institutional case manager, Intensive Supervision Officer, Long-Term Support Specialist, and community stakeholders or supporters for a family group conference 30 days prior to release in order to develop a release plan (Lattimore et al., 2004).

The chapter gives an extensive review of each model for several reasons. First, the use of family group conferencing has increased substantially because it has received solid legislative support. Second, family group conferencing is emerging strongly in the child welfare field internationally as a new and promising practice. Because child welfare is state supported, this development has important implications for vast numbers of children and their families. Third, family group conferencing (FGC), in comparison to VOM and Circles, has generated important questions in the restorative justice community about the extensive use of shame in the dialogue to effect offender change and about the use of police or other authority figures to facilitate the dialogue.

The research on family group conferencing for young offenders demonstrates that this approach, when legislatively stipulated, substantially decreases the number of cases sent to court and so reduces the use of incarceration. It also increases the support felt by offender families and the police. Over 90% of offender participants view the process as fair. The impact on recidivism, however, is somewhat mixed. Although the strength of this approach is its focus on the family of the offender, this emphasis makes the victim's presence less significant. This shifts the principal philosophical emphasis in restorative justice away from the harm to the victim and therefore threatens to again marginalize the victim as happens in the criminal justice system. The victim can feel used because the victim may feel undue and subtle pressure to give priority to what is good for the offender while their own needs get minimized.

Research on family group conferencing in child welfare also shows conflicting results. Although consumer satisfaction is high, some studies indicate that family involvement actually resulted in worse outcomes, that is, increased referrals to child protection. This model has a tendency to place more stress on staff because it requires that ownership of the problem and the problem be given back to the family. Staff report feeling more anxiety because they still feel responsible for the outcome but have less control.

FAMILY GROUP CONFERENCE, NEW ZEALAND STYLE

In New Zealand, FGC grew out of a crisis in the juvenile justice system. By 1980, the incarceration rate for young people was one of the highest in the world (MacRae & Zehr, 2004). Moreover, the Maori who were indigenous to New Zealand were overrepresented in the prison system. Although they made up 13% of the country's population, they comprised 50% of male prisoners and 56% of female prisoners (Tauri & Morris, 2003). New Zealand also had a high crime rate, which continues to this day. The Maori complained that the Western system of criminal justice undermined the family and disproportionately affected Maori youth based on institutional racism. They contended that law, religion, and education are three primary institutional pillars and when any of them disregards or undermines Maori values and traditions, a system of racism is in operation (MacRae & Zehr, 2004). In response to their complaints, the government initiated a process of listening to communities throughout New Zealand. The Maori recommended that the extended family and community be the source of any efforts to address juvenile offending from the perspective that responsibility for the harm lay not in the individual but in the lack of balance in the offender's social and family environment, which therefore required that the cause of the imbalance be addressed in a collective way (Tauri & Morris, 2003). FGC emerged as the answer because it both addressed the failures of the traditional juvenile justice and incorporated indigenous Maori values (Umbreit & Zehr, 2003).

Children, Young Persons, and Their Families Act of 1989

In 1989, the New Zealand legislature passed a landmark Act of Parliament. The Children, Young Persons, and Their Families Act made Family Group Conferences, not the courtroom, the hub of the entire youth justice system and the jurisdiction for these issues (MacRae & Zehr, 2004). This world pioneering legislation created a partnership between the state and family groups based on the perspective that the family is the social unit most suited to the needs of children and young people; that the well-being of children and young people requires a sense of continuity, identity, and stability that can only be provided within the immediate or wider family group; and that alternative care for children should be looked for within the wider family group (Doolan, 1999). Judge Fred McElra, a prominent New Zealand judge, commented on this groundbreaking Act by declaring that FGC was the first truly restorative system ever institutionalized within a Western legal system (Umbreit, 2000). Recent estimates suggest that over 50,000 conferences in New Zealand have been convened since 1989 (Harris, 2008).

As part of revamping the focus and process of juvenile justice, the Children, Young Persons, and Their Families Act of 1989 physically divided the function of the Family Court, which deals with care and protection matters involving children and young people under the age of 17 from the newly established Youth Court, which would deal with offending by young persons between 14 and 17 years of age. Neither court could make a decision on the disposition of a case unless an FGC had been held. New Zealand law identifies four types of youth justice FGCs based on differing circumstances (MacRae & Zehr, 2004) (1) Custody Conferences are held when a young person is placed in custody after denying the charges. (2) Charge-Proven Conferences are held when a young person has denied guilt but is then found guilty in court. (3) Intention-to-Charge Conferences are held when a young person is not arrested but a decision is needed about prosecution or an alternative.

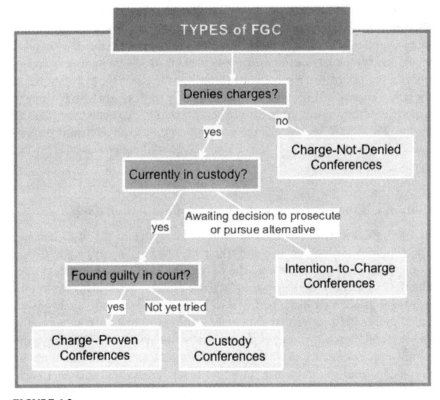

FIGURE 6.2

(4) Charge-Not-Denied Conferences are held when the young person is arrested and admits responsibility. (See Figure 6.2.)

Most FGCs do not involve the courts except for sentence recommendations, monitoring or enforcement of agreements, or the recommendation, under special circumstances, that charges be withdrawn from the court. This makes the community, not the court, the center of decision making. Only murder and manslaughter are not referred for an FGC.

Principles of Family Group Conference

Howard Zehr, widely regarded as a leading pioneer of restorative justice, has often stated that we must be clear about our principles, values, and philosophies and having accomplished that, to do what he calls "principled practice," a concept that refers to behaving in strict accordance with a person's commitment to foundational beliefs as a framework to guide practice. He references New Zealand as the quintessential example, noting that the Children, Young Persons, and Their Families Act of 1989 set down seven principles and seven goals for restorative practice. Practitioners virtually carry those principles and goals in their back pocket and for every decision they make, they refer to those principles (MacRae & Zehr, 2004).

The seven primary goals of youth justice in New Zealand are as follows:

1. Diversion to keep young people out of the courts and to prevent labeling them as offenders
2. Accountability by offenders accepting responsibility for their actions and to repair the harm they have caused
3. Involving the victim including the opportunity to be part of deciding the outcomes
4. Involving and strengthening the offender's family
5. Consensus decision making
6. Cultural appropriateness
7. Due process to ensure that the young person's rights are respected (MacRae & Zehr, 2004)

Seven guiding principles support the achievement of these goals:

1. Criminal proceedings should be avoided unless the public interest requires otherwise.
2. Criminal justice processes should not be used to provide assistance.
3. Families should be strengthened.
4. Children should be kept in the community if at all possible.
5. The child or young person's age must be taken into account.
6. Personal development should be promoted using the least restrictive option.
7. The interests of victims must be considered.

MacRae and Zehr (2004) are adamant that the success of the New Zealand model rests on following these principles and goals consistently not only to shape policy but also to guide decisions "in each case and each situation" (p. 24). Indeed, they place the importance of these goals and principles above standards of practice and ethical guidelines.

Procedures for Conducting a Family Group Conference

The Children, Young Persons, and Their Families Act of 1989 established statutory officials called youth justice coordinators who are responsible for convening and facilitating the FGC, monitoring the Act, recording agreements or plans, and communicating the results to appropriate people and agencies. The coordinator is most often a social worker (Hoyle, 2007). Possible participants in an FGC include offenders, family members of the offender, and

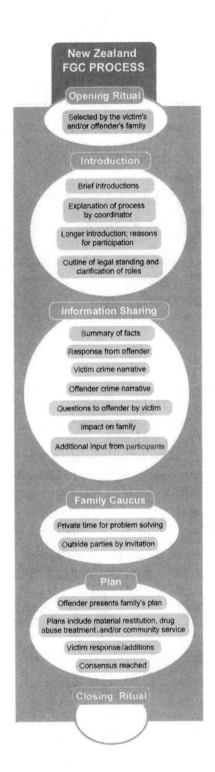

FIGURE 6.3

police representatives all of whom are mandated to attend. Others who may attend include extended family of the offender and his or her family, victims or victim representatives and supporters, youth advocates who are nonadversarial lawyers selected to safeguard the rights of the offender and assist the process, lay advocates to ensure the cultural appropriateness of the process, social workers, information givers (for example, community, school, or church representatives), and other caregivers. Figure 6.3 outlines the process.

Preparation

When the coordinator receives a case, letters are sent to victims, the offender, and the offender's parents explaining the process and asking for a response within 72 hours (MacRae & Zehr, 2004). The coordinator tries for an in-person meeting with the victim to build rapport and understanding, inform them of their rights, and to give them information about the conference. In New Zealand, victims can participate in three ways. They can attend and bring support people such as a family member, close friend, or representative of a victim support organization. They may send a support person, and that person may bring people from their own support network. Or they may choose to send information only either through the coordinator or through a video or audio message to be played during the Conference. Victims can also participate by phone, observe through a closed-circuit video link, or write notes to be read to the offender. Victims often fear revictimization and may need reassurance either in the form of safeguards that can be incorporated into the conference or from stories about what other victims have gained from their participating. In some cases, such as traffic offenses or drug charges, the community is considered the victim because there is no identifiable victim. Consequently, the police may represent the community, or surrogate victims may be involved.

The coordinator also meets with the offender's family to ensure understanding of the charge, explain the conference process, and advise them on the importance of their own responsibilities to both support and hold the youth accountable (MacRae & Zehr, 2004). Family members are briefed on the law that entitles them and the offender to have private deliberation time called the family caucus to devise a plan to address the youth's offense and related issues. The family is asked for a list of people they would like to invite for support. The list should include anyone who can help in developing a plan for the youth or helping to resolve it. Including people that the young person admires or who can serve as an advocate or who have a positive relationship with their child may also be important. If the offender's family does not have a network to draw from or the family may have difficulty carrying out supervision of the youth, the family can be put in contact with organizations that may be able to help them.

In-person preparation of the primary participants in a conference (the victim, the victim's immediate family, the offender, and the offender's immediate family) should occur to connect with the parties, build rapport and trust, provide information, encourage participation, and prepare them for the conference (MacRae & Zehr, 2004). Both the victim and offender's family may discuss how to start the conference, for example, with a prayer or blessing, songs, or other cultural protocol, and the coordinator can inform both sides of these wishes so everyone knows what to expect. The preparation process can help participants feel safe enough to participate in an open dialogue with one another, with the coordinator being as nondirective as possible.

The Conference

The conference usually begins with the ritual selected by the victim and/or offender's family and may be offered by a family member or support person (MacRae & Zehr, 2004). Brief introductions by name and official position are initially made followed by an explanation by the coordinator of the process for the FGC. Then participants introduce themselves including the reasons for being there. The coordinator outlines the legal standing of the conference and clarifies that it is the coordinator's role to make sure that the principles that guide the Youth Justice process are not compromised in the FGC or through the agreed outcomes.

The meeting then moves into information sharing (MacRae & Zehr, 2004). After a reading of the summary of the facts by the police, the offender is asked if the charges and what they mean are understandable and then asked to admit or deny the offense. The victim then shares the impact of the crime on them and their lives including feelings of hurt and/or anger. The offender responds by telling the story of committing the crime and why. Additionally, offenders are encouraged to talk about their feelings and to say something to the victim. Following these openers, victims ask questions of the offender, and the offender's family members speak about how the crime has affected them and any other statements they want to make about their child's actions or questions they may have. The professionals in attendance may offer further information to the offender's family as well, for example, school reports.

Following the information sharing, the family is given a list of the harms and impacts and preventive issues to address in the family caucus, a private time for the family to discuss their child's offending and related problems and devise possible solutions (MacRae & Zehr, 2004). The offender's family can invite any of the FGC participants to the caucus as well. The rationale behind the family caucus is that family members are able to investigate more personal issues like financial commitments or the need for support from the extended family such as time commitments, when they can deliberate in private. This time out also empowers family members to take charge, with support from the Youth Court, of the outcome and its potential for a constructive impact on the offender and the rest of the family.

When the family has completed its deliberations, the large group reconvenes and the offender presents the plan, which tends to put the focus back between the offender and the victim(s) (MacRae & Zehr, 2004). Plans may include restitution to the victim for material losses, drug abuse treatment, community service, and so on. Subsequently, the victim is asked first for input and can add or remove anything from the plan followed by feedback from the professionals and the police. The coordinator may offer options for the family to consider for successful implementation of the plan. For example, the victim may want to be kept informed, and the coordinator may suggest a range of possibilities from a letter to the victim written by the offender to reconvening the FGC to review the young person's progress. Each part of the plan including what is being requested of the jurisdictional agency, reparation, prevention, and monitoring is reviewed to ensure clarity and understanding. When there is full consensus on the plan, the conference is closed with a ritual.

Research Findings

Long-term follow-up on FGC cases in New Zealand from 1987 shows a large decrease in court cases from 600 per 10,000 in 1987 to about 250 per 10,000 in 2001 (Maxwell, Kingi, Roberson, & Morris, 2004). Incarceration also declined from 300 cases in 1987 to less than 100 in 2001 (MacRae & Zehr, 2004). Plans were successfully completed in 80% of cases. In Wellington, New Zealand, there was a two-thirds drop in youth offending within 3 years, and the number of conferences held also fell during the same period from 168 to 78.

Interviews with 520 offenders from conferences held in 1998 and interviews with 100 offenders from conferences conducted in 2000–2001 found that half of the offenders felt involved in making decisions and almost all of them understood and agreed with the decisions made (Maxwell et al., 2004). "It was good having my parents and having support from them" and "it was good—just saying my side and saying sorry and being able to have a say in the plan" (p. 125). Predictors of reconviction related to the conference include remembering the conference, completing tasks, feeling sorry and showing it, feeling the damage was repaired, not being made to feel a bad person, feeling involved in the decision making, agreeing with the outcome, and meeting the victim and apologizing to that person (Maxwell & Morris, 2001). Indeed, offenders who failed to apologize to victims were three times more likely to be reconvicted that those who had apologized (Morris & Maxwell, 1997).

Victims choose to attend only half of the FGCs (Maxwell et al., 2004). Interviews with victims about their nonparticipation found that not wanting to meet the offender and the offender's family was the primary reason followed by an inability to attend even though victims were interested in participating. Evidently, the degree to which victims are prepared for the conference also influences their participation rates. Reasons for participating include seeing FGC as a better way of resolving the situation, giving offenders another chance, knowing the offender, wanting to have a say or to confront the offender, wanting to see the offender, wanting to see the effects of the meeting in the offender's remorse, and seeking reparation.

Although recent findings indicate that victims are satisfied with conference outcomes (Maxwell et al., 2006), an early study showed that 60% of victims found the meeting helpful, and a quarter of the victims reported that they felt worse as a result of their participation (Maxwell & Morris, 1993). Reasons included the inability of the offender and offender's family to make reparation, the victims' inability to express themselves adequately, problems communicating cross-culturally, lack of support, perceived failure to show remorse to the victim, feeling their concerns were not listened, to and that others were uninterested or unsympathetic. These concerns are viewed as being rooted in poor practice and hence can be corrected through adequate preparation of both victims and offenders.

More recent findings show that only 5% of victims said that they felt worse, 90% said they felt they were treated with respect, and three-quarters said that their needs had been met at the conference. More than two-thirds said that the conference helped put matters behind them (Maxwell et al., 2004). They also indicated that they gained understanding of some of the reasons behind the offending; received some kind of repair in the form of an apology, reparation, or community work; were more satisfied with the agreements reached; felt less angry or safer; and gained a sense of closure (Maxwell et al., 2006).

Besides what FGC does for victims and offenders, offenders' families are also affected by the experience. They are given the support that enables them to be more effective with the offender and the offender's siblings, gain long-term support networks, and have the opportunity to remove the shame and sense of failure that come through the antisocial behavior shown by the offender (MacRae & Zehr, 2004). Police also feel empowered because they gain greater information about the community they police; build a closer and more effective relationship with the young people, their families, and communities; and feel better respected.

Application of Family Group Conference

Although FGC was developed for youth, the New Zealand model is also being used with adults in two projects for medium to serious crimes as a pretrial diversionary effort, Project Turnaround and Te Whanau Awhina, the latter having been developed for Maori offenders. Both groups of participants were less likely to be reconvicted a year later than their comparable control groups (Maxwell & Morris, 2001). Plans were completed by more than four-fifths of the sample in Project Turnaround and two-thirds of the sample in the Te Whanau Awhina sample. Research also found that those offenders who felt like a bad person were more likely to be persistent recidivists. Costs were $462 per offender at Project Turnaround. Savings on correctional outcomes for 100 participants compared to the 100 matched controls were $27,811 at Project Turnaround and $168,259 at Te Whanau Awhina. Savings on court appearances and associated costs with the savings on correctional sentences were estimated at $85,325.

Conclusion

The New Zealand model of FGC is unique because it is legislated and administered under the welfare and social sector rather than the criminal justice sector. Moreover, it is governed primarily by a set of principles, offers a family caucus, uses consensus decision making, and aims at cultural adaptability and appropriateness (MacRae & Zehr, 2004; Umbreit & Zehr, 2003). Because the circle of participants is inclusive of numerous family members and support persons, it contributes to the empowerment and healing of the community, including a wider range of people to be involved in assisting with the reintegration of the offender into the community and the healing of the victim. Most importantly, it acknowledges and regularizes the important role of the family in a juvenile offender's life (Umbreit & Zehr, 2003). Although this model originated in New Zealand, it is the dominant model today in both New Zealand and Australia (Hoyle, 2007). A graphic summary of the New Zealand model is shown in Figure 6.4.

FAMILY GROUP CONFERENCE, WAGGA WAGGA MODEL

In contrast to New Zealand, which created a national model, a local model was produced in Australia in 1991, when police in the New South Wales city of Wagga Wagga began to organize and conduct FGCs as part of a new cautioning process for young offenders under the context of community policing (Moore & Forsythe, 1994). Under British-style policing, a series of reprimands and warnings are issued in lieu of prosecution. The Wagga Wagga Juvenile Cautioning Process was entirely police based and aimed at a more effective use of police discretionary power not to charge young offenders, thereby reducing the number of first time offenders appearing before the court (O'Connell & Moore, 1992).

This community policing technique spread across Australia in the early 1990s largely through the efforts of Terry O'Connell, a police sergeant in Wagga Wagga, and the passage of legislation by separate states authorizing

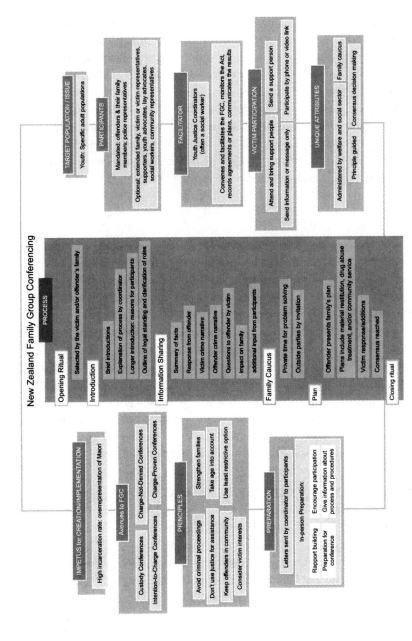

FIGURE 6.4

conferences (Zernova, 2007). In 1994, a 5-year conferencing program was launched in Canberra, which resulted in the training of over 100 police and the implementation of research known as RISE (Reintegrative Shaming Experiment) to evaluate the effectiveness of the Wagga Wagga model for youth crime (O'Connell, 1998). By 1995, however, there was intense debate about police-led cautioning (Hoyle, 2007), and the New South Wales Government funded Community Justice Centers to manage conferences instead of the police arguing that police were not seen as "independent" by either victims or offenders (O'Connell, 1998). In 1998, the Young Offenders Act gave responsibility for youth conferencing to Juvenile Justice, which meant that community representatives were trained and paid to facilitate conferences and the police were precluded from further conferencing. Today, only two Australian jurisdictions still use police-led conferencing, the Australian Capital Territory, which has been dwindling since the end of the RISE experiment in Canberra, and the Northern Territory (Hoyle, 2007).

Ironically, however, and in contrast to Australia, which shifted to the New Zealand model, the Wagga Wagga model has spread and proliferated rapidly in several countries due, in part, to its vigorous promotion by Terry O'Connell and Real Justice, a Pennsylvania-based organization employing conferencing to bring together young offenders, victims, their respective supporters, and community members to try to resolve the harm of crime (Umbreit & Zehr, 2003). Terry O'Connell introduced the model to the Thames Valley in England in 1994 as an experiment, and the project was implemented across the Thames Valley Police force by 1998. Moreover, the 1998 Crime and Disorder Act created a statutory system of strong, multiagency Youth Offending Teams staffed by persons from social services, police, probation, and others, who, together with community volunteers, bring together the juvenile, his or her family, and the victim for a conference, including reparation and a program of activity that is designed to prevent further criminal activity (Dignan & Marsh, 2003). Over 600 conferences took place with victims in the Thames Valley project during each of its first 3 years, and several thousand occurred in which the cautioning officer relayed the views of absent victims (Hoyle, Young, & Hill, 2002).

The Wagga Wagga model was also employed by the Bethlehem Police Department in Bethlehem, Pennsylvania, and evaluated through random assignment of juveniles to conferencing or traditional court referral (McCold & Wachtel, 1998; Zernova, 2007). In 1997, the Royal Canadian Mounted Police (RCMP) officially adopted the Wagga Wagga model as a discretionary option in dealing with nonviolent offenses (Chatterjee & Elliott, 2003). By the end of 1998, RCMP had trained 1,700 officers and community members across Canada to conduct what is called Community Justice Forums. In 2003, the Government of Canada implemented the Youth Criminal Justice

Act, which requires police to consider one of the extrajudicial options, such as FGC, to reduce the use of courts for less serious offenses.

Procedures for Conducting the Wagga Wagga Model

The conferencing scheme in Australia is incident-focused rather than victim- or offender focused (McCold, 1999). It is set up and facilitated by the police, usually in uniform, or someone in authority, for example, teacher, school principal (Umbreit, 2000). This individual decides which offenders are offered the service, who else to invite, how the meeting progresses and, to some extent, influences decisions about appropriate reparation (Hoyle, 2007). The police contact people, including the victim, by phone and only occasionally conduct in person prep meetings. Similar to New Zealand, participants include the offender, the offender's family members and others connected to the offender, the primary victim, if available, and people connected to the victim, and the arresting police officer or affected school or other public official.

In contrast to New Zealand, the Wagga Wagga model uses a prescriptive script, which allows for a more directed facilitation and structured discussion by the convener or coordinator about the harm caused by the offence and how this could be repaired. The script was written out for the convenience of the facilitator and was constructed from the predictable sequence of conference processes and outcomes that emerged over time (O'Connell, 1998). Participants are encouraged to trust the police and adhere to the script.

Conference protocols include having offenders talk about what happened, what they were thinking when they committed the offense, and who was affected followed by the victim's reaction, responses from victim and offender supporters, and the opportunity for the offender to offer an apology or respond to comments from any of the other participants. The conference then moves into negotiating a reparation agreement and an open-ended consideration of possibilities. After the agreement is complete, participants share an informal reintegration or social period where refreshments are served. If the conference does not reach an outcome, the matter is referred to a Youth Court judge or Youth Court magistrate. Figure 6.5 illustrates the process.

Theoretical and Explanatory Framework

The Wagga Wagga model is built on the criminological theory of reintegrative shaming advanced by Braithwaite (1989) and affect theory attributed to Silvan Tomkins (1992) and elaborated by Donald Nathanson (1992). These theories collectively explain the procedures used in FGC and the individual

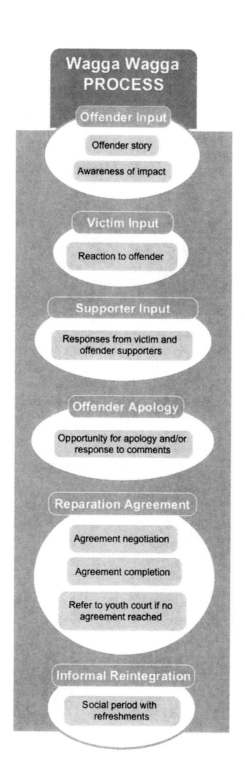

FIGURE 6.5

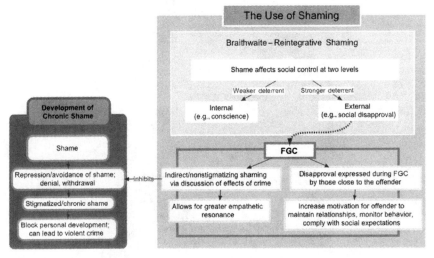

FIGURE 6.6

and collective dynamics that occur (Moore, 1994). Braithwaite contends that shame affects social control at two levels—external and internal. Social disapproval deters offending behavior through the external threat of a loss of status and affection. Pangs of conscience discourage offending behavior internally. Both generate shame, but social disapproval produces disgrace, which is more potent. See Figure 6.6 for an elaboration of this theory.

The use of FGC to address juvenile crime generates social disapproval but also serves to mollify the creation of stigmatized or chronic shame, which if repressed or defended against by shame avoidance mechanisms, for example, denial, withdrawal, can block a person's personal development and lead to rage and violent predatory crime. Conferencing draws on the use of disapproval from those persons close to the offender in order to cause shame, which, in the context of personal relationships, is a powerful motivator to continually monitor and work on those relationships and comply with social expectations. Because the shaming happens just through the gathering of persons impacted by the crime and through the discussion of its consequences, it is indirect and nonstigmatizing. Moreover, the feeling of remorse and offering of a genuine apology allow the offender to drop his or her shame avoidance mechanisms and generates an empathic resonance from the other participants based on the sharing of emotion and awareness of the collective vulnerability we all share (Van Stokkom, 2002).

The inducement of shaming is highly controversial in the restorative justice community. Scholars have expressed concern that an offender's reaction to shaming is unpredictable and, even with the best of intentions, may be interpreted as stigmatizing (Morris, 2002). Van Stokkom (2002) raises the possibility that planned shaming efforts might backfire and close down communication with the offender, generating disapproval from other participants instead of restoration. Indeed, the ideal outcome of regret, remorse, and forgiveness is frequently not achieved. Moreover, the meaning of shame varies based on whether the culture involved is individualistic or collective (Kitayama, Markus, & Matsumoto, 1995).

In the United States, for example, shame is often hidden with anger because it is interpreted as weakness, whereas in collectivist cultures, demonstrating shame to others is better and sanctioned because it helps maintain relationships and the value given to interdependencies between people. Umbreit and Zehr (2003) suggest that conference coordinators who use a more authoritarian style, such as police, might be perceived as causing harm through shaming and blaming or using a process that breaks down youth and then tries to build them up again. Morris argues that the most important mechanism in conferencing is not shaming but the eliciting of remorse as a result of empathy. Moreover, remorse is directed toward behavior rather than the self and does not involve any negative self-directed feelings (Taylor, 2002). Feminists view shame as a tool of oppression, and some regard the interest in reintegrative shaming as an attempt to revive shame as a socially approved mechanism of social control.

Braithwaite has countered these criticisms, in part, by revising the theory of reintegrative shaming (Braithwaite & Braithwaite, 2001). Although he does not alter his fundamental prediction that reintegrative shaming reduces offending, he posits that positive change occurs because reintegrative shaming allows offenders to cope with feelings of shame in more constructive ways. Consequently, what matters is not the experience of a type of shame but shame management. FGC, therefore, helps offenders and their supporters acknowledge, work through, and ultimately resolve the shame they are already experiencing (Harris & Maruna, 2006).

Rodogno (2008) argues, however, that conferencing is more complex than simply reducing it to shame management and that it is not possible to apply a single precept to all such meetings. Rather, success depends on the cultural and situational specificities, including knowledge of the perceived relations between victim and offender as well as the affective states of the others involved. Finally, it is important to remember that restorative justice is about healing harms, not creating new ones, even if done for good reasons. As Molly Baldwin, Executive Director of ROCA Inc., Chelsea, Massachusetts, reminds us, as a values-based process, restorative justice is predicated on the notion that we cannot "get to a good place in a bad way" (as cited in Chatterjee & Elliott, 2003, p. 356). This quote suggests that the means in restorative justice are as important as the ends.

The Role of Authority in the Wagga Wagga Model

Besides questioning the use of reintegrative shaming, scholars have also debated the use of police-led conferences. Police already control the processes of arrest, detention, and investigation. To empower them still further can seem counterproductive to restorative justice's efforts to move away from a retributive model. Moreover, police already have a variety of roles that, when combined with mediation, makes it more difficult for them to operate dispassionately, without bias, and to ensure a fair process (Hoyle, 2007). Police are steeped in an adversarial punitive system and with little training to manage the power differential between a young disadvantaged person and a group of adults (Palk, 1997). Not only does this conditioning increase the temptation to move from being neutral to using their power in ways that intimidate, but it also increases the potential for shaming of the offender, which can replicate the criminal justice system, subject victims to being used as shaming props, and may curtail the open sharing of feelings and thoughts (Umbreit, 2000). The practices of tying conferencing to the cautionary process, which operates on the basis of police discretion, and using the police themselves as the hub of the conferencing process raise the potential for net widening (Umbreit & Zehr, 2003). Finally, police-led conferences raise additional concerns about the misuse of power when dealing with indigenous and minority populations (Hoyle, 2007). Research has shown that police agendas are highly likely to result in white middle class participants being treated more fairly and more respectfully than those from ethnic or other minorities and those from less privileged backgrounds (Bowling, Phillips, & Shah, 2003; Sanders & Young, 2003). Indeed, Cunneen (1997) found that the police presence increased the reluctance of aboriginal people to attend meetings and contributed to a noncommunicative atmosphere for those who did participate.

In contrast to these criticisms, it has been argued that the use of police to implement and facilitate conferences reflects a shift in the philosophy of policing congruent with the thrust toward community policing (Hoyle et al., 2002). Proponents of restorative policing further maintain that having police involved in restorative justice can be used to bring about wider cultural change, including a move from a punitive legalistic approach to a more problem-solving and restorative approach (Braithwaite, 2002; O'Connell, 1998). Advocates of police facilitation also point out that making police central to the conference lends a serious tone to the proceedings and increases the likelihood that agreements will be successfully completed (Hoyle et al., 2002). Being in uniform can also make victims and other participants feel more secure.

Research findings on police-led practices are mixed. Studies from Canberra, Australia, and Bethlehem, Pennsylvania, suggest that offenders do not find FGCs oppressive nor do they perceive police facilitation as problematic (Sherman & Barnes, 1997). In the Bethlehem study, 95% of offender participants found the tone of the conference to be friendly, and in Canberra, 47% of young offenders said that they gained more respect for the police and felt that the police had been fair to them during the meetings. The Canberra study also showed, however, that only between 46% and 54% of the offenders who felt that they had control over the conference outcomes actually felt that they had enough control over the way things were run.

This same paradox emerges in a study of police-led conferences in the Thames Valley (Young & Goold, 2003). Only 9% of the 178 participants interviewed expressed disapproval of the police facilitation (Hoyle et al., 2002). However, tape recordings of 15 cautioning sessions show that the police insert themselves in overbearing ways into the dynamics of conferences (Young, 2003; Young & Goold, 2003). For example, the analysis of the tapes revealed detailed and judgmental questioning of offenders by police rather than their following the open-ended scripted questions they were supposed to be asking. Police also used information from the investigative file to verify or add to the offender's story, which became an additional and even competitive narrative to the offender's story. In the following example, "F" is the facilitator and "O" is the offender.

F: . . . At what point in your own mind then did you decide that you were going to take that and not pay for it. Was it before you went into the shop?

O: No, it wasn't . . .

F: No.

O: . . . preplanned or anything

F: OK, so once you're in there then, so did you have any money on you at the time, did you have enough money to pay for it?

O: Yeah, I did.

F: You did. [Checks police file and states value of items under ten pounds.] So you did have enough money on you to pay for that. [Pause—no verbal response.] How did you go about concealing it, how did you actually steal it.

O: I think it was just, putting it in my pocket or sleeve, I don't [trails off].

F: You put it in your sleeve in fact.

Because police-led conferencing is inherently problematic, suggestions have been made to help police-led facilitation achieve restorative outcomes.

Umbreit and Zehr (2003) advise cofacilitation with a trained community person. They also emphasize the need for police training in mediation and conflict resolution skills as well as training in cultural and ethical issues that might affect the conferencing process and the participants. Others recommend that training in restorative justice not be limited to a few officers but rather given across all ranks and departments in order to attain a cultural and attitudinal shift (McCold & Wachtel, 1998; O'Mahony, Chapman, & Doak, 2002). Hoyle and Young (2002) propose using other agencies to monitor police-led practices, feedback forms from participants, and independent and grounded research on the practices used in conferences. A recent study on how convener type (police vs. civilian) affects decisions to participate in conferences found that participants chose police-convened conferences as frequently as civilian-convened conferences (Sivasubramaniam & Goodman-Delahuntyh, 2008). The researchers suggest that preferences may be influenced by cultural issues and the ways people perceive power differences, and these preferences may be important to consider.

Research Findings

Studies on the Wagga Wagga model have focused on participant satisfaction, victim response, restitution, diversion, and reoffending. In U.S. studies, about 95% of victims indicate that the process and outcome were fair (Fercello & Umbreit, 1997; McCold & Wachtel, 1998; McGarrell, Olivares, Crawford, & Kroovand, 2000). In one of those studies, 89% of juvenile offenders felt that the resulting conference agreement was fair (Fercello & Umbreit, 1997). One of the strongest results was found in the Queensland Department of Justice conferencing program, where 98% of offenders thought that the conference was fair and 99% were satisfied with the agreement (Palk, Hayes, & Prenzler, 1998). Offender participants were also more likely to experience fairness in the justice system than court-referred youth (Hayes & Daly, 2003), more likely to have felt involved (84% vs. 47%) and to feel that they had an opportunity to express their feelings (86% vs. 55%) (McGarrell, 2000).

Victim involvement in FGC in Australia ranges from 75% to 80% (Strang & Sherman, 1997; Trimboli, 2000; Wundersitz & Hetzel, 1995). Young (2001), however, reports that the victim is not commonly present at restorative conferences in the Thames Valley area of England. Reasons for attending include that they wanted to try to help the offender, express their feelings, make statements to the offender, or ask questions like why me followed by curiosity and a service to have a look followed by responsibility as citizens to attend (Wundersitz & Hetzel, 1995).

Victims report changes in themselves as a result of their involvement. For example, in the RISE experiment, 60% of victims said that they felt quite or very angry at the beginning of the conference, but only 30% said so afterward (Strang & Sherman, 1997). Many said that they felt safer. Indeed, only 6% of conference victims feared further victimization compared with 19% of victims whose cases went to court. The proportion of victims who felt sympathetic to the offender almost tripled from 18% to 50% by the end of the conference (Strang, 2000). A recent and randomized controlled trial of victims of robbery and burglary found one-third fewer posttraumatic stress symptoms at 6 weeks than victims in the control group and 40% fewer symptoms at 6 months (Angel, 2005; Strang et al., 2006).

Restitution in FGC ranges from 83% compared with 58% completion in the control group (McGarrell, 2000) to the high 90% range (Fercello & Umbreit, 1997; McCold & Wachtel, 1998), and in one instance, completion of agreements achieved 100% (Walker, 2002). As part of restitution, Strang (2000) reports that 71% of the victims randomly assigned to conferencing got an apology compared to 17% in court assigned cases. Victims in conferences rated 77% of the apologies they received as sincere or somewhat sincere compared to only 36% of apologies received from offenders who went to court.

Diversion results are mixed. A program in Bethlehem, Pennsylvania made no difference (McCold & Wachtel, 1998). Outside the United States, however, the Wagga Wagga model appears to have had a significant impact. In Australia, a program reduced the total number of involving youth and increased the proportion of cases handled through cautioning from 38.2% to 51.9% rather than in court (Moore & Forsythe, 1995). Moreover, a school-based conferencing program in Colorado found that all of its conferencing cases amounted to having been diverted from the conventional justice system; 70% of cases were done in place of suspension and 35% (with some overlap) of cases were done in place of criminal charges (Ierley & Ivkor, 2003).

There have been four studies evaluating the effectiveness of the Wagga Wagga model on juvenile recidivism (Bradshaw & Roseborough, 2005). Moore and Forsythe (1995) used a single group pretest or posttest design (n = 693) and found statistically significant reductions in reoffense at 9 months follow-up, but after controlling for time there was no treatment effect on reoffense. McCold and Wachtel (1998) used random assignment to conferencing or a control group for property or violent offenses. The groups were nonequivalent. FGC property offense participants had greater rates of recidivism than the control group at 1-year follow-up. Violent offense conferencing participants had a statistically significant reduction in reoffense, which was negated later because of the self-selection process. McGarrell, Olivares, Crawford, and Kroovand (2000) used an experimental design with assignment to either conferencing (n = 232) or diversion (n = 226) programs. Rearrest was 40% lower in the conference group than that in the control group, an effect that decayed to 25%

reduction after 12 months (Braithwaite, 2002). Finally, Sherman, Strang, and Woods (2000) used four experimental studies to test the effectiveness of the Wagga Wagga model by crime type compared to a control group. Results specific to conferencing found an increase of six crimes per 100 per year for driving while intoxicated, no difference for juvenile shoplifting or property offenders, and a net reduction of 38 crimes per 100 per year for violent offenses when compared to offenders assigned to court. The drunk driving conferences did not include a victim and involved adult rather than juvenile offenders.

Summary

The Wagga Wagga style of FGC was pioneered as a community policing technique and as an extension of cautioning used in countries with British-style policing (McCold, 2006). The Wagga Wagga model, today, is also used in schools for attendance and behavior problems (Hayden, 2009). Although the conference process is similar to the New Zealand model in its recognition of the important role of the family and community of care in the offender's life, it differs in its use of a script, style of facilitation (e.g., nonhumanistic), lack of private family time, and stronger emphasis on the offense committed rather than the needs of the offender or the victim. The Wagga Wagga style also differs from the New Zealand model in that it is built on the change theory of reintegrative shaming, which serves to disapprove of the act but to do so in a way that is respectful of the offender as a human being. Although there is debate about the role of the state in police-led facilitation and potential for distortion of restorative justice principles, the Wagga Wagga style, if practiced according to restorative justice values, provides an avenue for developing more meaningful and vital relationships between communities of care, for example, family members and support persons of the offender and victim and representatives of the macro community. A summary of the Wagga Wagga style is provided in Figure 6.7.

FAMILY GROUP DECISION MAKING

Family Group Decision Making (FGDM) originated and was established in New Zealand under the Children, Young Persons, and Their Families Act of 1989 that brought under the Family Court the care and protection of matters involving children under the age of 17. FGDM is a family-focused, culturally sensitive approach to developing permanency plans for children who are in foster care or are at risk of entering foster care due to parental abuse or neglect. It draws on three sources of influence, namely empowerment, social support, and social pressure (Baumann, Tecci, Ritter, Sheets, & Wittenstrom, 2005).

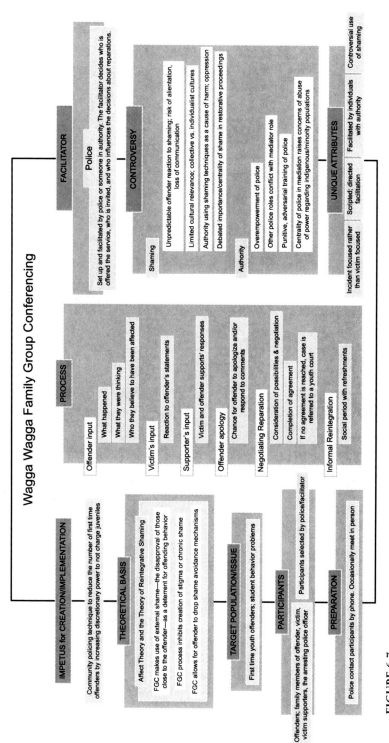

FIGURE 6.7

The philosophy underlying FGDM holds that families, when provided with the necessary pertinent information, are better able to devise plans to protect their own welfare than are professionals; that children need the sense of community, identity, and stability that only the family, in its various forms, can provide; and that families are more likely to find solutions that actively involve other family members, thus keeping the child within the care of the family, rather than transferring the care of the child to the state (Mirsky, 2003b). FGDM is initiated by child welfare agencies but uses a trained coordinator independent of the case to bring together the family group and agency personnel to create a plan to safeguard children and other family members. It uses processes that position the family to lead the decision making, and the agency personnel agree to support the family's plan as long as it adequately addresses the agency's concerns.

FGDM has spread rapidly to other countries including the United States. For example, FGDM grew from 5 in 1995 to more than 100 by 2000 in the United States (Merkel-Holguin, 2000). Four pilot programs that began in 1994 in England and Wales multiplied, and by 2000, 55 local authorities or nongovernmental groups had FGDM programs (Nixon, Merkel-Holguin, Sivak, & Gunderson, 2001). Today over 50% of communities in the United Kingdom are either using FGDM or considering doing so (Mirsky, 2003b). An online survey conducted by Nixon, Burford, and Quinn (2005) for the American Humane Society received 225 responses from 16 countries that have FGDM programs. In 1999, the American Humane Society established its National Center on FGDM with an international Advisory Committee of practitioners and researchers in the field and assumed a strong leadership role under its mission to build community capacity in order to implement FGDM processes congruent with the central values and beliefs of this approach.

Procedures for Implementation and Facilitation

FGDM is used for two types of child welfare cases. Assessment track cases involve neglect and dependency. Forensic cases involve abuse and the legal system. When a CPS social worker refers a family, a trained independent facilitator is assigned to the case and interviews potential "family members" who might include blood relatives as well as friends of the family and service providers involved with the case. The goal is to bring a diverse group of people to a meeting, and then, as a group, to construct a plan that works for the family members. The preparation is comprehensive and is used to explore family resources and begin to transform the relationship between the service providers and extended families, which is traditionally marked by a strong power imbalance and limited shared decision making. Numerous questions need to be explored for the meeting to be successful. For example, to get at the notion of family—which will be different in every case—it is important to ask the family, "How do you define family?" or "Who do you consider part of your family?" It is crucial that the definition is based on the family's perceptions, not those of the other professionals involved in the case. (Merkel-Holguin & Ribich, 2001). This quality preparation time takes 20–25 hours on average (Mirsky, 2003a).

The meeting itself takes place in a neutral setting and follows a format similar to FGC, New Zealand style (Mirsky, 2003b). (See Figure 6.8.) The meeting opens with a ritual or family tradition of some sort. Participants share their hopes for the day. Guidelines and safety plans are reviewed. Professionals then present brief reports about the child's situation and address bottom line issues such as a family's history of substance abuse. This review is followed by a concise discussion of the family's strengths. The group then adjourns for a shared meal break as a prelude to the family's private time.

The family members meet together without the professionals to devise a plan for the child. Nonfamily members, such as family supporters, are allowed in the room during private family time if the family requests and reaches consensus about this. When the family is ready, it presents the plan to the professionals who can ask questions. Professionals may ask for more detail on the plans sending the family back into private time. When the family is done, the plan is reviewed either by the professionals or, in some instances, by the relevant department and sometimes courts before endorsement is given (Harris, 2008). New Zealand requires unanimous agreement among family members, the Child Protection worker, and the facilitator to be accepted. In Texas, the FGDM conference lasts 3 hours, and private family time is less than an hour on average (Baumann et al., 2005). CPS accepts the family's recommendations 95% of the time.

Research Findings

FGDM receives high ratings consistently for consumer satisfaction in international research (Marsh & Crow, 1998). Few studies, however, have evaluated outcomes, and the studies done show conflicting results. Some indicate reductions in subsequent maltreatment, a decrease in the future involvement of child protection agencies, better placement stability, and increased placement with relatives (Crampton, 2003; Crampton & Jackson, 2007; Pennell & Buford, 2000; Sundell & Vinnerljung, 2004). Others show that involvement did not contribute to significantly different outcomes (Center for Social Services Research, 2004) or contributed to negative outcomes such as higher rates of subsequent referrals to child protection agencies and longer out of home placements (Sundell & Vinnerljung, 2004).

Moreover, most family group decision studies lack an equivalent control group. Several studies have attempted to create a matched comparison group.

FIGURE 6.8

The Newfoundland and Labrador FGDM project had more CPS events prior to the conferences and fewer events subsequently compared with the matched cases (Pennell & Buford, 2000). Follow-up interviews found that children in the FGDM project suffered less abuse than children in the comparison group and their parents were providing better care.

Texas has completed a recent study of FGDM that shows promising results (Baumann et al., 2005). FGDM is used in 37 Texas counties and continues to expand as a voluntary program offered to families following removal of a child and to youth who are preparing for adult living. Families were offered FGDM in a total of 993 instances. Conferences were held in 60% of these. Conferences are held within the first 30–45 days following removal. Over a 2-year period, foster care placements for families experiencing a FGDM meeting fell from 54% to 38%, and relative placements increased from 29% to 45%. By June 2006, more children whose families participated in at least one FGDM exited care (48%) compared to those who did not participate (33%).

The Texas study also showed strong impact of FGDM on families with African-American and Hispanic children. For African-American children, 32% returned home compared to 14% receiving traditional services. For Hispanic children, 39% returned home compared to 13% who did not experience FGDM. For White children, 22% returned home compared to 11% who did not experience FGDM. FGDM also made a difference in that children experiencing FGDM showed less anxiety and better adjustment to new living arrangements. Both parents and relatives felt more empowered, had a clearer sense of what was expected of them, and were better able to identify issues in the family plan of services as a result of having participated in the conference. FGDM also enhanced communication and family involvement, especially for fathers and the paternal family, and facilitated parental ownership of family problem. Some staff initially reported slight anxiety over the apparent loss of control. However, they also reported that working collaboratively with the families was inspiring to help to shift their perceptions of their roles. They liked seeing themselves as facilitators of change.

Summary

FGDM emerged in response to pressure to ensure that families had a say about the care of their children and to counter the habit of separating the needs of children and adult family members in the child welfare system. FGDM is both child focused and family centered (Buford & Hudson, 2000). Moreover, it emphasizes collective decision making and shared responsibilities. It also challenges professionals to truly share power and partner collaboratively with the families they serve rather than continue to reinforce an ideology of child protection with its emphasis on forensic investigation and risk management

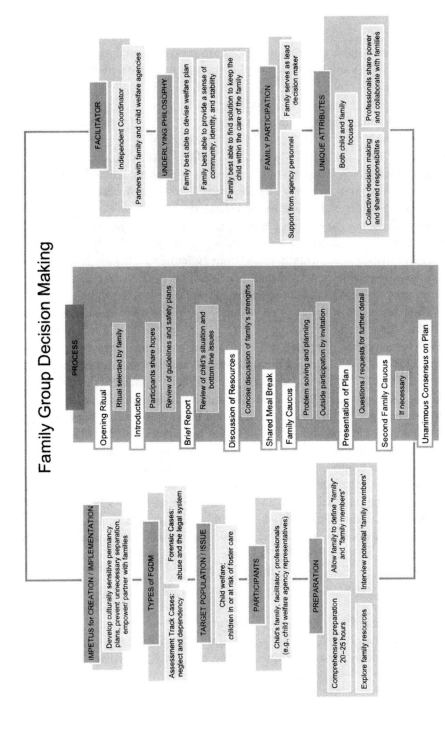

FIGURE 6.9

(Connolly, 2004). In a sense, the professionals' contribution is to provide space and get out of the way so that family groups can work with the tasks at hand, make the necessary decisions, and make them their own. A graphic summary of Family Group Decision Making is provided in Figure 6.9.

CONCLUSION

Family Group Conference, New Zealand style, Family Group Conference, the Wagga Wagga model, and Family Group Decision Making for both care and protection and youth offending, have significantly expanded the influence of restorative justice on tempering the retributive emphasis of the criminal justice system, especially as applied to juveniles.

In contrast to Victim-Offender Mediation and circles, FGC and FGDM have been strongly supported by legislative mandate or statutory authority as mechanisms to reduce overcrowded courts, respond with greater sensitivity to cultural mores of disadvantaged and overrepresented groups in the youth justice and child welfare systems, and empower families to respond more effectively to the needs of children and youth. Although the legal structures that attend FGC and FGDM provide for a partnership between the State and family groups, statutory officials must constantly monitor the use of power to maintain the integrity of their programs. Umbreit and Zehr (2003) spell out the possible risks when power is not harnessed including increased potential for victim and offender coercion, intimidation, lack of neutrality, and inflexibility through adherence to a prescriptive script-driven process.

Although more research is needed on all three modes of family conferencing, it is clear that victims, offenders, and family members show high rates of satisfaction both with outcomes and procedures and a strong sense of fairness. Indeed, satisfaction of participants with the fairness of the process and outcome is not to be discarded as soft evidence since, according to Chatterjee and Elliott (2003), it is the satisfaction of people who experience the justice system that validates and affords some faith in the system.

REFERENCES

Angel, C. (2005). *Crime victims meet their offenders: Testing the impact of restorative justice conferences on victims' post-traumatic stress symptoms*. Doctoral dissertation, University of Pennsylvania, Philadelphia.

Baumann, D. J., Tecci, M., Ritter, J., Sheets, J., & Wittenstrom, K. (2005). *Family group decision-making: Stage 2: Preliminary evaluation*. Austin: Texas Department of Family and Protective Services.

Bazemore, G., & Griffiths, C. T. (2003). Conferences, circles, boards, and mediations: The 'new wave' of community justice decisionmaking. In R. F. E. McLaughlin, G. Hughes, & L. Westmarland (Eds.), *Restorative justice: Critical issues* (pp. 76–93). Thousand Oaks, CA: Sage.

Bobbitt, M., & Nelson, M. (2004). *The front line: Building programs that recognize families' role in reentry.* New York: Vera Institute of Justice. Retrieved April 15, 2010, from http://www.vera.org/download?file=273/IIB%2BFront%2Bline.pdf

Bowling, B., Phillips, C., & Shah, A. (2003). Policing ethnic minority communities. In T. Newburn (Ed.), *Handbook of Policing* (pp. 528–555). Cullompton: Willan Publishing.

Bradshaw, W., & Roseborough, D. (2005). Restorative justice dialogue: The impact of mediation and conferencing on juvenile recidivism. *Federal Probation, 69*(22), 15–21.

Braithwaite, J. (1989). *Crime, shame, and reintegration.* Cambridge: Cambridge University Press.

Braithwaite, J. (2002). *Restorative justice and responsive regulation.* New York: Oxford Publishing.

Braithwaite, J., & Braithwaite, V. (2001). Part 1: Shame, shame management and regulation. In E. Ahmed, N. Harris, J. Braithwaite, & V. Braithwaite (Eds.), *Shame management through reintegration* (pp. 3–72). Melbourne: Cambridge University Press.

Buford, G., & Hudson, J. (Eds.). (2000). *Family group conferencing: New directions in community-centered child and family practice.* New York: Aldine de Gruyter.

Center for Social Services Research. (2004). *Title IV-E child welfare waiver demonstration project intensive services: Final report.* University of California at Berkeley.

Chatterjee, J., & Elliott, L. (2003). Restorative policing in Canada: The Royal Canadian Mounted Police, community justice forums, and the Youth Criminal Justice Act. *Police Practice and Research, 4*(4), 347–359.

Connolly, M. (2004). *Child and family welfare: Statutory responses to children at risk.* Christchurch, New Zealand: Te Awatea Press.

Crampton, D. (2003). Family group decision making in Kent County, Michigan: The family and community compact. *Protecting Children, 18*, 81–83.

Crampton, D., & Jackson, W. L. (2007). Family group decision making and disproportionality in foster care: A case study. *Child Welfare, 86*, 51–69.

Cunneen, C. (1997). Community conferencing and the fiction of indigenous control. *Australian and New Zealand Journal of Criminology, 30*, 1–20.

Dignan, J., & Marsh, P. (2003). Restorative justice and family group conferences in England: Current state and future prospects. In E. McLaughlin, R. Fergusson, G. Hughes, & L. Westmarland (Eds.), *Restorative justice: Critical issues* (pp. 105–116). Thousand Oaks, CA: Sage.

Doolan, M. (1999, August 7). *The family group conference: 10 years on.* Paper presented at the Building Strong Partnerships for Restorative Practices Conference, Burlington, VT.

Fercello, C., & Umbreit, M. S. (1997). *Client evaluation of family group conferencing in 12 Sites in First Judicial District of Minnesota.* St. Paul, MN: Center for Restorative Justice & Peacemaking, University of Minnesota.

Harris, N. (2008). *Family group conferencing in Australia 15 years on.* Australian Institute of Family Studies, National Child Protection Clearinghouse.

Harris, N., & Maruna, S. (2006). Shame, shaming and restorative justice. In D. Sullivan & L. Tifft (Eds.), *Handbook of Restorative Justice* (pp. 452–462). New York: Routledge.

Hayden, C. (2009). Family group conferences—Are they an effective and viable way of working with attendance and behavior problems in schools? *British Educational Research Journal, 35*(2), 205–220.

Hayes, H., & Daly, K. (2003). Youth justice conferencing and re-offending. *Justice Quarterly, 20*(4), 725–764.

Hoyle, C. (2007). Policing and restorative justice. In G. Johnstone & D. Van Ness (Eds.), *Handbook of restorative justice* (pp. 292–311). Portland, OR: Willan Publishing.

Hoyle, C., & Young, R. (2002). Restorative justice: Assessing the prospects and pitfalls. In M. McConville & G. Wilson (Eds.), *The handbook of the criminal justice process* (pp. 525–548). Oxford: Oxford University Press.

Hoyle, C., Young, R., & Hill, R. (2002). *Proceed with caution: An evaluation of the Thames Valley police initiative in restorative cautioning.* York: Joseph Rowntree Foundation.

Ierley, A., & Ivkor, S. (2003). Restoring school communities: A report on the Colorado restorative justice in schools program. *VOMA Connections, 13*, 1–4.

Kitayama, S., Markus, H. R., & Matsumoto, H. (1995). Culture, self and emotion: A cultural perspective on self conscious emotions. In J. P. Tangney & K. W. Fischer (Eds.), *Self-conscious emotions: The psychology of shame, guilt, embarassment and pride* (pp. 439–464). New York: Guilford.

Lattimore, P. K., Brumbaugh, S. M., Visher, C., Lindquist, C. H., Winterfield, L., Salas, M., et al. (2004). *National potrait of SVORI: Serious and violent offender reentry initiative.* Washington, DC: The Urban Institute.

MacRae, A., & Zehr, H. (2004). *The little book of family group conferencing: New Zealand style.* Intercourse, PA: Good Books.

Marsh, P., & Crow, G. (1998). *Family group conferences in child welfare.* Oxford, England: Blackwell Science, Ltd.

Maxwell, G., Kingi, V., Roberson, J., & Morris, A. (2004). *Achieving effective outcomes in youth justice research: Final report.* Wellington, New Zealand: Ministry of Social Development.

Maxwell, G., & Morris, A. (1993). *Family, victims, and culture: Youth justice in New Zealand.* Wellington: Social Policy Agency (Ropu Here Kaupapa) and Institute of Criminology, Victoria University of Wellington.

Maxwell, G., & Morris, A. (2001). Putting restorative justice into practice for adult offenders. *The Howard Journal, 40*(1), 55–69.

Maxwell, G., Morris, A., & Hayes, H. (2006). Conferencing and restorative justice. In D. Sullivan & L. Tifft (Eds.), *Handbook of restorative justice* (pp. 91–107). New York: Routledge.

McCold, P. (1999, August 5–7). *Restorative justice practice: State of the field.* Paper presented at the Building Strong Partnerships for Restorative Practices, Burlington, VT.

McCold, P. (2006). The recent history of restorative justice. In D. Sullivan & L. Tift (Eds.), *Handbook of restorative justice* (pp. 23–51). New York: Routledge.

McCold, P., & Wachtel, B. (1998). *Restorative policing experiment: The Bethlehem Pennsylvania police family group conferencing project.* Pipersville, PA: Community Service Foundation.

McGarrell, E., Olivares, K., Crawford, K., & Kroovand, N. (2000). *Returning justice to the community: The Indianapolis juvenile restorative justice experiment.* Indianapolis, IN: Hudson Institute Crime Control Policy Center.

Merkel-Holguin, L. (2000). Practice diversions and philosophical departures in the implementation of family group conferencing. In G. Burford & J. Hudson (Eds.), *Family group conferencing: Perspectives on policy, practice and research* (pp. 224–231). Hawthorne, NY: Aldine de Gruyter.

Merkel-Holguin, L., & Ribich, K. (2001). Family group conferencing. In E. Walton, P. Sandau-Beckler, & M. Mannes (Eds.), *Balancing family-centered services and child well-being* (pp. 197–218). New York: Columbia University Press.

Mirsky, L. (2003a). Family group conferencing worldwide: Part one in a series. *Restorative Practices eForum.* Retrieved January 5, 2010, from http://www.iirp.org/library/fgcseries01.html

Mirsky, L. (2003b). Family group conferencing worldwide: Part three in a series. *Restorative Justice eForum.* Retrieved January 5, 2010, from http://www.iirp.org/library/fgcseries03.html

Moore, D. (1994). Evaluating family group conferences. In D. Biles & S. McKillop (Eds.), *Criminal justice planning and coordination.* Conference proceedings no. 24. Canberra, ACT: Australian Institute of Criminology. Retrieved January 7, 2010, from http://www.restorativejustice.org/articlesdb/articles/815

Moore, D., & Forsythe, L. (1995). *A new approach to juvenile justice: An evaluation of family conferencing in Wagga Wagga.* Wagga Wagga, Australia: Centre for Rural Social Research.

Morris, A. (2002). Shame, guilt and remorse: Experiences from family group conferences in New Zealand. In I. Weijers & A. Duff (Eds.), *Punishing juveniles: Principles and critique* (pp. 157–178). Oxford: Hart Publishers.

Morris, A., & Maxwell, G. (1997). *Family group conferences and convictions.* Occasional paper no. 5. Wellington, New Zealand: Institute of Criminology, Victoria University of Wellington.

Nathanson, D. (1992). *Shame and pride: Affect, sex and the birth of the self.* New York: W.W. Norton.

Nixon, P., Burford, G., & Quinn, A. (with Edelbaum, J.). (2005, May). *A survey of international practices, policy & research on family group conferencing and related practices.* Retrieved January 5, 2010, from http://www.americanhumane.org/assets/docs/protecting-children/PC-FGDM-practices-survey.pdf

Nixon, P., Merkel-Holguin, L., Sivak, P., & Gunderson, K. (2001). How can family group conferences become family driven? Some dilemmas and possibilities. *Protecting Children, 16*(3), 22–33.

O'Connell, T. (1998, August 6). *From Wagga Wagga to Minnesota.* Paper presented at the North American Conference on Conferencing, Minneapolis.

O'Connell, T., & Moore, D. (1992). Wagga juvenile cautioning process: The general applicability of family group conferences for juvenile offenders and their victims. *Rural Society, 2*(2), 16–19.

O'Mahony, D., Chapman, T., & Doak, J. (2002). Restorative cautioning: A study of police-based restorative cautioning pilots in northern Ireland. *Northern Ireland and Statistical Services Report 4.* Belfast: Statistics and Research Branch of the Northern Ireland Office.

Palk, G. (1997). Conferencing in New Zealand and Australia. *VOMA Quarterly, 8*(2), 3–9.

Palk, G., Hayes, H., & Prenzler, T. (1998). Restorative justice and community conferencing: Summary of findings from a pilot study. *Current Issues in Criminal Justice, 10*(2), 138–155.

Pennell, J., & Buford, G. (2000). Family group decision-making and family violence. In G. Burford & J. Hudson (Eds.), *Family group conferences: New directions in community-centered child and family practice* (pp. 171–192). Hawthorne, NY: Aldine de Gruyter.

Rodogno, R. (2008). Shame and guilt in restorative justice. *Psychology, Public Policy and Law, 14*(2), 142–176.

Sanders, A., & Young, R. (2003). Police powers. In T. Newburn (Ed.), *Handbook of policing* (pp. 228–258). Cullompton: Willan Publishing.

Seymour, A. (2006). *The role of victims in offender reentry: A Community response manual.* Lexington, KY: American Probation and Parole Association.

Sherman, L., & Barnes, G. C. (1997). Restorative justice and offenders' respect for the law. *RISE Working Papers 3.* Canberra, ACT: Australian National University.

Sherman, L., Strang, H., & Woods, D. (2000). *Recidivism patterns in the Canberra reintegrative shaming experiments (RISE).* Canberra, ACT: Centre for Restorative Justice, Research School of Social Sciences, Institute of Advanced Studies, Australian National University.

Sivasubramaniam, D., & Goodman-Delahuntyh, J. (2008). Decisions to participate in restorative justice conferences: Effects of convenor identity and power-distance. *Psychiatry, Psychology and Law, 15*(2), 301–316.

Strang, H. (2000). *Victim participation in a restorative justice process: The Canberra reintegrative shaming experiments.* Canberra, ACT: Australian National University.

Strang, H., & Sherman, L. (1997). The victim's perspective. *RISE Working Papers 2.* Canberra, ACT: Australian National University.

Strang, H., Sherman, L., Angel, C. M., Woods, D. J., Bennett, S., Newbury-Birch, D., et al. (2006). Victim evaluations of face-to-face restorative justice conferences: A quasi-experimental analysis. *Journal of Social Issues, 62*(2), 281–306.

Sundell, K., & Vinnerljung, B. (2004). Outcomes of family group conferencing in Sweden: A 3-year follow-up. *Child Abuse and Neglect, 28,* 267–287.

Tauri, J., & Morris, A. (2003). Re-forming justice: The potential of Maori processes. In E. McLaughlin, R. Fergusson, G. Hughes, & L. Westmarland (Eds.), *Restorative justice: Critical issues* (pp. 44–53). Thousand Oaks, CA: Sage.

Taylor, G. (2002). Guilt, shame and shaming. In I. Weijers & A. Duff (Eds.), *Punishing juveniles: Principle and critique* (pp. 179–192). Oxford: Hart.

Tomkins, S. S. (1992). *Affect/imagery/consciousness* (Vol. 4). New York: Springer.

Trimboli, L. (2000). *An evaluation of the NSW Youth Justice Conferencing Scheme.* Sydney, ACT: New South Wales Bureau of Crime Statistics and Research, Attorney General's Department.

Umbreit, M. S. (2000). *Family group conferencing: Implications for crime victims.* Washington, DC: U.S. Department of Justice, Office for Victims of Crime.

Umbreit, M. S., & Zehr, M. (2003). Restorative family group conferences: Differing models and guidelines for practice. In E. McLaughlin, R. Fergusson, G. Hughes, & L. Westmarland (Eds.), *Restorative justice: Critical issues* (pp. 69–75). Thousand Oaks, CA: Sage.

Van Stokkom, B. (2002). Moral emotions in restorative justice conferences: Managing shame, designing empathy. *Theoretical Criminology, 6*(3), 339–360.

Walker, L. (2002). Conferencing: A new approach for juvenile justice in Honolulu. *Federal Probation, 66*(1), 38–43.

Wundersitz, J., & Hetzel, S. (1995). Family conferencing for young offenders: The south Australian experience. In J. Hudson, A. Morris, G. Maxwell, & B. Galaway (Eds.), *Family group conferences: Perspectives on policy and practice* (pp. 111–139). Munsey, NY: Criminal Justice Press.

Young, R. (2001). Just cops doing "shameful" business?: Police-led restorative justice and the lessons of research. In A. Morris & G. Maxwell (Eds.), *Restoring justice for juveniles: Conferences, meditations and circles* (pp. 195–226). Oxford: Hart Publishing.

Young, R., & Goold, B. (2003). Restorative police cautioning in Aylesbury—from degrading to reintegrative shaming ceremonies. In E. McLaughlin, R. Fergusson, G. Hughes, & L. Westmarland (Eds.), *Restorative justice: Critical issues* (pp. 94–104). Thousand Oaks, CA: Sage.

Zernova, M. (2007). *Restorative justice: Ideals and realities.* Hampshire, England: Ashgate.

7. Peacemaking Circles

> *In every one of us there is a deep desire to connect to others in a good way.*
>
> Judge Barry Stuart

> *I'm impressed with the gentleness of the Circle. It arrives at something in such a gentle way.*
>
> Circle participant in an alternative school

*E*verything the power of the world does, it does in the Circle. This sky is round, and I've heard that the Earth is round like a ball, and so are all the stars. The wind, in its greatest power, whirls. Birds make their nest in circles, for theirs is the same religion as ours. The sun comes forth and goes down again in the Circle. The moon does the same, and both around. Even the seasons form a great circle in their changing, and always come back again to where they were. The life of the man is a circle from childhood to childhood, and so it is in everything where power moves. (Neihardt, 1988)

Circles are a metaphor for how the universe operates in that everything is connected and unending. All parts of the circle are equal, since every point on the circle is in exactly the same relation to the center (Pranis, Stuart, & Wedge, 2003). Consequently, all participants, regardless of role or status, age or experience, are of equal importance, with equal voice. Equality is achieved, in part, by inclusivity and maintaining a balance in who and what are represented in the circle, including victim and offender, family members, community representatives, different points of view, and all facets of experience including the spiritual, mental, emotional, and physical dimensions of being. The concept of equality extends to personal worthiness and the need to convey respect and caring to all peoples. Barry Stuart who served as a judge in the Yukon makes the following observation on circles compared to the justice system:

> [A]s long as the discussion focused on whether or not the offender would go to jail, the bad aspects of the crime and the offender were underplayed while the offender's good points were overplayed. People couldn't get beyond discussing the offenders' fate, which left the victim's interests unaddressed.
>
> Once they realized that control over the outcome was to be shared equally, they dropped the debating stance, and we began to explore how to address everyone's interests. Sharing power among equals generated a dialogue

that elicited a more open and truthful exchange. The victim's experience and needs were no longer secondary. The Circle began to ask different questions concerning what to do not only about the offender and the victim but also about the underlying problems that gave rise to the crime. (2003, p. 38)

Circles are built on the recognition that we are all interconnected. Everything we do ripples out to affect others and comes back (Pranis et al., 2003). Therefore, if we leave anyone behind it affects all of us negatively. A case in point is the decision to put someone in prison as a way to get rid of a problem. Rather than solving the problem, this action comes round again in the form of increased violence due to aversive conditioning in prison, high recidivism rates, and public monies allocated to overcrowded prisons rather than education and health. The reality of our connectedness means that as a family or community, we bear some responsibility, when a crime occurs, for the harm that happened. We therefore have an obligation to make things right, including helping those who caused the harm to assume their responsibility. Consequently, we are all in some sense accountable to each other. Moreover, our interconnection is, in effect, a statement that we are all, as human beings, in need of help and that helping others helps us at the same time. Everyone, therefore, benefits from the collective wisdom of everyone in the circle (Pranis, 2005).

Circles are process oriented and process guided. This means that primary attention is given to creating a safe, if not sacred, space for dialogue and implementing practices that create the climate necessary for the work of the circle to proceed. A major practice is the delineation of commonly held values that participants uphold in their conduct in the circle (Pranis, 2007). The use of a talking piece for sharing in the group and decision making by consensus help reduce the potential for dominance or control. Instead of granting power to a leader, the circle requires that participants trust the process and not force its direction or its outcome. Participants therefore participate only as themselves. Participants discover that the use of process means that each circle is different and no one can predict what will happen. Indeed, what emerges is the paradoxical nature of circles (Pranis et al., 2003). They are structured and open, ordered and spontaneous, framed and free, and limited and unlimited. Instead of resolving the paradoxes, participants come to appreciate that the existence of each side allows the existence of the other and that the process of discovery pulls everyone to a new place. Although such outcomes may appear to happen spontaneously, circles are a carefully measured process and will not generate the energy necessary for healing unless the conditions that allow for such a process are thoughtfully preplanned.

Circles are built on four premises (Pranis et al., 2003): (1) Every person wants to be connected to others in a good way. (2) Everyone shares core values that indicate what connecting in a good way means. (3) Connecting

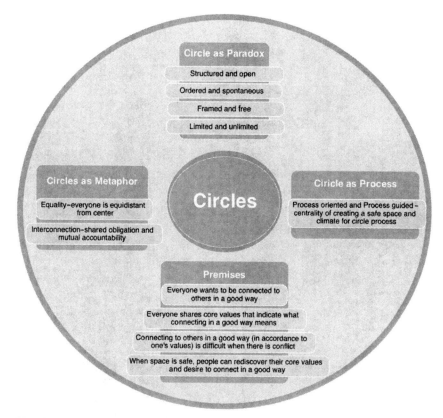

FIGURE 7.1

to others positively and in accordance with one's values is difficult and more so when there are conflicts. (4) When the space is safe, people can rediscover their core values and the deep desire to be positively connected. Collectively, these premises, about the basic human impulse to connect in a good way, call upon circle participants to access their common humanity and bring their best selves to the endeavor. "[T]he Circle is not about sitting in the physical space but about how to be in Circle when you are not in Circle. The meaning of 'being in Circle' has expanded to refer to . . . holding oneself 'in a good way' in one's relationship with others and oneself" (Boyes-Watson, 2002, p. 220). See Figure 7.1 for a pictorial illustration of these aspects of Circles.

This chapter examines the history and development of circles and delineates the attributes of the circle process. Circles, more than any of the other approaches, are explicitly values driven and thus are implicitly fueled by a strong spiritual dimension that shapes members' interactions. Even the values to be employed in the dialogue process are selected by the members and continually referenced, reviewed, and clarified so that the process has integrity and the consensus on values operates as a guide for a co-constructed and communal effort. Circles as a restorative justice approach, therefore, is distinct from VOM and FGC in its continual attention to the details that must be in place and tended in order for the work of the circle to be productive. Concentrating on the circle process is the focus in this chapter in the same way it is in constructing a circle dialogue meeting.

Although circles represent the oldest and the most original form of restorative justice practiced by some indigenous groups, it is less researched than VOM, FGC, and VOD. There are several explanations that account for this development. First, the use of circles, in contrast to the other approaches, has varied and diffuse purposes. They may be employed to address conflicts in schools or neighborhood disputes. They may be preferred for residential treatment as a support system for youth or to respond to the woundedness of parishioners after a clergyperson sexually abused one of them. It may be difficult, therefore, to know what to measure because the purpose and desired outcome are diverse.

Second, although sentencing circles are used for criminal wrongdoing, this practice is limited and often reserved for use with indigenous groups. Consequently, it is difficult to obtain adequate numbers to draw conclusions about the effectiveness of circles or to make comparisons with offenders from similar groups who are handled through traditional court processes.

Third, the principle intent of circles, regardless of their overt goals, is to develop or strengthen the community. This purpose usually requires a period of time and is part of an evolutionary process that can be difficult to assess quantitatively.

Fourth, except for sentencing circles, circles tend to be grassroots efforts that function outside of legislative processes and concerns. Consequently, there is less interest and investment in evaluating their effectiveness. In spite of these realities, anecdotal stories abound both about their effectiveness and the enthusiastic investment of circle members who feel honored to have been part of a vital effort to change the course of others' lives.

HISTORY

Circles derive directly from native traditions that used circles to resolve disputes and conflicts and specifically from the tradition of the talking circle, common among First Nation groups in Canada and Native American peoples in the United States (Coates, Umbreit, & Vos, 2003). This oral tradition was later complimented by the more contemporary practices of dialogue, consensus building, and dispute resolution, which furthered the development of the circle concept (Pranis et al., 2003). Indeed, the feminist movement employed formal circles, as represented by Baldwin in *Calling the Circle*, to explore values and build relationships (Umbreit, 2008). Talking circles within indigenous communities are a form of ceremony, with specific rituals to foster a spiritual connection. Circles, specific to restorative justice, combined the wisdom of the ancient traditions, not the specific ceremony, with these current concepts as a way to respond to harm through a group process that fosters connectedness, consensus, accountability, and healing.

Circles were first introduced into the criminal justice system in 1982 in Yukon, Canada, as an alternate way of sentencing (Stuart & Pranis, 2006). This practice became more publically known when Judge Barry Stewart of the Yukon territorial court convened a sentencing circle in the case of Philip Moses, a 26-year-old chronic offender with 43 prior convictions. As a result of gathering together and dialoguing with Moses' family and friends, Stuart suspended the sentence but ordered two years probation, residence with Moses' family, and alcoholism treatment to which Moses responded successfully (Cayley, 1998). Sentencing circles gained in popularity in the 1990s. Because they incorporated native beliefs and practices, they were more frequently employed in areas that had a significant aboriginal population.

The circle process also gained momentum in Minnesota under the leadership of Kay Pranis, Restorative Justice Planner for the Minnesota Department of Corrections who used circles to address staff conflict. Indeed, corrections practitioners found other applications including the use of circles to facilitate community reentry for offenders (Pranis, 2005; Walker, Sakai, & Brady, 2006) and to improve the effectiveness of community supervision for people on probation. Pranis et al. (2003) brought the theoretical and practical thinking about circles together in their seminal book, *Peacemaking Circles: From Crime to Community.*

Circles have been used in non–corrections-based settings as well. Roca, a youth development organization in Boston, embraced circles, for example, as an ongoing practice to address Roca's functioning as an agency, as a way to teach young people an alternative communication method for dealing with violence, pain, and suffering and for community peacebuilding (Boyes-Watson, 2008). Circles are increasingly employed in the classroom as a tool for preventing violence and containing conflict as well as addressing management issues in schools. They have also been effective for dealing with conflicts in families, workplaces, and communities.

Regardless of the context in which circles are used, the purpose of circles is to create a safe, nonjudgmental place to engage in a sharing of authentic personal reactions and feelings that are owned by each individual and acknowledged by others, related to a conflict, crisis, issue, or even to reactions to a speaker or film (Umbreit, 2008). In every setting, circles are fashioned so that community is central, and a process is co-constructed so that it has structural integrity.

Slumped in his chair, legs stretched out, arms folded, and head down, Jaime listened as the feather was passed around the Circle. People were talking about him or his crime. He heard anger, but mostly he heard people asking him in many different ways: Why? Why had he spent so many years lost to alcohol and crime? When was he going to change? What would it take for him to change? Did he not care about the people he hurt? He was now twenty-one; when was he going to grow up? When was he going to take responsibility for his life?

Jaime . . . was nervous, very nervous. He knew the feather would soon be passed to him. Soon he would have to talk and answer many questions. In court, anger, hostility, and a silent resignation to the process enabled him to slip through without being involved. Not here.

The feather came to him. He held the feather, twirling it in his hands. He passed, "I don't know what to say. I'm here because I want to change. That's it."

He passed the feather to John with a desperate hope that John might answer all the questions. . . . John held the feather but didn't speak. Jamie worried that John might pass the feather back to him. John reached into his pouch and pulled out another feather. This feather was hardly recognizable as an eagle feather. It was twisted and large gaps suggested strands were missing. It was bedraggled, unkempt, and obviously not cared for—not a sacred object. John held up the feather for everyone to see.

"This is an ugly feather. I don't know when I've seen such an ugly feather. This feather reminds me of myself when I was running wild and crazy. I was missing many strands, it seemed. I was twisted up inside, full of booze and anger, full of not caring for anyone, not even for myself. I was an ugly feather with lots of gaps in my life. I want everyone to see up close how ugly this feather really is, so I'm going to pass it around while I talk. Hold this feather for a while. Look at it, feel it, and see how ugly and uncared for it is."

As the feather passed around the Circle, John spoke about his youth and broken life . . . By the time John finished the story of his youth, the old, ugly feather had been around the Circle. Jaime held it for a moment, stroked it, and passed it to John. "Hold up the old feather," John said, "Now look how beautiful this old, ugly feather has become.". . .

Still holding up the feather, John said, "This feather is like me. Once I was ugly, mad, and twisted up by anger. There were big gaps in my life. Many important parts of living a good life were missing. Then Agnes and several others came into my life. They held me, cared for me, and changed me like this feather. That's what we all have to do with Jamie. If all of us touch him with caring hands, we can help him become like this feather. Everything is beautiful, is sacred. It takes caring to bring out beauty, to make someone realize they are sacred, and to make us realize they are sacred. So I'm asking all of us tonight to touch Jamie's life, to care for him, to bring out his beauty, his sacred spirit." (Pranis et al., 2003, pp. 3–6)

ATTRIBUTES OF THE CIRCLE PROCESS

Circles are explicitly values driven and built on a foundation of shared principles and circle keeping elements. Collectively, these components create the safety necessary for victims, offenders, and community members to express their thoughts and feelings without being diminished or harmed (Pranis et al., 2003). Rather than being imposed from the outside, these aspects of the process are either selected or constructed by circle members and exist as commitments made through consensus agreements. As such, the communal establishment of a process that builds a baseline of safety and the mutual responsibility for tending the process become nonverbal agreements among participants to honor each other, protect the space for the work, and engage in ways that are constructive. Indeed, the presence of these elements reminds participants of their promises to each other both inside and outside of the circle.

Values and Principles

The values that underline the circle process serve as a guide, with the goal being to learn to act in value-consistent ways (Pranis et al., 2003). Moreover, values help move participants beyond positional thinking by calling forth the best that is us—values that are essential to health, equality, and just relationships (Boyack, Bowen, & Marshall, 2004). The delineation of shared values, therefore, provides a compass for addressing conflicts in a different way. Values are not static. The ones selected for each circle are determined by the participants and are returned to for clarification, again and again, when in doubt about what to do or how to do it. Consequently, values and understanding their meaning grow over time.

There is no one set of values. However, certain values are core values and are most frequently named by participants as essential. They include respect, honesty, trust, humility, sharing, inclusivity, empathy, courage, forgiveness, and love (Pranis et al., 2003). These values are interdependent and reinforce one another. Values grow out of the question, "If we had a good process in the community to resolve conflict, what would you want the characteristics of that process to be?" They also grow out of the question, "What do I need to do to act out of my best self?" In circle trainings, Pranis elicits each person's value and what it means and from those, by consensus, develops the list of shared values for the group.

For example, the value of humility grows from recognizing our own limitations and, consequently, pulls us to focus more on discovering the wider truth than on advancing our own needs (Pranis et al., 2003). The value of courage doesn't mean the absence of fear but the ability to acknowledge fears and go forward in spite of them. These values and their meanings become the values standard for the group. They guide how to "be" in group. Because they are collectively determined, participants experience a reduced sense of authorship and social distance, which otherwise allows indifference to the pain of others. A circle keeper commented on the importance of spending time on the values.

> After an opening reading and some calming breathing, I spoke a long time about the talking piece. I had the feeling that the talking piece was going to hold this Circle together—and it did. We each wrote a value on a [paper] plate and put

the plates in the middle of the Circle. People referred several times to the values as well as to their commitment to the talking piece and to hearing each other out. I spoke several times of people's patience—a value someone had laid out. On one occasion, someone said, "I'm just glad I put "self control" in the middle there, because otherwise I wouldn't be using it." (Pranis et al., 2003, p. 137)

Principles give direction in answering questions about how to design and run circles with integrity. They help build the process by keeping the means and ends congruent. They also help translate shared values into practice. Pranis et al. (2003) have identified 13 principles.

1. Circles call us to act on our personal values. Consequently, participants need to regularly check their thoughts, decisions, and conduct against the shared values.
2. Circles include all interests. A broad participation increases the potential for a wide base of support and innovative, community-sensitive solutions.
3. Circles are easily accessible to all. The circle process must be transparent and barriers to participation, for example, baby sitting and expenses, must be removed.
4. Circles offer everyone an equal opportunity to participate. Circles are radically democratic based on the belief that each participant has thoughts, feelings, and experiences that lend balance to the circle.
5. Involvement in circles is voluntary. The circle affirms the participants' ability to choose for themselves including that the offender can always elect to return to court.
6. In circles, everyone participates directly as themselves. People are more likely to take responsibility for agreements when they participate directly.
7. Circles are guided by a shared vision. A shared vision developed through consensus becomes a force that unites and directs the community.
8. Circles are designed by those who use them. Circles are participant driven, and the community shapes its own process for each case.
9. Circles are flexible in accommodating unique needs and interests. Circles are responsive to the situation and adapt the process to fit the conflict by asking, "For whom, when, how often, and for what purpose?"
10. Circles take a holistic approach. Dialogues are not confined to the immediate issues but recognize that crime occurs in a context and problems must be tracked to their roots.
11. Circles maintain respect for all. Respect permeates the circle process that grows out of hearing, in a deep way, what others are saying.
12. Circles invite spiritual presence. By inviting all dimensions of people into the circle, for example, emotional, spiritual, cognitive and physical,

the engagement of their wholeness opens participants to a spiritual sense of each other.
13. Circles foster accountability to others and to the process. Circles inspire accountability through value-based action and connections formed within the circle.

Values and principles form an inner frame for the circle dialogue (Pranis et al., 2003). Once values are intentionally named and defined, they function from behind unless there is a need for reinstatement and change. Both values and the thirteen principles, therefore, form an implicit support that serves to guide and steer the process without being seen.

Circle Keeping Elements

The outer supports of a circle process consist of five structural elements, the purpose of which is to create a safe space for connection (Pranis, 2005; Pranis et al., 2003). Those elements include ritual, behavioral guidelines, a talking piece, circle keeping, and consensus decision making. (See Figure 7.2.)

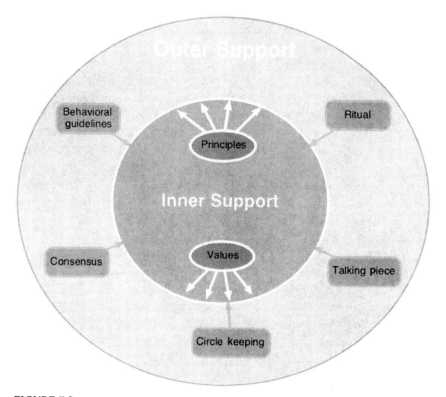

FIGURE 7.2

Ritual

Some type of ceremony is used to open and close the circle. The opening ceremony sets the time and space for the circle apart from the usual hustle and bustle of the day. It establishes the tone for the circle and moves participants to deeper or sacred places internally, where participants can experience themselves and others in different ways. It centers the person psychically and shifts his or her perspective inward from head to heart and from a focus on outer concerns to unseen forces that provide a sense of the universal connectedness of all that is. It fosters a sense of community and connection with others. Within Native American communities, ritual is well exemplified in smudging, a ritual that consists of the burning of sage, cedar, and sweet grass to cleanse a person of any bad feelings, negative thoughts, bad spirits or negative energy prior to entering the sacred realm. At AMICUS, a juvenile residential program for serious and chronic female juvenile offenders, approximately 40% of the clientele are Native American. Smudging ceremonies are characteristically used to open many of the support circles used extensively by the agency as a way to help participants be actively "present" (Gordon, 2004).

The selection of the opening ceremony is based, in part, on the purpose of the circle and its cultural context. Examples of themes to be considered include cleansing or purifying, welcoming, and a sense of possibilities and hopefulness. Ceremonies may include reading poetry or a meaningful passage, lighting candles, listening to music, and sharing something of personal meaning (Pranis et al., 2003). Ceremonies can also engage participants more actively. Roca uses an opening ritual where each person in turn asks themselves, "Am I my brother's keeper?" The answer is, "Yes I am" (Pranis, personal communication, June 19, 2008). Openings can also be light and fun. Participants can take turns introducing themselves as an animal or object or pantomime the activities they did in the morning before coming to the circle. The goal is to move people into a safe and encompassing space where they can share personal stories, express emotions, take risks, and be together in ways that are different from how they engaged before the circle was called.

The closing ceremony marks the transition to ordinary reality. It might include comments that honor the dialogue, people's participation and effort, or expressions of appreciation. Creating a sense of closure may also involve a celebration of accomplishments, a brief reading, group exercise, or question. In going back to the outside world, participants may also need to address what they are returning to. Above all else, the closing ritual inspires gratitude and helps participants to value the good that was achieved.

The selection of a ritual must be made with sensitivity to the participants. What is meaningful to some may be threatening to others. Staff from Roca report that in one circle, recent arrivals from Sudan had a negative reaction to the burning of sage at the opening ritual. "Having fled a region where religious conflict led to terrible violence, these young men feared any connection to any particular religion in their new home and immediately got up and left the room" (Boyes-Watson, 2008, p. 87).

Behavioral Guidelines

The guidelines of the circle are the commitments and promises participants make to one another about how they will behave in the circle. They provide the means for participants to come together in a good way (Pranis et al., 2003). Guidelines may be generated by the participants or selected and adapted by consensus from a preestablished list. In either case, participants are guided by what they want for themselves from others. Some beginning questions might be "What do you need in order to feel safe enough to express the thoughts and feelings that are important to you?" "How would you like to feel when you leave the circle and what would it take for you to get you there?" These types of questions elicit the participants' ideas and allow them to have a say in deciding what the circle process will be and how to make the circle safe for them.

Some guidelines circles have used include the following: we will respect each other's time and space; we will consider our ancestors, future relatives, and those unable to join us; and we will remember that we are all teachers and learners (Greenwood, 2005). Guidelines are not rules but rather are elastic and rooted in each person's own values. They help put the circles' shared values into action (Pranis, 2005). There are four guidelines, however, that are considered essential to dialoguing and setting the parameters for how participants will act.

1. Listen from the heart (Greenwood, 2005; Pranis et al., 2003; Umbreit, 2003). This guideline clarifies the conditions that allow participants to hear each other fully. It invites people to be attentive to what others are saying and sincere in receiving what is being shared. Instead of responding or reacting internally, participants recognize that experiencing what a person feels puts them in the position of bearing witness to another person's life experience and requires deep, compassionate listening.
2. Speak from the heart (Pranis et al., 2003; Umbreit, 2003). This guideline asks participants to talk from a place of honesty, to share their own journey, and to use their own true stories as their point of reference. It reminds participants not to be philosophical or abstract but to share feelings and state simply about how events have affected them. It also asks them to share feelings in respectful ways, honor differences with others, and consider how others might experience their words.

3. Remain in the circle (Pranis et al., 2003). This guideline requests that participants not leave the circle even when it feels hardest to stay. Because circles deal with conflict, emotions, volatile issues, and personal stories, participants need the reassurance that others will stay to work things through to the extent possible. Timely breaks assist in staying in because they provide an emotional breather and a chance to decompress from the intensity.
4. Honor confidentiality (Pranis et al., 2003). This guideline lets participants share freely and trust that what is said will stay confidential and with the circle participants and not be misused later. Confidentiality may have to be breached if a participant is legally required to report to the state information that involves personal or public safety. The circle can agree that this person will leave the circle if someone wants to reveal a crime or does not want to press charges. Confidentiality is also different for sentencing circles because the law requires that sentencing be a public process. In some instances, circle participants have decided to keep certain information, such as personal stories, confidential. Regardless of the exceptions, circles need to discuss confidentiality up front and before personal sharing begins.

In one circle, the power of the shared guideline to be honest startled one of the participants. Joe was a repeat offender and approached the circle with the same cynicism with which he approached the criminal justice system. He had rarely been honest with himself or others. When he received the talking piece, he passed it on with only a grunt. But the honesty and courage of others to speak their truths broke through his defenses. When he finally spoke, Joe discovered the power of his own honesty: "I did not believe what came out of me. I never had talked in court before. [In the circle,] I did not expect the reaction either in me or in them" (Pranis et al., 2003, p. 36).

Like values, guidelines need to be constructed at the start and also reviewed along the way. Participants may need gentle reminders or tactful conversations during breaks to keep everyone mindful. When guidelines are held thoughtfully with patience and tolerance, a climate of "enforcing of the law" is avoided. Moreover, participants tend to take a more active role in helping others and, consequently, share the leadership.

The Talking Piece

Circles grow out of the tradition of the Native American talking circle. An object called a talking stick gave each speaker the courage to speak the truth. Other members of the circle were to listen without interruption and focus on understanding the message. The talking piece could be a feather, walking stick, braid of sweet grass, a rock, or a pipe.

The talking piece builds on the tradition of the talking stick. It regulates dialogue through an object of special meaning or symbolism to the group. The talking piece is carefully selected by the circle keeper to foster respect for listening and reflection. A talking piece might be a symbol for a powerful story or tradition, reflect a value from the community where the participants live, or be a sign of peace or hope. It might be a natural object such as a rock or sea shell. A broken snail shell was used in a circle as a metaphor for our own brokenness, with the suggestion that the brokenness enabled participants to see the lovely, delicate inner spiral of the shell (Pranis et al., 2003). An old key to the cells in a prison was used for the staff as a metaphor for their shared work and for unlocking the doors to encourage more open talking (Pranis, personal communication, June 19, 2008).

Circles follow certain conventions in the use of a talking piece. The talking piece is passed clockwise from person to person around the circle signaling the opportunity to speak. When a participant receives the talking piece, that person may speak without interruption, hold the talking piece in silence, or simply pass it in silence to the next person (Greenwood, 2005; Umbreit, 2008). In one case, an elder simply held the feather for a while to create moments of silence for the young offender to prepare to speak. "I am holding on to this feather to give you time to find your voice, so you can speak from the heart. We're all here to help you . . . I know you have a good heart. Let us hear from your good heart" (Pranis et al., 2003, p. 97). Besides being passed consecutively, the circle keeper may place the talking piece in the center of the circle and allow free conversation after everyone has had a chance to speak.

The talking piece develops listening skills (Pranis et al., 2003). Participants have to wait to speak until the talking piece comes to them. This waiting brings deeper listening, and genuine reflection may change the way people respond when their turn comes. Jane, a community member whose friend's cabin had been broken into by Jake, was furious. Jake's father was initially angry in return, but his attitude changed. "I was ready to jump down her throat for speaking about my son in such a way. But as I waited to speak, I listened to people reaching out . . . to help my son deal with this in a good way. I spoke in a way that surprised me, and I think I set a better example for my son to speak" (Pranis et al., 2003, p. 102). Because of listening, participants like Jake's father may find that they have unexpected thoughts and feelings. They may find themselves moved by what is shared by others so that by the time they speak they are moved to more personal levels of sharing.

The use of a talking piece slows the pace, which relaxes participants so they become more thoughtful (Greenwood, 2005; Pranis et al., 2003). Because the talking piece prevents one-to-one debating, attacking, or domination, the slower pace fosters deeper conversation, more careful listening, and thoughtful expression (Umbreit, 2008). The slowness also gives participants time to modulate the expression of deep emotions.

Besides conveying orderliness and the time to be reflective, the passing of the talking piece sets the stage for each person to speak and to speak their truth honestly, calmly, and authentically (Pranis, personal communication, June 19, 2008). As such, each verbal contribution becomes an offering. Each monologue becomes an opportunity to be true, to speak in alignment with their best selves. In this public forum, participants tend to listen to themselves as others listen to them. All of this gives the talking piece more and more meaning.

Because the talking piece sends the implicit message that each person has something important to contribute, it ensures that all voices are heard, thereby affirming equality. Indeed, it opens the same space for everyone with no distinction of age, gender, education, or status. It also cultivates the conditions for consensus, which are built on each person having a voice in the decision making.

Circle Keeping

In circles, all participants share in the responsibility for establishing and maintaining a healthy process. One person serves as a guide or advisor for the healing process, often referred to as the circle keeper. This person is sometimes referred to as the circle facilitator. This person is a servant leader who is trusted and respected and chosen because of his or her personal qualities and ability to be a clear vessel for the flow of the circle (Pranis et al., 2003). Besides being humble and impartial, the circle keeper or facilitator is caring and accepting, nonviolent in word and behavior, skilled in listening, patient, flexible, creative, and positive. He or she is able to speak wisely and strongly while addressing issues with compassion. Most important, the circle keeper is personally grounded and centered.

The circle keeper sets the tone for the circle conveying a calm, unhurried, and reflective mood; a respect for differing views; and an appreciation of each person's efforts (Pranis et al., 2003). The circle keeper also works to establish a supportive environment based on openness that includes permission for the expression of spiritual and philosophical values (Greenwood, 2005).

Facilitating responsibilities include making arrangements for certain participants to welcome others, the preparation of refreshments, and the creation of a physical environment conducive to dialogue, for example, no interruptions, music to set the tone, and so on. During the circle, the circle keeper or facilitator maintains the focus by offering or asking questions for a round of responses, decides how to use the talking piece, and summarizes after a round of responses or before breaks, noting any common ground or progress made (Pranis et al., 2003). The circle keeper calls timely breaks, promotes brainstorming and the encouragement of new ideas, and offers guidance, for example, resources, while also furthering the circle's autonomy (Greenwood, 2005; Pranis et al., 2003).

Besides being servant leaders, circle keepers are members of the circle and therefore participate as participants too. Although circle keepers strive to be unobtrusive and take care not to alter the course of any conversation, they are also purposeful about their participation. For example, circle keepers often go first in answering the questions that they have asked the group in order to show that it is safe to be vulnerable (Pranis et al., 2003). When there has been a round that is focused on expressing views or opinions, circle keepers may go last to lend balance and show respect for all sides. In their summaries, they may use the space to affirm others and value the group's contributions. If necessary, they may raise the talking piece or give a signal to convey the need to move on if, for example, someone is taking too much time.

Although circle keepers guide the circle, much of their effort centers on what needs to be done to convene the circle or to follow up on the decisions or agreements made by the circle. Consequently, much of their work is done outside and before and after the circle. Finally, circle keepers are mindful of the need to take time for their own centering before and during circle breaks (Greenwood, 2005) and to remain cognizant of the fact that they are not responsible for the outcome of the circle.

Consensus Decision Making

In circles of different types, the need to reach agreements occurs at various points in the process, including the selection of values and guidelines for running the group, the determination of whether to accept an applicant for a sentencing circle, and the sentence to be served on an offender. In one circle, participants responded to a circle keeper's assignment to give a word or phrase that helped define consensus. Their replies included reluctant agreement, come out of support, unity, shared leadership, individuals coming together, general agreement, and understanding. When asked "What makes for consensus?," participants gave the following answers: flexibility, cooperation, trust, listening, compromise, not being stuck on your own idea, letting go, going to an uncomfortable place, and teamwork.

As implied in these responses, consensus decision making requires wholeminded solutions that incorporate everyone's interests as much as possible. The goal is to build something that is larger than any one person's preconceived ideas can imagine (Pranis et al., 2003). Yet, each person's interests must be integrated into the decision for consensus decision making to work. Consequently, consensus decision making is more democratic than majority rule because of the requirement that every interest must be attended to

(Pranis et al., 2003). Procedurally, areas of disagreement must be identified and given serious consideration. In the end, consensus decision making does not call for enthusiasm but expects that each person live with the decision and support its implementation (Pranis, 2005; Pranis et al., 2003). Clearly, the probability of reaching consensus is increased when participants feel that their concerns have been recognized and carefully considered by the circle.

Circles allow for consensus decision making to be more meaningfully attached to the deeper issues that emerge when the offender's wrongdoing is addressed. George was arrested for possessing drugs after he drove his car off the road. His nonresponsiveness to circle members made them frustrated and impatient. George responded by saying, "I don't care much about death. Dying doesn't bother me. I just care about having as much fun as I can."

> The dialogue abruptly changed. Participants spoke to his indifference not just to them but to life itself. Many remembered their own teenage angst and were now hearing similar attitudes from their own children. The new focus produced a very different outcome. The ultimate consensus targeted neither his dangerous driving nor his [drug use] but rather the underlying causes; namely, his indifference to life and hence his pursuit of reckless, even dangerous thrills. The sentence of the Circle, inspired in large part by George himself, was to complete a twelve-week hospice training. He did that and much more. (Pranis et al., 2003, pp. 78–79)

The requirement for consensus achieves several goals. Participants have a greater stake in making an agreement work when they have genuinely participated in building it (Stuart & Pranis, 2006). Moreover, their shared ownership of the decision fosters a shared accountability not just to the plan but to all other participants who were part of making it. Finally, the process of consensus decision making generates more than an agreement. It creates new respect and understandings between participants. It also forms new relationships between them.

The five elements of ritual, behavioral guidelines, the talking piece, circle keeping, and consensus decision making provide a format to engage participants in respectful, nonjudgmental deep listening and in sharing authentic personal reactions and feelings without interruption. Along with values and principles, these elements, when used, establish a self-governing process (Pranis et al., 2003) and offer participants a spirit of cooperation and collaboration; the chance to work through differences, difficult issues, and painful experiences; the opportunity to make decisions together; the opening to repair, heal, and build relationships in the sense of community; and the prospect of planning for the future (Greenwood, 2005). These elements are depicted graphically in Figure 7.3.

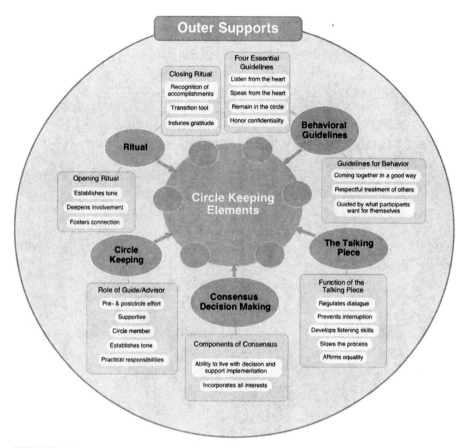

FIGURE 7.3

THE CIRCLE PROCESS

The circle process requires planning and preparation for bringing people together. It unfolds by following a flexible set of procedures. Core to the process is the sharing of stories related to the purpose of the circle. Accounts of the critical events that produced the harm and related thoughts and feelings are central to the circle's work, but participants other than the victim and offender may share stories from related experiences as a way to teach or as a backdrop or context for their contributions. The circle process also uses community both by drawing on the community that already exists for participation or resources and by building community through participants' experiences of being in the circle.

Planning and Preparation

The amount of time spent in planning and preparation varies according to the purpose of the circle. In sentencing circles, for example, there may be preparatory circles used so that everyone is ready to meet for the sentencing. Sarah had pulled a knife on the principal at her school and was subsequently arrested and placed at a long-term residential program. She had two circles of support with her school liaison before she felt ready to meet with the principal and others at the school, including some teachers who had made good connections with her (Gordon, 2004).

The calling of a community circle to address conflict may require individual meetings with each possible attendee. Indeed, planning and preparation usually mean separate meetings to invite potential participants to the circle, to hear their experiences, and to describe the purpose of the circle and the process (Greenwood, 2005). The circle keeper, for example, may explain that the purpose of the circle is to bring people together to work through and attempt to resolve the trouble; to come to terms with and resolve, to the extent possible, a crime that has occurred; to make peace with the past, and so on. In describing the purpose, the circle keeper can introduce basic concepts of restorative dialogue, for example, a focus on harms, the ability to deal directly with what has happened, sharing from the heart, and hearing all possible views. Participants are helped to weigh the possible benefits and risks of circles as part of considering whether they want to go forward (Greenwood, 2005). If they decide to participate, then they need to be prepared for the experience, including ascertaining their hopes and concerns, what they might choose to share in the circle, what questions they may want to ask of others, what possibilities exist for resolution or restitution, and what additional people they might want to include.

Outline of the Circle Process

Although the content and outcome of each circle is unique, the process itself follows a commonly used sequence of activities. Participants sit in a circle with no tables. In the middle of the circle is a centerpiece, which serves as a metaphor for the incident that led to the circle or the work to be accomplished and a reminder to the participants of the space they have entered. A small sculpture of people joined in a circle through their arms, a compact disc carrying case to symbolize what was taken in a robbery, and a patchwork quilt to show that diverse elements can coexist and enhance each other are examples of centerpieces used in circles.

The circle begins with a welcome from the circle keeper and a request for each participant to introduce himself or herself followed by brief comments about the purpose of the circle, the use of the talking piece and the circle keeper's role as a neutral guide (Pranis et al., 2003). The opening ritual may be part of the circle keeper's initial comments or interlaced as an exercise with the participants' brief introductions. As part of the orientation, the circle keeper invites a discussion, using the talking piece, about personal values to guide the work followed by reflection and consensus about the guidelines for dialogue.

The circle keeper then poses a question to reflect on that is often related to participants' needs and interests and passes the talking piece to the person on the left, going counterclockwise (Pranis et al., 2003; Umbreit, 2008). It is important not to start by talking about the issues that brought participants to the circle because the circle must first create a space that is emotionally safe (Pranis et al., 2003). The groundwork is done by first delineating guidelines and then asking questions designed to elicit trust like "What is a personal life experience that was pivotal to whom you are today?," "What do you appreciate about your community?," or "What do you hope will happen here and what do you wish for this gathering?" (Greenwood, 2005). The next round of passing the talking piece begins with sharing information about what happened to bring participants together, what has been done, and what they are experiencing. For example, the circle keeper may say, "I invite each of you to share with the circle what happened, what your experience was, how you felt about it, how it affects you now" (Greenwood, 2005, p. 7).

The questions for subsequent rounds are based on participants' answers and, based on the circle keeper's judgment about group process, may or may not continue with a formal passing of the talking piece. Ultimately, the circle keeper moves to explore options in response to the issue that brought people to the circle. Participants focus on what can be done to make things right, to promote healing, or implement change. Depending on the purpose of the circle, this phase may result in consensus about a plan or agreement along with possible follow-up if needed. Agreements may be recorded on paper and signed by participants who receive copies (Greenwood, 2005). The circle then moves toward closing with a focus on final thoughts and feelings, the good achieved, and everyone's efforts as circle members. The circle keeper may initiate a question for closing comments including an invitation for participants to reflect on their experience in the circle followed by the closing ritual (Pranis et al., 2003).

The size of the circle can vary from approximately 10 to up to 70 people (Boyes-Watson, 2008). The typical circle length is between 2 and 3 hours with breaks but usually shorter in schools (Coates et al., 2003). With large groups and limited time, chairs can be arranged with a speaker circle in the center surrounded by a support circle that offers brief comments or questions (Greenwood, 2005). Although circles follow a similar process, procedures are flexible and meant to conform to the needs of participants and the purpose of the circle. In more complex cases, many additional circles are often required.

TYPES OF CIRCLES

Different types of circles may modify the circle process depending on the purpose of the circle and who participates. Some circles function as before or after adjuncts to a primary circle, some circles require more than one meeting, and some circles include criminal justice officials.

Sentencing Circles

On May 7, 2002 a circle sentencing hearing was convened for a 28-year-old Aboriginal male offender. He had previously been convicted of driving under the influence of alcohol while . . . resisting police at time of arrest. When police attended the scene, they were abused. Further, the offender head-butted the police car and threatened suicide. Instead of arresting the offender they took him to his maternal grandmother who agreed to look after him. As the police were leaving the scene the offender spat on the window of the police vehicle.

A further assault occurred when he was on bail . . . During the course of the [circle] proceedings, the offender's solicitor began by explaining that the offender suffered from depression, alcohol abuse, and substance abuse to which one of the community representatives of the circle replied, "We know about his childhood. We've known him since he was born . . . ." Further subjective features of the case revealed that the offender was a childhood victim of domestic violence. He suffers from a psychiatric illness as a result of brain damage following a brutal assault. He had a significant criminal record including seven convictions for offenses involving violence . . .

Later [during the proceedings] the reason for the offender's animosity towards the police emerged. The offender had spoken of two occasions where the police were reluctant to assist him. One incident involved a gun pointed at his head and a second when he had been brutally beaten by two bouncers at a local hotel. The offender considered the police did nothing to protect him when he needed help.

OFFENDER: *The police never done anything for me, I've rung them and they haven't done anything for me. I feel like I've no rights whatsoever. I got hit over the head with a bar stool and they did nothing for me.*

SOLICITOR: *A person was charged, but the case dismissed:*

[Police] VICTIM: *Look, cops have baggage too. I've policed for 15 years and I don't have a heavy hand. My dealings with you have probably not been a good relationship, but I was giving him a lift home.*

[Community] REPRESENTATIVE 4: *I was a hot head as a young bloke, I haven't fallen in love with the Police force. You get good police and bad police, but you have to accept that they have a difficult job.*

[Community] REPRESENTATIVE 3: *Previous assault on you by others was not by the police, you shouldn't take it out on all the police.*

[Community] REPRESENTATIVE 4: *You can't dwell on the past for other injustices.*

[Police] VICTIM: *You are an angry man, you should get to appreciate that not all cops are a problem for you. You showed considerable respect for your [Mom]. I thought it was a huge imposition on her having regard to your intoxication, we were only too happy to take you to hospital but you didn't want to go.*

VICTIM SUPPORT: *We always take injured to hospital*

[Some time later]

PROSECUTOR: *You were a danger to the police. Parliament has recognized that police are a special class of victim. Police don't enjoy being vulnerable*

OFFENDER: *I'm sorry, I'm sorry to you and I'm sorry for my [Mom].*

[Police] VICTIM: *I accept your apology.*

[Traditional handshake taken in center of circle]

Three months after sentencing, the Aboriginal Project Officer presented a progress report . . . the report was very positive indicating that the offender's life had changed for the better. His grandmother reported that she was pleased with his progress and that he assisted her around the house. He remained drug and alcohol free. He had completed 120 hours of community service. He . . . was enrolled in a computer course. He was involved with organizing a cultural program to teach local Aboriginal youth traditional dance and was working towards recording local Aboriginal sacred sites. As part of his community service, the offender took clients of [a residential facility] on bush walks, informed them about local Aboriginal culture, resulting in employment prospects at the . . . [facility].

The offender appreciated receiving a second chance by not being sent to jail as this help him gain a little more faith in the criminal justice system. He also appreciated being dealt with by people he knew and respected, who demonstrated they cared about him and who assisted him in determining his future . . . The offender's community service involved him passing his Aboriginal cultural knowledge onto other Aboriginal people. The sentence places a strong value on the use of Aboriginal culture as a strong reinforcing element in the healing of the offender. (Potas, Smart, Brignell, Thomas, & Lawrie, 2003, pp. 16–20)

A sentencing circle (see Figure 7.4) is a community-directed process in partnership with the criminal justice system (Pranis, 2005). All of those affected by a crime are included in deciding the appropriate sentencing plan. Referrals may come from the police, judges, or probation officers. Participants in a circle could include, at a minimum, the offender, the offenders family, the victim and victim supporters, community members, and professionals from the system including the judge, prosecutor, defense counsel, and possibly a probation officer, social worker, or police (Pranis et al., 2003). Although the role of the judge is

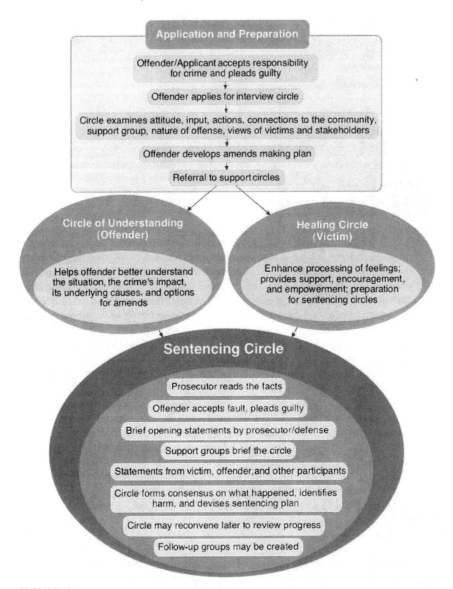

FIGURE 7.4

somewhat uncertain and variable within the circle process itself, the judge, with input from the circle, pronounces the actual sentence (Dignan, 2005). Because circle sentencing is a court hearing, the circle hearing is open to the public, and a record is made of the proceedings (Lilles, 2002). The sentencing decision is subject to appeal or reviews in the same manner as any other court decision.

To be considered for a circle process, the offender or applicant must first accept full responsibility for the crime and enter a guilty plea prior to making application for an interview circle (Pranis et al., 2003). This circle then examines the offender's attitude, input, and actions; his connection to the community; community resources and the strength of the offender's support group; the nature of the offense; the victim's view; and the views of the other stakeholders to see if he is suitable (Stuart, 1996). If the offender's application is accepted, the circle asks him to develop a plan for amends making and personal change (Lilles, 2002).

The victim is referred to a healing circle and the offender to a circle of understanding to prepare them for the sentencing circle (Pranis, 2005). These antecedent circles draw on support people who are willing to become involved, offer resources, and help monitor agreements that come out of the circle. The circle of understanding helps the offender and others better understand the situation, the crime's impact, its underlying causes, and the options for amends. Membership in the circle of healing is limited to the victim's choices. This circle allows for more in-depth exploration of what happened, what may have led up to the crime, or what happened afterward. Besides helping the victim to process feelings, the healing circle provides support, encouragement, and empowerment as well as preparing the victim for the upcoming meeting. The victim may elect to participate directly or through a representative, the formal court, only after sentencing, or not at all (Lilles, 2002; Pranis et al., 2003). These circles can meet regularly for weeks or months out of respect for each person's level of readiness.

At the sentencing circle, the prosecutor reads the facts establishing the charges, the offender accepts fault, and a guilty plea is formally entered (Pranis et al., 2003). The prosecutor and defense counsel may be asked to make brief opening statements. Support groups brief the circle, and then the circle is open for statements from the victim, offender, and other participants. If the preconference screening and preparation process works well, the sentencing circle becomes a recognition of what the offender is already doing and a chance for the victim and the offender to tell their stories (Bazemore & Griffiths, 2003). The circle moves to formulate a consensus about what happened, to identify the harm caused, and to devise an appropriate sentencing plan. Plans are often lengthy and detailed and may include attendance at treatment programs, restitution, and involvement in community projects and cultural rituals if aboriginal groups are involved (Lilles, 2002). The circle may reconvene several weeks or months later to review the offender's progress and make any necessary changes to the plan. Community volunteers may create follow-up groups to support the offender's compliance and help him turn his life around.

Other Types of Circles

Sentencing circles are multistage and refer to the entirety of the process including the actual sentencing. Other types of circles usually refer to one specific gathering (Praniset al., 2003). Their names reflect their function. Some of the common circles include the following:

Talking circles bring people together to talk about an issue. Some examples are what it takes to leave gangs, racism in the community, and responses to a new school policy. *Conflict circles* are held to address difficulties in a particular relationship and include others that are affected by the relationship. These are carefully planned events so that participants are prepared to deal with the underlying conflict. *Support circles* offer encouragement and support to someone facing a challenge or going through a personal transition such as losing a job or reintegrating into community after prison. *Healing circles* provide the opportunity to tell ones' story of trauma or loss where others serve as empathic witnesses for one another in order to provide emotional support and nourishment. *Organizational circles* are used for organization concerns including brainstorming sessions, strategic planning, and management supervision.

APPLICATION OF CIRCLE TYPES

Circles, regardless of type, are often referred to as peacemaking circles. This nomenclature refers to the fact that circles do not make peace but give participants opportunities to find a way to peacefully interact (Stuart & Pranis, 2006). Hence, the larger aim of circles is to bring peace by building communities (Pranis et al., 2003). Peacemaking circles are used in a variety of ways by different groups. The Methodist Church uses circles to work through congregational conflict. Some child welfare agencies use circles to help youth in foster care transition from their dependence on the state and move toward independent living when they reach 18 (Stuart & Pranis, 2006). Prisons have begun using restorative circles to help inmates draft a plan for reentry, reconcile with those harmed by their past behavior, and find ways to meet other needs for a successful life (Walker et al., 2006). In Minnesota, circles are being used by people who are chronically on probation. At Roca in Boston, staff employ a wide variety of circle types for reaching inner city youth and guiding them as they transition into adulthood (Boyes-Watson, 2008). Circles are also being used by communities. After 18 months of study, the South St. Paul Restorative Justice Council determined to humanize the justice system and created a sentencing circle process with community members to deal with a wide variety of cases referred by the police and judges (Coates et al., 2003).

Circles have been used extensively by schools to resolve issues of truancy, conflict, crime, and suspensions as well as preventatively so that concerns are raised at an early stage before they escalate in conflict (Amstutz & Mullet, 2005). Besides the fact that schools are a microcosm for how we live in community with one another, they are also a training ground for citizenship. Circles teach students self-discipline, individual and collective accountability, the core value of relationships, respect for differences, enhanced speaking and listening skills, and a problem-solving process through collaboration.

A number of school districts have implemented circles throughout their schools. For example, in Barron County, Wisconsin, all administrators, teachers, and staff are trained to infuse restorative discipline practices in the classrooms, hallways, playground, and extracurricular activities. Elementary school teachers use different types of circles in the classroom, including beginning and day circles, any-time circles, and end-of-day circles. A farewell circle includes a ritual of planting seeds as a metaphor for the seeds planted in the students through the relationships being honored that day.

Circle processes have also been developed for specific issues. Concern over elder abuse led community members involved with the Restorative Justice Approaches to Elder Abuse Project in Ontario, Canada, to seek a safe and healing approach that would decrease fear so elders would be less reluctant to disclose abuse and provide a fair and just way to deal with it (Groh, 2005). Many of the cases are complex because they involve ongoing relationships between the older adult and family members or trusted caregivers. First a referral is made. After a careful screening, two facilitators are assigned to make contact and hear the story of what happened from the older person and the offender and, with permission, contact supporters of both to gain a broader perspective on what happened. In one case, the victim, when everyone came together, talked about her love for her son who stole money from her. She admitted that she was sometimes afraid of him. She expressed regret that her son was abused by her husband. The son apologized and talked about how he had taken his frustration out on her but wanted to get his life together. He agreed to attend Alcoholics Anonymous and pay back the money he took. Circle participants agreed to provide caregiver relief hours for the son each week. The victim's daughter agreed to take on some of the responsibility for handling her mother's finances. Participants were contacted 3 months after the circle for follow-up. A circle participant noted that the use of circles allows elder abuse and neglect to be dealt with in a manner that does not destroy people's relationships and allows for a better understanding of the intertwining dynamics.

Circles of Support and Accountability (COSA) is a reintegration program for released sex offenders in Canada, the United States, and the United Kingdom (Wilson, Cortoni, & Vermani, 2008). The program provides a support network of four to six volunteers for high-risk sex offenders who commit to an offense-free lifestyle. These volunteers construct a community around the offender as part of the process of reintegration and sustainability in the community. These volunteers in this community-driven model are supported by professionals and engage with the offender around the practical, social, and emotional issues in his life. They serve in a variety of roles including befriending, supporting, advising, advocating, challenging, and mediating. The circle meets together regularly over a period of years. Weekly circles are held when the offender is first released. Circle members take turns contacting the offender daily, either in person or by phone. As the offender's needs diminish, the formal circles are held less often. Either the offender or a circle member, however, can always call a meeting if there is a problem or the offender shows signs of reverting to high-risk behavior. Evaluation of COSA found that sexual reoffending dramatically decreased by 83% in contrast to the matched comparison group and actuarial projections (2.1% vs. 12.8%) (Wilson et al., 2008). Offenders reported that they felt less nervous, angry, and afraid, as well as more realistic in their perspectives, more confident, felt more accepted, and experienced pride for not reoffending. Among nonvolunteers from the community at large, 100% reported they would feel better about a former offender living in the community if they knew he or she were part of a circle.

Circles work with energy, both the transforming of energy generated by and related to conflict or the building of energy for various needs, for example, support through a crisis, celebration, or learning (Stuart & Pranis, 2006). Indeed, the objective of circles, in part, is to engage this energy in ways that foster respect for differences and that improve relationships and connections to the community. The diversity in application of circles to various needs reflects the hugely creative potential of circles to move that energy in constructive ways.

EVALUATION OF CIRCLES

Research on circles is somewshat limited due, in part, to the fact that circles are often embedded in a broader community response to harm. Existing studies include information on sentencing circles, school violence and suspensions, and systemic reform.

One of the more extensive efforts to document the impact of circles occurred in the Hollow Water First Nation community located in Manitoba. These circles focused on community-wide change in response to Hollow Water's problems with intergenerational sex abuse. Circles included sex abuse victims, offenders, families, and community members at large. Findings were mixed (Lajeunesse, 1996). Some participants reported benefits that included having strength and commitment to change and healing, mutual respect, and renewed community or cultural pride. Others pointed to a lack of privacy, difficulty working with family members and close friends, embarrassment, unprofessionalism, religious conflict, and negative aspects of the circle process. A second study contends that the circles used to address this community-wide issue brought considerable monetary savings for provincial and federal governments and has a very low recidivism rate of approximately 2% over a 10-year period (Couture, Parker, Couture, & Laboucane, 2001; Native Counseling Services of Alberta, 2001).

Evaluations of other community-wide efforts include Washington County near St. Paul, Minnesota, that undertook system-wide reform by building a partnership among community participants, criminal justice decision makers, and court service personnel (Bazemore & Schiff, 2005; Coates, Umbreit, & Vos, 2004) and South St. Paul where a citizen's group has used restorative processes, including circles, for dealing with conflict in both the community and the schools (Coates et al., 2003). Evaluations from members in both communities are positive. Victim and offender participants in the South St. Paul project (n = 30) would recommend the circle process to others who were in similar circumstances. Without exception, offenders and their family members believed that the outcome of the circle process was fair (Umbreit, Vos, & Coates, 2005). Research on sentencing circles and recidivism rates is sparse. A recent study conducted in Australia found no difference between Aboriginal offenders dealt with in a normal court proceeding and those dealt with by a sentencing circle for frequency of offense in the 15 months following the circle sentence compared to the 15 months prior to the circle (Fitzgerald, 2008). Libin (2009) reports that these findings may be similar to statistics from Saskatchewan, which has a large aboriginal population and has seen a reduction in the use of sentencing circles from 39 in 1997 to just 5 in 2008. Throughout this period, crime rates and reoffense rates of aboriginals rose. The Director of the Australian Bureau of Crime Statistics and Research feels, however, that circle sentencing should be strengthened rather than abandoned by including more opportunities than just self-reflection to address factors such as drug and alcohol abuse (NSW Bureau of Crime Statistics and Research, 2008).

Studies on sentencing circles in Canada, which have been used principally in First Nations communities, suggest that there may be concerns with the power accorded victims (Cunliffe & Cameron, 2007). A study of trial decisions found a general disregard for the victim relative to her presence or absence in the circle, the nature of her participation, and attention to her safety and emotional well-being. The researchers conclude that the voice of the victim and her experience of violence are being silenced and that she is being placed at risk by a practice that is viewed as helping Aboriginal communities.

Studies on circles in schools as part of restorative processes are promising. A study in St. Joseph Missouri at four middle schools found changes in behaviors of students who participated in a circle prior to returning to the school from which they were suspended (Amstutz & Mullet, 2005). Comparisons in behaviors before and after the circle found decreases in disrespect to staff (71% to 26%), incomplete assignments (26% to 6%), and refusal to work in class (55% to 23%).

In Minnesota, almost half of the school districts use some form of restorative practices, including circles, and some are using them extensively (Karp & Breslin, 2001). The Seward Montessori Elementary School, for example, witnessed a 27% reduction in the number of suspensions and expulsions during the first year of the project. Lincoln Center Elementary School, which has data from 1997, saw the number of referrals for violent behavior decrease by more than half. After 2 years of restorative practices, the number of reports of violence decreased from seven per day to fewer than two. In South St. Paul High, the number of out-of-school suspension days dropped to 110 in the first year of the program and to 65 in the second year. A report on the school districts in Minnesota noted that consistent application of restorative principles and practices, for example, circles, to repair harm resulted in significant yearly reduction of behavior referrals and suspensions. Acts of physical aggression in one elementary school dropped from 773 to 153 over 3.5 years of application (Riestenberg, 2002).

Although these studies suggest that circles in schools and communities have potential to influence crime and misconduct, studies are missing on the more elusive effects of circles on community building. Research on community-wide efforts in South St. Paul and Washington County is particularly important because these communities are models for how to implement and sustain the community effort generated by circles.

ONGOING TENSIONS IN CIRCLE IMPLEMENTATION

There are a number of ongoing tensions in implementing circles that can affect their quality and generate concerns that can influence how widely they are used (Coates et al., 2003). They include issues about preparation, recruitment of community volunteers, diversifying referral sources, the spiritual nature of circles, and time.

Circles, and particularly sentencing circles, require extensive preprocess preparation (Bazemore & Griffiths, 2003). Indeed preparation seems critical because of the need to bring together so many diverse perspectives and the complexity of cases, including the possibility that there could be multiple offenders and/or victims. Victims and offenders may not want to take the time for preparation. One participant noted, "We're so used to this quick, fast-paced society. Everything happens, and it's question-answer, 'Let's get this done.' Circles are not like that; they are completely different, and I think that is what people have the most difficulty with" (Boyes-Watson, 2008, p.191). Some community representatives have indicated that they do not want to be biased by knowing about a case ahead of time. Others have been concerned that without structure and sufficient planning, the circle can be co-opted by those who want to dominate.

Circles lean heavily on community volunteers to provide support at the local community level (Coates et al., 2003). Recruiting and retaining volunteers is pivotal to the sustainability of the circle process. Because of the work involved in soliciting and building interest, it is often easier to use veteran volunteers who are trusted, know what to do, and are low maintenance. Volunteers who feel overburdened by the time demands, however, can burn out, which further uses up the resources needed to sustain the circle process. Although it is time intensive to line up new recruits and train them, new volunteers bring their own experiences and skills to bear on a group, which may be regarded by others in the circle as a valuable new addition or as disruptive.

Similarly, to generate a pool of community volunteers, it takes additional effort to diversify referral sources by doing outreach and education and building relationships with community organizations (Coates et al., 2003). Referral sources have major implications for the number of cases generated. Where cases come from also impacts how the circle is run because referral sources such as courts or a particular prison may have their own requirements and personnel may have their own attitudes about circles. In one case, for example, some criminal justice professionals felt that "circles require you to be human, to talk from your heart," whereas others felt that "there are no checks and balances in a circle that are part and parcel of the court process" (Coates et al., 2003, p. 274).

Circles have a strong spiritual dimension (Coates et al., 2003). Among proponents of circles, the view is shared that spirituality is at the heart and core of circle work. The rituals, passing of the talking piece, purposeful elevation of and respect accorded the unfolding of the circle process, and being connected in profound ways are elements that feed the spiritual nature of circles. However, faith tradition practices such as smudging or Christian prayers used to open or close a meeting may become negatively fused with religion. Moreover, the use of spiritual practices associated with particular groups, for example, Native American, by those who are not members of those groups may appear superficial or even disrespectful to some.

Circles are time intensive (Coates et al., 2003). It takes time to build relationships with referral sources or key community players, for the preparation of participants, the planning for a circle, and being in the circle. One participant clarified some of the issues with time.

> I've heard that folks are sometimes put off by how long it takes to go around the Circle, and it does take time, but then I think it depends on what it means to you to listen to people. Some people don't have that patience and are constantly on the go, but the Circle slows you down. It gives you an opportunity not only to deal with your own thoughts but also to listen to other people. (Boyes-Watson, 2008, pp. 191–192)

The natural tensions and conflicts that arise within the group over time as it refines its values and guidelines and time taken for the unfolding of the group process further increase the time commitment for both the circle keeper and circle members. Moreover, there may not be much that can be done to reduce the time without it seriously compromising the circle process. Although circles may ultimately save time and money, for example, the cost of incarceration or therapy, the immediate experience and perception are that the time necessary for circles may create an additional burden on an already overtaxed school or criminal justice system.

Although these tensions are endemic to circles in the real world, some of them can be lessened. For example, having a large cadre of well-trained volunteers can help with the time demands on any one person. Participants can be informed, prior to the circle, about the spiritual nature of circles and possible use of spiritual or religious traditions so that they can make decisions about their participation accordingly.

CONCLUSION

Circles counter the misplaced responsibility given to professionals for what has unfortunately been missing in communities. They show that individuals do make a difference, that citizen involvement is necessary for the health of a society, and that the challenges to communities are not too complex for lay people to handle. Circles are a way of getting the most complete picture people can have of themselves, of one another, and of the issues at hand. They make visible the far-reaching implications of crime (McCold, 2004). For example, participants, by listening to others, can learn how community values are threatened, how the sense of relationship is injured, how fear and incivility are increased, and how order and predictability are jeopardized. The presence of community members in circles is empowering for community building because it helps participants think about how to change conditions, develops participatory skills, and provides a sense of the collective capacity to make a difference. The use of peacemaking circles as a mechanism to involve the community and build community is growing, particularly in settings such as schools, which have a strong community-building agenda. The likelihood for a successful, satisfying and, at times, transformative outcome is high provided adequate attention is given to preparation.

REFERENCES

Amstutz, L. A., & Mullet, J. H. (2005). *The little book of restorative discipline for schools*. Intercourse, PA: Good Books.

Bazemore, G., & Griffiths, C. T. (2003). Conferences, circles, boards, and mediations: The "new wave" of community justice decisionmaking. In R. F. E. McLaughlin,

G. Hughes, & L. Westmarland (Eds.), *Restorative justice: Critical issues* (pp. 76–93). Thousand Oaks, CA: Sage.

Bazemore, G., & Schiff, M. (2005). *Juvenile justice reform and restorative justice: Building theory and policy from practice.* Portland, OR: Willan Publishing.

Boyack, J., Bowen, H., & Marshall, C. (2004). How does restorative justice ensure good practice? In H. Zehr & B. Toews (Eds.), *Critical issues in restorative justice* (pp. 265–276). Monsey, NY: Criminal Justice Press.

Boyes-Watson, C. (2002). *Holding the space: The journey of circles at Roca.* Boston: The Center for Restorative Justice at Suffolk University.

Boyes-Watson, C. (2008). *Peacemaking circles and urban youth.* St. Paul, MN: Living Justice Press.

Cayley, D. (1998). *The expanding prison: The crisis in crime and punishment and search for alternatives.* Cleveland, OH: Pilgrim Press.

Coates, R., Umbreit, M. S., & Vos, B. (2003). Restorative justice circles: An exploratory study. *Contemporary Justice Review, 6*(3), 265–278.

Coates, R., Umbreit, M. S., & Vos, B. (2004). Restorative justice systemic change: Washington County, Minnesota. *Federal Probation, 68*(3), 16–23.

Couture, J. Y., Parker, R., Couture, R., & Laboucane, P. (2001). A cost-benefit analysis of Hollow Water's community holistic circle healing process. *Aboriginal Peoples Collection 2001.* Ottawa, Canada: Solicitor General Canada.

Cunliffe, E., & Cameron, A. (2007). Writing the circle: Judically convened sentencing circles and the textual organization of criminal justice. *Canadian Journal of Women in the Law, 19,* 1–34.

Dignan, J. (2005). *Understanding victims and restorative justice.* Berkshire, England: Open University Press.

Fitzgerald, J. (2008). Does circle sentencing reduce Aboriginal offending? *Contemporary issues in crime and justice* (Vol. 115). New South Wales: NSM Bureau of Crime Statistics and Research.

Gordon, K. G. (2004). *From corrections to connections: A report on the AMICUS Girl's Restorative Program.* Minneapolis, MN: Amicus.

Greenwood, J. (2005). *The circle process: A path for restorative dialogue.* St. Paul, MN: Center for Restorative Justice and Peacemaking, University of Minnesota.

Groh, A. (2005). Restorative justice: A healing approach to elder abuse. In E. Elliott & R. M. Gordon (Eds.), *New directions in restorative justice: Issues, practices, evaluation* (pp. 175–192). Portland, OR: Willan Publishing.

Karp, D. R., & Breslin, B. (2001). Restorative justice in school communities. *Youth and Society, 33*(2), 249–272.

Lajeunesse, T. (1996). *Community holistic circle healing, in Hollow Water, Manitoba: An evaluation.* Ottawa, Canada: Solicitor General Canada, Ministry Secretariat.

Libin, K. (2009). Sentencing circles for aboriginals: Good justice? *National Post.* Retrieved January 7, 2010, from http://www.nationalpost.com/news/story.html?id=1337495

Lilles, H. (2002). Circle sentencing: Part of restorative justice continuum. In A. Morris & G. Maxwell (Eds.), *Restorative justice for juveniles: Conferencing, mediation and circles* (pp. 161–179). Oxford: Hart Publishing.

McCold, P. (2004). What is the role of community in restorative justice theory and practice? In H. Zehr & B. Toews (Eds.), *Critical issues in restorative justice* (pp. 155–172). Monsey, NY: Criminal Justice Press.

Native Counseling Services of Alberta. (2001). *Cost-benefit analysis of Hollow Water's community holistic circle healing process.* Alberta, Canada: Aboriginal Corrections Policy Unit, Solicitor General Canada.

Neihardt, J. G. (1988). *Black Elk speaks: Being the life story of a holy man of the Oglala Sioux.* Lincoln, NE: University of Nebraska Press.

NSW Bureau of Crime Statistics and Research. (2008). Circle sentencing evaluation *Media Releases.* NSW Bureau of Crime Statistics and Research.

Potas, I., Smart, J., Brignell, G., Thomas, B., & Lawrie, R. (2003). *Circle sentencing in New South Wales: A review and evaluation.* Sidney, NSW: Judicial Commission of New South Wales.

Pranis, K. (2005). *The little book of circle processes: A new/old approach to peacemaking.* Intercourse, PA: Good Books.

Pranis, K. (2007). Restorative values. In G. Johnstone & D. Van Ness (Eds.), *Handbook of restorative justice* (pp. 59–74). Portland, OR: Willan Publishing.

Pranis, K., Stuart, B., & Wedge, M. (2003). *Peacemaking circles: From crime to community.* St. Paul, MN: Living Justice Press.

Riestenberg, N. (2002, August 8–10). *Restorative measures in schools: Evaluation results.* Paper presented at the "Dreaming of a New Reality," the Third International Conference on Conferencing, Circles and other Restorative Practices, Minneapolis, MN.

Stuart, B. (1996). Turning swords into ploughshares. In B. Galaway & J. Hudson (Eds.), *Restorative justice: International perspectives* (pp. 193–206). Monsey, NY: Criminal Justice Press.

Stuart, B., & Pranis, K. (2006). Peacemaking circles: Reflections on principal features and primary outcomes. In D. Sullivan & L. Tifft (Eds.), *Handbook of restorative justice: A global perspective* (pp. 121–133). New York: Routledge.

Umbreit, M. S. (2003). *Talking circles.* Retrieved January 5, 2010, from http://www.cehd.umn.edu/ssw/rjp/Resources/RJ_Dialogue_Resources/Peacemaking_Healing_Circles/Talking_Circles.pdf

Umbreit, M. S. (2008). *Peacemaking circles.* St. Paul, MN: Center for Restorative Justice and Peacemaking, University of Minnesota.

Umbreit, M. S., Vos, B., & Coates, R. (2005). Restorative justice in the 21st century: A social movement full of opportunities and pitfalls. *Marquette University Law Review, 89*(2), 251–304.

Walker, L., Sakai, T., & Brady, K. (2006). Restorative circles: A solution-focused reentry planning process for inmates. *Federal Probation Journal, 70*(1), 33–37.

Wilson, R. J., Cortoni, F., & Vermani, M. (2008). *Circles of support and accountability: A national replication of outcome findings R-185.* Ottawa, Ontario: Correctional Service of Canada.

8. Victim-Offender Dialogue in Crimes of Severe Violence

> "I feel human for the first time in twelve years since the murder of my daughter. You can't imagine what that feels like, it feels good . . . . I think the program is the best thing that's ever happened to me. Before, he was just, you know, a murderer. After having met with him for several hours, I realized he was still a human being despite having killed my precious daughter."

> "I think I'm more alive now than I ever have been at any one point in time since I committed the murder. I feel like I'm actually living life now, instead of just existing? Very much at peace. I felt a great burden had been lifted off my shoulders. I felt joy."

On the morning of June 9, 1998 in the chapel of the Alfred D. Hughes Unit in Gatesville, Texas where White was an inmate, Thomas Ann Hines sat across the table from the murderer [White] of her son. The mediator sat at the side. He had prepared them for this moment, and now there was no turning back. They sat in silence for a few minutes, as Hines sought the strength to speak, dabbing at unceasing tears. "This is so hard for me," she said to him at last. "And I know it's hard for you . . . the hardest thing, though, was to bury Paul . . ." White, who had been waiting apprehensively and listening intently, hung his head as tears welled up in his eyes. Hines choked back her sobs. "I appreciate your doing this," she said, "and please know that I will not be unkind to you in any way. That's not why I'm here . . ." White's head lowered more. "You were the last person to see Paul alive, and it's really important that I know the last things he said, and the last things that happened in his life."

It took White a few moments to reply. "I don't know how to start," he said, and barely more than a whisper. "I don't know how to explain. It was just a stupid thing. Just stupid . . ."

And so commenced a conversation that was to begin to restore two individuals whose lives had become inextricably entwined 13 years before.

"I don't blame you for how you feel about me," he said. "I didn't know I was going to cause so much pain."

The emotional session lasted eight hours, with a 40 minute break for lunch." I went in there totally for <u>me</u>," admits Hines, "but it changed for me as he <u>listened</u> to me, *and I <u>listened</u> to him. At one point, I remember saying, 'If you knew how much I loved him you wouldn't have shot him, I just know you wouldn't,' and he just folded . . . That sad, troubled boy let me see inside his soul. I began to feel such compassion."*

In a year and a half since the meeting, White has changed. The inmate who averaged more than 10 serious infractions a year before the meeting has had just two minor ones since. No day passes without Hines thinking about her lost son . . . but her work with others, particularly victims and inmates in need, keeps her going. (Wilson, n.d.)

Victim-Offender Dialogue (VOD) in crimes of severe violence is an outgrowth of Victim-Offender Mediation (VOM). In its early years, no one foresaw that the processes used for VOM might be appropriate in cases of severe violence such as murder, vehicular homicide, or serious felony assaults. Any potential for repairing harm after a person had been killed seemed impossible to envision. Moreover, it seemed inconceivable that victims of such great injury would ever wish to meet the offender who had caused it, much less speak to that person in a face-to-face meeting (Umbreit, Vos, Coates, & Brown, 2003).

However, unlike the initial impetus for VOM, which grew out of concern for a more effective approach to dealing with juvenile offenders, the impetus to expand VOM into the domain of serious and violent crime has been victim driven. In Texas, for example, the momentum originated with Cathy Phillips who after the death of her daughter in 1990 wanted answers that only the offender could give. When her request to meet was turned down by officials, Phillips, undaunted, pressed all the way to the Governor's Office before permission was given for the dialogue (Wilson, n.d.). This perseverance both in Texas and other states has paid off. Today, VOD is an increasingly accepted restorative justice practice that is offered to victims and victim survivors whose loved one was murdered, by Departments of Corrections in 25 states (Wilson, 2009), Belgium (Peters & Aertsen, 2000), and Canada; through the Fraser Region Community Justice Initiatives Association (CJI) in Langley, British Columbia (Gustafson, 2005); and the Collaborative Justice Project in Ottawa (Correctional Service of Canada, 2009). See Figure 8.1 for the similarities and distinctions between VOM and VOD.

Like the chapters on VOM, FGC, and Circles, this chapter explains VOD, its history and development, its characteristics, and its procedures. In contrast to the other approaches, however, VOD is strictly victim initiated, not stipulated by the court, and occurs post conviction during incarceration rather than, like the others, at the front end of the criminal justice process. These differences are significant. The offender may be incarcerated for years or never be released. Consequently, the usual questions about the impact of restorative practices on recidivism and community safety are not relevant. Instead, what matters are the victim's questions, for instance, about what happened to their loved one or the motivation for or explanation of the offender's actions. These

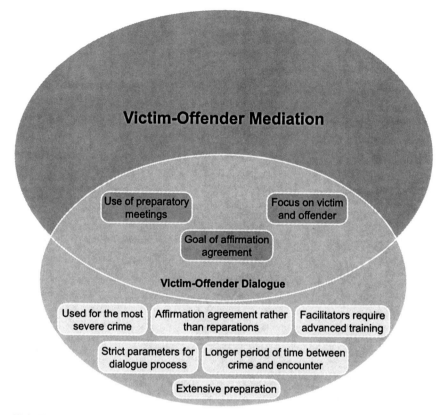

FIGURE 8.1

questions never stop lingering and haunt both parties because the answers are central to the victim's healing and because only the offender has the answers.

Another difference between VOD and the other approaches covered in previous chapters is that the establishment of a relationship between the victim and offender, as noted in Chapter 2 on values, is central to being able to willingly give and receive answers that evoke strong emotional reactions. Indeed, a relationship already exists, albeit involuntary, situationally induced, and filled with anger and hostility. However, with careful preparation of both parties the VOD meeting actualizes that relationship but channels it through the pain in ways that foster healing and accountability. Participants report that the engagement with each other is life changing in a positive way. When this kind of result can occur in meeting between the surviving family member and the murderer of a loved one, it underscores the fundamental interconnectedness of human beings and the transcendent significance of human relationships beyond individual behaviors.

The dialogues associated with VOM, FGC, and Circles may involve issues of remorse and forgiveness between victim and offender. Concerns about forgiveness, however, are more explicit in VOD because the nature of the crimes involves the taking of human life or other heinous act and the impossibility of ever returning life to the one murdered or restoring a survivor's life to what it was before the murder.

Finally, in contrast to the other approaches, many cases that go through the preparation phase never proceed to a dialogue meeting. Every step of the VOD process is emotionally demanding and time intensive. Facilitation requires a vast knowledge and a disposition that can absorb a wide range of psychological dynamics from rage to emotional meltdown, with exquisite understanding of the needs of both offender and victim. States, therefore, have reason to question the cost efficiency of VOD. Remarkably, states have been eager to implement it and to offer victims a solid resource to advance their healing.

HISTORY AND DEVELOPMENT

Part of the cautiousness about the use of restorative justice for violent crime was concern that it might revictimize victims. Understandably, victim service professionals and others warned that this practice, if it were to be used, had to be carefully constructed because of the degree of harm victims have endured. Reactions to violent crime, for example, are often protracted and difficult to treat. Studies of family members of homicide victims have found, for example, that posthomicide distress does not dramatically lessen over time (Thompson, Norris, & Ruback, 1998) and family survivors are significantly more likely than other direct crime victims to have lifetime PTSD (Freedy, Resnick, Kilpatrick, Dansky, & Tidwell, 1994). Studies of sexual assault victims show a slower recovery rate from sexual than nonsexual assault (Gilboa-Schechtman & Foa, 2001), increased vulnerability to panic disorder (Leskin & Sheikh, 2002), and chronic posttraumatic stress if psychological disorders are also present (Darves-Bornoz, Choquet, Ledoux, Gasquet, & Manfredi, 1998). In contrast to victims of minor crimes, victims of violent crime suffer significantly more distress including loss of confidence (41% vs. 11%), loss of self-esteem (37% vs. 2%), sleeplessness (27% vs. 9%), headaches, and other physical symptoms (41% vs. 5%) (Strang, 2002).

In the United States, therefore, states have proceeded slowly and carefully while looking closely at each other's experiences before developing their own protocols. Information and research on existing programs therefore have played a critical role in answering states' questions and creating statewide procedures. The first study of VOD (Umbreit, 1989), for example, found that in four cases, offering a mediated dialogue was very beneficial to the victims, offenders, and community members or family members who were involved in the process. The second study (Flaten, 1996), involving juvenile offenders incarcerated in a juvenile correctional facility in Alaska, substantiated the previous study and found very high levels of satisfaction with the process and outcomes, from both victims and offenders in four cases.

The third study (Roberts, 1995) moved beyond case reports and reported specific results by participant group for 22 offenders and 24 victims who had participated in a VOD program in Langley, British Columbia, initiated in 1991. Prior to implementing the program, a small survey had found that victims and offenders involved in severely violent crime would be interested in meeting with each other in a safe and structured manner, after intensive preparation, if such a service were available (Gustafson, 2005; Gustafson & Smistra, 1989). The results showed that VOD was a powerful intervention. The overall effects for victims included the following: they had finally been heard; the offender now no longer exercised control over them; they could see the offender as a person rather than a monster; they felt more trusting in their relationships with others; they felt less fear; they weren't preoccupied with the offender anymore; they felt peace; they would not feel suicidal again; and they had no more anger.

For offenders, the overall effects of a mediated dialogue included discovering emotions; increasing awareness of the impacts of their acts; increasing self-awareness; opening their eyes to the outside world, rather than closed, institutional thinking; feeling good about having tried the process; and achieving peace of mind in knowing one has helped a former victim. These results exposed both the potency of VOD for emotional healing and increased awareness of need relative to the conditions otherwise endured by victims of severely violent crime, for example, mistrust, fear, helplessness.

Against this backdrop, two states ventured forth to implement VOD through their Departments of Corrections. Texas began its program in 1993 through the Victims Services Division of the Texas Department of Criminal Justice (TDCJ) (Umbreit et al., 2003). After visiting and studying other jurisdictions where dialogue had been used in violent crimes, developing the program philosophy and protocols, and beginning the process of preparation for the first victims and offenders, it facilitated its initial dialogue in 1995. By 1996, there were 200 mediation requests from victims on file. Ohio began its program in 1995 through the Office of Victim Services housed within the Department of Rehabilitation and Corrections (Umbreit et al., 2003). Like Texas, it received its opening request from a victim or survivor to meet with an offender. Within 6 months, there were 14 more such requests. Ohio created a 20-member planning committee with widespread representation including skeptics and critics along with proponents and supporters. Visits were made to other states, like Texas, where VOD was being considered for serious and violent crime. The initial dialogue occurred in 1996.

From 2000 to 2002, Umbreit and colleagues (2003) conducted an ethnographic study of the programs in Texas and Ohio. Although other states had also begun initial programs, for example, New York and Pennsylvania, the study of Texas and Ohio publicized the emerging practice and, as such, established a blueprint for other states. The study examined the following questions:

- How did the programs develop?
- What were the critical issues for replication in other areas?
- Who participated in the VOD process and why?
- What was involved in the actual VOD process?
- What were the outcomes for participants including their satisfaction levels?
- What were the implications for training and practice?
- What were the policy implications for other jurisdictions considering a similar initiative?

The flow of information between states continues through the efforts of Jon Wilson, the Director of JUST alternatives, and Karen Ho, Director of the Office of Victim Services in Ohio. Wilson regularly updates an ongoing survey of the states with VOD programs and distributes the findings to the appropriate staff. Wilson and Ho facilitate an annual VOD summit for professionals responsible for their state's VOD operations, which give staff from across the country the opportunity to collaborate and explore issues together such as funding, facilitation models, and program evaluation.

CHARACTERISTICS OF VICTIM-OFFENDER DIALOGUE IN CRIMES OF SEVERE VIOLENCE

VOD is an outgrowth of VOM and is similar in its central focus on the relationship between victim and offender. Support people, if present, have no active role in the dialogue, which is facilitated by either a single facilitator or co-mediators. Like VOM, VOD requires preparatory meetings and often culminates in an affirmation agreement that, instead of specifying financial restitution as happens in VOM, allows the victim and offender to concretize particular requests of the victim that the offender agrees to, such as involvement of the offender in prevention efforts or a commitment to changes in their in-prison behaviors (Umbreit et al., 2003).

Beyond being similar in structure, however, VOM and VOD are vastly different. VOD deals with the most serious crimes imaginable: criminal negligence causing death, driving while intoxicated and causing bodily harm or death; aggravated assault; armed robbery; kidnapping; sexual assault; attempted murder; and homicide offenses including manslaughter, first- and second-degree murder, and multiple murders (Gustafson, 2005). These crimes can cost people their lives and create a lifetime of trauma for direct victims and survivors that strips them of their self-worth, dignity, and emotional endurance. For offenders, these crimes keep them behind bars for years, if not for the rest of their lives, and, in some instances, result in their executions.

Entering such territory requires a process that is exquisitely sensitive to emotional wounds, the courage it takes to meet together, and the readiness of each party to encounter one another. Typically, therefore, there is a longer time lapse between the occurrence of the crime and the victim's request to meet with the offender, often extending many years (Umbreit, Coates, Vos, & Armour, 2006). Encounters generally take much more preparation ranging from several months to over a year, prior to any joint meeting. Facilitators, either as volunteers or professional staff, must have advanced training including the ability to work with intense emotions understanding trauma, clarity about the boundary between mediation/dialogue and therapy, and knowledge about working with correctional institutions. Many, if not most, draw upon their work experiences as staff in the criminal justice system, clergy, mental health professionals, victim advocates, teachers, and so on.

Moreover, VOD programs have strict parameters around the dialogue process between victim and offender that are designed to ensure adequate safety for participants and the Department of Corrections (Wilson, 2009). The rules include the following:

- Participation does not affect an offender's legal status.
- Participation is voluntary for both victims and offenders. Either may discontinue the program at any time.
- Participation is not a guarantee that a face-to-face meeting will occur.
- Victims must be 18 or older (of legal age) to participate.
- In order to participate, both victim and offender must sign a release relieving the Department of Corrections from liability and declaring their intentions to not cause harm.
- Program policy includes a confidentiality statement.
- All parties agree not to call the facilitator/mediator to testify in court or to subpoena material from the dialogue (yet others who may be involved cannot necessarily be prevented from doing so).
- The dialogue must focus on the offense on record.
- The facilitator/mediator will not impose solutions or expectations. No particular outcome is guaranteed.

- No dialogue can take place as long as a stay away or no contact order is in place.
- Facilitator is responsible for halting dialogue if attitudes or actions become disruptive or destructive.

Although there are substantive differences between VOM and VOD, the evolution of current dialogue and pursuing cases of violent crime rest on the foundation of VOM practice, which was well established by the time VOD was introduced at the state level. In many instances, the push toward expanding VOM processes took place because facilitators already had a strong positive base on which to build (Umbreit et al., 2003).

REASONS FOR MEETING

In their quest for meaning and healing following the death of their loved ones, surviving family members of homicide victims from both criminal and political violence are seeking to meet the offender through restorative dialogue opportunities in North America, Europe, Israel/Palestine, South Africa, and other parts of the world.

The most striking characteristic of participants' reasons for seeking to meet or agreeing to meet with their counterpart is their great variation (Umbreit, Vos, Coates, & Armour, in press). There is no single guiding motivation for family members who wish to have some type of encounter with the person who took their relative's life. Billie Lee wanted the offender to know how she felt about her son, and she wanted to make a change in his life. "I wanted to make such an impression on him that his life would never, ever be the same. Mine's not. Nor is my son's. I told him, 'When you asked my son for a ride, our three lives were cemented together for eternity'" (Umbreit et al., 2003, p. 47). Betsy whose 7-year-old daughter had been sexually abused by the child's stepfather wanted to know how long the abuse had been going on. She also wanted to hear the offender take direct responsibility for what he had done rather than hide behind the plea bargain, and she wanted him to own the consequences of his actions (Umbreit et al., 2003). Sandra was shot unintentionally as part of a robbery. She wanted to demystify him, to "look him [the offender] in the eye and have a conversation, find out what he was like as a person, what he thought about the shooting, what had it been like in prison for him" (Umbreit et al., 2003, p. 181). Danny's wife, his friend, and his friend's wife all died as a result of a heavy equipment truck "accident." The driver's blood alcohol at the time of the accident was more than double the Ohio limit of 0.10. Danny initially wanted to meet the offender to get questions answered but by the time of the meeting said, "Time heals, and you learn to deal with your emotions, so my frame of mind had changed . . . The thing that I most wanted to do was to cleanse my heart and forgive" (Umbreit et al., 2003, p. 190).

Reasons why offenders meet are equally varied (Umbreit et al., in press; Umbreit et al., 2003). Carl was serving a 10-year sentence for sexually assaulting a woman. When the victim's mother asked to meet with him, he felt it would give him the chance to make things right. He thought that she had received misinformation about what happened, and he wanted to set that straight. He also wanted her to see him as a person "and not some kind of monster, let her now I'm somebody who made a mistake, not Jeffrey Dahmer or somebody like that" (Umbreit et al., 2003, p. 60).

Nick was serving time for murder. He wanted to meet the victim's daughter because he wanted her to see who he is today. "I think I make a lot more sense than I had back then" (Umbreit et al., 2003, p. 62). In addition, he wanted her to know that he had no problem with her protesting his parole because he would have done the same thing in her situation. Mike had kidnapped and shot his former girlfriend in the thigh. He wanted to meet because it was a way for him to take responsibility directly, and he hoped for some level of closure and perhaps acceptance or even forgiveness.

Besides the victim-focused reasons for meeting, some offenders realize that a face-to-face dialogue may also include possible benefits for themselves. One person, for example, said, "Helping myself get rid of some of the guilt, stuff I've been holding on for the past nine years" (Umbreit et al., 2003, p. 268). Some offenders have remarked that they wanted the victim to know something positive about them. Others have maintained, among other reasons, that talking with the victim would help them take responsibility, contribute to their own rehabilitation or healing, or provide an opportunity to seek forgiveness.

In addition to these explicitly stated goals, victims and offenders are often haunted by deeper and often unexpressed questions that guide their desires for dialogue (Gustafson, 2005). Victims, for example, may ask, "What is it about what happened that keeps me so stuck in painful memories? Why is it so difficult to break free and begin to thrive again? Why do I feel such responsibility, such enormous shame, when I'm the innocent victim and the shame ought to be on the offender's shoulders" (Gustafson, 2005)? Offenders grapple with questions about their own behaviors. "How did I allow my life to get so out of control that I acted in the way I did bringing such painful consequences to others including myself and my family? How did I get power, shame, sexuality and rage so badly cross-wired? How did I get so 'bent' that I could believe that shaming and degrading someone else would rid me of my own shame and degradation? Is there any way back? I feel forever barred from the free world for what I did" (Gustafson, 2005). Although participants may not be conscious of these yearnings or able to state them openly, they may play under the dialogue process as unspoken hopes to varying degrees.

VOD PROCEDURE

All states that offer VOD through their Departments of Corrections mandate that only direct victims or victim survivors can initiate a dialogue request (Wilson, 2009). With few exceptions, the victim's request does not proceed unless the offender has taken responsibility for the crime. Moreover, although the victim makes the initial request, the offender's participation is not coerced and must be voluntary (Umbreit et al., 2003). Some states, such as Texas, subscribe to the following procedure in order to assess the offender's sincere acceptance of responsibility. The facilitator pays an unannounced visit to the offender to tell him that the victim or victim survivor wants to meet with him.

The offender's initial reaction to the news provides important information that the facilitator uses to determine the offender's appropriateness for a dialogue. Individual reactions vary. Some claim their innocence or blame the victim for being incarcerated. Others are shaken or even crying with relief that finally they will have the chance to address what they did to another person's life. If the facilitator assesses that the offender admits wrongdoing and accepts responsibility and the offender wants to participate in the dialogue, the process moves forward. Most states use a screening process to assess the offender's suitability or potential for adverse effects to self and others by checking for possible appeals, security, and mental health issues (Wilson, 2009).

Some states, such as Minnesota, have added an additional mechanism for offenders who want to write letters of apology to the victims of their crime (Minnesota Department of Corrections, n.d.). Offenders may write such letters, which, after review by the Victim Assistance program at the Department of Corrections, are held in an apology bank and distributed only when and if the victim completes an apology letter notification form asking for such a letter if it is received in their name. Victims may, at the time of engaging in the apology letter process, initiate a request for victim-offender dialogue (Minnesota Department of Corrections, n.d.). In Texas, offenders who initiate a request for a dialogue are assessed for motivation and readiness. Although the process does not move forward unless and until the victim makes a request, offenders are offered the option of being a surrogate

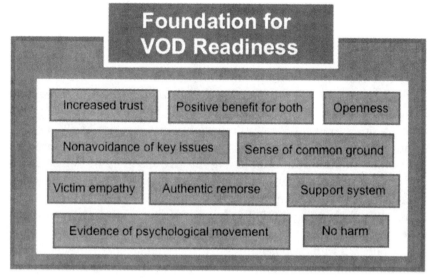

FIGURE 8.2

for other victims who want a meeting but whose offenders refuse or are not appropriate candidates for a dialogue (Wilson, 2009). Figure 8.2 displays key elements of VOD readiness.

Once both parties agree to participate, the process moves forward. It consists of three stages: (i) preparation, (ii) meeting, and (iii) follow-up.

Preparation

To ensure that the upcoming meeting is responsive to their needs and mutually constructive, victims and offenders need to be as clear as possible about their goals and expectations, aware of what they might encounter during the dialogue, cognizant of their fears and concerns about the meeting, and ready with the words they want to express to each other. Because the crime was so violating and emotionally laden, the prospect of meeting together, in some instances, may awaken intense feelings and reactions that need to be addressed as part of preparing to meet. States vary in the amount of time given to preparation ranging from "no set time" to at least two predialogue meetings each with the victim or offender (Wilson, 2009). The range in time is illustrative of differences in program philosophies and reasons for meeting. The underlying premise of the Ohio program, for example, is that victims and offenders define their own needs regarding meeting each other and that the program exists to facilitate that meeting in a manner that is safe for all involved (Umbreit et al., 2003). Given that the range of needs for some may be quite narrow and centered on one or two specific questions, preparation may be brief.

Because preparation is centered on readiness for the dialogue, facilitators may ask victims and offenders to complete questionnaires that help them explore the details of the crime, their reactions, and their hopes and fears about the dialogue session (Umbreit et al., 2003). Facilitators may also explore potential risks. Victims may worry that meeting the offender could make things worse because of getting so close to the emotional wound, being revictimized by the offender or by the bureaucracy, being lied to by the offender, or experiencing rageful feelings that had not previously surfaced (Umbreit et al., 2003). Offenders may worry about what victim survivors will do including physical repercussions, the size and intensity of the victim's anger and rage, or the possibility that the dialogue would have a negative impact on their parole (Umbreit et al., 2003). Although the facilitator meets separately with the victim and offender, the facilitator may also use this time to bring the two together metaphorically by sharing information, with permission, about each with the other. In a situation, for example, where an offender can conceive only of the victim's anger, the facilitator may share how a victim wanted to learn more about the offender's life or expressed recent concern for the offender's well-being. This kind of sharing makes each less on guard, more real to the other, and engages them from a distance.

There are few definitive indicators to determine the readiness of victims and offenders to meet. Readiness is guided by a program's philosophy and is determined, in part, by the goals each has for the meeting. Readiness, however, is also determined by the facilitator's assessment of the conditions needed for participants' safety as well as other factors, for example, the level of the offender's awareness of what he did or remorse, the victim's fear, and so on. At a VOD summit held in May 2002, facilitators suggested the following criteria:

1. Neither party will harm each other.
2. There is a positive benefit for both victim and offender.
3. Both victim and offender have the psychological strength to proceed as indicated by a diminishment in the avoidance of key issues and emotions.
4. Both victim and offender have a support system in place.
5. Evidence of movement on psychological issues that otherwise block movement for either offender and/or victim.
6. Sense of openness to each other.
7. Sense of common ground to further the development of empathy.
8. Evidence of increased trust in the facilitator, the mediation process, or oneself.
9. Evidence of authentic remorse.
10. Evidence of victim empathy, social awareness, and social responsibility.

A survey of the states that do VOD indicates that the readiness to move to dialogue is usually done by the facilitator in consultation with the victim or victim survivor and offender followed by receiving approval from the program administrator (Wilson, 2009).

The readiness issue has particular relevance because of the high number of cases that do not proceed to the meeting stage. A recent study of VOD in Ohio (Borton, 2008), for example, found that three-fourths of cases fail to proceed. These cases included a myriad of circumstances, some of which were unrelated to preparation: instances where the offender refused to participate (20%), the victim's request for dialogue was considered inappropriate (9.5%), the facilitator lost contact with the victim (15%), the victim backed out (12.6%), the victim was satisfied with less than the meeting (5.7%), the offender denied guilt (4.4%), and the offender was out on parole (4.4%).

An examination of the factors that frustrate or facilitate progress toward actual dialogue found no evidence for race of victim and offender or length of time from crime to request for dialogue. The study did find that crimes involving male victims are more likely to complete the dialogue than those involving female victims. Moreover, direct victims who had a relationship with the offender prior to the crime were significantly less likely to complete the dialogue than those victims who did not know the offender previously. Finally, nonvictim parties, that is, victim survivors, were more likely to complete the dialogue than actual crime victims. These findings suggest that more time for preparation and attention may need to be given to cases where a relationship existed prior to the crime and to those cases where a request to meet is made by a direct victim.

Meeting

Unless the offender is on parole, the dialogue session is usually held at the prison where the offender is incarcerated. The physical location may be the prison chapel or a private room away from the rest of the inmates. In some states, the victim visits the prison facility the day before the session both to increase the victim's familiarity and comfort with the setting and to see where the offender is housed (Wilson, 2009). Although the victim is given the option to suggest seating arrangements and determine who speaks first, victim and offender usually sit across from each other and the facilitator sits at the head of the table, an arrangement that ensures face-to-face engagement and symbolically expresses that the dialogue belongs to the two parties, not the facilitator. There is no time limit on the meetings, which can run anywhere from less than an hour up to 8 hours (Umbreit et al., 2003; Wilson, 2009).

Both parties are understandably nervous about meeting each other. A parent of a murdered child said, "You will never, ever be prepared; you just won't" (Umbreit et al., 2003, p. 108). Another victim explained, "I was scared. I kept thinking, what's the big deal, then all of a sudden he walked in and it was just really scary at first" (Umbreit et al., 2003, p. 241). Although some offenders feel neutral or positive about meeting, more often their feelings range from merely nervous or anxious to terrified and scared. One man remarked, "I felt like I was being led to the electric chair. I was more nervous about that [meeting the victim] than being sentenced and going in from of the parole board combined. Because (those people), I didn't actually cause them pain . . ." (Umbreit et al., 2003, p. 273).

The dialogue sessions do not follow a rigid format, leaving plenty of room for the victim and offender to express themselves, ask questions, and carry on the conversation until it reaches a natural ending. The facilitator, however, usually begins the meeting including an introduction of names, a review of the purpose of the meeting, procedures for interaction and for taking breaks, an explanation of the facilitator's role, ground rules, and the designation of the person who will be the first speaker (Umbreit, 2001). The facilitator's opening statements and body language serve several functions. They outline the procedures but also serve to set the tone for the dialogue and give encouragement to both the victim and offender (Szmania, 2006). The following facilitator statement is an example of creating the climate for dialogue, although many facilitators say very little in the opening statement since the climate of safety in dialogue and the connection with the involved parties, while remaining impartial, was well established during the separate preparation process with each person.

> Like I said earlier, the preparation we have done for these many months has now led us and given us the foundation for what we are about today. For you, Rachel [victim], to have the opportunity to meet with you, Bill [offender], to facilitate healing and recovery. What we are about can be very personal and very emotional. Even intimate. We presume it is difficult, awkward, maybe painful. What we're doing today is based on creating a safe place built on trust and openness, honesty, sensitivity. Toward the end of establishing personal safety, what is done and said here is said in confidence, is confidential. Each of you, well all of us, have signed confidentiality forms, including the corrections officer outside. You are free to share and not share as you choose. This is y'all's day. My role is the same as it's been from the beginning. I'm just here to help both of you, to help, if need be, to facilitate any dialogue between . . . [you]. To help clarify questions, any needs, issues, or purpose you may have. And I'm not here to impose my expectations or solutions. Like I said, it's . . . [your] day to encourage how you feel and to own your feelings. Our ground rules together. I have basically covered them

with . . . [you] earlier. There's just no name-calling, no obscenities, or any kind of disruptive actions. When one of you is talking, don't interrupt the other. And I've given both of . . . [you]paper and pen, and you can jot it down, and you can remember to ask later. Our time here, our time together, is, will be according to your own needs, your own individual needs, your own mutual needs. We'll take breaks whenever necessary . . . if I don't take one soon enough . . . just let me know. As far as the dialogue itself, as I said earlier, we'll begin with Rachel. And I'll ask you to give a brief opening statement. You know, just a couple of sentences. And then I'll ask the same of you, Bill. Then we'll go back to Rachel, and she'll start the actual dialogue between . . . [you]. At the conclusion of our dialogue together . . . we'll have the option to develop together an affirmation agreement. I want to affirm your commitment and trust of this process and also acknowledge both your hard work and willingness to be vulnerable today. Other than that, are . . . [you] ready? Okay. Rachel if you wanna go ahead and just, like I said, just give an opening statement on your purpose for being here and what you want to accomplish. (Szmania, 2006, pp. 124–125)

Victims, family members, and offenders describe the process of the meeting as a conversation (Umbreit et al., 2003). The interaction is respectful, and most of the time, the conversation flows back and forth among participants unaided by any facilitator action. Victims and family members report that the major focus of the dialogue is on the impact of the crime on themselves, on the direct victim (if different), and on other family members and persons connected to the victim. Offenders report that they share information about the crime followed by information about their lives before the crime (Umbreit et al., 2003). Some talk about taking ownership, apologizing, and assuring the safety of the victim or victim survivor.

Betsy described the significance of learning new information in the meeting about the sexual abuse of her daughter. The abuse had been going on much longer and was far more frequent than she had ever known. She found it difficult to listen to the details, but she was grateful for herself and the offender that he was honest and direct about it. Nick recalled the victim's opening statement. "We sat down and she looked me in the eye and said, 'Nick, many years ago you left some trash on my front porch and I am here to give it all back to you'" (Umbreit et al., 2003, p. 63). Then for the next 2 hours she proceeded to tell him how his actions affected every member of her family. In another case, Sondra asked David if he wanted to hear what she had written about being shot and how it had affected her life (Umbreit et al., 2003). David said yes, so she read what she had written. Sondra did not realize how deeply her story was affecting him until the facilitator picked up on David's distress, asked him how he was feeling, and accompanied him to a side room for several minutes so he could get his composure back.

These examples illustrate the vast array of experiences that occur during the dialogue session. In some states, victims and offenders are expected to develop an affirmation agreement. Common components include a commitment by offenders to pursue more education or stay in treatment. In one case, the offender agreed to visit the victim's grave annually once he was paroled. In another, the offender contracted upon release to send a dollar once a month to the victim as evidence that he still remembered what he had done to her (Umbreit et al., 2003).

Immediate reactions once the meeting is over suggest that the experience is exceedingly powerful for both victims and offenders. Offenders describe positive reactions including happiness, relief or release, and feeling a weight has been lifted. Typical comments include "I just really felt at peace for the first time in a long time, and I slept really good that night" (Umbreit et al., 2003, p. 162). "I think that is the tiredest [sic] I've been in years, emotionally exhausted. It was like having a personal open heart surgery" (Umbreit et al., 2003, p. 162). Victims, too, emphasize relief or release and exhaustion. "I was euphoric" (Umbreit et al., 2003, p. 250). "I was released from my own prison that day" (Umbreit et al., 2003, p. 250). Others express sadness or disappointment. "There was no joy. It was heaviness; it was sorrow, because my daughter isn't there" (Umbreit et al., 2003, p. 250).

Upon reflection, participants describe important achievements accomplished during the mediation session including results they had not anticipated or sought. A common theme is the human nature of the encounter. "One thing I did get accomplished was I did see him face-to-face" (Umbreit et al., 2003, p. 117). Participants also stress the importance of the answers or information they receive from the offender including the actual events of the crime as well as getting to ask questions they wanted to ask. Offenders, too, convey the significance of looking into each other's eyes. "You can see it in their face, see what you did. It was almost like reliving it" (Umbreit et al., 2003, p. 168).

Follow-Up

After the session is over, the facilitator debriefs the victim and offender separately (Umbreit et al., 2003; Wilson, 2009). This practice helps participants transition back into their everyday life and provides an opportunity to assess if either or both need additional support. Most states conduct in-person or telephone follow-up sessions within weeks of the session and again within 1–3 months (Wilson, 2009). Some states routinely videotape the actual meeting and show it to victims and offenders as part of the follow-up (Umbreit et al., 2003). In the intensity of the moment, participants may forget that entire topic areas were discussed. The record of what happened in the dialogue can be critical as victims, for example, begin to second-guess their own experiences. The video validates what they went through. With the video, the facilitator can also guide the victim or offender to notice their accomplishments or reflect on the unrealized significance of something one or the other might have said during the session.

The VOD procedure requires substantial time. Even though some needs may seem straightforward, the idea of meeting together can trigger strong and ambivalent emotions as participants approach the trauma of the murder experience again. Because each participant's emotional process is different, the procedures cannot be rushed. Indeed, part of the safety that allows victim and offender to finally meet is created by giving each sufficient time and space for reflection in preparing to meet, for speaking one's truth during the session, and for integrating the experience after the session is over. Gustafson (2005) comments on the significance of revisiting the trauma for victims. He notes that this time because of the dialogue process the victim or victim survivor approaches memories and related emotions accompanied by others who are trusted companions. Rather than feeling overwhelmed by life-threatening associations, survivors can experience along with their fear states a new sense of mastery that over time begins to prevail.

THE ROLE OF THE FACILITATOR

Because of the intensity of the crime and personal nature of the violation, facilitation of the dialogue process requires extensive involvement with each of the parties. Victims and offenders are reentering a nightmare that has brought horrific consequences and speaking about topics that, heretofore, may never have been addressed and speaking about them with the actual person responsible, that is, the offender or the person harmed, that is, the victim. The ability to revisit this territory and engage with such volatile material requires time and building of trust in the facilitator and the process. Participants, for example, often need time to tell their story over and over again just to be able to identify the questions they have about what happened or what they want to know about each other. Participants need time as well to address their fears about meeting together or sharing their stories. As one offender commented, I was "wondering if they were coming to get me, I know by being in here [prison], if you want to bring something in, you can bring it in . . . scared because I didn't know if they had a gun or not" (Umbreit et al., 2003, p. 147).

In preparing to tell their stories to each other including the impact on their lives, participants commonly find themselves at a loss for words to adequately express their thoughts and feelings. Participants need time, therefore, to find their voice and help to say what is in their hearts. In some instances, offenders cannot remember what happened and need time for the details of the crime to reemerge and to address their reactions to their memories. Participants may also need time and assistance to gain courage to ask the difficult questions. Participants may encounter negative reactions from family members about their decision or agreement to meet together (Umbreit et al., 2003). The decision to proceed in spite of the family members' objections may cause considerable conflict among them. As one person remarked after his sister chose to meet the man who killed their mother, "I didn't want him to be a human being."

These issues require the facilitator to be emotionally attuned to a myriad of needs with the knowledge and foresight that attending to them will likely bring each party closer to the table. The sense of attunement requires deep compassionate listening, being fully present and supportive of the involved parties, and being profoundly nonjudgmental (Umbreit et al., 2003). Although this process can sound deceptively simple, it requires a true integration of knowledge about trauma, conflict resolution, case development, and problem solving in concert with comfort with experiencing powerful emotions, the vicissitudes of the healing process, and ambiguity in direction. It also requires recognition of and respect for the healing found in silence, the significance of bearing witness to another's truth, and the need for honoring the strengths and inner wisdom of participants (Umbreit et al., 2003).

The facilitator's most active work occurs during preparation. Although the dialogue belongs to the victim and offender, the facilitator begins the process, helps with transitions, invites breaks as needed, and remains a constant, readily alert, and cementing presence throughout. Facilitators speak very little during the face-to-face dialogue. Their presence is vital, but it is most often a supportive nonverbal presence that is comfortable with moments of silence and bearing witness to the strength and resilience of the involved parties. As noted in Chapter 2, what happens in these nonverbal moments are often referenced by participants as spiritual, unexplainable, and ineffable. In one case, an offender started sharing material that the offender had specifically named during the preparation as off limits. "It kind of blew me away. I just sat there and just listened to what he had to say" (Umbreit et al., 2003, p. 248). In another case, the victim was amazed at her own reactions. "The biggest surprise was that at the end I noticed I was feeling forgiving toward the offender" (Umbreit et al., 2003, p. 248).

States vary in the use of paid staff or volunteers to be facilitators (Wilson, 2009). At the present time, four states use only paid staff, five states use community volunteers, four states use both staff who volunteer as well as community volunteers, and 10 states use both paid staff and volunteers. States also differ in whether they use a single facilitator or a co-facilitator model (Umbreit et al., 2003; Wilson, 2009). Currently, nine states use co-facilitators, nine states use a single facilitator, and six states use both options. Facilitators are assigned based, in part, on availability and geographic location by program administrators of victim service units in each state's Department of Corrections. They undergo rigorous and thorough training including victim sensitivity, inmate sensitivity, exploration of cultural difference, communication, self-care, spirituality and forgiveness, case studies, videos of actual dialogues, and in some states, mock scenarios (Umbreit et al., 2003). The mock scenarios involve bringing others in as actors to play the parts of victim and offender. Facilitators are also educated on departmental policy and procedures. Increased sensitivity to victims is regarded as crucial by trainees. One facilitator who worked within her state's department of corrections stated, "After a decade in the department of corrections you become very brash and matter of fact about things. Things don't shock you like they do other people. Can't be that way around victim survivors. Need to watch what (we say) and how we say something may offend or upset them" (Umbreit et al., 2003, p. 205).

DEATH ROW CASES

Eleven states do VOD with death row cases (Umbreit et al., 2003). There is an inherent controversy in choosing to offer mediated dialogue in capital cases where the outcome for offenders is ultimately death. Some have argued that "restorative justice" programs have no place in such a context because the premise of restorative justice, which is to restore victims, offenders, and community members, is incongruous with the death penalty, which creates a new group of profoundly injured people: the offender's family, and that the only truly restorative response would be to eliminate the death penalty (Radalet & Borg, 2000; Umbreit, Vos, Coates, & Brown, 2006). Despite the seeming contradiction, however, there remain the needs of victim survivors and that the decision to participate is voluntary on the offender's part. "Moreover to ban VOD from death penalty cases would strip those most directly affected by the horror of the crime of the opportunity to find some degree of meaning, healing and closure: a fundamental pillar of restorative justice" (Umbreit, 2000, p. 95).

The VOD process including preparation, dialogue session, and follow-up uses the same format as used in non-death penalty cases. Like non–death penalty cases, the reasons for meeting varied, underscoring that there is no one way to heal and no single "correct goal" for VOD in serious and violent crime. Despite the reality of the offender's having received a death sentence, offenders and victim survivors who have done VOD report satisfaction with the process (Umbreit et al., 2003; Umbreit, Vos, et al., 2006). They have expressed that the VOD experience served to humanize each to the other and gave both parties a chance to tell their stories, apologize, and, if desired, share forgiveness. Both victims and offenders found the experience powerful and healing, and they were relieved and renewed. From the offenders' perspective, each felt grateful to have been able to help family members begin to heal. Each man also described that participation in the mediation made it easier to face his impending death. "And it actually makes it a lot easier to face the execution . . . that you've done something positive, that at least something positive will come out of this" (Umbreit, Vos, et al., 2006, p. 366).

THE QUESTION OF FORGIVENESS

Restorative justice practices are frequently associated with the concept of forgiveness because of their ability to achieve emotional healing for the victim through processes that reduce vengefulness and increase empathy (Armour & Umbreit, 2005, 2006). Some even draw the erroneous conclusion that restorative justice explicitly promotes forgiveness. Forgiveness is a flashpoint of controversy among victim groups and victim advocates in part because crime victims have been told by their clergy that they must forgive in accordance with the tenets of their religion. These prescriptions to forgive have created much guilt and consternation in victims who are not able to do so. Many subsequently leave their church in search of another faith institution that is more sympathetic to their needs or no longer practice their faith.

Restorative justice does foster the possibility for forgiveness (Gehm, 1992). It recognizes the contribution forgiveness can make to the well-being of both victim and offender (Zehr, 1985) by helping release the victim from the negative power of the crime (Zehr, 1990), raising the offender back to the status of a human being (Van Biema, 1999), facilitating the offender's reintegration into the community (Cragg, 1992), restoring the victim's peace of mind (Van Stokkom, 2002), and potentially contributing to the victim's mental (e.g., Coyle & Enright, 1997; Freedman & Enright, 1996) and physical health (e.g., Witvliet, Ludwig, & Vander Laan, 2001). However, within the context of serious and violent crime, forgiveness is often referred to as the "f" word meaning that it is a dirty word within the survivor community and facilitators should exercise caution because of the emotional volatility associated with the word.

Relevance of Forgiveness to VOD

Out of all the restorative justice practices, VOD is the most vulnerable to being seen and misinterpreted as a forgiveness intervention because of the personal nature of the violation and the belief on the part of some people that forgiveness is necessary for true healing and inner peace. Program staffs for VOD take the position that forgiveness is not a part of the VOD agenda or its goal. Facilitators do not want to build up the expectation that forgiveness is possible or desirable. They are, however, willing to talk about it if the victim brings it up. The ethnographic study of VOD in Texas and Ohio (Umbreit et al., 2003) found that even though facilitators did not raise the issue themselves with participants nor did the researchers, over half the research sample made some mention of forgiveness issues during their interview. Among the victims who spoke about forgiveness, 15 out of 24 reported that they had forgiven the offender either prior to or during the dialogue session. Another eight volunteered that they had not forgiven, indicating that they never would or might someday. Among the offenders who spoke about forgiveness, 10 of the 25 who mentioned forgiveness reported that family members had shared forgiveness with them and the experience was quite moving for all of them. An additional four offenders reported changes in how victims or victim survivors felt toward them that led them to feel that they had come close to being forgiven.

This information is important because it suggests that forgiveness, though playing naturally in the background, is significant at some level to many victims and offenders. Extreme care must be exercised, however, in highlighting this aspect of the process because it can easily overshadow other critical factors such as the ability of VOD to restore victim safety and security (Armour & Umbreit, 2005, 2006).

Defining Forgiveness in Restorative Justice

The propensity for others outside of restorative justice to identify VOD or other restorative practices with forgiveness is related to the fact that the field of restorative justice has shied away from defining forgiveness in the context of restorative justice (Armour & Umbreit, 2006). Indeed, the ambivalence about forgiveness is heightened by the lack of agreement about just what it is. It is frequently defined by what it is not. "It does not imply forgetting, condoning, or excusing offenses, nor does it necessarily imply reconciliation, trust or release from legal accountability" (Exline, Worthington, Hill, & McCullough, 2003, p. 339).

When it is defined, there is often a division about what forgiveness entails beyond a change in motivation toward the offender. For some, forgiveness requires positive feelings toward the offender. For others, the absence of

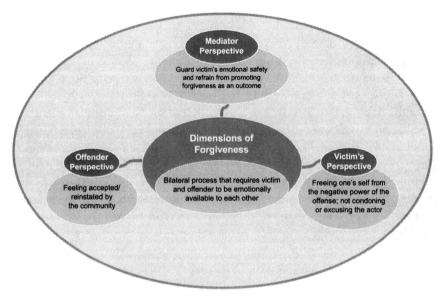

FIGURE 8.3

negative feelings is enough. Variability also exists as to whether or not victim forgiveness is defined as a decision or a journey, unconditional or obligatory, superficial or deep, and partial or full (Armour & Umbreit, 2006).

Although facilitators rightly respect the standard that victims and offenders must be the ones to initiate the topic of forgiveness and must always define it for themselves, it is also useful to the field of restorative justice and others to explicate the current and implicit dimensions of forgiveness in restorative justice. Moreover, because restorative justice is systemic in its focus, forgiveness is not one dimensional and must be viewed from multiple perspectives (Armour & Umbreit, 2005, 2006). (See Figure 8.3.)

The Victim's Perspective

From the victim's perspective, forgiveness refers to a conscious decision to free himself or herself from the negative power of the offense and the offender while not condoning or excusing the actor (Zehr, 1990). This letting go of the negative power usually refers to disconnecting from the trauma or releasing bitterness and vengeance (Armour & Umbreit, 2005, 2006). The reduction in negative motivations neither precludes nor includes positive feelings toward the offender. Victim forgiveness may be implicit, and its communication is not dependent on the use of explicit language or the occurrence of specific behaviors. Indeed, forgiveness may occur as a by-product that is communicated through a shift in attitude (e.g., letting go of anger) or behavior (e.g., no longer fighting against the offender's parole).

The Offender's Perspective

From the offender's perspective, the experience of being forgiven is associated with feeling accepted by representatives of the community (e.g., victim, mediator, neighborhood resident) who participate in a restorative justice conference (Armour & Umbreit, 2005, 2006). The feeling of being reinstated in the community as a moral citizen (Van Biema, 1999) occurs as the outgrowth of offender engagement in a process of accountability, remorse, and reparation.

The Facilitator's Perspective

Mediators refrain from promoting forgiveness as an outcome (Armour & Umbreit, 2005, 2006). Mediators guard the victim's emotional safety and the opportunity for authentic dialogue by remaining personally de-invested in the outcome, other than to support a process of healing that may include a change in the victim's attitude toward the offender.

Forgiveness as a Bilateral Process

Forgiveness, in the context of restorative justice dialogue, is a derivative of a bilateral process that requires victim and offender to be emotionally available to each other (Armour & Umbreit, 2005, 2006). Change may be created in both victim and offender as a result of their impact on each other. The victim's pain, for example, may reduce the offender's denial and elicit the remorse necessary for offender self-accountability and victim healing. Similarly, the offender's remorse may reduce the victim's anger and vengeance and foster empathy. If appropriate and desired, the mutuality in this kind of interpersonal influence may advance the conditions for victim forgiveness.

Notwithstanding the forgoing comments, restorative justice advocates also recognize and accept that many persons initiate and choose to forgive because granting forgiveness is congruent with their personal or religious beliefs (Armour & Umbreit, 2005, 2006). If a victim elects to offer unconditional forgiveness to an offender, the facilitator supports the victim's decision and helps facilitate the interchange.

Forgiveness in the context of restorative justice and VOD remains a paradox (Armour & Umbreit, 2005, 2006). The practice for facilitators of allowing it to play in the background unimpeded and instead to focus on creating a safe place for dialogue increases the likelihood that many victims will feel safe enough to travel the path of authentic forgiveness, if that is what they truly desire.

RESEARCH ON THE IMPACT OF VOD

The ethnographic study of Texas and Ohio (Umbreit et al., 2003) collected information on participants' satisfaction and the impact of VOD on participant lives. All but one of the 78 or 99% of participants who responded reported that they were satisfied, and 65% of them indicated that they were "very satisfied." In addition, 73 participants found the dialogue session to be helpful, and 96% of them found the meeting to be "very helpful." Among victims, 85% said they would recommend VOD to others in similar circumstances, and 97% of offenders felt that any similar offender who was offered the opportunity to meet with a victim should do so.

A total of 63 participants or 80% of the sample reported that participation in the VOD process had a profound effect on their lives (Umbreit et al., 2003). Specific changes for victims and family members included personal growth and healing, feelings about the offender for the better, outlook on life for the better, and strengthened spirituality. In discussing the reasons for these changes, victims and family members talked about letting go of hate, obtaining answers, placing the anger where it belongs, having a human encounter, and/or experiencing the offenders' ownership and remorse as having been important factors.

Specific changes for offenders included personal growth and healing, outlook on life for the better, strengthened spirituality, and thinking that victim's feelings about them had changed for the better (Umbreit et al., 2003). In discussing the reasons for these changes, offenders pointed to being accountable, seeing their victim as a person, understanding the impact of their actions, being able to give something back, feeling the victim/family member's opinion of them had changed for the better, and being more open to feelings.

Participants were also asked about any regrets they had about their participation (Umbreit et al., 2003). Only one person reported regrets and that was an offender who, despite his very high satisfaction with his participation and his positive assessment of its impact on his life, nonetheless feared that in some way the state might use his participation against him, which might negatively impact his case. Participants were also asked about any negative consequences that they would not otherwise have incurred. Two offenders reported events that could be considered a negative consequence. For one offender, confidentiality regarding his case was breached when the victim's family member used real names in a presentation at which a reporter was present. For another offender, the participating victim reported that as a result of the meeting, she would continue to fight the offender's parole. This latter case may not in fact be an instance of harm; the victim in this case already was in opposition to the offender's release and simply did not change her position.

Fraser Region Community Justice Initiatives Association (FRCJIA), a community-based nonprofit organization in Langley, British Columbia, operates a VOD program for crimes of severe violence. FRCJIA has facilitated over 350 cases over 15 years. A survey of the reasons for the program's effectiveness by participants includes the following (Gustafson, 2005):

1. The "reality of the process," which refers to the fact that the dialogue session is not a role-play or some kind of psychotherapy but takes place between the "real" principles
2. The degree of safety, respect, and empowerment experienced at each stage of the process
3. The "values commitments," professionalism, skills, personal traits, and attributes of facilitators such as humanness, warmth, care, trustworthiness, and tenacity
4. The trust relationships between participants and facilitators
5. The power of the process for discovering (or creating) empathy in offenders
6. The validation of the victim's perception of truth by the offender

The results from FRCJIA and the ethnographic study of Texas and Ohio suggest that VOD is a powerful and beneficial practice for both victims and offenders. It also holds promise as an initiative that can unlock traumatic experience and free victims and offenders, to some extent, to move forward with their lives (Gustafson, 2005).

CONCLUSION

Although emerging out of VOM, VOD has unique characteristics as a restorative justice practice because its focus on serious and violent harm requires concentration on issues of extreme loss and trauma. In 15 short years, VOD has grown into a full-fledged program that is supported by Departments of Correction in 25 states. Indeed, it likely has more institutional support nationally than do many other restorative justice practices. It is also unique because it is a postconviction practice and is solely victim initiated at least in the United States. Although not psychotherapy, it does provide an opportunity for deep healing that is entirely client driven. It requires intensive training for facilitators, time for the process to unfold for both victim and offender, and tight coordination with the bureaucracy of the prison system. Because of the level of injury and emotional need, VOD has both the challenge and potential to provide a transformative process for crime victims, offenders, family members, and other support people in their search for meaning and healing in the aftermath of serious and violent crimes. At its core, the process of VOD is about engaging those most affected by the horror of violent crime in the process of holding the offender truly accountable; helping the victim gain a greater sense of meaning, if not closure, concerning the harm resulting from the crime; and helping all parties to have a greater capacity to move on with their lives in a positive fashion (Umbreit et al., 2003).

REFERENCES

Armour, M., & Umbreit, M. S. (2005). The paradox of forgiveness in restorative justice. In E. L. Worthington, Jr. (Ed.), *Handbook of forgiveness* (pp. 491–503). New York: Brunner-Routledge.

Armour, M., & Umbreit, M. S. (2006). Victim forgiveness in restorative justice dialogue. *Victim and Offender, 1*(2), 123–140.

Borton, I. M. (2008). *Victim offender communication in felony cases: An archival analysis of Ohio's Office of Victim Services Dialogue Program.* Bowling Green, OH: Bowling Green State University.

Correctional Service of Canada. (2009). *Victim-offender mediation: A brief overview.* Retrieved Janaury 5, 2010, from http://www.csc-scc.gc.ca/text/rj/vom-eng.shtml

Coyle, C. T., & Enright, R. D. (1997). Forgiveness intervention with postabortion men. *Journal of Consulting and Clinical Psychology, 65*, 1042–1046.

Cragg, W. (1992). *The practice of punishment.* London: Rutledge.

Darves-Bornoz, J. M., Choquet, M., Ledoux, S., Gasquet, I., & Manfredi, R. (1998). Gender differences in symptoms of adolescents reporting sexual assault. *Social Psychiatry and Psychiatric Epidemiology, 33*, 111–117.

Exline, J. J., Worthington, E. L., Jr., Hill, P., & McCullough, M. E. (2003). Forgiveness and justice: A research agenda for social and personality psychology. *Personality and Social Psychology Review, 7*, 337–348.

Flaten, C. (1996). Victim offender mediation: Application with serious offences committed by juveniles. In B. Galaway & J. Hudson (Eds.), *Restorative justice: International perspectives* (pp. 387–402). Monsey, NY: Criminal Justice Press.

Freedman, S. R., & Enright, R. D. (1996). Forgiveness as an intervention goal with incest survivors. *Journal of Consulting and Clinical Psychology, 64*, 983–992.

Freedy, J. R., Resnick, H. S., Kilpatrick, D. G., Dansky, B. S., & Tidwell, R. P. (1994). The psychological adjustment of recent crime victims in the criminal justice system. *Journal of Interpersonal Violence, 9*, 450–468.

Gehm, J. R. (1992). The function of forgiveness in the criminal justice system. In J. Messmer & H. Otto (Eds.), *Restorative justice on trial* (pp. 541–550). Boston: Kluwer Academic Publishers.

Gilboa-Schechtman, E., & Foa, E. B. (2001). Patterns of recovery after trauma: The use of inter-individual analysis. *Journal of Abnormal Psychology, 110*, 392–400.

Gustafson, D. (2005). Exploring treatment and trauma recovery implications of facilitating victim-offender encounters in crimes of severe violence: Lessons from the Canadian experience. In E. Elliott & R. M. Gordon (Eds.), *New directions in restorative justice: Issues, practice, evaluation* (pp. 193–227). Portland, OR: Willan Publishing.

Gustafson, D., & Smistra, H. (1989). *Victim offender reconciliation in serious crime: A report on the feasibility study undertaken for the Ministry of the Solicitor General (Canada)*. Langley, BC: Fraser Region Community Justice Initiative Association.

Leskin, G. A., & Sheikh, J. I. (2002). Lifetime trauma history and panic disorder: Findings from the National Comorbidity Survey. *Journal of Anxiety Disorders, 16*, 599–603.

Minnesota Department of Corrections. (n.d.). *Victim assistance program: Apology letters*. Retrieved January 5, 2010, from http://www.doc.state.mn.us/crimevictim/apology.htm

Peters, T., & Aertsen, I. (2000). Towards restorative justice, victimization and victim support and trends in criminal justice. In Council of European Union (Ed.), *Crime and criminal justice in Europe* (pp. 35–46). Strasburg, Germany: Council of Europe Publishing.

Radalet, M., & Borg, M. (2000). Comment on Umbreit and Vos. *Homicide Studies, 4*(1), 88–92.

Roberts, T. (1995). *Evaluation of the victim offender mediation project*. Victoria, BC: Focus Consultants.

Strang, H. (2002). *Repair or revenge: Victims and restorative justice*. Oxford: Clarendon Press.

Szmania, S. (2006). Mediators' communication in victim offender mediation/dialogue involved crimes of severe violence: An analysis of opening statements. *Conflict Resolution Quarterly, 24*(1), 111–127.

Thompson, M. P., Norris, F. H., & Ruback, R. B. (1998). Comparative distress levels of inner-city family members of homicide victims. *Journal of Traumatic Stress, 11*, 223–242.

Umbreit, M. S. (1989). Violent offenders and their victims. In M. Wright & B. Galaway (Eds.), *Mediation and criminal justice* (pp. 337–352). London: Sage.

Umbreit, M. S. (2000). Reply to Radalet and Borg. *Homicide Studies, 4*(1), 93–97.

Umbreit, M. S. (2001). *Victim meets offender: The impact of restorative justice and mediation*. Monsey, NY: Criminal Justice Press.

Umbreit, M. S., Coates, R., Vos, B., & Armour, M. (2006). Victims of severe violence in mediated dialogue with offender: The impact of the first multi-site study in the U.S. *International Review of Victimology, 13*(1), 27–48.

Umbreit, M. S., Vos, B., Coates, R., & Armour, M. (in press). Victim offender dialogue in cases of homicide: Participants' experience. *Journal of Community Corrections*.

Umbreit, M. S., Vos, B., Coates, R., & Brown, K. (2003). *Facing violence: The path of restorative justice & dialogue*. Monsey, NY: Criminal Justice Press.

Umbreit, M. S., Vos, B., Coates, R., & Brown, K. (2006). Facilitated dialogue on death row: Family members of murder victims and inmates share their experiences. In J. R. Acker & D. R. Karp (Eds.), *Wounds that do not bind: Victim-based perspectives on the death penalty* (pp. 349–375). Durham, NC: Carolina Academic Press.

Van Biema, D. (1999). Should all be forgiven? *Time, 153*, 55.

Van Stokkom, B. (2002). Moral emotions in restorative justice conferences: Managing shame, designing empathy. *Theoretical Criminology, 6*(3), 339–360.

Wilson, J. (2009). *U.S. corrections based victim offender dialogue programs in crimes of severe violence: An overview of policies and protocols.* Somerset, Maine: Just Alternatives.

Wilson, J. (n.d.). Crying for justice. *Hope Magazine,* 9–14.

Witvliet, C., Ludwig, T. E., & Vander Laan, K. (2001). Granting forgiveness or harbouring grudges: Implications for emotion, physiology, and health. *Psychological Science, 12,* 117–123.

Zehr, H. (1985). *Retributive justice, restorative justice*: Mennonite Central Committee, U.S. Office of Criminal Justice.

Zehr, H. (1990). *Changing lenses: A new focus for crime and justice.* Scottsdale, PA: Herald Press.

9. The Facilitator's Role in Restorative Justice Dialogue

> *Please remember, it is what you are that heals, not what you know.*
>
> Carl Jung

From the 1970s through the early 1990s, the term *restorative justice was, for many, synonymous with one model of practice called victim-offender reconciliation (VORP) or victim-offender mediation (VOM). The standard for facilitation within restorative justice grew out of that practice thereby setting the stage for how to facilitate FGC, peacemaking circles and VOD. Initially, these other models were positioned as distinct from each other with the primary focus on the differences among them* (Roberts, 2004).

Although outlining the specifications for each practice is helpful for delineating one from the other and for understanding what is unique about each one, separating them out from each other does not represent what has been happening in real time. Indeed, there has been a gradual shift toward looking at the similarities and overlaps between and among all the restorative justice dialogue models. More and more hybrids have been developed, as characteristics of each practice have been mixed and matched to better meet the needs of participants and the social issues involving harm. Consequently, a facilitator might use a talking piece to manage a conference or a multi-problem VOM. A case might involve an initial meeting between victim and offender and a follow up meeting might include family and community members to address underlying issues relevant to the offender and his family. Facilitators therefore must have skills that can not only be used for specific traditional models but also skills that can be adapted for the variations within models as well as among them.

Facilitation varies, to a large extent, based on the seriousness of the crime committed, the purpose and intent of the dialogue, and the number of participants. (See Figure 9.1.) Specifically, the protocol for how to handle an hour-long meeting between a victim and offender that results in a reparation

240   RESTORATIVE JUSTICE DIALOGUE

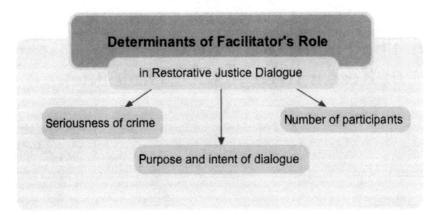

FIGURE 9.1

agreement about how the offender will pay the repair costs for vandalizing the victim's car makes different and lesser demands on a facilitator than one that involves a 6-month protocol for preparing a victim and offender for a dialogue about the impact on the victim of the offender's attempt to take her life.

Likewise, the pressures on the facilitator for meeting with a single victim and offender are significantly different from the level of stress occurring when a facilitator conducts a sentencing circle with community members or a family group decision-making conference where extended family members determine who will raise a child. It is important, therefore, to recognize that although there are foundational principles that guide facilitation in restorative justice forums, facilitators need particular knowledge and skills to mediate complex interpersonal dynamics as well as the ability to work with cases involving highly dramatic, severe interpersonal violence (Gustafson, 2004; Wilson, n.d.). This is especially true for facilitation involving criminal offenses with a power base component, notably sexual abuse and domestic violence (Gustafson, 2004). Although these power dynamics may be blatant, they more often manifest themselves in subtle and hidden ways even from the participants themselves. Facilitator education and experience, therefore, are critical in working with these dynamics, which include a thorough grounding in the victim experience, trauma, and posttraumatic syndromes. Ensuring that practitioners are competent to facilitate at the highest level demanded by the case is crucial to the safety of program participants.

There has been debate in the restorative justice community about what to call the person who serves as a guide for the dialogue. Some have felt that the term *mediator*, which is the same term used in the legal field of dispute resolution, might be confusing or even misleading. Consequently, the term *facilitator* was introduced as an alternative. When peacemaking and sentencing circles were introduced, the term *circle keeper* became popular as a way to express that the ownership of the process rested with the circle. In this chapter, the terms *mediator* and *facilitator* will be used interchangeably.

This chapter examines three subjects: (1) the differences in facilitating a settlement-driven versus dialogue-driven mediation, (2) the concept of introducing a humanistic approach to mediation and dialogue, (3) the characteristics and qualities of an effective mediator in relation to the victim and offender, the facilitator's responsibilities during preparation, the dialogue itself, and follow-up, including the significance of self-care. Nowhere else in the restorative justice process is the principle of respect and being nonjudgmental more critical than in how the facilitator treats the victim, offender, and other key stakeholders. Indeed, the facilitator's respectful interaction with the parties sets the tone for how they need to engage with each other.

Answers in the restorative justice community to questions about who should facilitate dialogues or what qualifications are necessary remain general, imprecise, and ambiguous in the restorative justice community. The field has been reluctant to offer certification or suggest a required path to follow in order to gain the skills necessary to conduct circles, family group conferences, or victim-offender mediations. Indeed, in the interests of not being restrictive or exclusionary, the field, in effect, has taken a laissez-faire approach to skill development. However, restorative justice leaders also advise that facilitating dialogues requires strong relational skills, extreme sensitivity to the simultaneous needs of a diverse group of people, deep compassion, and the ability to understand and attend to process over outcome.

These same leaders warn as well that although a certain type and level of education is necessary, education alone is insufficient and can through words used, manner of dress, assumptions made about being "better than" or being "the expert," though unintended, create the kind of social distance that mars the chances for genuine engagement. These kinds of mixed messages may retard growth in the understanding of restorative justice facilitation, which is actually quite complex and demanding. This chapter attempts to explicate the dimensions of the role so that the personal characteristics, competencies, and skills that are needed are more clearly defined.

DIFFERENCES BETWEEN SETTLEMENT-DRIVEN AND DIALOGUE-DRIVEN MEDIATION

There are many types of mediation, including divorce mediation; disputes related to guardianship, trusts, and probate matters; and so on. In these situations, the parties are called disputants and the assumption made that both are

242 RESTORATIVE JUSTICE DIALOGUE

contributing to the conflict and both must compromise to reach an agreement. Mediation, therefore, focuses on reaching a settlement, with less emphasis on discussing the full impact of the conflict on the disputants' lives. Moreover, contemporary mediation practice places a strong emphasis on procedural fairness and the need to develop a mutually acceptable agreement in the quickest and most efficient manner possible (Umbreit & Burns, 2002). See Figure 9.2 for the differences between settlement-driven and dialogue-driven mediation.

Settlement-driven mediation is generally practiced within a conflict resolution context, not a healing paradigm (Gold, 1993). Indeed, the mediation has a strong task orientation focused on problem solving (Umbreit & Greenwood, 2000). Healing, though valued, is not the primary goal but rather a hoped for bonus based on a collaborative, constructive process aimed at resolution. Moreover, the mediator's role is defined narrowly and within the parameters of remaining neutral and impartial with no vested interest in the outcome. This practice does not take into account the relationship between client and mediator or the "'presence" the mediator brings to the negotiation sessions (Gold, 1993).

In contrast, dialogue-driven mediation recognizes that most conflicts develop within a larger emotional and relational context characterized by powerful feelings of disrespect, betrayal, and abuse. When these feelings about the past and current state of the relationship are suppressed or not aired in a healthy manner, an agreement might be reached but the underlying emotional conflict remains. Little healing of the emotional wound is likely to occur without an opening of the heart for genuine

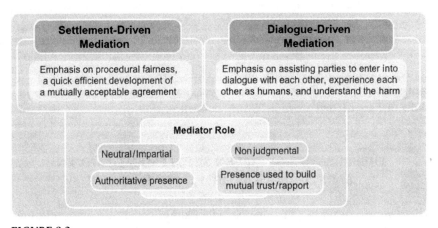

FIGURE 9.2

dialogue, empowerment, and recognition of each other's humanity despite the conflict (Umbreit & Burns, 2002). Indeed, with criminal offenses and cases involving harms as horrendous as murder, settlement is not what motivates participants to become involved with each other (Gustafson, 2005). Dialogue-driven mediation within the context of restorative justice also rests on the fact that one faction has clearly committed a criminal offense and admitted to it, whereas the other faction has clearly been victimized. Therefore, the parties are not equal. In addition, the issue of guilt or innocence is not mediated, and crime victims are not expected to compromise or settle by requesting less than what they need to restore their losses (Umbreit & Greenwood, 2000). Although a restitution agreement or reparation plan may be arrived at, the priority is given to the dialogue between the victim and offender or among the stakeholders. The emphasis in the actual dialogue is on the emotional and information needs of victims that are at the forefront of the purpose to empower the victim and develop empathy in the offender, which hopefully will inhibit future criminal behavior.

In dialogue-driven mediation, the mediator's role is to assist parties to enter a dialogue with each other, experience each other as human beings along with the harm that has occurred, and facilitate a process of mutual aid. The mediator's role appears to be deceptively simple. The mediator must put aside his or her own biases in order to be nonjudgmental and so that he or she can focus solely on the needs of the involved parties. Instead of remaining emotionally distant to ensure neutrality, the mediator works to connect and build trust and rapport through deep and compassionate listening. Indeed, being nonjudgmental means being open to hearing other people's stories and being self-aware about what pushes a mediator's personal buttons because "if you are not at peace with your stuff then you cannot feel the pain" of others (Umbreit, Vos, Coates, & Brown, 2003, p. 375).

In addition, it requires being fully present and supportive of the involved parties; honoring their strength and inner wisdom; respecting their needs and choices; using a very nondirective style of mediation; and being mindful of not speaking too much while honoring the enormous healing power often found in silence. In a humanistic approach to mediation and dialogue, the mediator's role is not at all simple. It requires an exceptionally strong exercise of self-discipline and personal integrity. The mediator's role in dialogue-driven mediation, therefore, has more to do with being than with doing. See Table 9.1 for a summary of the differences between problem-solving mediation (settlement driven) and humanistic mediation (dialogue driven).

TABLE 9.1 Comparison of problem solving and humanistic mediation

	Classic Problem-Solving Mediation	Humanistic/Transformative Mediation
Primary focus	Settlement driven and problem focused.	Dialogue driven and relationship focused.
Preparation of parties in conflict	Mediator has no separate contact with involved parties, prior to mediation. Intake staff person collects information.	Mediator conducts at least one face-to-face meeting with each party prior to bringing them together in joint mediation session. Focus is on listening to their stories, building rapport, explaining the process, and clarifying expectations.
Role of mediator	Direct and guide the communication of the involved parties toward a mutually acceptable settlement of the conflict.	Prepare the involved parties prior to bringing them together so that they have realistic expectations and feel safe enough to later engage in a direct conversation/dialogue with each other facilitated by the mediator.
Style of mediation	Active and often very directive, speaking frequently during the mediation session and asking many questions.	Very nondirective during the mediation session. After opening statement by mediator, the mediator fades into the background and is reluctant to interrupt direct conversation between parties. Mediator is not, however, passive and will intervene if parties indicate a need.
Dealing with emotional context of conflict	Low tolerance for expression of feelings and the party's "storytelling" related to the history and context of the conflict.	Encouragement of open expression of feelings and discussion of the context and history of the conflict. Recognition of the intrinsic healing quality of "storytelling" when speaking and listening from the heart.
Moments of silence	Few moments of silence. Mediator uncomfortable with silence and feeling the need to speak or ask questions of the parties.	Many prolonged moments of silence. Mediator reluctant to interrupt silence and honors silence as integral to genuine empowerment and healing.
Written agreements	Primary goal and most likely outcome of mediation. Agreements focus on clear tangible elements.	Frequently occur but secondary to the primary goal of dialogue and mutual aid (the parties helping each other through the sharing of information and expression of feelings). Agreements may often focus on symbolic gestures, personal growth tasks, or affirmations of the new relationship between the parties.

HUMANISTIC MEDIATION

Dialogue-driven mediation is often referred to as humanistic mediation (Umbreit, 1997; Umbreit & Greenwood, 2000). This concept is based on the work of Carl Rogers, a pioneer in humanistic psychology, who emphasized the importance of empathic understanding, unconditional positive regard, and genuineness. It is also rooted in the formulations advanced by three social workers: Virginia Satir, Dennis Saleeby, and William Schwartz.

Virginia Satir was a world renowned family therapist, teacher, and trainer who identified the supreme importance of the presence of the therapist. Satir, who was steeped in the humanistic tradition, regarded authentic human connection as being fundamental to change processes (Gold, 1993).

Dennis Saleeby (1992) and his colleagues built a theory of helping based on the strengths perspective, which recognizes that humans possess inherent power to transform their own lives. Saleeby noted that helping ". . . occurs through a kind of dialogue; a give-and-take that begins with the demystification of the professional as expert, an operating sense of humility on the part of the helper, the establishment of an egalitarian transaction, the desire to engage clients on their own terms, and a willing to disclose and share" (1992, p. 420).

William Schwartz highlighted mediation as the core function of social work specific to relationships between people, including the helper (Schwartz, 1976). He delineated the process by dividing it into four processes: (1) "tuning in," (2) the beginnings, (3) the tasks, and (4) transitions and ending. These phases are analogous to the self-preparation of the mediator, preparation of dialogue participants, the dialogue meeting, and follow-up. Schwartz emphasized that the social worker as mediator sensitively holds the realities of more than one constituent and further the mediator must "not only help people talk but help them talk to each other . . . purposeful talk that is related to [what] brings them together . . . it must have feeling in it . . . and be about real things" (Schwartz, as cited in Berman-Rossi, 1994, p. 315).

Humanistic mediation refers to the mediator's presence, which is much deeper than physical presence and central to helping change happen because humanistic mediation is rooted in the belief that "the way we stand in relation to each other fosters healing" (Gold, 1993, p. 59). It also refers to particular qualities that the mediator must cultivate to be competent and effective in conducting different types of dialogues.

Mediator "Presence"

Presence refers to a mediator's bearing, personality, or appearance. His or her unique persona or personal being is what the mediator uses to engage with

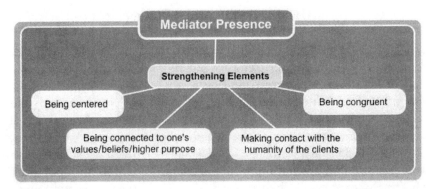

FIGURE 9.3

others and through which he or she expresses thoughts and feelings specific to furthering the dialogue process. A mediator's professional "being," and hence presence, is shaped, in part, by the steadfastness of his or her beliefs in the principles or values that undergird restorative justice work. Presence is additionally strengthened by the mediator's attention to four key elements: (1) being centered; (2) being connected to governing values, beliefs, and highest purpose; (3) making contact with the humanity of clients; and (4) being congruent (Gold, 1993). (See Figure 9.3.)

Being Centered

Before mediators can listen fully or connect empathically with victims, offenders, or other stakeholders, they must clean away the clutter that otherwise clogs their ability to hear and feel (Umbreit, 1997). This clearing the clutter requires a conscious decision to move away from their own lives and enter a space that allows them to focus fully on what they are observing and experiencing in the present without interfering with it. This transition internally aligns mediators with what is around them, opens them to see anew because thinking and judgment are suspended, lets them view others from the heart, and grounds them in a sense of reverence for human existence, personal truth, and the healing that needs to happen (Gold, 1993). When mediators are centered, they project a sense of calm that helps pull others in the same space so that participants can unreservedly reflect their own emotional realities.

Being Connected to Values, Beliefs, and Highest Purpose

Besides the governing values that define humanistic mediation, mediators must cultivate their emotional commitment to and connection with the highest principles they assign to the dialogue work (Gold, 1993). Those personally held principles may be about the power of honesty; the importance of human interconnection, self-determination, or a reverence for personal growth as an antidote to life-diminishing experiences; and so on. When those principles become clearer, more conscious, and amplified, they become a guiding force that organizes the facilitator's behavior at even an unconscious level and reduces the ambivalence that can otherwise impede the level of sharing or risk taking necessary to make change happen.

Connecting With the Humanity of the Participants

Connecting with the humanity of others requires mediators to be aware of the shadow side of themselves and the reality that each of us is capable of evil as well as good (Williams & Williams, 1994). Also, feelings are sloppy work (Doerfler, 2004), and mediators have to grow a tolerance for ambiguity and uncertainty without trying to "fix" things. This tolerance includes the self-discipline to just listen (Umbreit, 1997). Pure listening is extremely powerful because it places the spotlight on the other person, which permits, even obliges, that person to set their thoughts in order and look at the causes and consequences of their actions (Williams & Williams, 1994). Listening to the human side of those who have violated others or been wounded by another's wrongdoing—the side not seen or recognized by others—also helps the other side to see.

Being Congruent

Having an authentic connection with others requires "congruence," a condition of being emotionally honest with yourself in which there is consistency in your words, feelings, body and facial expressions and actions (Umbreit, 1997). Because mistrust of the other is a natural consequence of wrongdoing for both victims and offenders, mediators must expect to be questioned and tested for their authenticity. Indeed, in many ways, the facilitator is a stand in for the actual person victims or offenders will encounter in the dialogue. Are you who you say you are? What is your intent? Mediators must therefore be transparent. Their ability to be who they are, unencumbered by "shoulds" and self-consciousness, makes them real and gives permission to victims and offenders to do the same. Indeed, it is the congruence in a victim's or offender's presence and not the content of what either says that makes each believable to the other.

Qualifications and Qualities of a Mediator

Restorative justice is a movement that is rooted in community. Although mediators may be credentialed as social workers, criminal justice officials, clergy, or other type of specialist, they may just as likely have no formal degree

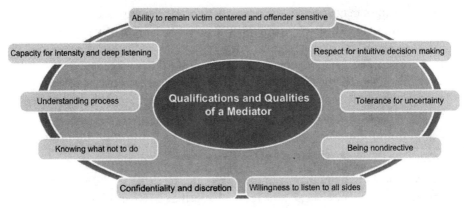

FIGURE 9.4

but rather have passion for the values and tenets of restorative justice or deep commitment to giving offenders a way back or furthering safety in their neighborhoods. Indeed, there is little support in the field for greater professionalism in the mediator's role because it can lead to exclusionary practices and the placing of professional or financial self-interest over genuine concern for others. Consequently, mediator competence is defined broadly as "the confluence of knowledge, honed skills, character, personality traits, attitudes and experience" (Gustafson, 2004, p. 309). A recognized director of a mediation or conferencing program advises others to "hire for the heart; teach for the skills" (Gustafson, 2004, p. 309).

Dialogue practices vary widely in terms of the degree of mediator knowledge and specific skills necessary to be effective. Facilitating a peacemaking circle in an elementary school will require a different level of proficiency than conducting a dialogue between a victim and offender of domestic violence or being the keeper for a sentencing circle with community members related to a hate crime. Facilitators of humanistic mediation, however, need to develop their abilities widely if they are planning to mediate a variety of issues or expect to facilitate dialogues involving severe violence or power dynamics (see Figure 9.4).

Willingness to Listen to All Sides

Facilitators must have a tolerance for a wide range of viewpoints. It may be difficult to listen sympathetically to the chilling account of a planned robbery or not join forces with a family who is outraged with an uncle for raping his niece. The mediator must remember, however, that he or she needs to be able to hear all voices with the idea that the ultimate goal is for them to begin to hear each other.

Ability to Remain Victim Centered and Offender Sensitive

Jon Wilson, a noted mediator from Maine, argues that restorative justice has become increasingly synonymous with expectations of forgiveness and reconciliation, instead of addressing harms and enabling accountability (2005). He contends that this slippage is due to the fact that practitioners lack an understanding of victim awareness. Their ignorance is costly because it leads them to presume that they know best what victims need or to insist on some sort of theoretically prescribed balance between the needs of the victim, offender, and community.

Wilson (2005) and others (Armour & Umbreit, 2005, 2006) insist that VOD is not about forgiveness or reconciliation—unless that is absolutely and unequivocally what the survivor wants it to be about. Wilson proposes that the term *restorative justice* be modified to *victim-centered restorative justice* in order to reduce the ambiguities about the purpose of restorative justice and reanchor it in the harms of victimization. He says, It is ". . . no longer a question about how restorative justice is defined when it is victim-centered. And with that ambiguity gone, the promise of this approach for healing and justice and accountability returns. Not just for victims/survivors, but for offenders, and for the community, as well" (Wilson, 2005, p. 63).

Confidentiality and Discretion

Wrongdoing results in the breaking of trust and a sense of separation. Victims feel alone, violated, and vulnerable (Sharpe, 1998). Offenders feel defiant and justified. The effect from wrongdoing extends outward into the community. Both victims and offenders find that others feel threatened because of the fear others feel around them. The decision to meet often runs headlong into the concomitant pull to avoid the pain associated with betrayal, loss, isolation, and feeling an outcast. The ability to help participants feel safe, therefore, is paramount. Confidentiality is of particular concern because each party knows that the mediator is also meeting with others including the other party. Unless participants can trust that what they share alone with the facilitator or what they express to each other in the dialogue will remain private, they will hold back on what they say, which can undermine the potential for healing.

If there are limits on disclosure due to the nature of the case, that is, child abuse, policies of an agency, or a lack of legal protections specific to disclosure (for example, admission of prior offenses, threat to commit future crimes including harm to others, abuse and/or neglect of children and/or vulnerable adults), these should be discussed with all parties at the outset

(Reimund, 2004). However, mediators must also use discretion, deciding what, when, and how to make suggestions or share information that will help bring the parties to each other.

Capacity for Intensity and Deep Listening

Although the purpose and depth of dialogue practices vary, the facilitator must recognize that nothing is simply what it appears to be. Mediators, therefore, must encourage talk that is not only purposeful but expressive of feelings. Moreover, because healing by nature is multilayered and multidimensional, mediators need to be able to help victims and offenders process, when appropriate, what is deep in their hearts, not just what is immediate and from the head (Doerfler, 2004).

Tolerance for Uncertainty

Inherent in humanistic mediation is the expectation that the dialogue belongs to the participants and the facilitator does not get in the way of what needs to happen between people. Consequently, mediators need to be patient with a victim who remains ambivalent about whether or not to participate in the process of understanding of an offender whose denial continues to block the full realization of what he did. One facilitator described the time it took for the victim to draft the list of questions he had for the offender. "We wanted to know what he expected . . . We kept talking and talking. Each time he would come up with another question. Finally there were several sessions when the list was set" (Umbreit et al., 2003, p. 376).

Respect for Intuitive Decision Making

Because each dialogue is a process rather than a product and rests on a multitude of factors including the severity of the crime, the harm done, the needs and expectations of individual stakeholders, the type of dialogue and when it occurs in the criminal justice process, and so on, mediators cannot follow a preset plan. Rather they have to make countless decisions in dealing with stakeholders and bringing them together, including their readiness to meet, what to ask, when to challenge perceptions, when to introduce topics for their consideration, and so on. Mediators, therefore, rely on their intuition to help guide them. Intuition is the act of knowing or sensing without the use of rational processes. Indeed, mediators often describe the decisions they made as coming from their gut. In response to a question about knowing when participants are ready to meet, a facilitator spoke about decision making regarding his own readiness, "Ultimately and honestly, you trust your gut. The reason multiple meetings are needed is not just for the parties. It is for you too" (Umbreit et al., 2003, p. 378).

Understanding Process

Restorative justice dialogue is a process rather than a product. It involves a number of sequential and concurrent actions. The results of any one change influences what comes next in time. Sometimes it's a small change. A facilitator described what happened after an offender watched a videotape of the victim expressing her thoughts to him. "As he felt her sincerity, things began to really change in him. At several points he could see his common ground with the victim." A mother talked about her decision to meet with the offender after her ex-husband had done it. "My ex-husband kept on me . . . 'You've just really gotta do it to be able to go on with your life. It will just be so helpful to you and you can just get all these things answered. I don't wanna tell you all the things he said, I want you to find out—I want you to experience it. I want you to experience what I have felt.'—You know, now, I'm glad that he did. If he hadn't have done it, you know, I probably would never have done it."

Process is about movement. Rather than being attached to any particular outcome, mediators have to learn to read and stay with the process and to know that each action that a person takes opens up possibilities that move things forward. They must also be sensitive to the smallest detail recognizing that where people sit, who accompanies them to the dialogue as support, the frequency of the contact kept by the mediator, the words a facilitator selects, or tone of voice used to express the lack of resolution felt by a group all impact safety and movement.

Being Nondirective

The practice of humanistic mediation requires mediators to be noncontrolling, accepting of what they do not know, and continually returning the decision-making process to the parties involved. Although they may provide leadership or assistance, it is done only in accord with the ultimate goals and usually in the form of a question that helps the participant discover their own answers. This level of respect also engenders humility or the lessening of ego so that mediators can see themselves as part of a world larger than themselves. Being nondirective results in the mediator most often speaking little during the session and allowing plenty of room for silence as people may need space for reflection or as they may struggle to find their voice.

Knowing What Not to Do

Although a humanistic approach to mediation and dialogue may have therapeutic benefits to the participants, therapy is not the focus of restorative dialogue. Mediators, therefore, must take care not to violate the boundaries of vulnerable participants and impose their own agendas about health and healing onto others. The goal of the dialogue is to bring people together to address the harms done. The facilitator's job is to empower and support participants through the process by drawing on their strengths and yearnings for resolution.

Mediators must also maintain boundaries about personal self-disclosure. The relationship with participants exists for the purpose of facilitating their dialogue. Although mediators may selectively share information about their own lives as a way to connect, demystify themselves to participants who may otherwise ascribe attributes and powers to the facilitator that he or she does not have, or prompt movement in a victim or offender, they must remember that their relationship with participants is time limited and exists for the participants' needs, not their own.

In an interview, mediators were asked to describe what they would look for if they were hiring mediators or seeking volunteer facilitators to work within the humanistic approach (Umbreit et al., 2003). Mediators said the following things: "They need to be open to hearing other people's stories and act in a way that is nonjudgmental, not condemning." Being self-aware was important. "You may have all the skill and all the understanding up in the head on trauma and recovery, but if you are not at peace with this stuff—if you are not able to be with suffering in a way that you do not run from it—then you cannot feel pain." The capacity for deep listening is paramount. "To hear the story is to recognize and embrace the incredible healing power of storytelling—uninterrupted storytelling. Not active listening, not paraphrasing, but when you are fully present to listen from the heart. And time stops. Everything else is gone and you just listen" (Umbreit et al., 2003, pp. 374–375).

THE FACILITATOR'S ROLE WITH VICTIMS AND OFFENDERS

The mediation process is generally divided into three phases: referral and preparation, dialogue session, and follow-up. The tasks involved and facilitator's role vary based on the phase of the process and whether or not the facilitator is working with the victim or offender.

The Facilitator's Role With the Victim

When a wrongdoing or crime occurs, victims feel helpless because someone, other than themselves, made a decision that affected their lives. Consequently, it is important to respond to the involuntariness and force of what happened to them by giving them constant choice about what they want to do or what they need in the mediated dialogue. That includes the right to say no to the mediation or to stipulate the conditions under which they will participate without feeling any pressure (Umbreit & Greenwood, 2000). In talking to the victim about the prospect of a dialogue, the facilitator describes the process, the experiences of others who have done it, and the research findings on satisfaction. The facilitator also outlines the risks and benefits but emphasizes how important it is that the victim thinks carefully about why they would meet and what they would want to say to or ask the offender. Although the length of preparation or procedure for preparation will vary based on the type of dialogue practice, the facilitator always elicits the victim's story out of a genuine desire to understand fully what happened and how it affected the victim's world. The facilitator listens carefully for the yearning of victims. What do they long for? What would make a difference? They also assess where they are in their healing process and the reality of their expectations about what they hope for from the offender. Victims may want to know something about the offender's state of mind and circumstances that the mediator can give only with the offender's permission (Umbreit & Greenwood, 2000). The facilitator makes sure that the victim has adequate emotional support. Suggestions may be given that the victim consults with his or her therapist, clergy person, or close friend before proceeding. The facilitator also discusses who the victim might want as a support person(s) when the meeting occurs. In circles, a preparatory healing circle may be held with the victim for this review and support before moving forward.

All of these decisions give victims choice, thereby reminding them that this time they will feel safe when they meet with the offender because it will be on their terms and with adequate protections. After the victim decides to proceed, the facilitator prepares the victim by again giving a range of choices. In some dialogue practices, victims decide how they want to be involved. In a family group conference, they may decide to send a tape of what they want to say to the offender rather than appearing in person, or they may want to observe the conference from behind a one-way mirror. In a victim-offender dialogue (VOD), victims may want to correspond with the offender or ask questions of the offender in writing before deciding to meet face to face. This experience of choices and decision making also occurs as the facilitator reviews what will happen at the time of the dialogue meeting. Victims are reminded that no date will be set until they feel ready. They will decide where they will sit, who will speak first, and what they need back from the offender. They are also encouraged to ask any questions that may possibly occur to them. The goal of this preparation is for victims to feel set to go forward and for surprises to be minimized, allowing them to concentrate on the underlying issues, not external logistics or distractions, so they can move in the dialogue meeting to core issues and feelings if appropriate. This helps build the safety that allows victims to give full attention to their internal process and what they want to do in meeting with the offender.

Victims frequently have unrealistic expectations about the offender and what will happen as a result of the dialogue. Some imagine that the offender will be deeply remorseful or able to answer fully why they committed the offense. They may expect that after the meeting, they can put the wrongdoing behind them or receive complete reparation for what was taken from them. The facilitator may need to help victims scale back their hopes because the offender's response, if not complete, may otherwise feel like a negation of the victim. A 15-year-old boy will likely not understand fully the motivation that drove him to steal, may have trouble expressing emotions, and probably will not be able to earn the amount of money necessary to replace what was stolen. However, a sensitive analysis of what is possible can also open up conversation about other ways the victim's needs and losses might be considered, including possibilities that may not involve the offender making concrete restitution.

Mediators may use various tools to help prepare victims. They may suggest watching videotapes of other dialogues in order to see what is possible. They may suggest that victims write out their story of the crime or do artwork or other nontraditional forms of expression to encourage self-awareness and communication. They may ask victims to reflect on various questions in between times that they meet. Mediators recognize that apart from their preparatory sessions, victims need time alone to consider what was discussed and to process and incorporate their learning. Indeed, this time is just as, if not more important than, the preparation meetings done together.

The Facilitator's Role With the Offender

Offenders need similar considerations in determining whether to participate in a dialogue. As with a victim, the facilitator has to establish some measure of trust so that offenders can focus on the issues instead of their concerns for their personal safety. If they are incarcerated as happens in VOD cases, they will be understandably wary of participating because the prison environment has taught them to trust no one. They may also fear the victim's rage, or if they are young and considering participating in VOM or FGC, they may dread having to listen to their family's disappointment in them for what they did. They may also feel defiant and justified, rationalizing that what they did was not wholly their fault. Although offenders may be motivated to participate to avoid a criminal record or to receive a less severe sanction, engaging them in the process for what they owe the victim or community or even for their own healing may be more difficult. If, however, the facilitator treats offenders with dignity and respects their right to be involved in the decisions about how they will make amends, offenders will more likely begin to feel some respect for themselves, which can make the dialogue a positive and remedial experience for them.

Besides the offender considering their options about whether or not to participate, the facilitator too has to assess whether the offender accepts sufficient responsibility for the harms caused to move forward. This requirement is critical because it is tied to protecting the offender's right to a formal courtroom trial unless that right is voluntarily waived (Sharpe, 1998). Indeed, without an admission of responsibility, the case will go to court, where the court must prove it is justified in claiming that this person is responsible. Moreover, the purpose of the dialogue is addressing the harm done to victims including their needs for amends making from the offender. If the offender denies responsibility, the aims of the dialogue cannot be realized and victims will again feel betrayed and wounded.

Mediators listen carefully to the offender's story of what happened, both to understand the offense from the perspective of the wrongdoer and to gain clues about what bothers the offender about what he or she did, how the offender is minimizing his or her actions, and what motivated the offender's behavior. The facilitator can use these meta-level aspects of the story to raise questions with the offender as part of preparing for the dialogue.

Mediators also review the dialogue process, its relationship to the judicial system, and the offender's rights (Umbreit & Greenwood, 2000). The offender may have questions about the victim and the victim's feelings toward him or her, which the facilitator can share if given permission by the victim. As part of what they need to consider, mediators review with them what will happen in the dialogue, the risks and benefits of their participation, the experiences of others who have done it, and the research ratings on offender satisfaction and offender perceptions of fairness. Offenders, like victims, may elect to have a friend, relative, or other support person with them at the dialogue session. The presence of these people can reinforce the seriousness of what happened and the dialogue process (Umbreit & Greenwood, 2000). These people may also provide support and encouragement to the offender in going through the process and be available afterward to ensure that offenders fulfill the reparation agreements. They may also help offenders be more at ease and feel safer, which can strengthen the confidence of offenders in their ability to participate as well (Sharpe, 1998).

In preparing for the dialogue, offenders need to reflect on their wrongdoing and their feelings about it. For some, this will be the first time they have faced themselves or thought in depth about what happened and what they did to the victim, victim's family, and/or the community. This is a highly sensitive time because the facilitator must use this review to confront offenders with the real human costs of their actions. To move them out of their self-centered view marked by denial, minimization, manipulation, or rationalization, the facilitator has to challenge in ways that both express caring and the demand for self-honesty and support the courage it takes to look at oneself critically rather than using techniques that bully or shame offenders into submission. Offenders might watch videotapes, reflect on their own victimization or the victimization of family members or friends, answer questions on self-reflection surveys, or talk to others in order to better understand the impact of what they did and begin to face themselves. As expressed by David Doerfler, former Director of the Victim-Offender Mediation and Dialogue program in Texas, offenders often feel that "I'm not so afraid of the cold and darkness around me as I am afraid of the cold and darkness inside of me." The work with offenders, therefore, is to bring them to themselves and persevere in challenging them to be accountable to themselves for what they really know.

As part of preparation, the facilitator also asks offenders to consider what they want from the dialogue and why they are doing it. What do they want to share about themselves with the victim? What questions do they have of the victim? What do they want to say about the harm they caused? What do they expect back? As with the victim, facilitators must ensure that the expectations of offenders are realistic and do not place undue pressure on the victim for a particular response back. For example, does the person expect forgiveness? Does the person think that an apology should make things all right? If so, the facilitator needs to help offenders realize that their desire is understandable, but asking the victim to meet it is misplaced, inappropriate, and self-serving given that the purpose of the meeting is to address the harm done to the victim.

The facilitator also needs to ask offenders to think about the victim's needs, both tangible and intangible, and what they might do to respond to the harm. What would it take to repair the harm? Given that some of what happened cannot be repaired, what else might matter to the victim? As part of this discussion, the facilitator should also explore offenders' resources in the context of their age, income that can be generated through jobs, and/or the type of services offenders might offer to make actual or symbolic reparation (Umbreit & Greenwood, 2000).

Bringing Each to the Other

Many proponents of restorative justice dialogue frequently make the following assertion about the most key task of the process: "preparation, preparation, preparation." Indeed, without adequate preparation, the dialogue session will likely falter. Preparation is more than a review of what will happen in the dialogue meeting or the participants' goals. Preparation really begins the dialogue because although the participants are not in direct contact, they have begun the conversation with each other through the facilitator. Consequently, part of the facilitator's job during the preparation phase is to bring each party to the other.

The facilitator accomplishes that task in a variety of ways. By talking to each party about what they want from the other or discussing possible options for repairing the harm, the facilitator metaphorically brings the other party into the room. As part of getting ready for the meeting, the facilitator may role-play the dialogue session with the offender to help prepare him or her for the kinds of questions victims often ask. Or the facilitator may role-play with victims helping them to ask the questions or selecting the words they want to use to communicate intense feelings while ensuring that the offender can really hear them and not become defensive, which would shut down honest dialogue.

The concept of bringing each to the other, however, principally refers to giving information about each to the other that disrupts the preconceptions that each has about the other or noting what they hold in common that they each may not have recognized about the other. This process metaphorically plants each person inside the other so that each becomes more real to the other and each is answerable to the other. An offender, for example, may believe that the victim is vindictive and really wants to hurt him when they meet. Because of what he did, he cannot believe that her intentions with him are altruistic. He sees himself as bad because of what he did. It's hard for him to see that there is any good in himself. The mediator, however, can suggest that the victim, through the dialogue process, is actually giving the offender a place to be good. He may embed the idea by noting what the victim is saying symbolically through her desire to meet him. "I know you can do good. You deserve it. We are all trying to make something good come out of this. We are on the same side. If I help you do good for yourself, then it will be good for me." There are other points of commonality. For example, a victim realizes the similarity between herself and the offender as she struggles with the anger she knows is there but can't feel. "I can't reduce myself down to that level. If I did I would be like him." Another says, "My office and your cell are about the same size. My wall has built up over 10 years."

The mediator is the bridge between offender and victim as well as the bridge between them and others who may also participate in the dialogue. The mediator helps clear the path so that people can discern what they want. The mediator also clears the path so that people can hear. In so doing, the mediator establishes emotional safety for each so that each can come to the other.

The Facilitator's Role During the Dialogue

Although mediators are active during the preparation phase, they are less active during the dialogue, often withdrawing so that their presence is barely noticeable. If the preparation has been done well, the parties will be ready to meet, share, and question each other without needing much direction. Mediators may take time to center themselves prior to the meeting. One facilitator said, "I'm a firm believer that there is a power in the universe that connects us . . . and so part of my work for me is being able to feel, being in touch with that in a way that I can really hand the meeting off to that presence." Mediators may check in with participants before bringing them together. Mediators recognize that this gathering is emotionally charged and may review with participants what will happen before they go into the room. Most often, there is a bit of silence after everyone is seated. Honoring the power of silence is central to humanistic mediation, whether during preparation or during the actual face-to-face encounter (Umbreit & Coates, 2004).

Mediators usually start by offering a brief opening statement welcoming and thanking each person for attending. Participants are reminded that the conversation belongs to them and that the facilitator will not do much talking. Parties can ask for a break at any time. The facilitator reiterates the ground rules, which are "to listen respectfully and speak respectfully to each other, and that no one does anything to intentionally hurt anyone." This opening sets the stage for what comes next. Consequently, these comments help create the safe if not sacred place for dialogue. One mediator advises, "It is less important what you as a facilitator say than how you say it. If you are nervous or sound like a stiff professional, that will not be conducive to people being vulnerable. I want to be fully present and authentic. I also want to establish an informal but dignified atmosphere." These introductory comments are, in some ways, an induction into a healing and cooperative process (Gold, 1993).

Based on the dialogue practice being used, participants may have an opening ritual that has been planned in advance. A person may light a candle, read a poem, or the facilitator may pass the talking piece silently before the dialogue begins. Typically, the order in which participants will speak initially will have been decided earlier. The opportunity is frequently given to the victim to speak first as a symbolic rectification of the fact that he or she was not able to do so in the criminal justice process. In some instances, the victim elects to have the offender or someone else initiate the dialogue.

This is a pivotal moment when the mediator lets go of the preparation and trusts what is about to unfold. The mediator may ask the victim a question such as, "Could you think back, not just to how you are feeling now but when all this began and the effect on your life? Could you tell (the offender's name) what it was like?" The mediator may help with transitions such as, "We've talked a lot about what has happened. Do you have any other questions or do you have anything you'd like to say about what happened that you have not already said?" The mediator may check in with participants about their needs for a break. Unless the dialogue practice uses a prepared script or follows a specific procedure such as a family caucus, the mediator does little until the end of the dialogue when the mediator assists in the construction of a formal agreement if one is needed. Although the mediator is relatively silent, he or she remains actively involved nonverbally in the encounter and is able to respond at any moment required, particularly when people get stuck and indicate a need for assistance.

Mediators though quiet are exceedingly attentive throughout the dialogue, bearing witness to what happens. They remain aware of the fact that victims need to feel heard by the offender because too often they are completely anonymous to their offenders who are anything but anonymous to them (Wilson, personal communication). As one victim said, "Just as I could never forget your face, you could never remember my face." They stay mindful that true accountability is moving the wrongdoer to see himself or herself through the eyes of the victim. As such, the offender sees that he or she is much more than who they are as defined solely by the crime. Mediators anchor themselves in the goal that the dialogue needs to keep participants from living in the past by bringing them right into the present, which is broader, opens things up, lets them go on, and encourages them to look to the future. Mediators focus all their energies on the present moment because the coming together makes what happened completely real and starts to thaw what has been frozen, complete what has been incomplete, and resolve what has been irresolvable.

The Facilitator's Role During Follow-Up

There is no set procedure for follow-up in restorative justice dialogues other than what may be required by the sponsoring agency. Follow-up sessions between the parties, however, may be scheduled because the issues are too complex to resolve in one meeting, the subsequent meetings are part of the monitoring arrangement for reparations, or a problem has arisen in the offender's ability to complete the agreement. Most often, the facilitator maintains telephone contact with the participants to see how they are doing after the dialogue meeting. Participants may need help with referrals for further assistance. Occasionally, the victim or offender may have been overwhelmed and need to talk about the experience, perhaps even seeking clarification or confirmation of what was said. They may also just need to process the dialogue and its impact on them or their family members. Because there remains a fine line between the usual follow-up regarding unanswered questions, recall of what actually happened during the mediation, and moving on with one's life versus the longer-run care issues, the facilitator has to use some discretion in determining how much contact is necessary and when and how to pull back or say goodbye.

When a reparation agreement requires monitoring, there may be extensive follow-up with offenders. Sometimes the follow-up is shared with other participants who volunteer to check in or ensure that the person is fulfilling his or her obligations. Victims too may ask for a monthly written progress report on the person's progress. This aspect is critical because the follow through by offenders is often the action necessary to reestablish trust from victims, family, or community members and to build pride in what they accomplished. Indeed, for offenders their actions may become the mechanism for belonging or reentering their communities in a different way.

Finally, the facilitator should establish procedures for evaluation of all mediations as part of the follow-up. Evaluations should measure participant satisfaction and perception of fairness as well as other topics to help improve services. The 10-item *Victim Satisfaction with Offender Dialogue Scale* can be used for these purposes and modified to fit the particular dialogue practice (Bradshaw & Umbreit, 2003).

ALTERNATIVE PROCEDURES

Although dialogue practices may be centered in VOM, FGC, VOD, or peacemaking circles, there are a variety of alternative procedures that can be employed when the facilitator determines that they can advance the dialogue or be an effective response to victims' needs. These procedures include the use of audiovisual aids or the use of surrogates when the real person is not available to meet.

Facilitators recognize that bringing people together in the aftermath of crime and wrongdoing may require adaptations given the specifics of a particular case. Victims, for example, may want to meet with offenders but feel too apprehensive for a face-to-face dialogue. In these instances, the mediator can offer alternatives such as sending a close friend or relative in their place to the FGC, attending via conference call or Skype, or writing a letter that they will read at the meeting. Because the work of preparation is about gradually bringing participants together, facilitators may also use audiovisual aids to access emotionally "shut-down" areas in offenders or to provide victims with more first-hand information so they can assess for themselves the genuineness of a wrongdoer's feelings. In one instance, for example, a mediator decided to use videotaping so that the victim and offender could see each other first on tape. He also used the taping to help both participants move forward. First and with the permission of the victim, he asked her to tell the full story of the crime so he could videotape it. He then showed it to the offender and videotaped the offender, with his permission, as he watched the tape of the victim so that the victim could subsequently watch this tape and see his reactions. The facilitator also had the offender watch the videotape of himself as way to give feedback to the offender about his responses. The offender was surprised. "I look like a criminal. Look at that body language." As the offender felt the victim's sincerity through the videotape, things also began to change in him.

Although the goal of doing a dialogue is to give those most directly affected by wrongdoing the chance to come together to address the harms done, the primary parties may not always be available. Victims may decide that they do not need or want to meet. A facilitator may decide that an offender in a VOD case is not an appropriate candidate or the offender may pull out during the preparation. In these instances, it may be possible to use a surrogate victim or offender instead. The facilitator will want to select someone whose story is similar to the actual case so that what the surrogate shares or how the surrogate responds will be as real and meaningful as possible. One such dialogue took place between a victim who wanted to meet with the offender who murdered her mother and an offender who wanted to meet with his daughter after killing his wife (Jones, 2005). Since the two cases were not found suitable for direct victim/offender mediation, the two individuals met with each other as surrogates. These arrangements often have benefit to surrogates who themselves may never have had the opportunity to meet with the person responsible for the harm or the person who was hurt. Meetings between surrogates can also help prepare victims and offenders for an anticipated meeting at some point in the future.

SELF-CARE

Humanistic mediation calls upon facilitators to live their beliefs recognizing that it is not possible to perform in a congruent way as a mediator unless the person also embodies restorative justice principles in the ways they live their lives (Sullivan & Tifft, 2001). "The choices we make about how we respond to the world we live in reflect not only our perspective on justice but also our moral stances in life; and it is through these stances that each of us reveals our essential being to others" (Sullivan & Tifft, 2001, p. 179). The giving of oneself to others, however, requires attention to self-replenishment. This requirement is difficult to meet because it seemingly contradicts the mandate to be attentive to others and to surrender self-interest in the service of meeting the needs of participants. Self-care, however, has to become a top priority to avoid the burnout that is otherwise inherent in this work. Experienced mediators often integrate self-care into their lives as a form of disciplined practice. Some watch carefully what they eat or are fastidious in getting adequate sleep. Some have a regular routine that includes meditation or daily prayer. Others find release in physical exercise taking time regularly to lift weights, run, do yoga, or square dance. Still others do lots of reading, watch sports, or cultivate their passions for raising horses, playing music, photography, cooking, or sailing. Because dealing with human pain is exceedingly intense, mediators must select activities that are intense or absorbing enough to break the grasp of the work so that they can enter a different realm for some period of time. Consequently, what matters is not the specific interest or practice but rather its ability to interrupt the level of engagement in their work so that mediators can return to that work refreshed.

The facilitation of humanistic mediation brings facilitators close to themselves. Indeed, it is likely not possible to be involved with the issues raised by crime, conflict, and victimization without being changed in a deeply personal way. Some mediators even claim that mediators must experience the deeper layers of their own feelings and questions in order to facilitate the process for others. Primarily, however, facilitators are touched and grow personally because they are privileged to work with the extremes of the human condition including deep pain, devastating violence, and human anguish as well as profound moments of intimacy, the resurrection of inner peace, and the growth that comes with the agony of unrealized sorrow.

REFERENCES

Armour, M., & Umbreit, M. S. (2005). The paradox of forgiveness in restorative justice. In E. L. Worthington Jr. (Ed.), *Handbook of forgiveness* (pp. 491–503). New York: Brunner-Routledge.

Armour, M., & Umbreit, M. S. (2006). Victim forgiveness in restorative justice dialogue. *Victim and Offender, 1*(2), 123–140.

Berman-Rossi, T. (Ed.). (1994). *Social work: The collected writings of William Schwartz*. Itasca, IL: F. E. Peacock.

Bradshaw, W., & Umbreit, M. S. (2003). Assessing satisfaction with victim services: The development and use of the victim satisfaction with offender dialogue scale (VSODS). *International Review of Victimology, 9*, 71–83.

Doerfler, D. (2004). Victim offender dialogue: Healing on a deeper level. *Kaleidoscope of Justice: Highlighting Restorative Juvenile Justice, 4*(3), 4–6.

Gold, L. (1993). Influencing unconscious influences: The healing dimension of mediation. *Mediation Quarterly, 11*(1), 55–66.

Gustafson, D. (2004). Is restorative justice taking too few, or too many, risks? In H. Zehr & B. Toews (Eds.), *Critical issues in restorative justice* (pp. 303–314). Monsey, NY: Criminal Justice Press.

Gustafson, D. (2005). Exploring treatment and trauma recovery implications of facilitating victim-offender encounters in crimes of severe violence: Lessons from the Canadian experience. In E. Elliott & R. M. Gordon (Eds.), *New directions in restorative justice: Issues, practice, evaluation* (pp. 193–227). Portland, OR: Willan Publishing.

Jones, M. (2005). Surrogate mediation for murder victim's daughter. *The Crime Victims Report, 9*(1), 8, 10.

Reimund, M. E. (2004). Confidentiality in victim offender mediation: A false promise? *Journal of Dispute Resolution, 401*, 401–427.

Roberts, A. W. (2004). Is restorative justice tied to specific models of practice? In H. Zehr & B. Toews (Eds.), *Critical issues in restorative justice* (pp. 241–252). Monsey, NY: Criminal Justice Press.

Saleeby, D. (1992). *The strengths perspective in social work practice*. White Plains, NY: Longman.

Schwartz, W. (1976). Between client and system: The mediating function. In R. Roberts & H. Northern (Eds.), *Theories of social work with groups* (pp. 177–197). New York: Columbia University Press.

Sharpe, S. (1998). *Restorative justice: A vision for healing and change*. Edmonton, Alberta, CA: Edmonton Victim Offender Mediaton Society.

Sullivan, D., & Tifft, L. (2001). *Restorative justice: Healing the foundations of our everyday lives*. Monsey, NY: Willow Tree Press.

Umbreit, M. S. (1997). Humanistic mediation: A transformative journey of peacemaking. *Mediation Quarterly, 14*, 201–213.

Umbreit, M. S., & Burns, H. (2002). *Humanistic mediation: Peacemaking grounded in core social work values*. St. Paul, MN: University of Minnesota.

Umbreit, M. S., & Coates, R. (2004). *Restorative justice dialogue: A multi-dimensional, evidence-based practice theory*. Center for Restorative Justice and Peacemaking, School of Social Work, University of Minnesota.

Umbreit, M. S., & Greenwood, J. (2000). *Guidelines for victim-sensitive victim-offender mediation: Restorative justice through dialogue*. Washington, DC: Office of Victims of Crime, U.S. Department of Justice.

Umbreit, M. S., Vos, B., Coates, R., & Brown, K. (2003). *Facing violence: The path of restorative justice & dialogue*. Monsey, NY: Criminal Justice Press.

Williams, S., & Williams, S. (1994). *Being in the middle by being at the edge: Quaker experience of non-official political mediation*. London: Quaker Peace & Service.

Wilson, J. (2005). Victim-centered restorative justice: An essential distinction. *Crime Victims Report, 9*, 49–63.

Wilson, J. (n.d.). Characteristics of VOD facilitators. Retrieved September 8, 2009, from http://justalternatives.org/

10. Dimensions of Culture in Restorative Dialogue

> *If we could read the secret history of our enemies we should find in each person's life enough sorrow and suffering to disarm hostilities.*
>
> Henry Wadsworth Longfellow
>
> *Three-fourths of the miseries and misunderstandings in the world will disappear if we step into the shoes of our adversaries and understand their viewpoint.*
>
> Mahatma Gandhi

A *power imbalance is created between a victim and offender whenever an offense occurs and always in the offender's favor.* Victims commonly feel degraded by the offense and, according to Murphy and Hampton (Murphy, 1988), feel a kind of intangible and moral injury or sense of violation. The purpose of restorative justice, therefore, is to redress the abuse of power and the resulting imbalance. Some of the correction happens by giving the victim power to decide if he or she will agree to a meeting with the offender, having the victim decide who will speak first or who will sit where they meet, and making the victim and the victim's needs pivotal to what the offender must do for restitution.

Putting right the imbalance also happens during the dialogue process. For example, the offender's show of remorse for what he has done to the victim and others puts the victim in a raised position in relation to the offender. Likewise, the victim's expression of forgiveness, if such occurs, is elevating both because the victim has the power to withhold or grant grace and because the act of forgiving makes the victim the "bigger" person.

The presence of power inequities in restorative dialogue is much broader, however, than the imbalance created by a specific crime or wrongdoing and includes social inequities that are deeply rooted in attitudes, cultural traditions, economic disparities, and histories of social conflict. When a Maori youth comes together with a Pakeha (person of predominantly European ancestry) crime victim for a conference facilitated by a Pakeha official facilitator, differences between cultures and differences in social relations marked by societal ascribed power and privilege as well as differences in experiences of oppression are all present. Likewise, when a victim of domestic violence from an indigenous group elects to address the abuse through a restorative rather than retributive process, power inequities are still pervasive specific to gender and age if elders are involved. Moreover, family violence may be a familiar outlet for accumulated trauma related to the historical realities of oppressive practices associated with colonization. Members in a community sentencing circle, therefore, may be more concerned with the power relationships between themselves and the governmental officials who allow or disallow the restorative justice practice than with the magnitude of the harm done to a female crime victim.

An analysis of the intersectionality of gender, race, class, culture, religion, and sexual orientation is critical to understanding victimization, crime and wrongdoing, and the role of restorative dialogue in addressing harm and furthering meaningful accountability and community safety. Such an analysis, however, requires more than a factual description of cultural differences because the meaning of those differences is imbued with the interconnections between power, privilege, and oppression (Almeida, Dolan-Del Vecchio, & Parker, 2007). Consequently, attention to the dimensions of culture in restorative justice practices refers not only to differences among peoples but also to the broader contextual issues including societal prescriptions and the vicissitudes of power, privilege, and oppression that earmark relationships between peoples.

Three such dimensions of culture are considered in this chapter. The first dimension focuses on issues practitioners must be sensitive to when they are working with people who are different from themselves and different from each other. Although differences may include race, ethnicity, gender, sexual orientation, religion, and class, the significance of the differences will depend on the historic relationships of power and privilege between them and may not emerge until all the parties consider engaging with each other.

The second dimension centers on the nature of the crime or wrongdoing, specifically hate crimes and interethnic conflict. Besides being a criminal act, hate crimes target individuals because of their race, ethnicity, religion, sexual orientation, disability, age, or gender. Groups that are already oppressed become object lessons to others about what can happen to them or their loved ones in the future. Interethnic conflict is often the product of group and cultural factors related to ethnic membership and self-identity, historic misunderstandings and miscommunications between conflicting ethnic in groups and out groups, long-held cultural stereotypes, or the influence of colonization and subjugation.

The third dimension concentrates on the emerging interest in restorative justice by non-Western or non-Westernized cultures often located in diverse corners of the world. Unfortunately, this trend means that restorative practices as conceptualized in the West are being exported to indigenous groups, some of which are in underdeveloped countries. As much as globalization promotes intercultural understanding and connections among disparate groups, it also can trample indigenous or local customs through imposing Western and capitalist values. If restorative justice proponents are not aware of historic relationships of power between indigenous or dispossessed groups and majority culture or import practices without regard to context and tradition, restorative justice can inadvertently become a colonizing influence itself.

MULTICULTURAL IMPLICATIONS OF PRACTICE

The biggest dangers in examining cultural differences are to be superficially valuing of differences and to overgeneralize, which contribute to the stereotyping of groups. Moreover, by compartmentalizing various ethnic groups, they are decontextualized, and little to no attention is given to differences within cultures, relationships between groups, intersectionalities such as class or gender, and systems of power, privilege, and oppression that organize interaction (Almeida et al., 2007). Although seemingly invisible, these critical components of social relations play out in restorative dialogues often in the nuances of behaviors or in what is not said. A focus on distinct cultural characteristics by group also negates the growing reality of multiculturalism or the mixing of ethnicities through marriage or procreation such that any given individual may claim identity with a variety of groups or may self-identify with one core group over others.

Facilitation of restorative dialogues requires sensitivity to the fact that differences between participants and between participants and the facilitator may exacerbate the sense of trauma or victimization or block constructive engagement between participants. Consider the following example:

> "The hell you say. I won't stand for it." Banging the table with his fist, the Black store owner shouted, "You're not gonna get off that easy!" The Native American teen shoplifter cowered in silence. She worked hard at keeping her lips from trembling and her stare fixed on an old picture hanging on the wall to the right of the Black man. With churning stomach, the Anglo facilitator believed the entire mediation was torpedoed by the store owner's angry outburst. He tried to think of a way of aborting the session with some semblance of civility. Frustrated, the Black man looked with disgust at the other two. He expected, he wanted a response. But neither individual looked alive. (Umbreit & Coates, 1999, p. 4)

Although the crime victim, in this situation, is loud in expressing his frustration and is likely acting within the cultural dictates of his community that call

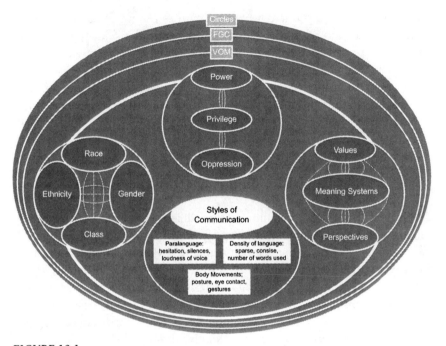

FIGURE 10.1

for "harsh" handling of misbehavior in children, his affect, declarations, and fist banging are received as threatening, and the facilitator reacts in fear rather than understanding the meaning of the victim's behavior or translating the meaning of the victim's behavior to the offender so that she could stay engaged rather than psychologically disappearing. Similarly, the Native American teenager, in contrast to the facilitator and crime victim, is female, from a different culture, and young. Her looking away may be a mechanism to control her tears but likely reflects a cultural prescription to avoid eye contact with an authority figure as a sign of humility and respect. Without direction from the facilitator about the possible meaning of the offender's reaction, the victim is left alone, may feel guilty about his outburst, or may erroneously conclude that the offender could care less about what she did. The offender too is left alone, may internalize the victim's disgust, or may erroneously feel victimized herself by the offender because of his outburst or conclude that she is a failure.

Participants raised in different cultures will probably have different styles of communication (see Figure 10.1). Those differences will typically be as evident in the way points of view are communicated as in the message being relayed (Sue & Sue, 1990). Just as this example illustrates, African Americans tend to be more comfortable speaking with less distance between themselves and others than are Anglos. An Anglo facilitator who is comfortable with more distance may be seen as backing away, which to a Latin-American victim or offender may appear as having a sense of superiority and as if "he believes he is too good for me." These assumptions unfortunately reinforce misunderstandings, making it harder, if not impossible, for the facilitator to establish the safety necessary for genuine dialogue between parties.

The ability to communicate effectively across different cultural backgrounds requires attention to many of the nuances that accompany verbal expression. Those nuances are evident in body movements, paralanguage or other verbal cues, and the density of language. When the facilitator or participants are not familiar with the meaning of these nuances, they can readily create misunderstandings that block communication.

Body Movements

Body movements often speak louder than words. Posture, smiling, eye contact, laughing, gestures, and many other movements communicate. How we interpret what we hear and see may vary greatly from culture to culture (Sue & Sue, 1990). Asians may be puzzled and offended by a White mediator, for example, who wants to express herself—her likes and her dislikes—with facial grimaces and smiles. The White mediator may interpret the Asian who has been taught to tightly control his feelings as having no feelings. It may be inappropriate to expect an individual raised to value control of emotions to shed tears as signs of remorse for having burglarized a home, even if that person may be feeling very remorseful. Avoidance of eye contact may not mean avoidance of an issue, poor self-confidence, submissiveness, or guilt and shame but rather reflect a Liberian person's discomfort with face-to-face interaction, because communication in his culture when talking of intimate matters occurs sitting side by side.

Paralanguage

Paralanguage or other vocal cues, such as hesitations, inflections, silences, loudness of voice, and pace of speaking, also provide ample opportunity for misinterpretation across cultures (Sue & Sue, 1990). Rural Americans tend to talk at a slower pace than their urban counterparts. Put a northern Minnesota farmer in the same room with a New York City taxicab driver, and they may find it difficult to speak with each other not because they don't share things in common but because they don't exercise the patience to work at communicating with each other. The New Yorker would feel that an eternity had gone by before the Minnesotan had completed a thought. The latter would have difficulty straining to comprehend the fast-paced patter of the New Yorker.

In Native American culture, silence is valued as sacred (Sue & Sue, 1990). Each person must have the opportunity to reflect, to translate thoughts into words, and to shape the words not only before taking a turn at speaking but also while speaking. Anglo-Americans often feel uncomfortable with silence. Frenchmen might regard silence as a sign of agreement. To a person who is Asian, silence may be considered as a token of respect or politeness.

Related somewhat to pace and silence is hesitation. For persons who speak rapidly and feel uncomfortable with silence, hesitation on the part of another is a cue to begin speaking. To the one who hesitates, the breaking of the silence by another might be taken not as an interruption but as an intentional, grievous insult. Asians are given to speaking softly as if not to be overheard; many Asians find U.S. speakers brash and loud. Arabs on the other hand may find U.S. speakers soft spoken. They may prefer volume. Similarly, persons of Asian descent may find Anglo-Americans too direct, blunt, and frank. The former will go to great lengths not to hurt feelings; the latter is often unaware when feelings are hurt.

Density of Language

Density of language also differentiates speakers from different cultural backgrounds (Sue & Sue, 1990). Some Blacks tend to be sparse and concise. In exchanges among Blacks, many shared codes are used requiring little further information. Even the simple "uh, huh" is loaded with meaning when taken in the context of the social situation. To outsiders, some Blacks may appear terse and uninterested.

Asians and Native Americans will often use many more words to say the same thing as their White colleagues (Sue & Sue, 1990). The poetry of the story may be more important than the content of the story and may actually be the point of the story. Much patience is required of Blacks and Whites to hear what is being said when conversing with Native Americans or Asians. There is potential for obvious problems when doing mediation work across these groupings that possess very contrasting communication patterns.

With the reminder that generalizations are problematic, Sue and Sue (1990) provide an overview of communication styles associated with the largest ethnic groups in the United States. Native American, Asian-American, and Hispanic manners of expression are described as low keyed and indirect. Whites seem objective and task oriented; Blacks affective, emotional, and interpersonal. Blacks will interrupt or take a turn at speaking when they can. Whites will nod to indicate listening or agreement. Native Americans and Asians seldom provide cues to encourage the speaker; they listen without a lot of nonverbal engagement.

In addition to these potential pitfalls of misunderstanding based on different communication styles, other meta factors such as cultural values loom over the attempts to build restorative justice with participants from differing cultures. For example, the emphasis on individualism, competition, taking action, rational linear thinking, and "Christian principles and Protestant work ethic" may to a large extent reflect values of the dominant U.S. White culture but not values particularly shared by all Whites, let alone persons from different ethnic groups. Asians, Hispanics, and Native Americans are instead apt to place more emphasis on the needs of the collective over the individual and place higher value on the community fabric and kinship networks. Native Americans and others would move a step further by cherishing the place of the individual within the context of the entire natural world. Without the latter, many believe the individual has no value. Persons from religious perspectives other than Christianity, which emphasizes "individual salvation," may see the individual as equal to all living things, as journeying toward individual fulfillment, or even as insignificant in the total scheme of things. Although no one worldview is the correct one to have, worldviews often clash (too often literally in the waging of war) and may undermine attempts to repair wrongs experienced as a result of crime.

Differing values, perspectives, and meaning systems also affect core understandings related to restorative dialogue. Cunneen (2004), for example, criticizes restorative justice for its portrayal of victim and offender as uncomplicated and homogeneous categories of self and for its globalizing assumption that peoples from vastly different groups subjectively experience what it is to be a victim or an offender in identical or similar ways. He contends that the larger reality for oppressed populations is more varied than dichotomous and simplistic.

For example, particular racial and ethnic groups are overrepresented in the criminal justice system and have become linked with criminality. Indeed, the vast majority of prisoners today are Black and Latino who represent 26% of the U.S. population but comprised 63% of all inmates under state or federal custody in 2003 (Belk, 2006). Similarly, the idea of justice may vary across cultures. It is not difficult, for example, to imagine that Native Americans who adhere to traditional values would seek to restore more than a personal relationship after commission of a crime. The communal or tribal relationship would need to be repaired, and likely even the relationship of the individual with the universe, for violations within the tribal context rip the fabric of the whole that holds all together.

Impact of Racism on Perceptions

Speech patterns, intensity of communication, interpretation of nonverbals, and many other nuances of interaction are influenced not just by a person's culture but the place of that culture in the broader sociopolitical context and all dimensions of a person's social location. In particular, the experience of racism is a powerful dynamic in how Whites, Blacks, and other persons of color perceive others and respond to messages. Although Blacks from different social classes and different regions of the United States communicate and handle conflict in the different ways, the fact of being Black is likely a key determining factor in how they perceive the world and how others perceive them. Being on guard, lack of openness, being passive or aggressive, and choosing what role to play in an interaction will be affected by previous experiences of individual or institutional racism.

The impact of racism will also be a potential contextual variable in restorative justice programs where participants are of different races. Because Whites, in particular, are race privileged, they will have more resources than other groups including political power, which will impact the interaction in a dialogue with participants of color. In locations where Blacks have more political power than Hispanics, Hispanics have more political power than Native Americans, or Asian Americans have more political power than Whites, racism will play out differently.

Rather than a set of rules to follow, facilitators of restorative dialogues, to be truly effective, have to develop a critical consciousness about their own social location in order to illuminate realities about how the world operates and to better understand how each participant's gender, race, sexual orientation, sexual identity, culture, and ethnicity in concert with those who are different from themselves play out when the parties encounter each other (Umbreit & Coates, 2000). With that filter, facilitators can probe whether reactions to participants including themselves and all other participants reflect a reality or biased attitudes. For example, a Native American youth offender sitting before us comes from a broken family of alcoholics, is lazy, and has no goals. Such descriptors may, in fact, describe a particular youth. However, when they are assumed because of the youngster's skin color, then racist attitudes based on erroneous prejudicial assumptions are operating.

For participants in a restorative dialogue, racism may be a justification used by the offender for committing the crime or may play into why and how the victim wants not an "ounce of flesh," but a "pound of flesh." When a mediator realizes that racist assumptions or accusations may occur between offender and victim, he or she will need to be prepared to act as interpreter or buffer during separate premediation meetings and during any actual face-to-face encounters be they in the form of mediation, healing circles, conferences, community boards, or other restorative justice programs (Umbreit & Coates, 2000). As part of preparation, facilitators will need to help participants understand the viewpoints and different communication styles that they will be exposed to when they meet each other. This information will help prepare them for the encounter and what they might normally regard as insulting or disrespectful behaviors. Also, each participant may be moved to some self-awareness, thereby tempering behaviors that might be interpreted as offensive by others.

To illustrate some possibilities of preparing participants for cultural differences, let us return to our opening scenario involving a Black male store owner owner, a female Native American shoplifter, and an Anglo facilitator. In that illustration, the facilitator had not done any homework on himself or others. Had he spent sufficient time with the store owner, the following scenario might have occurred. The facilitator has absorbed the businessman's sense of invasion and loss. He knows the man wants to work with the teen to prevent a repetition of shoplifting, but he does not want to see her dealt with harshly. The man volunteers that he grew up on the streets and knows how difficult it is. His casual conversation is punctuated by gestures. His voice booms, particularly as he speaks of how the system generally rips off kids and people of color in general. The man wants his economic loss recovered and assistance for the girl. Essentially, he is sympathetic to meeting with the teenager for his benefit as well as hers or he wouldn't "take the time out of a busy schedule to do so."

When the facilitator meets with the Ute teenager, he discovers a very different way of communication. She is more subservient than he is comfortable with. She will answer only direct questions. There is much spacing between her sentences. Sometimes he thinks she is done speaking when she adds still another thought. Rarely does she make eye contact with him. The mediator leaves the young woman perplexed, feeling that he is not yet ready for the face-to-face meeting.

Through a mutual friend, the mediator is able to identify and connect with an elder of the tribal band to which the teen belongs. He asks questions. He listens, seldom to direct answers, but he gets the information he needs. The facilitator comes to understand that the girl was not being surly or uncooperative. She was demonstrating respect by not looking him in the eye. She did not ask questions because such an insult would have suggested that he had not been thorough in his work with her. Her slow speech pattern was consistent with her upbringing and culture. The silences he experienced demonstrated how important it was for her to answer his questions as well as she could.

After gaining the kind of appreciation for the participants that he needed, he was ready to proceed. He went back to each participant in turn. With the girl, he shared how the Black man would likely be perceived by her as coming on quite strong. The man would speak rapidly to her, seeking to make direct eye contact, and he would probably raise his voice, but these things would not mean he was angry with her or trying to put her down. They were simply his ways of conversing about things important to him. The facilitator informed the girl that he did not expect the store owner to change his ways but that she should focus more on what the man was saying than on the mannerisms and style, which would make her want to withdraw.

With the Black store owner, the facilitator talked of how the Ute girl would not look the store owner in the eye. In her culture, it was a sign of respect not to challenge authority. And certainly she would view the man whose store she violated as being in a position of authority. He encouraged the man to refrain from interrupting the girl until she had worked through her thoughts and spoke her mind. Again, the slowness of speech did not indicate a learning disability or any other weakness. It simply reflected the speech patterns of her culture.

As the facilitator moves back and forth between the victim and the offender, he is also working on his own awareness of how cross-cultural differences may affect his efforts to work with these two. With new information, he is also exploring his own reactions: his initial discomfort with the Black man's seeming abrasiveness, with the Ute teen's excessive meekness and seeming inability to articulate, and with his wonderings about his own ability to work with two people so diametrically opposed in style, if not worldview.

Relieved and enlightened by all these discoveries, the facilitator is now ready to bring the two participants together. Having prepared, the mediator is comfortable and better prepared for the usual unpredictable directions that such encounters take and hopeful that positive resolution will be agreed upon by persons who had very little in common other than sharing opposing sides of a conflict and wanting to right a wrong.

To repair or restore relationships, personal or communal, damaged by criminal or delinquent acts is a challenging goal in any circumstance. When participants—including victims, offenders, family members, support people, and program staff—are of differing cultures, typical patterns of communicating and expressing values can lead to confusion if not complete disruption of the process. In order to arrive at a just and healing response to the crime by those most directly affected by it, the views of all involved parties need to be considered. However, the likelihood of repair and restoration of relationships is increased by the extent to which facilitators take the time to know and understand the differing communication styles and worldviews of the participating individuals.

HATE CRIMES AND INTERETHNIC CONFLICT

In response to a racial incident, a group of 30 community members including both victims and offenders come together in a peacemaking circle to openly discuss what led up to this crime, its impact on the community, the need for greater understanding and tolerance among diverse community members, and a detailed plan for both repairing the harm and meeting several more times to foster healing within the community.

The use of dialogue for hate crimes and interethnic conflict is a second example of the interface between restorative justice and culture expressed through violence related to power, privilege, and oppression. Indeed hate promotes violence. In the United States, law enforcement agencies report that racial prejudice motivates more than half of all the reported single-bias incidents (51.3%) followed by incidents related to a religious bias (19.5 %), a sexual orientation bias (16.7%), and an ethnicity or national origin bias (11.5%) (U.S. Department of Justice, 2008). The remaining incidents are ascribed to a disability bias. Hate conveys that behind a crime is an aversion to an individual because of his or her individual or social attributes. Moreover, the offender's views are often shared by the wider communities to which they belong, and the offender's motive and even behavior may have their tacit approval.

There are similarities between hate crimes and interethnic conflict in that both are motivated by bias and prejudice related to a person's or people's identity or group membership. (See Figure 10.2.) Both emerge out of a long historical lineage. Both intend to subordinate the "other" through intimidation related to the politics of difference that holds that individuals do not merit treatment as equals or that they deserve blame for various social problems. They are different in that interethnic conflict involves mass violence, open conflict between two of more groups, and reciprocal harm and offending by members of both groups even though one group may dominate another, for example, Apartheid (racial), conflict between the British as a colonial power and the Irish (religious).

Hate Crimes

The national response to escalating rates of bias-motivated violence and intimidation has been to criminalize it through legislation. Most recently, it has been hoped that the vast underreporting of incidents will be reduced by federal legislation named the Matthew Shepard and James Byrd, Jr. Hate Crime Prevent Act signed into law in October 2009. The act, named after a gay Wyoming man who died after being kidnapped and severely beaten and

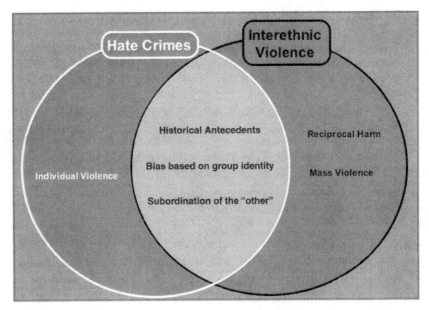

FIGURE 10.2

an African-American man dragged to death in Texas, seeks to strengthen the protections against hate crimes by giving the Department of Justice the power to investigate and prosecute bias-motivated violence.

Although this response is necessary and encouraging, restorative justice, because of its focus on community and community resources as well as its ability to mobilize efforts to address issues that gave rise to the initial dialogue, is in a unique place to advance healing not just for the immediate victim but for others from the same community who are indirectly targeted by the offender (Umbreit, Coates, & Vos, 2003). Indeed, hate-charged situations are often embedded in the communities that are impacted by hate, and consequently members of that community often experience fear, particularly of repeat attacks, anger, depression, physical ailments, and trauma.

The following is an account of a community response to a 9/11 hate crime as a result of a restorative justice intervention (Umbreit, Lewis, & Burns, 2003).

> Within hours after watching footage of a terrorist attack on television, a man in Eugene, Oregon, went to his phonebook, looked up the Islamic cultural center in his area, and made a call. The director of the Center, a prominent leader of the local Muslim community, answered the phone. The caller, raging and spewing profanities, made a death wish to all Muslims. Later, he made a second call to the community mosque, leaving a similar message on the answering machine.

The director of the Islamic cultural Center, Tammam Adi, immediately contacted the human rights commission to enlist their help and protection. They were able to trace the call, and by that evening, the caller had been identified. He was taken into custody, and after a short time, released.

The decision was made to try to use restorative conferencing. First the mediators met with the caller, a 33-year-old man named Christopher Younce. Younce described to the mediators how he had acted out of rage, yelling into the phone to blame and scare the Muslim leader. He explained that the news had run stories implicating Osama bin Laden that morning. And that he confused Arab Muslims with terrorist extremists in his thinking. Afterwards he felt badly about what he had done. Younce spoke of his long history of anger problems, describing a steady buildup over the years that reached crisis levels over the death of his son and a recent job loss. Younce said he wanted to apologize in person to the Muslim leader and his family, and do whatever was asked of him to make things right. He wanted the opportunity to show them that he is a better man than his actions suggested. "I'd like a peaceful solution," he said.

The husband and wife who ran the Islamic Center had two main concerns. First, they have been dramatically affected by the phone call and second they were committed to finding some way of mending harm. The first meeting included a discussion of the current political climate and the way it was affecting the Muslim family. The nation was at war and Muslim Americans were being mistaken for the enemy. As a result, the Adi's lives had changed drastically over night. A police officer was assigned to protect them; he would open their mail, check their car, and accompany them to speaking engagements. Mrs. Adi, like many Muslim women fearing retaliation, stopped wearing the traditional scarf around the head. From the Adi's perspective, in order for this matter to be resolved, the issue of negative stereotyping would have to be addressed. "Everyone knows about the stereotypes," said Mrs. Adi, "But nobody knows about the religion."

At the first face-to-face meeting, twelve community members of the Community Accountability Board were present along with the victims and offender. Although Younce apologized early on, the Adi's were dissatisfied with his answers to their questions and doubted his sincerity. Younce though appreciative of the process, was overwhelmed by all the questions from the victims and the community members, and felt pressure to provide the right answer. At one point, a community member pointed out that Tamman Adi was not able to make eye contact with the offender, though his wife was able to. It seemed that he came to this joint meeting feeling more fearful, more vulnerable than he had realized.

After the first meeting, everyone agreed to meet again. Younce, however, shared his apprehensions about the meeting and how he had felt a bit under fire. It had hurt him when a community member expressed reservations about his raising a child, given his rage and racial prejudice. Younce had earlier told the mediators about the loss of his 20-month-old son six years earlier. He had died on September 14, and every year at this time Younce experienced bouts of anger and depression. Following the first meeting, the Adis also struggled with questions like, "Did he act alone or as a member of a racist group?" Was this a first time racist act, or part of an ongoing pattern?" "What went on in his mind between the time of seeing the news and picking up the phone?" In short, the victims wanted to hear Younce state why he did it, and why he wouldn't do it again.

At the second meeting each party waited in separate rooms, while the community members took time to debrief the previous meeting and get oriented for the follow up session. The community members spoke again of expectations and of the impact of the crime on the larger community. Younce began by providing an update on his progress with counseling, and mentioned that he had told his employer about the whole situation, which impressed the victims. Most important, he brought up the death of his infant son, helping the Adi's to understand the very real, human suffering behind Younce's misdirected rage. Tammam Adi again had a string of questions for the offender, only this time, Adi was better able to take in the answers offered. "I'm satisfied with what I have heard," he said in response. "I think we can move forward." A palpable shift took place in the room. The group began to discuss options for restitution. The Adi's wanted a public letter of apology to the Muslim community. They also asked that Younce attend two upcoming lectures on the religion of Islam. They requested that Younce cooperate in news coverage of the case, commit to continue his counseling, and speak to teens in juvenile detention about his experience.

Since then, Younce has attended the two lectures on Islam. Attending the first lecture, he was met by Adi at the door where they shook hands. After the lecture, he indicated that he had enjoyed being there, had learned a lot, and was motivated to attend additional lectures on his own. He also submitted his apology letter, which was printed on the editorial page of the local paper. The same edition featured a front-page account of the Younce-Adi story.

In the mist of the volatile cultural climate following the September 11 terrorist attacks, the case involving Younce and the Adi's embody the courageous journey from hatred to healing. It offered hope for peaceful, creative solutions to conflicts rising out of misguided rage and racial prejudice. It allowed a grieving community to play a cathartic role in responding to a local hate crime that had great symbolic meaning in the context of a national tragedy.

For hate crimes, there may be numerous preparation meetings to identify appropriate participants and topics of common interest (Umbreit, Coates, Vos, & Armour, 2006). During preparation, individuals should be encouraged to articulate about their concerns regarding hate in their community, of past experiences of being targets of hate, or of harboring their own hatreds. In bigger dialogue settings involving larger numbers of people, the dialogue may initially be restricted to a panel of participants followed by comments by the larger group of observers. It is expected that dialogue around issues and consequences of hatred will need to be ongoing. Indeed, it is advisable that an ongoing community dialogue follow from the original victim-offender mediation. The ongoing dialogue provides a way to maintain and nurture relationships in order to prevent or respond in the future to crimes of hate.

Interethnic Conflict

Restorative justice is increasingly seen as a viable mechanism for addressing long-standing interethnic conflict. It addresses the harm associated with recent and historic violence in order to promote the transition to a new phase of peaceful coexistence. Although less common, restorative justice has also been employed with parties in current conflict such as Palestinians and Israelis living in Israel and the occupied territories.

The South African Truth and Reconciliation Commission (TRC) is an exemplar of how restorative justice has been used to help society transition in ways that both address the injustices of the past and pave the way for a more just successor regime. The TRC was charged with investigating gross human rights abuses that occurred between 1960 and 1994 in order to create an accounting of the atrocities of that period (Borer, 2004). Perpetrators were offered amnesty in exchange for full disclosure about their past crimes. Victims were to receive reparations. The success of the South African TRC is hotly debated. Many, if not most, now conclude that the goal of national unity and reconciliation in order to create a nation democratically at peace with itself may have been achieved, but interpersonal or individual reconciliation has not happened (Borer, 2004).

Besides South Africa, truth commissions have been implemented in approximately two dozen countries around the world including Nigeria, Rwanda, and Sierra Leone. Indeed, the first known TRC in the United States took place in Greensboro, North Carolina, in 2004 (Magarrell & Wesley, 2008). Its purpose was to resolve questions and bring healing and closure to the survivors of activists gunned down in 1979 by members of the Ku Klux Klan and American Nazi party as they gathered in a Black neighborhood for a Death to the Klan rally and a conference for racial, social, and economic justice. All of the accused were subsequently acquitted by all-White juries. The Greensboro city government never backed the TRC commission, and a resolution to seriously consider its recommendations was rejected by a majority of city council members. This effort, however, resulted in numerous books and a documentary film, *Greensboro: Closer to the Truth*, to encourage deep and sustainable dialogue to promote community healing.

Many consider the use of restorative justice and dialogue extremely unlikely in ongoing conflict such as that between Arabs and Jews in Israel. Feelings of fear and vulnerability are ever present on all sides. The bombs set by Palestinian suicide bombers periodically pierce into the daily routine of Israelis while the Palestinians view the actions of Israel as imposing a state of terrorism on the daily lives of Palestinians.

The Parents Circle-Families Forum is precedent setting because it invites victims from both sides of the Palestinian-Israeli conflict to embark on a joint reconciliation mission while the conflict is still alive and violent. One of the forum's two offices is located in Ramat Efal, which is a suburb of Tel Aviv, and the Palestinian office is located in A-Ram, north of Jerusalem. Half of its' several hundred members are Palestinian and half are Israeli. Every participant has lost family members to the violence in Israeli and the occupied territories and understand better than most about the tragically high cost of continuing generational vengefulness.

Indeed, Robi Damelin, an Israeli activist in the organization whose son was killed while in the reserves by a Palestinian sniper, and Ali Abu Awwad, a former Palestinian revolutionary whose brother was shot and killed by an Israeli soldier, appear together to speak internationally as peace campaigners. Robi recently wrote a letter to the Palestinian sniper, Hamad, about her son, the depth of her pain, and her decision to work for reconciliation (Ben-Simhon, 2009). She began the letter stating, "This is one of the hardest letters I'll ever have to write." Although the response she received back from Hamad was a rejection with the statement, "I cannot address the soldier's mother directly," Robi wrote back. Her older son supported her continued effort and in response to Hamad's letter said, "Mom, this is also the beginning of a dialogue."

The Parents Circle-Families Forum is a grassroots organization that uses restorative processes to promote reconciliation as an alternative to unrelenting hatred, revenge, and violence. This vision humanizes the conflict between the parties by taking the toxic power of hatred's consequences out of it. The group's numerous programs include, among others, face-to-face reconciliation meetings; dialogue meetings for youth and adults; a television drama series called "Good Intentions"; a weekly radio program on the "All for Peace" radio station; professional training for activists, lecturers, and spokespeople; and children and youth meetings and summer camps.

The use of restorative dialogue for hate crimes and interethnic conflict requires awareness that participants will use the dialogue differently because the power imbalances between parties usually reflect larger issues of social justice. The Greensboro TRC, for example, reflects both an effort to bring together various factions to address the harm done as a result of the massacre and to make visible the ongoing refusal of the city council and police to get involved in the Greensboro TRC just as the police were conspicuously absent at the rally in 1979 (Magarrell & Wesley, 2008). Although these power imbalances affect the dynamics of the process, the dynamics of the process also have a powerful effect on the power imbalances between parties. The meetings between Younce who made the death threat calls to the Muslim Center and the Adis clearly altered the power imbalance between a White offender and members of a targeted minority group. Publicizing the meetings may have increased their impact because others who are part of the socially prescribed power imbalance between Whites and Muslim immigrants may have been reached as well.

GLOBALIZATION OF RESTORATIVE JUSTICE

In just 30 years, restorative practices have spread with amazing speed into justice systems, community organizations, and religious groups all over the world. The United Nations, in particular, has become one of the largest and most politically credible organizations promoting restorative practices. Beginning in 1999, the UN Economic and Social Council requested that the United Nations establish a set of standards for the international use of restorative justice practices. In 2002, the UN publicly declared that all countries should use restorative justice whenever possible and assembled an international expert group to develop an official set of principles to be made globally available. This group published the "Basic Principles on the Use of Restorative Justice Programmes in Criminal Matters," which was followed by the *UN Handbook on Restorative Justice Programmes*, published in 2006 (Wachtel, 2007).

Although the basic principles of restorative justice may have universal application, often the specific methodologies and/or assumptions about social behavior are not universal. Indeed, despite the 2006 publication and subsequent distribution of the handbook, it has still not been fully translated into a language other than English (Kirkwood, 2007). Part of the difficulty is that restorative justice itself is a delicate process that is often focused on the nuances of language and behavior between parties. The task of sensitively translating written restorative justice materials therefore is immense. Just the core concept of *circle keeper* presents difficulties because in English it implies guardianship and custodianship, whereas in Spanish the term implies leadership or directorship (Kirkwood, 2007).

Difficulties with exporting restorative justice also reflect the fact that Western concepts do not readily transfer to groups who have different philosophies about justice, different historical contexts, and different social traditions. Groups like the Mayas in Guatemala, for example, have been systematically stripped of any sense of social cohesion, traditions, culture, land, and other basic human rights and have no community justice program, as stipulated by the United Nations, on which to build a restorative justice model. Moreover, they are alienated from

Guatemalan government and justice due to the people's general mistrust of the Ladino-led government (Kirkwood, 2007). Indeed, for Third-World countries that continue to struggle with the establishment and maintenance of the rule of law, implementation of a "Western" style restorative justice program would seem superfluous in the face of a basic lack of social order.

Restorative Justice and Indigeneity

The movement to export restorative justice rests, in part, on the fact that restorative justice's philosophy and practices embody aspects of dispute resolution familiar to indigenous groups. Publications commonly reference First Nations groups from Canada, Native Americans, and the New Zealand Maori as examples of cultures grounded in the community, focused on the well-being of the collective, and steeped in the traditions of consensus decision making, face-to-face interaction, and the practice of restitution to the victim or victim's family (Kirkwood, 2007).

The overwhelming focus in the literature on these three indigenous groups as the indigenous link in restorative justice is problematic. Indeed, there are an estimated 300 million indigenous people in more than 70 countries across the world, which suggests a rich complexity and tremendous variation in how conflict is handled (Cunneen, 2004). Sanctions used by indigenous peoples that fall outside of prescribed restorative justice norms may be ignored, particularly if they include temporary or permanent exile or withdrawal and separation within the community (Cunneen, 2004). In many instances, sanctions may be based on avoidance rather than a face-to-face encounter between victim and offender.

Moreover, it could be argued that the similarities drawn by restorative justice proponents about indigenous groups from across the globe, such as holding a collective versus individual worldview, may more accurately reflect the need of the culture to think in collectivist terms about its own survival in the face of colonialism. This assertion is supported by the United Nations draft declaration on the rights of indigenous people authored in 1982 by 400 different indigenous delegations over 8 years (Holder & Courtassel, 2002). Agreement on the drafting of the document was easy because it reflected a common indigenous experience with colonialism and the need to unify agendas to maintain spiritual and political autonomy and the protection of rights as distinct peoples (Holder & Courtassel, 2002). In addition to elevating certain groups as models of indigeneity and disregarding sanctioning practices contrary to restorative justice beliefs, restorative justice must also watch that its claim to indigenous roots as its pedigree can appear patronizing and its importation of indigenous traditions taken out of context can trivialize otherwise sacred practices (Cunneen, 2004).

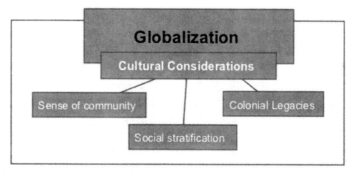

FIGURE 10.3

Cultural Considerations

The responsibility to train the UN's member nations is commonly given to Western restorative justice leaders, many of whom lack cultural fluency about the groups they are educating. One example is an Australian restorative justice practitioner was asked to speak at a conference in Thailand based on his previous international work. He acknowledged that he arrived completely unprepared to speak to a room of hundreds of Thai lawyers and due to his lack of knowledge on Thai culture admits that, "I am sure that I totally botched an opportunity" (Kirkwood, 2007, p. 101). Any examination of restorative justice and its application to a particular culture must include more than a cursory understanding of its key characteristics. An analysis of cultural considerations should include the group's indigenous and minority influence, religion, political system, legal and judicial system, and civil society (Kirkwood, 2007). Particular attention should be given to the group's sense and structure of community, the interface between a socially stratified society and restorative justice as democratically based, and the lasting effects of colonization (see Figure 10.3).

Variations in the Concept of Community

In restorative justice, the community is considered to be the embodiment of culture and values and the third major stakeholder after the victim and offender. For some groups, however, the current community is not indigenous per se but formed directly as a result of policies of the forced relocation of tribal groups, for example, Native Americans. Like indigeneity, community too has tended to be idealized and expected to be a strong, cohesive, and highly participatory entity that can achieve what institutions alone cannot (Bauman, 2001). Neighborhoods, however, may be torn apart by crime and violence or by genocide, mass murders, and government-sponsored terror. In these situations, a collective identity, or sense of community, may actually have formed around the violence and terror itself, for example, gangs (Kirkwood, 2007).

Globalization may also have created transnational communities or a sense of community that does not fit neatly into the Western conception of community (Kirkwood, 2007). Though an individual may live in a certain geographical area, the group to which they most closely identified could be located in another part of the world altogether.

Kirkwood (2007) describes a fictional example of how a myopic view of community could create additional harm. René, a young Haitian migrant in New York City was charged with stealing from a grocery store in which he works. A victim-offender mediation was arranged. The offender, store owner, arresting officer, and two employees who witnessed the event were invited. These participants were chosen as community representatives. As a result of the meeting, it was agreed that René would no longer be employed at the current store, but he would not be deported, and an arrangement would be worked out in which he would cover the cost of the stolen goods. In the view of this facilitator, the mediation was a success, and a sense of order and peace returned to these community members. René, however, had lived in New York for 5 years but still felt closely tied to the small coastal town where he grew up. He regularly sent back a part of his monthly earnings to his mother and two sisters in Haiti. Because of the financial assistance they received, René's family had been able to start a small business with the neighboring family. They baked goods that they sold in front of their home and that brought in enough income to pay the electricity bills and send the children of both families to school. Now that Renée has lost his job and can no longer send remittances, another set of victims has been created who were never touched by the traditional restorative process. These two families never receive justice, and Renée does not have the opportunity to make the amends within the community to which he considers himself to belong. It is imperative for the facilitator to uncover and promote the understanding and disclosure of all pertinent information that may influence the outcome from all parties' perspectives.

As this example demonstrates, the concept of community is mercurial and may reflect historical and current politics rather than indigenous culture. Moreover, micro communities do not exist in a vacuum but hold status based on the power and privilege accorded a population's race or ethnicity and the position of that community in relation to the dominant society or macro community. Communities, therefore, may not be peaceful, conflict free, or in support of restorative justice and may not even exist.

Socially Stratified Cultures

Democracy is characterized by a respect for the rule of law, strong legal and governing institutions, and a respect for human equality. Restorative justice, as it is currently understood and practiced, operates under these same assumptions.

Respect and equality are considered the most basic tenets of the philosophy as is the expectation that crime will be officially recognized and responded to as such. In a society where none of these prerequisites exist and/or cannot be created, the introduction of restorative justice practices will encounter major obstacles. What is to be done, for example, in weak democracies or even in fully nondemocratic countries?

Moreover, aid to developing countries after World War II was accompanied by the promotion of legal development assistance, which was justified as "a rational and effective method to protect individual freedom, expand citizen participation in decision making, enhance social equality, and increase the capacity of all citizens rationally to control events and shape social life" (Trubek & Galanter, 1974, p. 1063). Such justification parallels the goals of restorative justice. Restorative justice seeks to put decisions back in the hands of those who were harmed and to give them the ability to control events that shape their lives. It also promotes community participation in the responses to crime and expands citizen participation in decision making.

What happens, however, when restorative justice encounters cultural structures built on systems of social hierarchy, privilege, and inequality? In the case of Latin America, for example, 80% of Latin Americans define themselves as Catholic (Sanchez, 2005). The church is structured hierarchically, and its long influence in the region has transformed some of these principles to society itself. For example, traditional Roman Catholic teaching emphasizes the glories of eternal salvation (Vanden & Prevost, 2002). Catholics are taught that suffering is a part of life and that it will be rewarded in Heaven. Latin-American culture, and even the Spanish language itself, are often described as fatalistic (Kirkwood, 2007), and inhabitants of Catholic-affiliated Latin-American countries may perceive of themselves as victims of their circumstances (Claudet, 1992). Within the church philosophy, the idea of repairing harms caused by crime to the victim may be primarily reserved for the afterlife.

Society in India is another example of a socially stratified culture. The 3,500-year-old caste system survives today. This social system of gradation is religiously sanctioned and upheld by the *panchayat*, which has been the traditional institution of community justice in India, consisting of village councils. In 1992, The Congress Government passed an amendment that gave *panchayats* constitutional status at the village, block, and district levels (Vincentnathan & Vincentnatnathan, 2006). What does this mean for the international spread of restorative justice? Social and political hierarchies and cultural outlooks on life are often based on religious tradition. In dealing with Third-World cultures, awareness of these distinctions may need to go beyond typical religious sensitivities because they may influence directly how restorative justice is introduced, received, and incorporated into the existing social structure.

Colonial Legacies

Many, if not most, indigenous cultures show the effects of colonization, which was marked by exploitation and violence followed by efforts to uproot a people's culture—their language, religion, spirituality, ritual, and art—and replace it with the invader's own culture (Wonshe, 2004). Besides virtually destroying indigenous cultures and traditions, the conquerors imposed power disparities including the marginalization of ethnic groups. These unequal power relationships and oppressive structural frameworks in the developing world have resulted in a host of injustices and large-scale harms.

For example, when colonization in Melanesia took place, it involved the arbitrary partitioning of territories with little attention to existing social and political groups and boundaries (Dinnen, 2006). Christian missions and commercial plantations followed and also had a profound effect. Colonial justice consisted of the introduction of selected Western laws and specially adapted tribunals and processes for dealing with offenses. European district officers would draw on a limited knowledge of local customs to hold native courts that dealt with alleged breaches of specially designated native regulations. With time, the old colonial systems were dismantled in favor of institutional modernization and the modern nation-state. This transition, however, has been difficult, and local systems of self-regulation tended to exert a more direct influence on the daily lives of native inhabitants than did modern law and justice. At the same time, rapid social and economic change generated new sources of tension including escalating law and order problems; landowner conflicts over levels of compensation for mining development, which led to 9 years of civil war (May & Spriggs, 1990; Spriggs & Denoon, 1992); increasing alcohol and drug abuse; and declining levels of respect among young people for village leaders and traditional authority (Dinnen, 2006).

It's important to note that in places like Melanesia, the colonizing offender is considered European or the West, which is also the home of restorative justice. Consequently, restorative justice practitioners who educate non-Western communities in the philosophy and practices of the field must be aware of their potential to misuse their power and implant concepts without regard for the histories of the area in which they are going to be working. They need also to recognize circumstances in which communities might still be struggling with the effects of colonization and postcolonization (Kirkwood, 2007). The struggle for restorative justice is to locate itself within the realities of formerly colonized countries, find a way to deal with the historic injustices, and promote establishing a sense of reconciliation.

The global trend of restorative justice raises important questions about how to successfully transplant the Western notion of restorative justice to widely disparate cultures located in different corners of the world. Although restorative justice has a universal paradigm, it must be aware of its tendencies to romanticize (Cunneen, 2004) and inaccurately equate itself with indigeneity; the need to deconstruct its homogenizing concept of community in order to incorporate constructs that are more complex, varied, and reflective of the current circumstances of indigenous groups; the potential difficulties of using constructs associated with democracy when working with socially stratified groups; and the pervasive presence of colonialism and decolonization in today's indigenous cultures, which must be understood and incorporated to address crime and social injustices effectively.

DIMENSIONS OF CULTURE IN THE RESTORATIVE JUSTICE COMMUNITY

The field of restorative justice itself is not immune to issues of power, privilege, and oppression specific to gender, race, class, culture, religion, and sexual orientation. (See Figure 10.4.) Racism, in particular, stands at the center of restorative justice because criminality today is practically synonymous with Black and/or Hispanic due to the vast overrepresentation of men and women of color in the criminal justice system. Yet the number of persons of color who are practicing restorative justice, leading its organizations, or receiving services is substantially underrepresented. As a movement, therefore, restorative justice proponents must ask how culture, class, and gender, in particular, affect the practice of restorative justice.

Peacemaking circles, its principles, and rituals, including smudging and the talking piece, which have deep symbolic and emotional significance, are "borrowed" directly from First Nations groups in Canada. How does the field of restorative justice explain the absence of Native American representatives on restorative justice boards or the use of White practitioners instead

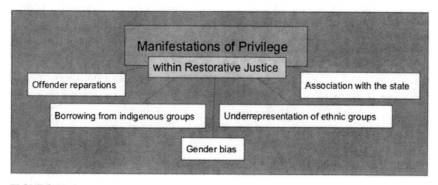

FIGURE 10.4

of Native Americans to explain a process that is theirs to claim, to offer, and to welcome (Raye, 2004)? To what extent does the field exclude others and use trainers and facilitators who embody Anglo norms including appropriate attitudes, communication skills, professionalism, and knowledge about boundaries? Too often male-led training consists of participants, volunteers, and staff who are mainly White, middle-class women who likely have time, resources, and social connections and can devote their efforts to something like restorative justice. The few participants who are persons of color end up feeling isolated or, worse yet, a token representative from the same socially marginalized groups that restorative justice is trying to reach. More efforts, therefore, should be made to get volunteers up to speed culturally and encourage leaders in minority communities to endorse restorative justice as a way of addressing crime.

There are increasing concerns about how decisions get made, about which offenders are referred to a restorative practice, and which offenders must go through court. In Australia, for example, Aboriginal youth are more likely to be referred to court and less likely than non-Aboriginal youth to be referred by police to family group conferencing (Cunneen, 2002). Legitimate questions might be raised about the ability of victims and/or offenders from particular groups to participate in restorative practices or be self-disclosing when they mistrust the process because of its association with the state or when the facilitator reflects the middle-class values associated with those in power.

Frequently, the mediation agreement requires that the offender perform services for the community that typically take the form of unskilled labor, such as picking up trash on the highway or in parks, painting over graffiti, raking leaves, or other menial services. Such services, including services to victims, churches, or other groups, rarely occur in the neighborhood where the offender lives. Reparations of this sort do little to benefit offenders or lead them to new job opportunities but rather can contribute to the race and class bias that may lay hidden underneath humanitarian concerns (Delgado, 2000).

The health of the restorative justice community and its future success rest on giving major consideration to these issues. A final concern that receives little mention is the potential for gender bias in the field. Although there are increasingly more female leaders in the restorative justice community, it, like the criminal justice system, has been male dominated. Many of its processes, however, including attention to relationships, belief in interconnectedness, and power balance/harmony within relationships and with the earth, are also feminine (Raye, 2004). Besides developing a critical consciousness about the potential within the restorative justice community to reproduce racist practices, it is just as essential "to explain the absence of women's names as founders, leaders, and "experts" in processes that have been theirs for generations" (p. 331).

The fact that we, as students and practitioners, find that biases of gender, race, and class are within our own subculture is not surprising. After all, we share a similar social conditioning based on society's constructs of power, privilege, and oppression and therefore are predisposed to replicate them if the awareness necessary to change them is lacking. As current and future supporters and practitioners of restorative justice, it is necessary to spend as much energy on manifestations of our own privilege as we spend on addressing harms and fostering accountability in others.

REFERENCES

Almeida, R., Dolan-Del Vecchio, K., & Parker, L. (2007). *Transformative family therapy: Just families in a just society*. Boston: Allyn & Bacon.

Bauman, Z. (2001). *Community: Seeking safety in an insecure world*. Cambridge, England: Polity.

Belk, A. (2006). *A new generation of native sons: Men of color and the prison-industrial complex*. Washington, DC: Joint Center for Political and Economic Studies Health Policy Institute.

Ben-Simhon. (2009). Forgiveness of dead IDF soldier's mother leaves Palestinian killer cold. *Haaretz.com*. Retrieved January 7, 2010, from http://www.haaretz.com/hasen/spages/1124595.html

Borer, T. A. (2004). Reconciling South Africa or South Africans: Cautionary notes from the TRC. *African Studies Quarterly, 8*, 19–38.

Claudet, P. T. (1992). *La cultura del pobrecito* (Editorial). San José: Universidad de Costa Rica (EUCR), pp. 27–28.

Cunneen, C. (2002). *Conflict, politics and crime*. Sidney: Allen and Unwin.

Cunneen, C. (2004). What are the implications of restorative justice's use of indigenous traditions? In H. Zehr & B. Toews (Eds.), *Critical issues in restorative justice* (pp. 345–354). Monsey, NY: Criminal Justice.

Delgado, R. (2000). Prosecuting violence: A colloguy on race, community and justice. *Stanford Law Review, 52*, 751–775.

Dinnen, S. (2006). Restorative justice and the governance of security in the Southwest Pacific. In D. Sullivan & L. Tifft (Eds.), *Handbook of restorative justice: A global perspective* (pp. 401–421). London: Routledge.

Holder, C. L., & Courtassel, J. J. (2002). Indigenous peoples and multicultural citizenship: Bridging collective and individual rights. *Human Rights Quarterly, 24*, 126–151.

Kirkwood, H. J. (2007). *A cultural critique of the globalization of restorative justice*. Master of Arts thesis, The University of Texas at Austin, Austin, Texas.

Magarrell, L., & Wesley, J. (2008). *Learning from Greensboro: Truth and reconciliation in the United States*. Philadelphia, PA: University of Pennsylvania Press.

May, R. J., & Spriggs, M. (1990). *The Bougainville crisis*. Bathurst, Australia: Crawford House Press.

Murphy, J. G. (1988). Forgiveness and resentment. In J. G. Murphy & J. Hampton (Eds.), *Forgiveness and mercy* (pp. 14–34). Cambridge: Cambridge University Press.

Raye, B. E. (2004). How do culture, class and gender affect the practice of restorative justice? (Part 2). In H. Zehr & B. Toews (Eds.), *Critical issues in restorative justice* (pp. 229–240). Monsey, NY: Criminal Justice.

Sanchez, M. (2005). Catholic church needs liberalized dogma. *Seattle Post-Intelligencer*. Retrieved January 5, 2010, from http://www.seattlepi.com/opinion/219252_sanchez08.html

Spriggs, M., & Denoon, D. (1992). *The Bougainville crisis: 1991 update*. Canberra: Department of Political and Social Change, Research School of Pacific and Asian Studies, Australian National University.

Sue, D. W., & Sue, D. (1990). *Counseling the culturally different* (2nd ed.). New York: John Wiley & Sons.

Trubek, D., & Galanter, M. (1974). Scholars in self-estrangement: Some reflections on the crisis in law and developing studies in the United States. *Wisconsin Law Review, 4*, 1062–1102.

U.S. Department of Justice. (2008). *Hate crime statistics, 2008*. Retrieved January 5, 2010, from http://www.fbi.gov/ucr/hc2006/index.html

Umbreit, M. S., & Coates, R. (1999). Multi-cultural implications of restorative juvenile justice. *Federal Probation, 65*(3), 44–45.

Umbreit, M. S., & Coates, R. (2000). *Multicultural implications of restorative justice: Potential pitfalls and dangers*. Washington, DC: U.S. Department of Justice Office of Justice Programs.

Umbreit, M. S., Coates, R., & Vos, B. (2003). *Victim offender mediation: Three decades of practice and research*. St. Paul, MN: Center for Restorative Justice and Peacemaking, School of Social Work, University of Minnesota.

Umbreit, M. S., Coates, R., Vos, B., & Armour, M. (2006). Victims of severe violence in mediated dialogue with offender: The impact of the first multi-site study in the U.S. *International Review of Victimology, 13*(1), 27–48.

Umbreit, M. S., Lewis, T., & Burns, H. (2003). A community response to a 9/11 hate crime: Restorative justice through dialogue. *Contemporary Justice Review, 6*(4), 383–391.

Vanden, H. E., & Prevost, G. (2002). *Politics of Latin America: The power game*. New York: Oxford University Press.

Vincentnathan, S. G., & Vincentnatnathan, L. (2006, November 1). *Democratization and the fate of community justice in India*. Paper presented at the Annual Meeting of the American Society of Criminology, Los Angelos, CA.

Wachtel, J. (2007). United Nations releases "Handbook of Restorative Justice Programmes". *Restorative Practices eForum*. Retrieved December 27, 2009, from http://www.iirp.org/pdf/unhandbook.pdf

Wonshe. (2004). How does the "who, what, where and how" affect the practice of restorative justice? In H. Zehr & B. Toews (Eds.), *Critical issues in restorative justice* (pp. 253–264). Monsey, NY: Criminal Justice Press.

11. Emerging Areas of Practice

> *If you want a future that's distinct from the past, you have to be with people who you aren't used to being with and have conversations that you're not used to having.*
>
> Peter Block
>
> *Intuition is the source of scientific knowledge.*
>
> Aristotle

*I*n the first chapter, we noted a number of opportunities for expanding the potential applications of restorative justice. Some of these opportunities included the use of restorative dialogue in work settings among co-workers, surrogate victim-offender community dialogue as a partial response to the large volume of crime victims whose offenders are never caught, and truth and reconciliation commissions to respond to the past injustices done by the dominant culture to the many ethnic groups and communities of color within a country. Broadening the net, however, raises important questions about the viable parameters of restorative justice. What are its limits? What determines whether an emerging practice is "restorative?" What does "justice" mean in light of the social issue being addressed? Enlarging the vision also elicits concerns about quality control and implementation. What mechanisms are in place to ensure that expansion of the field does not dilute its effectiveness? What training should be offered to instill principled practices? What are the challenges new applications pose to voluntarism and lay participation? This final chapter describes some of these innovations and the research to support their effectiveness, explores developments in the conceptualization of restorative justice based on the emergence of new practices, and explores some of the reasons for the effectiveness of restorative justice as a movement and restorative dialogue as application.

This final chapter describes some of the more recent restorative justice innovations and the research that substantiates their usefulness. It also explores developments in the conceptualization of restorative justice based on the emergence of new practices and looks at some of the reasons for the effectiveness of restorative justice as a movement and restorative dialogue as application. Some of the innovations draw on the approaches covered in previous chapters. For example, practices used for student misconduct on college campuses include VOM and a modified type of Sentencing Circle. Both Family Group Conferencing (FGC) and Family Group Decision Making (FGDM) have been used for domestic violence. As hybrid programs or new approaches develop, the field is not clear about what makes them restorative. Is harm to the victim the organizing principle? Is it necessary to be inclusive and have all sides participate in the process? Is the process voluntary and consensual? What about the process' contribution to transforming negative or toxic energy into a power that produces healing? Questions are also raised about the nature of facilitation and the qualities of the facilitator who prepares for and tends the dialogue. Is adequate time given to preparation? Does facilitation tap the strengths of the parties, empowering them to trust and engage openly with each other? These evaluative questions draw on the information covered in Chapter 4 about what makes a program restorative and in Chapter 8 about facilitator's role in restorative dialogue. Finding some answers safeguards the essence of the restorative justice movement from opportunistic superficiality and trendy programs that can be advertised as "restorative" when they are not.

As the growth of legitimate programs in the restorative justice field accelerates, dealing with the complexity that emerges from the movement's way of dealing with conflict requires the ability to perceive what is happening from a higher level of abstraction in order to understand what is so generative about restorative justice practices. One such explanation of this perceptual requirement has been introduced by Twila Hugley Earle, one of the founders of contemporary innovative theory and field practice design in criminal justice in the United States (Earle, 1996, 1998). Earle's groundbreaking work in the application of chaos theory principles to contemporary criminal justice innovations illuminates factors in successful restorative justice practices that reflect the underlying basic principles of nonlinear dynamics that govern self-organizing systems identified by chaos and complexity physics (Earle, 1998, 1999). Chaos theory offers a better way to view the coincidental timeliness of the emergence of restorative justice as a deeper way of dealing with human conflict that is more appropriate for the higher levels and more complex layers of conflict (Earle, 1998).

In the shift now occurring, both individuals and societies who linger in the more short term, oversimplistic, two-dimensional, either/or, black/white, dependent/independent, us versus them, win/lose mindset of the second millennium do not tend to fare as well as those who are able to adapt to more complex three-dimensional, interdependent, integrative, win/win, holistic depth perceptions that encompass the more contextual, comprehensive, interactive, faster-paced, and longer-term synergistic impact thinking required to meet the demands of the third millennium (T. H. Earle, personal communication, February 14, 2009).

Chaos theory postulates that there is order in what appears to be an otherwise chaotic situation created by change. Indeed chaos theory illuminates that underneath change is a pattern that replicates itself anew but with regularity each time certain conditions, such as conflict, rise to the level of causing chaos and reach a threshold where change is necessary. Chaos theory outlines those conditions. From the vantage point of chaos theory, which will be described later in the chapter, the diversity of programs, the complexity of the process, and growth of restorative justice as a movement during the past 30 years appear understandable and indicative of the fact that societies are undergoing a major shift as they discard old systems of managing conflict that are outdated and no longer useful.

INNOVATIONS IN PRACTICE

David Gustafson, Co-Director of the Fraser Region Community Justice Initiatives Association in Langley, British Columbia, has asked the question, "Is restorative justice taking too few, or too many, risks?" This question reflects not only Gustafson's appreciation for the explosion of growth in restorative justice around the globe but also his concerns that such rapid growth requires more risk relative to the attention that must be given to the quality of practice. Indeed, the lack of a solid foundation in emerging practices could compromise the quality of service delivery, which could turn participant involvement into a "perilous journey" (Gustafson, 2004, p. 311). Whenever a new area of restorative justice practice develops, therefore, it requires an assessment of what needs to be done to ensure the safety for all participants so that the conditions for a constructive dialogue can be met and also the competencies that are crucial for principled facilitation can be determined.

Among the many innovations, we review four restorative justice practices that have opened up areas for future growth. Those practices include the use of restorative practices for student misconduct in institutions of higher education, the establishment of surrogate dialogue programs in prisons between unrelated crime victims and offenders, the creation of restorative justice initiatives for domestic violence, and the development of methods for engagement between crime victims and members of defense teams who represent the accused offender.

STUDENT MISCONDUCT IN HIGHER EDUCATION

The use of restorative practices in schools began in the mid-1990s (Morrison, 2007) to address a range of wrongdoing including bullying, assaults, drugs, and property damage. Restorative practices in schools provide a secondary benefit. They build the skills of children and youth in conflict resolution and community building and contribute to the safety of the school community. In addition, restorative practices develop students' social and emotional intelligence. Hence, they embody both proactive processes to enhance teaching and learning and reactive processes to respond to harm and wrongdoing.

Although restorative practices are an increasing mainstay in schools at the elementary, middle, and high school levels (Morrison, 2007), their entry into higher education campus judicial affairs is more recent. Indeed, traditional adjudication approaches remain primary on most college and university campuses and fixed on the breaking of rules as articulated in university policies and codes of conduct (Allena, 2004). The close associations between student judicial systems, excessive legalism, the adversarial model, and concern for the preservation of student rights have been shaped by court rulings over the past 40 years (Footer, 1996; Lowery & Dannells, 2004), most notably *Dixon v. Alabama* (1961), which was considered precedent setting for issues related to due process in American higher-education law. In a review of cases before the Supreme Court related to academic processes, Lake (2009) notes that the Supreme Court has carefully avoided interfering with college's prerogatives to manage students on their own campuses, and some courts have questioned the wisdom of attempting to use legalistic approaches and court-like processes in institutions of higher learning.

Indeed, colleges have turned over their concerns to lawyers who have had a tendency to offer legalistic solutions to all types of problems and issues. This trend toward legalisms, codes, and discipline has created unique obstacles to the introduction of restorative justice on campuses despite the fact that student judicial services are philosophically grounded in the educational mission of the institution, which includes fostering the student's sense of civic responsibility and moral development (Lowery & Dannells, 2004). The introduction of restorative justice into higher education, therefore, is more complex than at the elementary or secondary school levels. Besides having to address important policy issues, there are also thorny considerations about what kinds of behaviors warrant or require restorative processes, who has been impacted and the extent of the harm, what is required organizationally to train staff, what amount of time is involved, and at what cost (Lowery & Dannells, 2004).

Student misconduct involves different behaviors than seen at the secondary or elementary school levels. Cheating, plagiarism, misuse of alcohol, hate crimes, sexual assault, and hazing misconduct are common violations of student codes of conduct as well as destruction of property, which may also constitute a municipal infraction.

Finally, students on college campuses pose unique challenges because of their developmental stage. Specifically, many are living for the first time independent of parental authority. Their living in dorms and residential halls, belonging to fraternities and sororities, or operating in the context of a campus community and cultural environment may promote behaviors such as cheating (McCabe & Trevino, 1996) or underage and heavy drinking (DeLong & Langenbahn, 1996) due, in part, to pressure from peers, the desire to belong, and anxiety about succeeding. The vulnerability of college women to sexual harassment and the incidence of off-the-field violence by college athletes are additional realities of campus life. Many students have not developed strong internal controls to regulate their behavior. Moreover, because the student population turns over regularly, responses at the individual level do little to change campus norms, build community, or resolve community-level problems. Consequently, student misconduct calls for a restorative approach that builds prosocial norms; greater community investment; direct participation from students, faculty, and staff; and the recognition that development of students' character, either in response to their wrongdoing or as a member of the responsive community, is part of the educational mission.

Although numerous colleges and universities are considering adding restorative practices for student misconduct, a few institutions, including Clemson University, Guilford College, and Michigan State, have begun restorative justice to varying degrees. The most fully developed programs, however, are at Skidmore College, the University of Colorado—Boulder, Colorado State University, and the University of Michigan.

Skidmore College

Skidmore College is a small liberal arts institution in upstate New York that uses an integrity board to handle student misconduct (Karp, 2004). An integrity board hears from the student responsible for the misconduct. An integrity board is composed of a cross section of the community and is drawn from a pool of members that includes four students, one staff member, and one or two faculty members. Initially, cases primarily involved alcohol or marijuana but also included harassment, assault, theft, fraud, weapons, hazing, and academic integrity violations (D. Karp, personal communication, March 31, 2009). An integrity board consists of board members, victims who are called "harmed parties" and a support person, wrongdoers who are called "respondents," affected parties such as a campus safety officer, and a representative of the Student Affairs Office called a "judicial officer," in addition to the board members (Karp, 2004). The judicial officer presents the facts of the case as they have been determined by administrative inquiry. The chair of the integrity board is always a student whose job is to facilitate the process following a script.

Although not currently happening, training for student members in the past was conducted over the course of the Fall semester with readings, guest speakers, role-plays, discussion of philosophy, debriefing recent cases, and evaluation of practice and policy (Karp, 2004). Under this model, students received academic credit for their participation in the board training, and their subsequent involvement in cases was considered a service-learning component. Besides providing integrity boards with a regular pool of student volunteers, the training gave students an opportunity to contribute to the campus community, involved them in the study of the Skidmore community, and promoted dialogue about community values and social problems. In cases that are pursued simultaneously by the criminal court, Skidmore has established a relationship with the Saratoga County District Attorney's office for the DA to review the integrity board's findings in hopes that the court will accept what has been negotiated with the respondent.

A successful integrity board hearing has five steps: (1) The establishment of common ground that encourages full participation of all parties and creates a space for social support and encouragement; (2) the determination of responsibility for wrongdoing based on objective weighing of the evidence; (3) respondent's acceptance of responsibility and evaluation of respondent's commitment to make things right; (4) identification of harm including physical, material, and communal harm; (5) identification collectively of ways to fix the damage done including ways to help the respondent become a responsible community member (Karp, 2004). Besides restitution to repair material harm, emotional harm is addressed through apology letters, which are submitted to the integrity board for approval before being sent to the harmed parties. Community service is used to repair harm to the community and is expected to be educational, meaningful, and rewarding. Reparations may also include a reflective essay, alcohol abuse screening, academic tutoring, and an initial visit for psychological assessment. If a student fails to complete the reparative contract, that student cannot register for classes until the contract is met. Consequently, in making the decision to not complete the agreement, the student, in effect, suspends himself or herself.

The University of Colorado—Boulder

The University of Colorado in Boulder operates Community Accountability Boards, which grew out of tensions between students and permanent residents that occurred in the 1990s related to drinking and property offenses (Gina Bata, personal communication, April 1, 2009). Based on the actions of a city judge who wanted to send student offenders through a restorative justice program, the university established the CU Restorative Justice Program

(CURJ). CURJ runs three different models: the Community Accountability Board Conference (CAB), the Victim-Offender Conference (VOC), and the Mutual Responsibility Conference. Models are selected for particular cases based on the type of offense and the circumstances surrounding it.

The CAB is used for low-level offenses, for example, nuisance party, unreasonable noise. It comprises two facilitators and two to three community members. These conferences do not include the victim or anyone else who was directly involved. Community and student volunteers belong to a pool, are trained by the restorative justice coordinator in basic processes, and receive advanced training (University of Colorado at Boulder [UCB], 2007). The offending student must be a first-time offender, take responsibility, though not necessarily plead guilty, and is given the choice to participate in the program or go through the regular court system for municipal violations as part of a plea bargain. There is a discussion with the student to identify who was harmed, how they were harmed, and what can be done to repair the harm. A reparative agreement is drawn up by all members of the conference including the student. Fulfillment of the written agreement is monitored by the restorative justice coordinator (UCB, 2007). CABS are held four times a week in the evening. The volunteer pool contributes over 1,860 hours annually to serve about twice per month to service approximately 400 cases each year (UCB, 2007).

VOC is used when there is an identifiable victim. The offense is usually more serious as well, for example, vandalism and third-degree assault. The restorative justice coordinator prepares the student responsible for harm and the victim by interviewing them about the incident, educating them as to their role in the conference, and suggesting that they identify ideas about repairing the harm related to the incident. Both victim and offender can bring support persons and family members to the conference if they wish. VOCs are conducted by highly trained facilitators. At the conference, facilitators introduce each person and their roles and purposes for being there and lay out the ground rules that guide the conference, emphasizing values such as deep listening, speaking respectfully, empathy, honesty, courage, and so on (UCB, 2007). The offending student tells their story of what happened, which establishes their sense of personal responsibility for the harm caused, followed by the victim's story and input from other affected community members.

The restorative justice program is mostly funded through a $135 fee that the responsible student must pay (L. Bloom, personal communication, May 2, 2009). About half the cases are "nuisance party" violations, which are usually related to drinking (UCB, 2007). The program does not deal with all cases because third-degree assault is the highest level of case that the municipal court handles (UCB, 2007). One of the major strengths of this program, according to Gina Bata, Restorative Justice program coordinator, is that people in the community have an outlet and a chance to offer input to students to help them understand their community and to talk about how their actions affect others living near them (Swenson, 2009).

The University of Michigan

Acting on awareness that the Office of Student Conflict Resolution (OSCR) was eager for a new vision and approach for responding to student misconduct, Jennifer Meyer Schrage introduced a new model for more effectively infusing restorative justice practices into conduct administration when she took over the directorship of OSCR in 2006 (L. Bloom, personal communication, May 2, 2009). The new vision focused on providing services to the students, staff, and faculty in a way that would "build trust, promote justice and teach peace" (OSCR University of Michigan, 2008). The relative ease of making a paradigm shift was due to the fact that Residence Education and Housing was already using restorative approaches to address conflicts in student residence halls and Schrage's ability, with OSCR staff team, to introduce restorative practices by drawing on a diversion clause for mediation that was already written into the conduct policy (L. Bloom, personal communication, May 2, 2009).

Today, OSCR operates according to a Spectrum Model, which places adjudication as but one option on a "Spectrum of Resolution Options" menu with multiple pathways for conflict resolution (Schrage, 2009; Schrage & Thompson, 2009). This development was based on the fact that "providing student-driven, educationally focused and socially just conflict resolution services is not possible if you have a one-size-fits-all" process for every incident that happens on campus (OSCR University of Michigan, 2008). Consequently, when a potential complainant comes into the OSCR, they are presented with both Formal Conflict Resolution (FRC) and Alternative Conflict Resolution (ACR) options. An extensive intake process provides complainants time to talk about their objectives. The process is also designed to help the complainant deconstruct the socialization around formal conflict resolution and consider how alternative dispute resolution options might address the harm done more comprehensively. ACR is not used for sexual assault or other incidents involving serious physical or emotional injury or for significant, long-term hostility between parties (OSCR University of Michigan, 2008).

If the parties involved elect ACR, an intake is scheduled with a student employee who explains OSCR's policies and menu of options. Parties can choose among various modes of informal conflict resolution including ACR for alcohol and other drugs, restorative justice circles, conflict coaching, facilitated dialogue, social justice mediation, and/or shuttle negotiation (OSCR University of Michigan, 2008). Conflict coaching provides consultation when there is a student in conflict with another who is unwilling to engage in meaningful dialogue. Social justice mediation is used for incidents that involve cultural differences and issues of power, privilege, and oppression. For example, an international student engaged in personal cultural practices without realizing that the activity violated the campus residence life policies. On many campuses, this act usually would have triggered a disciplinary process for the student. Because the Spectrum Model permits consideration of how the student's social identity and culture offered context and value in considering the most educationally effective intervention, mediation was invoked to negotiate the intersection between cultural practices and university violations (Schrage & Thompson, 2009). Shuttle negotiation refers to a process in which a facilitator works with parties in separate private caucuses to generate a negotiated agreement that resolves a conflict (OSCR University of Michigan, 2008).

After the ACR selection is made, a second meeting is held to review the procedures and process associated with the chosen option, including the fact that the responsible person needs to take ownership for the behavior before they can participate in a restorative justice circle. Staff is careful to prepare all the participants involved in a circle and continuously evaluate whether the circle is an appropriate venue for the conflict. On occasion during this preparation phase, staff may determine that another venue is more appropriate if it appears that the respondent or another participant seem unprepared for the circle. Of the restorative practices available, circles are used most frequently and are facilitated by an OSCR professional staff and an OSCR student intern. All facilitators complete extensive training on conflict resolution and how social identity informs process. Moreover, reparation agreements are monitored by the circle members (J.M. Schrage, personal communication, April 20, 2009).

The OSCR Spectrum Model program is run by the director, two assistant directors, two full-time resolution coordinators, student staff, and three student interns (J. M. Schrage, personal communication, April 20, 2009). Facilitators are drawn from a pool of students, faculty, and staff who receive a 40-hour social justice mediation training and who themselves refer cases (OSCR University of Michigan, 2008).

The vast majority of the cases come from the residence halls, but the Department of Public Safety and police are a major referral source, as well, for alcohol and other drugs (OSCR University of Michigan, 2008). OSCR does not have jurisdiction over scholastic dishonesty as cases are handled by the separate colleges at the University of Michigan. The use of ACR has grown exponentially. In 2006–2007, only 4% of new cases referred to OSCR were resolved in ACR. In 2007–2008, over 70% of cases were resolved in ACR (OSCR University of Michigan, 2008).

Although institutions of higher education are generally viewed as forward thinking, campus judicial responses have lagged behind in using new, effective strategies. Some colleges and universities have begun to infuse restorative practices into campus life thereby reinforcing a different set of values from those embodied in punitive responses. When students are compelled to reflect on the consequences of their actions, take active responsibility for making amends, and become prosocial members of the community, they actively integrate values that are more in line with their own educational aspirations.

A potential issue for higher education is that preparation of the parties, in some cases, focuses more on making students aware of restorative justice options and ascertaining their level of responsibility for their misconduct and less on their story, their expectations and fears about going through the process, an exploration of the impact their behavior may have had on others, or helping them begin to consider what they might do to make reparations. Likewise, it appears that, in some situations, little time is spent with preparing community representatives for the meeting including a review of their reactions, what they might say to the wrongdoer, and what ideas they might have about repairing the harm. Although some institutions, such as the University of Colorado at Boulder, have the referral source and student complete a form that asks some of these questions, it is possible that the process would be richer, more internally satisfying, and the effect more sustaining if the preparation process were more comprehensive, engaging, and focused on the relationship between the wrongdoer and victim or the wrongdoer and the community.

SURROGATE DIALOGUE PROGRAMS IN PRISONS

With the exception of Victim-Offender Dialogue in crimes of severe violence, restorative justice initiatives have been identified as primarily, if not exclusively, useful as a "front-end" diversionary option reserved for nonviolent property crimes and minor assaults. Relatively few restorative justice programs exist, therefore, within adult correctional settings that bring crime victims and offenders together. Indeed, most restorative justice in-prison programs rely on prison-based ministries that aim to facilitate the offender's character transformation through the development of religious practice and/or moral orientation (Armour, Windsor, Aguilar, & Taub, 2008).

Several programs are experimenting, however, with bringing together unrelated or "surrogate" victims and offenders to address the harm and suffering from criminal acts on victims, offenders and their family members, and the community (Armour, Sage, Rubin, & Windsor, 2005). These initiatives are voluntary; occur during an offenders' incarceration; are held at prisons, jails, or halfway houses; rely on a cadre of victim volunteers and community facilitators; and involve time-limited group meetings. They do not affect the status of offenders including any changes for commutation of sentence or for any kind of clemency action. Some of the programs combine faith-based and restorative justice philosophies and practices, whereas others are strictly secular. Although the format of the programs varies, they provide a safe place in the prison where the offender can learn about the effects of their offending and crime victims can learn about the reasons for offending.

In-prison programs generally are not used as tools to reduce recidivism. Rather, they are a means toward empowering offenders to take responsibility for their actions and make amends to victims and their communities. Because over two-thirds of released prisoners reoffend within 3 years (Bureau of Justice Statistics, 2002), innovative and effective prerelease programs are needed that promote successful transition and reentry by offenders into the free world.

Bridges to Life

Bridges to Life (BTL) is a manualized, faith-based, 14-week, in-prison program that uses a restorative justice approach to help prerelease offenders come to terms with their offenses and learn to deal with them in rehabilitative and redemptive ways. BTL (also referred to as Restoring Peace) is based in Houston, Texas. It operates in over 20 prisons in Texas and has expanded to other states including Colorado, Mississippi, and Florida. It uses a book, *Restoring Peace: Using Lessons From Prison to Mend Broken Relationships* (Blackard & Sage, 2005), and a study guide (Blackard & Sage, 2006) as well as in-person stories from unrelated or "surrogate" crime victims to sensitize offenders to the consequences of their crimes.

BTL uses two different program models. The first model consists of 5–8 small groups each of which comprises five offenders, two victims, and a community facilitator. The small-group format is used for victims to tell the story of their victimization to offenders who have hurt others like themselves and for offenders to tell the story of their broken lives and criminal behavior, and eventually to acknowledge to the victims the pain their actions have caused innocent others like the victims in the group. The sharing of stories and interaction with victims over a period of weeks can have substantial impact, because inmates may not have recognized that their drug-related crime, for example, has affected anyone other than themselves. Without the victim's voice, inmates can minimize and deny the significance of their criminal behavior, often seeing themselves only as the victim of a punitive justice system (Indermaur, 1994).

The second model called "Restoring Peace" consists of 4–6 breakout groups of 10 offenders and two community facilitators, one of which might be a crime victim. The small groups are used for offenders to tell their own stories and to discuss study questions related to a weekly topic (e.g., responsibility and repentance) and to verbally share their written answers to journal assignments. In both models, offenders from all the breakout groups gather at the beginning of each weekly session to hear first from a victim impact panel or view a video of a crime victim's experience. In both models, offenders are assigned readings during the week related to specific topics (e.g., accountability, confession, forgiveness).

Besides completing "homework" and talking in small groups about the crime committed, offender participants are asked to write two amends letters (not to be sent) that they read aloud in their small groups at the end of the program (Armour, 2004). The first letter is to a victim of the offender's crime. If the identity of a specific victim is not known, the letter is written to society. The second letter is written to a family member who has suffered because of the offender's crime. The final session is for graduation (Armour et al., 2008). At graduation, offenders remain in a large group and volunteer to take turns coming to the front of the room to share their personal changes and feelings about going through the Restoring Peace program. Offenders receive certificates of completion and appreciation followed by refreshments prepared by inmates at the close of the graduation.

BTL is a promising program. A survey of BTL graduates (n = 1,021) found an appreciatively lower recidivism rate than the general population of released inmates (Armour et al., 2005). Out of 8,338 offenders who have completed the program, only 17% of those who have been released have returned to prison for new crimes (10.7%) and technical violations (6.6%) (Bridges to Life, 2007). Only 1% of offenders released have returned for violent crimes. A comparison study of BTL participants with nonparticipating offenders housed at the same unit found that BTL participants had a recidivism rate of 13.4% compared to 18.7% for the nonparticipating offenders (Bridges to Life, 2007).

A study of the BTL change process found that participants were affected by seeing things from the victim's side, that is, with victim eyes, felt cared about by victims who had been hurt by people like themselves, gained self-knowledge as a result of personal insights and the accountability process for how they treated others, felt motivated by experiences that stimulated their hunger and drive for personal growth, and felt transformed by the quality of their changes (Armour et al., 2005). A study of the Restoring Peace model examined changes in moral motivations (n = 102) and found significant differences in offender's empathy and related compassion for others, relationship and interaction with others, forgiveness from others and God, vengefulness, and spirituality or religiousness (Armour et al., 2008). Moral motivations are motivational forces that inspire a person to "do good" while inhibiting behaviors that have negative consequences.

The "Sycamore Tree" project is another faith-based restorative justice program that operates internationally under the auspices of a Christian voluntary organization called *Prison Fellowship*. Similar to BTL, small groups of crime victims and unrelated offenders meet together for a period of 5–8 weeks to address concepts of responsibility, confession, repentance, forgiveness, amends, and reconciliation in the context of crime and justice (Prison Fellowship International, n.d.). Results from studies of attitude changes and recidivism are similar to the findings from BTL.

Secular Programs

Some prisons have instituted secular in-prison restorative justice programs. Although the values that frame secular and faith-based programs are similar, for example, responsibility, accountability, restitution, secular models can be delivered directly by corrections staff and more easily institutionalized into the correctional system because they are not affiliated with any faith tradition. In the United States, secular programs have been conducted at Washington State Reformatory (Lovell, Helfgott, & Lawrence, 2002), Shakopee Women's Center (Burns, 2001), and prisons under the Minnesota Department of Corrections (MDOC) (Wilson, 2009).

The restorative dialogue program offered through MDOC is called the VOCARE Project, which is an acronym for Victims, Offenders, Community, A Restorative Experience (Wilson, 2009). The word "VOCARE" is Latin for "to call, to summons, invoke, invite or to gather" (Minnesota Department of Corrections, n.d.). Approximately 10–12 victims, offenders, and community representatives are carefully screened and selected to meet together in a VOCARE group either over multiple weeks or for an intensive weekend. Crime victims and offenders share their stories of victimization or offending in detail. Community members serve as support persons to victims and offenders. Groups are led by two experienced facilitators trained in the restorative dialogue process.

The VOCARE Project is slated to be held at all 10 of the state prisons. MDOC is experimenting as well with themed groups by bringing together participants who share histories specific to sex offending, domestic violence, or drunk driving (Wilson, 2009).

The program at Washington State Reformatory also focuses on the sharing of personal narratives about harm but uses more of a seminar format with group discussion on topics including "What does justice mean?" or "What does the public want from offenders?" (Lovell et al., 2002). A qualitative evaluation of this program found that (1) remorse was seen as essential to the healing process; (2) empathy was demonstrated through attentive listening, accurate reflection, and affect; (3) participants showed personal growth and change by moving beyond stereotypes, increased awareness of restorative justice, and having a sense of healing because the seminars were a safe place to process the impact of crime on people's lives; (4) shifts in attitudes and beliefs were created by the coeducational process between participants and by recognizing their commonalities; and (5) increases in accountability and taking of responsibility.

Still another example is seen in the work of the Marquette University Law School Restorative Justice Initiative. For a number of years, Professor Janine Geske, founder of the RJ Initiative, has provided victims the opportunity to speak with circles of serious offenders in the Green Bay and Columbia maximum security correctional facilities, often bringing along law students and community members. Victims feel empowered when speaking about how crime has affected their lives, and offenders are encouraged to share how they better understand the negative impact of their crimes.

A survey of participant responses at Shakopee Women's Prison in Minnesota found changes in victims' attitudes about offender motivation for participation and evidence of offender remorse (Burns, 2001). Offenders felt that they better understood the victim's experience and felt that engagement with victims was helpful to them.

The emergence of restorative dialogue programs in prisons suggests that a surrogate model offers crime victims and offenders an avenue for sharing their stories with people who symbolically carry substantial weight and may serve as catalysts for healing because they share similarities either to the offenders who harmed them or to the victims that they harmed. Moreover, because these projects use a small- or large-group format and multiple meetings, they create communities of support and accountability that reduce isolation, foster empathy and remorse, cultivate trust, reinforce similarities between seemingly disparate groups, and lessen the distance and stereotypical judgments about each other that otherwise block healing.

DOMESTIC VIOLENCE AND RESTORATIVE DIALOGUE

Building largely on the success of Victim-Offender Mediation, Family Group Conferencing, and circles for violent and nonviolent offenses, practitioners during the past decade have begun to explore the possibility of using restorative justice to address domestic violence. Interest in the potential of restorative justice for crimes of domestic violence arose, in part, from the inadequacies of the criminal justice system. According to Hudson (2002), most women do not want criminal justice intervention; they simply want the violence to stop, particularly if they have children and the offender is the children's father. Recent mandatory arrest and no-drop prosecution policies force women who do not want to break up their families to decide between protecting the abuser and relying on a system that does not consider their interests or wishes (Grauwiler & Mills, 2004). Many of the current practices have resulted in unintended emotional and economic consequences that have worsened the plight of victims and offenders and failed to significantly stem the use of violence.

Interviews with victims of domestic violence have found that victims are stunned to discover how little attention was paid by the criminal justice system to their concerns and needs and were upset that they were only allowed to give victim testimony at the request of the prosecution. Victims also thought that their offenders manipulated the system with ease, often with the complicity of authorities. Overall, they felt the process did very little to address their needs, instead favoring "those who lacked moral scruples and would fight to win at any cost" (Herman, 2005, p. 583). Perhaps, it is not surprising that domestic violence is severely underreported (Herman, 2005) and suffers from low prosecution rates and even lower conviction rates (Hudson, 2002).

The suggestion that a restorative justice approach might better respond to the needs of victims, however, has brought strong reservations and vocal resistance from domestic violence advocates, psychotherapists, and restorative justice pioneers who, despite their alliance with restorative justice principles, fear that the application of restorative justice along conventional lines is inherently risky to victims because they lack adequate safety measures. Indeed, they argue that the usual approaches are ill advised for domestic violence because it differs from the kinds of crimes restorative justice traditionally addresses. For example, in domestic violence, the offender is not a stranger; it is someone the victim loves, with whom an intimate relationship, and possibly children, are shared (Stubbs, 2004). Second, because the abuse happens within the context of an ongoing relationship, victim safety is a concern that extends beyond the time immediately following a violent incident (Bazemore & Earle, 2002). Third, significant power imbalances exist between the offender and the victim that do not exist in other crimes (Frederick & Lizdas, 2003). Fourth, perpetrators of domestic violence often intentionally isolate the victim from family and friends thereby depriving her of a supportive community (Herman, 2005). Finally, domestic violence, unlike most other crimes, is control based and ongoing (Stubbs, 2002).

Historically, the focus on restorative justice has been on incident-based crimes, whereas domestic violence involves a long-term or committed relationship that usually involves multiple injuries over time rather than a one-time criminal act. The relationship between the victim and offender may include other and dependent stakeholders including children and extended family members. Restorative justice facilitation is generally indirect, which, in the context of domestic violence, can exacerbate the power differential between the victim and offender because there is no strong, authoritative overseer of the dialogue process. Restorative justice assumes that victims can negotiate freely and fully for what they need, whereas victims of domestic violence are more likely to negotiate for what they can get since they do not have the autonomy of a crime victim who is otherwise the offender's equal in status. Restorative justice relies on shared values, for example, honesty, accountability, and the belief that the perpetrator's future behavior can be controlled. In crimes of domestic violence where control and manipulation are central, values may not be shared and the facilitator will have little to no control over the perpetrator's reactions to meeting with the victim once the dialogue is over. Finally, restorative justice assumes that a meaningful community exists for either the victim or offender or both. Indeed, the available community may include members who reinforce the offender's violent behavior, or there may be no community for either party due to the history of enforced isolation of the victim or hiding the domestic violence from others including family members.

The potential risks of using restorative justice to address domestic violence have prompted many domestic violence advocates and restorative justice practitioners to think twice about developing and implementing restorative programs to deal with domestic violence. Indeed, the warnings have been so extensive and the concerns so great, that only a handful of restorative approaches have been tried. Consequently, there is almost no literature describing these approaches, little or no empirical evidence regarding their success or failure, and virtually nothing known about whether or not restorative processes are appropriate for domestic violence.

Several restorative approaches, however, are being used that appear promising for domestic violence. None of them, however, uses restorative dialogue in conventional ways. Rather these approaches include creative and innovative ways of addressing domestic violence that do not endanger the victim further while still adhering to the basic principles of restorative justice. Most of them meet the criteria explicated by Busch (2002) who states that in order for restorative justice to be completely successful it must be culturally specific, engage in thorough preprocess planning, and have the safety of all participants as its primary focus.

Family Group Conferencing

The North Carolina Family Group Conferencing Project uses family group conferences (FGC) to build partnerships aimed at safeguarding child and adult family members (Pennell, 2008). This project uses the New Zealand model of FGC. The intent of the model is to widen the circle of support for victims by including formal and informal resources for battered women and abused children including legal measures, advocacy for support of abused women, batterer's counseling, drug and alcohol assistance, and the support of families and friends. Representatives from these systems come together with the victim and relevant family members to plan a coordinated approach to safety planning for women and children under the auspices of a domestic violence program, drawing on formal and informal services and supports. Pennell (2005), who is the originator of this model, has published an extensive examination of safety issues in FGC that have wide application to any restorative approach to violence against women.

The safety planning model derives from earlier projects developed by Pennell in Newfoundland and Labrador and later researched in Edmonton, Alberta, Canada (Salucka, 2006). In Canada, Pennell brought together victims and offenders in low to medium cases for a mediated dialogue. Referrals were made post charge but also accepted from domestic and family violence services agencies, child welfare agencies, substance abuse centers, and agencies targeting multicultural communities. Heterosexual couples were assigned to male or female teams who worked extensively in same gender dyads with victim and offender prior to bringing them together for the mediated dialogue. The goal of the preparation was to get each person's perceptions of the events that precipitated the dialogue and to determine what each participant would like to express during the session. When the team and couple came together, the facilitators took turns retelling the victim's and offender's stories. Neither participant was encouraged to speak until both sides of the story had been told. The goal of the Canadian project was neither to encourage separation nor to encourage reconciliation. Rather, the challenge was to meet the needs of both participants and ensure the victim's safety regardless of her choice to stay or leave.

Research on Pennell's early work in Newfoundland and Labrador found that FGC brought multiple forms of abuse out into the open, decreased safety risks, and resulted in satisfactory plans for the majority of families (Pennell & Buford, 1995). Victims reported feeling safe during the conference if they were adequately prepared, had a support person, and perceived it safe to talk. Indicators of domestic violence (including economic, verbal, emotional, and physical abuse) significantly decreased in the majority of families. Results also indicated that conferencing helped change men's attitudes toward women and rethink their rigid adherence to traditional gender roles (Pennell & Buford, 2000). In the Canadian project, abuse and neglect declined by half following the conferences (Pennell & Buford, 2000). No violence occurred during these meetings or as a result of these meetings (Pennell, 2005).

Domestic Violence Surrogate Dialogue

The Domestic Violence Surrogate Dialogue (DVSD) program in Hillsboro, Oregon, brings together surrogate or unrelated offenders and victims for a dialogue about their experiences with domestic violence (Salucka, 2006). The offender and victim have no previous history or relationship to each other. The goals of the programs are (1) to allow victims and offenders to share their stories with each other; (2) to encourage the offender to understand the physical, emotional, and mental harm he caused his own victim; and (3) to enable the victim to identify and avoid violent behavior in future relationships by listening to the offender reveal his own insights, motivations, and manipulation tactics.

Restorative dialogues are the result of collaboration between local community corrections, a domestic violence agency, and batterer's intervention program (BIP). Community corrections provide the space and security (dialogues take place in a courthouse with metal detectors). Although DVSD accepts self-referrals and referrals from local counselors, the majority come from the domestic violence agency and BIP.

In order to be considered for DVSD, offenders and victims must be embedded in a counseling program for at least 3 months prior to participating in a dialogue (DVSD, n.d.). They must also agree to continue counseling for at least 3 months after the dialogue (Salucka, 2006). Prior to the dialogue, counselors work individually with their clients to obtain a detailed account of the circumstances surrounding the violence experienced or perpetrated. Victims and offenders are screened to determine their motivation. Those who are not motivated by anger; seek answers to specific, realistic questions; and who view the dialogue as an opportunity to repair the harms they have suffered or committed are considered good candidates. Offenders are required to take full responsibility for the crimes they admitted to in court.

DVSD program counselors work together closely to determine which victim should be paired with which offender. Once an appropriate pairing is decided upon, a complete background check is done to ensure that no previous relationship existed between victim and offender. The dialogue is facilitated by a male or female team who meets separately with each party in same sex dyads to explain the process and the room setup, review ground rules, which require that each person respect the other and listen carefully when not speaking, and answer questions. Facilitators complete a specific training for DVSD. The dialogue itself can occur within a few days to months of the preparation meetings and lasts 2–2.5 hours. Each party has a counselor present as a support person from his or her respective program. Only the facilitators, however, guide the dialogue. A debriefing session directly follows the dialogue to assess the participants' immediate reactions and ensure that they have scheduled follow-up counseling sessions. All sessions are audiotaped to provide the counselors a means of reviewing the session with each party and a mechanism for challenging inaccurate statements made by either offender or victim during the dialogue. These inaccuracies are addressed in the follow-up counseling sessions.

Victim participants have commented that the DVSD experience empowered them to speak their mind more openly and to tackle challenges that were previously daunting (Salucka, 2006). They feel clearer and have a stronger sense of ownership of their own lives and decisions (DVSD, n.d.). Offenders indicate that DVSD provided them with a chance to give back and to listen, more empathy for victims of domestic violence, and a stronger sense of self-accountability for their own actions.

The use of surrogate partners who have no prior history is an innovative approach that helps bypass many of the concerns raised by those who oppose the use of restorative justice for domestic violence including issues of safety and power imbalances. In some ways, the absence of history leaves both parties free to more fully engage with and learn from each other. As noted on the DSVD website (n. d.), victims are encouraged to participate through the statement, "If you have had questions for your abuser that, for safety reasons, you have never asked, DVSD offers a safe and honest environment to obtain your answers." Likewise, offenders are reminded that "[t]his is a unique chance for you to hear the effects of abuse on a survivor. You are able to address questions that only an offender can answer. DVSD provides a supportive place for you to honestly talk about your past in order to help another person."

Cultural Context Model

The Cultural Context Model (CCM) is a social justice approach offered through the Institute for Family Services in Somerset, New Jersey, to working with families where there is domestic violence (Almeida, Dolan-Del Vecchio, & Parker, 2007; Almeida & Durkin, 1999). As a feminist intervention, it is built on dismantling the linkages of power, privilege, and oppression that account for oppressive social forces including sexism, racism, homoprejudice, and classism. Healing is guided by the principles of critical consciousness that create awareness of how social forces, for example, idealized masculine roles and instill oppressive practices as well as the principles of empowerment and accountability. Although CCM does not advertise itself as a restorative justice approach, its philosophy of healing and the methods used for change embody restorative justice principles.

As a social justice model, CCM seeks to raise consciousness around the intersections of gender, race, age, culture, socioeconomic status, religion, and sexual orientation with family functioning and, by doing so, aims to bring nonviolence to the lives of couples regardless of whether or not they choose to remain in the relationship (Almeida et al., 2007; Almeida & Durkin, 1999). The CCM emphasizes examining individuals within the context of their families and the larger community in order to holistically respond to the violence. By dismantling power imbalances and restructuring power both inside and outside of the relationship, the CCM strives to both impact individual lives and affect institutional inequalities.

The CCM uses same sex groups and sponsors who have completed the program successfully and return to help current participants go through the program (Salucka, 2006). The model consists of three phases. In the first phase, the couple meets briefly for an intake session that includes separate meetings with each person to obtain the couple's history of violence and their goals for going through the program and a reconvening of the couple for an explanation of the CCM model and description of agency policies. For the second phase of the process, each individual participates in a small, same-gender socioeducational circle where participants watch film segments intended to educate and stimulate discussion about how the problems in their relationships connect to larger systems of power, privilege, and oppression related to race, ethnicity, gender, culture, and class.

During this 8-week phase, individuals also meet their sponsors who assist them in deconstructing the socioeducational materials (Salucka, 2006). Sponsors are the same gender as the participant and are recruited from the community. Sponsors fulfill several other roles in addition to working with victims or offenders in socioeducational circles. Male sponsors hold offenders accountable for the violence they have inflicted; mentor them on living a life of nonviolence; teach offenders that using violence is a choice that impacts their partners and children; provide an expanded definition of masculinity that incorporates vulnerability, nurturing, and empathy; and model respect for women, children, and people of different races, ethnicities, cultures, and sexual orientations (Almeida & Durkin, 1999). Female sponsors similarly contribute to the healing process of victims by modeling equitable relationships, breaking isolation, and engaging victims in expanded conversations about family life (Hernandez, Almeida, & Dolan-Del Vecchio, 2005).

For the third phase, couples alternate between large, same gender, and mixed gender "culture circle" in which they each address relationship issues pertaining to themselves, their partner, family of origin, children, and friends (Almeida et al., 2007; Salucka, 2006). The circles are structured differently for men and women. Men are encouraged to understand the impact of their actions on others and are held accountable for their violent and destructive behaviors by their sponsors. The men are also required to write a letter to their victim and their children acknowledging the harms they have committed against them, for example, intimidations, threats, male privilege, emotional and economic abuse, denying and blaming behaviors, and so on. Sponsors critique and edit the letters and assist the men in determining what restitution or reparation they can make to their victims.

For women, the circles encourage them to experience anger, rather than guilt, as a healthy response to the harms they have suffered (Almeida & Durkin, 1999). They are also empowered to take less responsibility for the total well-being of their families. Women also work with their sponsors to write letters, but their letters are designed to create personal narratives of liberation. The mixed gender culture circle is used for men and women to share their letters with their partners and the larger community.

Throughout the circle processes, traditional rules of privacy do not apply (Salucka, 2006). Clients, sponsors, and therapists are not required to maintain confidentiality. Clients are also encouraged to socialize outside the weekly meeting as a way to build ongoing communities of support and accountability. The CCM is designed this way for three reasons: to disrupt the secrecy and isolation that often accompany violence, to ensure victim safety, and to "dismantle access to power and social opportunity via open dialogues that focus on the principles of empowerment and maintaining accountability over time" (Parker, 2003, p. 276).

Referrals to the program come primarily from the courts. In cases where the offender is mandate to the CCM, the victim is contacted and asked to share her story or participate in the process. The victim's participation is strictly voluntary. For women, success means they are able to maintain safe lives after the program, regardless of whether or not they chose to stay with their partner, and they are able to manage their children and keep them from repeating the violent behaviors they witnessed. For the men, success means they successfully completed the program and committed to working as sponsors for the next 2 years.

Minnesota Circle Sentencing

The Minnesota Circle Sentencing (MCS) is operated through the Tubman Family Alliance in Minneapolis (Salucka, 2006). It is modeled after the First Nations circle sentencing project in the Yukon, Canada. After a victim calls the police or files a police report on the offender, the Tubman Family Alliance, which contracts with law enforcement to work with domestic violence crimes, offers the MCS process as an option for resolving the case. Victims are always able to pursue traditional criminal justice remedies, if desired. Volunteers follow up with the victims and explain the MCS process. If selected by the victim, offenders first participate in an Offender application Circle that typically includes a probation officer, a victim advocate, community members, and trained Circle Keepers. The Application Circle serves as a tool to screen the offender and make a "Social Compact," which is essentially a promise to change. It often includes a wide variety of creative conditions such as completing substance abuse treatment, establishing a closer relationship with one's children, or adjudicating oneself for other offenses such as failing to pay child support.

If the offender agrees to complete a Social Compact, the Application Circle ends and the PreSentencing Circle begins (Salucka, 2006). The circle series meets biweekly and lasts approximately 3 months. Victims are invited but are not required to attend. Even if they choose not to attend, they are given the opportunity to provide their input on what should happen to the offender. Each PreSentence Circle begins with a "check-in" time during which the offender is asked what parts of the Social Compact have been completed. If the offender needs assistance in completing certain requirements, for example, getting a job, community participants assist by using their own innate abilities and conventional wisdom to ensure that the offender is successful.

Following the PreSentence Circle series is the actual Circle Sentencing that includes the judge, prosecutor assigned to the case, the defense attorney, a victim's advocate, the victim if he or she decides to attend, and community members (Salucka, 2006). The victim and offender are also encouraged to invite family and friends to participate and support them through the Circle Sentencing process. To control for power imbalances and ensure that every voice is heard, a talking piece is employed. The person who holds the talking piece is the only person allowed to speak. After all information is presented, including the offender's performance during the Application and PreSentence Circles, members work to consensus to determine an appropriate sentence for the offender, which must include a probation period during which the offender is required to attend regular Follow-Up Circles.

Before the offender goes through the entire MCS process, the case must be granted a "stay of adjudication," which requires that the offender admit guilt and take full responsibility for the crime committed (Salucka, 2006). If the offender successfully completes the process and is not convicted of a same or similar offense during the course of the MCS process, the case is dismissed. Otherwise, it reverts to the traditional criminal justice process.

At the same time that the offender's MCS process is occurring, victims are given the opportunity to participate in Healing Circles, in addition to participating in or providing input for the offender's circle series (Salucka, 2006). Healing Circles are also offered to other community members who have experienced domestic violence in some way.

Of the approximately 25 offenders who have gone through the MCS process, 95% of them have not committed any subsequent violent crimes (Salucka, 2006). Evidence of widespread support is illustrated by a 1999 Minnesota Supreme Court decision to uphold sentences determined through community-based Circle Sentencing.

In addition to the four programs reviewed, two additional programs deserve mention. Construyendo Circulos de Paz (CCP) is a program in Nogales, Arizona, a predominantly Catholic, Latino or Latina community (Salucka, 2006). This postarrest intervention brings together willing victims, the offender, and their care communities for 26 weeks to work on the issues identified in a Social Compact. The facilitator and Circle Keepers work with the family and care community to identify their strengths, understand the underlying causes of violence, and develop consequences for the offender should he or she not comply with the Social Compact.

The Resolve to Stop the Violence Project (RSVP) is a jail-based violence prevention program implemented by the San Francisco Sheriff's Department that targets male offenders with current or prior felony convictions for violent crimes, both domestic and random violence (Salucka, 2006). The program incorporates three major components: offender accountability, victim restoration, and community involvement. Offender accountability is built on the Man Alive Violence Intervention and Prevention Curriculum. A Survivor Restorative Advisory Committee comprising domestic violence advocates and representatives from social service agencies provides direct practical and emotional support for the victims of the RSVP perpetrators. Community involvement encourages community participation in developing and providing opportunities for offenders to make reparations to victims and the community.

Summary

We have examined numerous examples of small programs that show promise for using restorative justice principles in responding to domestic violence. Notable is the fact that all programs require substantial modification of conventional restorative justice approaches in order to respond effectively to the challenges of domestic violence. For example, a number of the programs reviewed treat men and women separately or bring them together limitedly with others such as other men and women (CCM) and community members

(MSC and FGC). The DVSD program uses a surrogate model rather than the actual victim and offender. All programs, however, have commonality and are centrally focused on addressing victim harm, offender accountability, and community participation. In addition, all of them include multiple sessions or ongoing engagement in the change process thereby acknowledging that domestic violence is not incident based and requires social reconditioning and close monitoring. Moreover, the modifications made provide for victim safety usually through separation of victim and offender, ongoing monitoring, or by widening support and accountability by the community. Although facilitators, in some instances, remain less active, for example, MSC and DVSD, others such as sponsors (CCM, CCP) or community members (FGC, MSC) serve to dilute the conditions that might contribute to a power imbalance.

DEFENSE-INITIATED VICTIM OUTREACH

Nowhere is the adversarial nature of the criminal justice system more evident than in capital murder cases. The stakes are exceedingly high for both the prosecution and the defense because cases involve the possibility of death for the offender. Consequently, the goal of "winning" trumps all other considerations. In such cases, the divide between the prosecution and defense is exceedingly wide. Victim survivors, whose loved ones were killed, easily turn the defense into monsters because of their association with the alleged offender (defendant) and instinctually keep their distance. Likewise, the defense team perceives the victim survivor as hating them. Not knowing how to respond and fearful of the intensity of the victim survivor's feelings, they too keep their distance. These stereotypic and dehumanizing attitudes buttress the emotional climate long associated with the adversarial process in and out of the courtroom. Moreover, they add significantly to the ongoing trauma experienced by victim survivors in the aftermath of their tragedy. Indeed, a number of studies confirm that going through the criminal justice process negatively affects crime victims (e.g., Goodrum & Stafford, 2001; Tontodonato & Erez, 1994).

Defense-Initiated Victim Outreach (DIVO) is a modified restorative justice program that seeks to address the judicial needs of victim survivors throughout the justice process by providing a link between the survivors and the defense, especially in capital cases (Armour & Frogge, 2009; Branham & Burr, 2008; Leonard, 2006). A significant departure from traditional criminal justice-based victim services, DIVO serves as a mechanism by which survivor families, if they choose, may have access to the defense team and the defense team, in their discretion, in return can consider requests from them.

DIVO grew out of the bombing of the Oklahoma City federal building and the desire by the defense to reach out in some way to survivors and to acknowledge the depth of their pain and suffering (Armour & Frogge, 2009). To that end, DIVO was created with the objective of reducing unnecessary tension with the defense for victim survivors who already bear the brunt of the crime. Subsequent to the trial of Timothy McVeigh, his defense attorney Richard Burr, Dr. Howard Zehr of the Center for Justice and Peacebuilding at Eastern Mennonite University, and Tammy Krause, a graduate of the program, developed the DIVO process.

DIVO recognizes that that crime, especially murder, creates an involuntary relationship between the victim and offender in the sense that it is forced upon victim survivors as a result of the crime (Armour & Frogge, 2009). This destructive tie has profound consequences for victim survivors' ability to cope and move on from the crime. DIVO seeks to acknowledge that relationship and the corresponding obligation for the defense, as *proxy* for the defendant, to respond to victim survivors' needs for information, accountability, and redressing of the harm done to the extent possible. The requests from victim survivors may also offer an opportunity for the defense to work with the defendant toward recognizing the significance of what he did and what he might begin to do to make amends.

DIVO is used at the federal level and is gaining momentum at the state level through the efforts of the Georgia Council for Restorative Justice at Georgia State University, School of Social Work (Armour & Frogge, 2009). Because the Georgia model is readily transferable, it was brought to Texas and Louisiana through a grant from the Department of Justice, Office of Justice Programs. The American Bar Association has issued guidelines in support of the connection between the defense and victim survivors through the services of a liaison called a Victim Outreach Specialist (VOS).

DIVO is considered a modified restorative justice practice because it occurs between the victim and the defense team rather than the defendant. Moreover, there is no direct interaction between the victim survivor and the defense unless it is requested by the victim survivor. Contact between victim survivors and the defense is otherwise done through a VOS who serves as an intermediary between the parties. Communication between the VOS and victim survivor is confidential unless the victim survivor requests that the VOS share information with the defense (Armour & Frogge, 2009). Although the VOS is hired by the defense, the VOS is there only for the victim survivor's needs and is not part of the defense team and, therefore, operates independent of the defense.

The needs of survivor families specific to the defense may include having representatives of the offender hear their story and acknowledge the loss they have suffered or listen patiently and compassionately to the anger victim survivors feel toward the defendant (Armour & Frogge, 2009). They may want information about how and why a crime happened and specifics about their loved ones in the last moments of their life. They may want to know why the defendant pled not guilty after giving a 20-page confession. They may want information about timing and location of legal processes. Even without specific requests from survivor families, greater sensitivity to their needs may be available from the defense in the form of stipulating to a photograph of a keepsake so the family can have the keepsake back or referring to the victim by name in court proceedings. It may also be helpful to survivor families to be asked whether the scheduling of pretrial hearings or the trial itself will be a hardship because survivors may have to arrange in advance to travel long distances and miss work or other commitments. If it doesn't otherwise hurt their case, the defense team's acting with civility toward the survivor family can provide them with some dignity, create a less hostile environment, and lessen, to some extent, aspects of the adversarial judicial process that tend to retraumatize them.

Although there is no immediate or guaranteed advantage for the offender, DIVO increases options and opens up the possibility that the defense team's expressions of civility and sympathy to the survivors throughout the process, may, paradoxically be reciprocated. To that end, DIVO offers an ethical, principled bridge between the survivor family and the defense counsel in capital cases that can be used at different stages in the criminal justice process: during the trial, appellate and postconviction proceedings, or whenever it may be initiated by the defense team. It also offers a more active and empowering role for victim survivors in death penalty cases without compromising the due process rights of capital defendants.

Although DIVO is principally used for capital cases, there is interest in applying it to other crimes at the adult and juvenile level. Indeed, in cases where VOM or FGC is not available, DIVO could provide the opportunity for a healing connection either through direct or indirect contact. Moreover, its presence opens the door for a better informed and sensitive response from the defense toward victim survivors and their needs.

IMPACT OF GROWTH IN PRACTICE ON RESTORATIVE JUSTICE THEORY

Restorative justice has moved over the decades from Victim-Offender Mediation (VOM) as the sole dialogue approach to VOM, family group conferencing, and peacemaking circles as three core practice models and from this trio to a multimodel, mixed practice that blurs the purity of separate approaches in the interests of which ones would be most effective to use in concert with the others given the nature of a specific case. Currently, however, restorative practice is also inventing new and creative responses to the harms associated with particular social issues, for example, domestic violence or social contexts, such as student misconduct in higher education. These new forms of practice have emerged from the ground up and have required modifications of the traditional approaches but with strict adherence to restorative justice values and principles.

These recent applications have contributed to the conflicts and debates about restorative justice and its future. One of the core questions has been about which practices to include under the framework of restorative justice (Sharpe, 2004). In response to what he considers a vaguely defined paradigm and the emergence of programs claiming to be restorative, Paul McCold, for example, is concerned that restorative justice is too vaguely defined and therefore vulnerable to including practices that are at best minimally restorative. He calls for a purist model of restorative justice and a classification of programs as fully or partly restorative based on the extent to which they address the interests of all three parties, namely victim, offender, and community. He defines the purist model as holistic because it "focuses equally on the needs of victims, offenders and communities, and it seeks to meet those needs simultaneously" (McCold, 2000, p. 401). Under this delineation, victim-offender mediation is considered only "partly" restorative (as are victim impact panels, community service sanctions, Truth and Reconciliation Commissions, DVSD, DIVO, Bridges to Life, etc.) because it does not, by definition, include the community of care. The purist model focuses on process rather than outcome and on the membership used to accomplish healing and accountability.

In contrast, Bazemore and Walgrave contend that restorative justice is not a limited set of programs but aspires to different degrees a variety of initiatives, programs, and systems and that "all options and actions that aim at putting right as far as possible [the harm caused by crime] . . . can be included in the restorative justice concept" (Walgrave, 2008, p. 21). The aim of the maximalist model is to provide restorative outcomes to a maximum number of crimes and in a maximum number of possible situations and contexts. Hence, the focus under this definition is on the aims of restorative justice.

The argument between the purist and maximalist models reflects a deeper concern in restorative justice, which is heightened by the introduction of new practices, namely the need to define the determinants of what makes a practice restorative. For McCold, the determinants rest on who is present in the dialogue. For Bazemore and Walgrave, the determinants are identified by examining the objectives of an approach. The need to define the determinants of what makes a practice restorative is justified because rapid growth without parameters could lead to the dilution or "McDonaldization" of the field. The argument is also made that without clear definitions, it is difficult to evaluate practice and substantiate claims of effectiveness. Indeed the identification of a program as "restorative" can be confusing because others cannot determine if the word refers to the movement's values and principles, its aims and outcomes, its specific processes, its programs, or combinations thereof. Some of this vagueness, however, is intentional. There is worry within the restorative justice movement that the privileging of selected characteristics followed by a premature standardization of practices and procedures based on that selection might otherwise restrict growth in a relatively young and developing field. To that end, the use of membership as the prime determinant of a practice's restorativeness demonstrates some of the problems in even attempting to delineate the determinants of restorativeness because membership alone does not necessarily reflect the level of participation in a dialogue. Victims, for example, may be present in an FGC or a peacemaking circle, but the focus may center principally on the offender or the community's needs rather than on the harm done to the aggrieved party. VOM, on the other hand, may lack substantial community participation, but the focus more likely will remain on the victim's need, which supports the movement's professed aim.

Besides raising questions about the criteria for what constitutes restorative practices or the kinds of practices or range of activities included under the restorative justice umbrella, new applications also demonstrate unrecognized needs and how to meet them. As such, these applications suggest that the field may be moving toward a needs-led, multimethod approach and a careful, albeit cautious expansion to a wide variety of social issues. This elasticity underscores the vast untapped potential of restorative justice to redress human conflict in multiple settings. More importantly, some of these developments broaden its scope to include moral wrongdoing, which according to Llewellyn (2007) elevates and further illuminates restorative justice to be a theory about the very meaning of justice and not just a response to criminal justice. In this regard, these emerging practices clarify and highlight that restorative justice is about the relational nature of justice and that the response to wrongdoing requires appreciation and restoration of "right" relationship in the aftermath of harm. Llewellyn comments on this evolution and the critical interplay between practice and context (2007). "Restorative justice maintains that what justice requires depends upon the particular relationships at issue and what is necessary to restore them. It is this contextual and complex nature of restorative responses that enables them to be tailored to the particular context" (2007, p. 360). She warns as well that knowledge or experience of the specific context is essential to providing a model of practice. She as well as others maintain that the worthiness of new approaches should be assessed in terms of the extent to which they reflect restorative justice values and principles.

Those principles are universally understood to include (1) the acknowledgment and repair of harm caused by wrongdoing; (2) the taking of appropriate responsibility for addressing the needs and repairing the harm; and (3) the involvement of those affected, including the community, in the resolution. The values of restorative justice are those values that are essential to healthy, equitable, and just relationships, namely respect, honesty, humility, mutual care, accountability, and trust (Boyack, Bowen, & Marshall, 2004). These values and principles together increasingly define restorative practice and contribute to the description of restorative justice as a values- or principles-based movement. The use of restorative justice for student misconduct at institutions of higher education and domestic violence as well as the use of restorative justice in prison settings and for outreach by the defense to crime victims demonstrate applications that embody restorative justice principles and values and the pursuit of justice as a relational endeavor.

WHAT MAKES IT WORK: RESTORATIVE JUSTICE AND CHAOS THEORY

Restorative dialogue often has a magical quality. Victim, offender, and community come together and can transform conflict into a healing endeavor for all. What accounts for its success both as a movement and on a case-by-case basis? Attention must certainly be paid to understanding the meaning of restorative justice, planting a firm values base, adequate preparation of all parties, trained facilitators, and time for the process to unfold. These elements, however, do not account for the sense of transformation that is often associated with restorative dialogue.

"The very notion of complexity is that there is a natural tendency toward higher levels of order" (Dell, 2009). How that order emerges from seeming chaos is the work of chaos theorists. T. H. Earle (personal communication, February 14, 2009) suggests that the emergence of restorative justice is in part an evolutionary process throughout the world toward diversification and complexity. She also relays that her work regarding chaos theory and restorative justice principles was inspired and guided by Nobel Physicist Ilya Prigogine (awarded the Prize for his revolutionary work in chaos theory), his sense of the relevance of his work in human systems on many levels including formal policy making, and the great hope he held for what he termed "the reunification of human culture" (Prigogine, 1996).

Determining how that order emerges from seeming chaos is the work of chaos theorists. Chaos theory maintains that structures tend toward self-organization (Rickard, 2005). However, there has to be a sufficient degree of conflict and turbulent energy in the system before it can self-organize. There also has to be a process that is conducive to operating with mutual respect and a tone set to encourage mutual respect to emerge (Earle, 2000, 2009). Respect, in this regard, becomes the safety container for the turbulence necessary to generate movement into a new or different pattern. These elements are present in the dynamics of restorative dialogues (T. H. Earle, personal communication, February 14, 2009). First, because the world comprises interdependent relationships and interactive dynamics, when people are brought together for dialogue they self-organize. Second, the diversity of viewpoints coupled with the energy of the conflict generates interactions and movement between participants. Third, with mutual respect, differing points of view are included, which increases the complexity. Out of the turbulence and energy of conflicting harms and needs, or seeming chaos, comes a new or higher order that has greater strength and resilience than what existed previously (Bazemore & Earle, 2002). Chaos theory, therefore, is about paradox in that seeming disturbance and confusion actually provide the conditions for change (Earle, 2009). Likewise in restorative justice, bringing people together with different experiences coupled with the pain, anger, and confusion that results from criminal acts or wrongdoing often generates unexpected insights and reactions. Suddenly, the victim sees similarities between himself or herself and the offender, which disturbs his or her stereotypical, dichotomous thinking. Unexpectedly, the offender begins to see things with the eyes of the victim, which shakes him to his core because he experiences a powerful psychological dissonance between his previous behaviors and what he knows now. These experiences also disturb the linear or expected arrangements between people, which both creates chaos and also opens the door for unanticipated and startling connections and movement. This sense of discovery is often experienced as transforming (T. H. Earle, personal communication, February 14, 2009).

The growth and implementation of restorative dialogue in criminal and noncriminal contexts attests to the enormity of the need for relational healing and the failure of current institutions to adequately respond to that need. Concerns about burgeoning programs and how they fit and do not fit under the restorative justice umbrella, however, reflect larger concerns about the future of the field. Because restorative justice is an emerging social movement in many parts of the world, and because it is relatively young and fundamentally idealistic, it is therefore, vulnerable to society's hunger for quick answers and cultural prescriptions for rapid responses to intractable social issues. Indeed, with these pressures, the movement is open to cooption by mainstream groups who may try to short-circuit the carefully developed processes, proven successful for a true restorative outcome. For participants, any rush to implementation risks susceptibility to unsatisfactory outcomes or unintentional harmful consequences. All such circumstances will likely result in impeding the credibility and inhibiting the acceptance of effective restorative practices. For restorative justice to live up to its promise, it must remain vigilant that its core values are uncompromisingly present in the preparation and implementation process, that the full time necessary be allowed for the preparation of participants and the natural unfolding of the dialogue, and finally, the condition of safety for all participants must be present throughout the process to enable the generative and unpredictable outcome to occur.

The theory of restorative justice is grand in its concept and general in its definition of core values—such as (1) the centrality of victim harm and healing; (2) offender responsibility, accountability, and return to community; and (3) disruption of community peace and a return to safety. The possibilities for the application of restorative justice practices, like the universe, are infinite and expanding. The preparations for restorative justice practices most used have been inherently complex including the training and high skill level required of the facilitator, determining the appropriate participants in the process, and taking the time necessary to fully prepare the participants for the dialogue and guiding them through it. Because restorative justice practices are varied, multilayered, and developed for different purposes from bad behavior of youth in schools to those guilty of violent crimes, the practices cannot be reduced to a one-size-fits-all formula. Each individual, each community, each culture, each government, each school and university, each employment setting, each religion, and so on has to develop a restorative dialogue system that works. In the final analysis, the search for restorative justice is best served by not standardizing the means of getting there through restorative justice practices. It is vital that the possibilities of Restorative justice practices remain open to ever-expanding social situations. These situations arise whenever a legalistic approach to laws, rules, and customs of society and institutions unnecessarily overreaches in terms of the broad scope of individuals (i.e., age, race, ethnicity, type of offense) included in the net of strict enforcement and the resort to punishment and permanent stigmatization of the offender. Restorative justice practices will more and more occur in those situations where attending the personal physical and psychological harm experienced by the victim becomes the top priority while providing the offender a way back to respect as part of the community that was disrupted by the behavior. Restorative justice has an important part to play in the future of contributing to the healing and peace of all types of communities and the world. It is therefore critical that the implementation of restorative justice

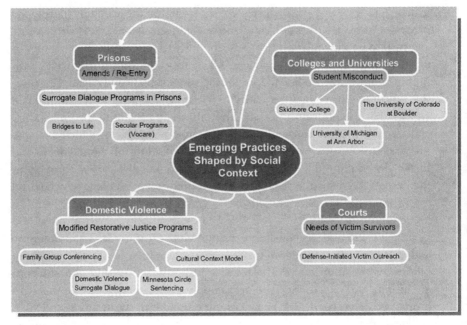

FIGURE 11.1

practices be not too tightly structured but guided by broad core values that fit the particular situation and careful preparation by a skilled facilitator whose guidance allows the outcome to be the result of the dialogue among and between the participants.

REFERENCES

Allena, T. (2004). Restorative conferences: Developing student responsibility by repairing the harm to vicitms and restoring the university community. In D. R. Karp & T. Allena (Eds.), *Restorative justice on the college campus: Promoting student growth and responsibility, and reawakening the spirit of campus community* (pp. 48–60). Springfield, IL: Charles C Thomas.

Almeida, R., Dolan-Del Vecchio, K., & Parker, L. (2007). *Transformative family therapy: Just families in a just society.* Boston: Allyn & Bacon.

Almeida, R., & Durkin, T. (1999). The cultural context model: Therapy for couples with domestic violence. *Journal for Marital and Family Therapy, 25,* 169–176.

Armour, M. (2004). Bridges to Life: A promising faith-based prison intervention for substance use. *Offender Substance Abuse Report, 4*(6), 81–94.

Armour, M., & Frogge, S. (2009).*Implementing defense-initiated victim outreach in Texas.* Austin, TX.: Institute for Restorative Justice and Restorative Dialogue.

Armour, M., Sage, J., Rubin, A., & Windsor, L. C. (2005). Bridges to Life: Evaluation of an in-prison restorative justice intervention. *Medicine and Law, 24,* 831–851.

Armour, M., Windsor, L. C., Aguilar, J., & Taub, C. (2008). A pilot study of a faith-based restorative justice intervention for Christian and non-Christian offenders. *Journal of Psychology and Christianity, 27*(2), 159–167.

Bazemore, G., & Earle, T. H. (2002). Balance in the response to family violence: Challenging restorative principles. In H. Strang & J. Braithwaite (Eds.), *Restorative justice and family violence* (pp. 178–190). United Kingdom: Cambridge University Press.

Blackard, K., & Sage, J. (2005). *Restoring peace: Project coordinator/facilitator guide.* Houston, TX: Bridges to Life.

Blackard, K., & Sage, J. (2006). *Restoring peace: Using lessons from prison to mend broken relationships.* Victoria, BC: Traford Publishing.

Boyack, J., Bowen, H., & Marshall, C. (2004). How does restorative justice ensure good practice? In H. Zehr & B. Toews (Eds.), *Critical issues in restorative justice.* Monsey, NY: Criminal Justice Press.

Branham, M., & Burr, R. (2008). Understanding defense-initiated victim outreach and why it is essential in defending a capital client. *Hofstra Law Review, 36*(3), 1019–1033.

Bridges to Life. (2007). *Evaluation of Bridges to Life: Program outcomes and evaluation.* Retrieved December 5, 2009, from http://www.bridgestolife.org/the-program/bridges-to-life-information

Bureau of Justice Statistics. (2002). *Reentry trends in the U.S.: Recidivism.* Retrieved December 5, 2009, from http://www.ojp.usdoj.gov/bjs/reentry/recidivism.htm

Burns, H. (2001). *Citizens, victims and offenders restoring justice project: Minnesota Correctional Facility Lino Lakes.* St. Paul, MN: University of Minnesota, School of Social Work, Center for Restorative Justice & Peacemaking.

Busch, R. (2002). Domestic violence and restorative justice initiatives: Who pays if we get it wrong? In H. Strang & J. Braithwaite (Eds.), *Restorative justice and family violence* (pp. 223–248). United Kingdom: Cambridge University Press.

Dell, A. (2009). System theory. Retrieved December 8, 2009, from http://adamdell.com

DeLong, W., & Langenbahn. (1996). *Setting and improving policies for reducing alcohol and other drug problems on campus: A guide for administrators.* Washington, DC: U.S. Department of Education, Higher Education Center for Alcohol and Other Drug Prevention.

DVSD. (n.d.). Domestic Violence Surrogate Dialogue. Retrieved Janaury 5, 2010 from http://www.dvsdprogram.com/participate.php

Earle, T. H. (1996, April).*Achieving safety in the community.* Paper presented at the National Summit on Promoting Public Safety Through the Effective Management of Sex Offenders in the Community, U.S. Dept. of Justice, Office of Justice Programs, Washington, DC.

Earle, T. H. (1998, September). *Through a whole new looking lass: Questions of liberty and justice and all.* Paper presented at the Executive Session on Sentencing and Corrections, University of Minnesota Law School, U.S. Dept. of Justice, National Institute of Justice, Minneapolis, MN.

Earle, T. H. (1999, May). *Chaos and order: The paradox of new justice in the real world*. Paper presented at the State of Michigan's First Juvenile Justice Conference on Balanced and Restorative Justice, Boyne Mountain, MI.

Earle, T. H. (2000, September). *Chaos theory and exceutive excellence*. Paper presented at the Executive Excellence Program, National Institute of Corrections, U.S. Dept. of Justice, Dallas, TX.

Earle, T. H. (2009, June). *Chaos theory and the challenge of leadership*. Paper presented at the Executive Excellence Program, National Institute of Corrections, U.S. Dept. of Justice, Denver, CO.

Footer, N. S. (1996). Achieving fundamental fairness: The code of conduct. In W. L. Mercer (Ed.), *Critical issues in judicial affairs: Current trends in practice* (pp. 19–33). San Francisco: Jossey-Bass.

Frederick, L., & Lizdas, K. C. (2003). The role of restorative justice in the battered women's movement. *Battered Women's Justice Project*. Retrieved September 29, 2005, from http://data.ipharos.com/bwjp/documents/restroative_justice.pdf

Goodrum, S. D., & Stafford, M. C. (2001). *Homicide, bereavement, and the criminal justice system*. Doctoral dissertation, The University of Texas at Austin, Austin.

Grauwiler, P., & Mills, L. G. (2004). Moving beyond the criminal justice paradigm: A radical restorative justice approach to intimate violence. *Journal of Sociology and Social Welfare, 31*(1), 49–69.

Gustafson, D. (2004). Is restorative justice taking too few, or too many, risks? In H. Zehr & B. Toews (Eds.), *Critical issues in restorative justice* (pp. 303–314). Monsey, NY: Criminal Justice Press.

Herman, J. L. (2005). Justice from the victim's perspective. *Violence Against Women, 11*(5), 571–602.

Hernandez, P., Almeida, R., & Dolan-Del Vecchio, K. (2005). Critical consciousness, accountability, and empowerment: Key processes for helping families heal. *Family Process, 44*(1), 105–119.

Hudson, B. (2002). Restorative justice and gender violence: Diversion of effective justice? *British Journal of Criminology, 4*, 616–634.

Indermaur, D. (1994). Offenders' perceptions of sentencing. *Australian Psychologist, 29*, 140–144.

Karp, D. R. (2004). Integrity boards. In D. R. Karp & T. Allena (Eds.), *Restorative justice on the college campus*. Springfield, IL: Charles C Thomas.

Lake, P. F. (2009). Student discipline: The case against legalistic approaches. *The Chronicle of Higher Education, 53*(322), A31.

Leonard, P. (2006). All but death can be adjusted: Recognizing the needs of victims in death penalty litigation. *The Champion*, 40–43.

Llewellyn, J. (2007). Truth commissions and restorative justice. In G. Johnstone & D. W. Van Ness (Eds.), *Handbook of restorative justice* (pp. 351–371). Portland, OR: Willan Publishing.

Lovell, M. L., Helfgott, J. B., & Lawrence, C. (2002). Narrative accounts from the citizens, victims, and offenders restoring justice program. *Contemporary Justice Review, 5*, 261–271.

Lowery, J. W., & Dannells, M. (2004). Contemporary practice in student judicial affairs: Strengths and weaknesses. In D. R. Karp & T. Allena (Eds.), *Restorative justice on the college campus: Promoting student growth and responsibility, and reawakening the spirit of campus community* (pp. 16–26). Springfield, IL: Charles C Thomas.

McCabe, D., & Trevino, L. (1996). What do we know about cheating in college: Longitudinal trends and recent developments. *Change, 28*, 28–33.

McCold, P. (2000). Toward a mid-range theory of restorative criminal justice: A reply to the maximalist model. *Contemporary Justice Review, 3*(4), 357–414.

Minnesota Department of Corrections. (n.d.). *Victim assistance program: Apology letters*. Retrieved Janaury 5, 2010, from http://www.doc.state.mn.us/crimevictim/apology.htm

Morrison, B. (2007). Schools and restorative justice. In G. Johnstone & D. W. Van Ness (Eds.), *Handbook of restorative justice* (pp. 335–350). Portland, OR: Willan Publishing.

OSCR University of Michigan. (2008). *2007–08 Annual Report*. Ann Arbor, MI: University of Michigan, Division of Student Affairs.

Parker, L. (2003). A social justice model for clinical social work practice. *Affilia, 18*(3), 272–288.

Pennell, J. (2005). Safety for mothers and their children. In J. Pennell & G. Anderson (Eds.), *Widening the circle: The practice and evaluation of family group conferencing with children, youths, and their families* (pp. 163–181). Washington, DC: NASW Press.

Pennell, J. (2008). Stopping domestic violence or protecting children? Contributions from restorative justice. In D. Sullivan & L. Tifft (Eds.), *Handbook of restorative justice: A global perspective* (pp. 286–298). New York: Routledge.

Pennell, J., & Buford, G. (1995). *Family group decision making: New roles for "old" partners in resolving family violence, Implementation report* (Vol. 1). St. John's, Newfoundland: Memorial University of Newfoundland.

Pennell, J., & Buford, G. (2000). Family group decision-making and family violence. In G. Burford & J. Hudson (Eds.), *Family group conferences: New directions in community-centered child and family practice* (pp. 171–192). Hawthorne, NY: Aldine de Gruyter.

Prigogine, I. (1996, June 20). Chasing the arrow of time. *On Campus Magazine*. University of Texas at Austin, Austin.

Prison Fellowship International. (n.d.). *Sycamore Tree Project*. Retrieved December 5, 2009, from http://www.pfi.org/cjr/stp

Rickard, R. L. (2005). Transforming chaos into order: Applying physics to human systems. *International Alliance of Holistic Lawyers, 14*(1).

Salucka, A. C. (2006). *Restorative justice: Is Austin, Texas ready for an alternative approach to domestic violence?* Master of Arts thesis, The University of Texas at Austin, Austin.

Schrage, J. M. (2009). The Spectrum Model: Answering the call for a new approach to campus conduct and conflict work. *Journal of Student Conduct Administration, 2*(1), 20–25.

Schrage, J. M., & Thompson, M. C. (2009). Providing a spectrum of resoluton options. In J. M. Schrage & N. G. Giacomini (Eds.), *Reframing campus conflict: Student conduct proactice through a social justice lens* (pp. 65–86). Sterling, VA: Stylus Publishing.

Sharpe, S. (Ed.). (2004). *How large should the restorative justice "tent" be?* Monsey, NY: Criminal Justice Press.

Stubbs, J. (2002). Domestic violence and women's safety: Feminist challenges to restorative justice. In H. Strang & J. Braithwaite (Eds.), *Restorative justice and family violence* (pp. 42–61). Cambridge: Cambridge University Press.

Stubbs, J. (2004). Restorative justice, domestic violence, and family violence. *Australian Domestic and Family Violence Clearinghouse* (Issues Paper 9). Sydney: University of New South Wales.

Swenson, G. (2009, January 13). Students make amends through restorative justice. *Inside CU: The CU-Boulder Faculty/Staff E-Newsletter.* Retrieved Janaury 5, 2010, from http://www.colorado.edu/insidecu/editions/2009/1-13/story1.html

Tontodonato, P., & Erez, E. (1994). Crime, punishment, and victim distress. *International Review of Victimology, 33,* 49–51.

University of Colorado at Boulder (UCB). (2007). Restorative justice program academic year report: August 1, 2006–May 11, 2007. Retreived February 23, 2010, from http://www.colorado.edu/studentaffairs/judicialaffairs/downloads/fullreport.pdf

Walgrave, L. (2008). Focusing on restorative justice. *Restorative justice, self-interest and responsible citizenship* (pp. 11–43). Portland OR: Willan Publishing.

Wilson, S. R. (2009, May 13–15). *The VOCARE project: Creating the power of the individual narrative.* Paper presented at the 2nd National Restorative Justice Conference, San Antonio, TX.

Index

A

Aboriginal Project Officer, 199
Aboriginals, 5–6, 14, 162, 205
"Aha moments", 77
Amends, making, 24, 46, 100
American Bar Association (ABA), 11, 13, 315
American Humane Society, in 1999, 168
American Nazi party, 279
Apartheid (racial), 15, 275
Apologies, 23, 56, 75, 100, 131, 135, 165. See also Remorse, expressing
Application Circle, 312
A-Ram, 280
Assessment track cases, 168
Austin, Texas, 120
Australia, 23, 85, 95–96, 155, 157, 158, 162, 164, 165, 205, 288
Australian Capital Territory, 157
Austria, 12, 16
Authority
  role, in Wagga model, 162–164
  sharing of, 42
  statutory authority, 116, 117
Awwad, Ali Abu, 280

B

Balance and harmony, 75–76
Baldwin, Molly, 161, 183
Barron County, Wisconsin, 57, 203
Basic Principles on the Use of Restorative Justice Programmes in Criminal Matters, 281
Bata, Gina, 298
Batterer's intervention program (BIP), 308

Bazemore, G., 317
Beck, Elizabeth, 38
Behavioral guidelines, of circle process, 189–190
Bethlehem, Pennsylvania, 57, 157, 162, 165
Bethlehem Police Department, 157
Body movements, 269
Braithwaite, J., 160, 161
Bridges to Life (BTL) program, 55, 56, 301–303
Buford, Gail, 38
Burglary, 122, 131
Burr, Richard, 315
Byrd, James, Jr., 275

C

Canada, 5–6, 14, 157, 183, 205, 307
Canadian project, 307, 308
Canberra, 157, 162, 163
The Center for Justice and Peacebuilding at Eastern Mennonite University in Pennsylvania, 57
Center for Restorative Justice and Peacemaking, 37, 57
Changing Lenses, 7
Chaos theory and restorative justice, 292, 293, 319–322
Charge-Not-Denied Conferences, 148
Charge-Proven Conferences, 147
Child welfare agencies, 62, 168, 202
Child welfare cases, 96, 144, 168
Children, Young Persons, and Their Families Act of 1989, 24, 47, 147–148
Christie, Nils, 3, 115
Chronic shame, 160
Circle keeper, concept of, 192–193, 241

328   Index

Circle of understanding (offender), 200, 201
Circle process, 180, 181, 183, 195
 attributes of, 184–195
 behavioral guidelines, 189–190
 circle keeper, 192–193
 circle keeping elements, 187–195
 consensus decision making, 193–195
 outline of, 196–197
 planning and preparation of, 195–196
 ritual, 188–189
 talking piece, 190–192
 values and principles, 185–187
Circles, 19, 21, 61. *See also* Healing circles; Peacemaking circles; Repair of harm circles; Restorative justice circles; Sentencing circles
 evaluation of, 204–206
 history and development of, 182–184
 metaphor as, 179, 181
 ongoing tensions in implementing, 206–208
 paradox as, 180, 181
 premises, 180–181
 process of. *See* Circle process
 types of. *See* Circle types
Circles of Support and Accountability (COSA) program, 203, 204
Circles types, 197
 application of, 202–204
 in classroom, 203
 conflict circles, 202
 healing circles, 202
 organizational circles, 202
 sentencing circles, 198–201
 support circles, 202
 talking circles, 202
Colonial legacies, 286–287
Common human bond, 73
Communication styles, 268
Community, 41
 corrections, 308
 involvement, 313
 members, 17, 18, 47, 57, 92, 99

 support development, 18, 119
 variations in, 283–284
 in Victim-Offender Mediation (VOM), 114–115
 volunteers, 94, 120, 201, 207
Community Accountability Board Conference (CAB), 297
Community conferencing. *See* Family group conferencing (FGC)
Community Corrections Advisory Board, 16
Community group conferencing. *See* Family group conferencing (FGC)
Community Justice Forums, 157
Competence
 effectiveness, 58–59
 training, 56–57
Confidentiality, 190
 and discretion, 249–250
Conflict circles, 202
Conflict coaching, 299
Confronting Oppression, Restoring Justice (2003), 38
The Congress Government 1992, in India, 285
Connectedness/belonging, 72–73
Consensus-based agreements, 100
Consensus decision making, 193–195
Construyendo Circulos de Paz (CCP) program, 313
Cook County, Chicago, 36
Cost, 133–134
Council of Europe, 12
Counseling Female Offenders and Victims: A Strengths-Restorative Approach (2001), 38
Crime and Disorder Act, 1998, 157
Crime victims, 4, 90–91, 303
Crimes of severe violence
 Victim-Offender Dialogue (VOD). *See* Victim-Offender Dialogue (VOD)

Criminal justice system, 4, 7
  and restorative justice, different
    views of, 8
  and social work, 36–39
CU Restorative Justice Program
  (CURJ), 296–297
Cultural Context Model (CCM), 309–311
Culture dimensions. *See* Dimensions
  of culture
Custody Conferences, 147
Czech Republic, 115

D

Dakota County, Minnesota, 25
Damelin, Robi, 280
Death row cases, with Victim-Offender
  Dialogue (VOD), 229–230
Deep listening, 76, 104, 250
Defense-Initiated Victim Outreach (DIVO)
  program, 26, 38, 61, 314–316
Departments of Corrections, 14, 15, 56,
  145, 212, 217, 220, 229
Determinants, 317–318
  of facilitator's role, 239–240
Dialogue. *See also* Restorative justice
  dialogue; Surrogate dialogue
  programs in prisons
  facilitator's role during, 258–259
  meaning of, 83–84
  meeting of, 98–100
Dialogue-driven and settlement-driven
  mediation, 241–244
Dialogue process, stages for
  dialogue meeting, 98–100
  follow-up, 101
  preparation, 97–98
  reparation agreement, 100
  statistics, 96
  storytelling, as personal truth, 99–100
Dignity and worth of person, social
  work value of, 47
  dual responsibility, 51
  holistic response, 48–49

respect, 48
self-determination, 50–51
strengths perspective, 49–50
Dimensions of culture, 265
  association with state, 288
  body movements, 269
  borrowing from indigenous groups,
    287–288
  density of language, 270–271
  gender bias, 288
  globalization. *See* Globalization
  hate crimes, 275–279
  interethnic conflict, 279–281
  multicultural implications
    of practice, 267
  offender reparations, 288
  paralanguage, 269–270
  racism impact, on perceptions,
    271–274
  in restorative justice community,
    287–289
  underrepresentation of ethnic
    groups, 287
Director of the Australian Bureau of
  Crime Statistics and Research
  feels, 205
Dixon v. Alabama (1961), 294
Doerfler, David, 256
Domestic violence and restorative
  dialogue, 304
  Cultural Context Model
    (CCM), 309–311
  Domestic Violence Surrogate
    Dialogue (DVSD) program,
    308–309
  family group conferencing (FGC),
    307–308
  Minnesota Circle Sentencing (MCS),
    311–313
  summary, 313–314
Domestic Violence Surrogate
  Dialogue (DVSD) program,
  60, 308–309
Dual responsibility, 51

E

Earle, Twila Hugley, 292, 319
Effectiveness, of restorative justice, 58–59
Emerging areas of practice, 291
  Bridges to Life (BTL), 301–303
  chaos theory and restorative justice, 319–322
  Defense-Initiated Victim Outreach (DIVO), 314–316
  domestic violence. *See* Domestic violence and restorative dialogue
  impact of growth in practice, on restorative justice theory, 316–319
  innovations in practice, 293
  secular programs, 303–304
  student misconduct, in higher education, 293–300
  surrogate dialogue programs in prisons, 300–304
Empowerment, 45–47
England, 4, 10, 12, 115–116
Europe, Victim-Offender Mediation (VOM) development in, 115–116
European Committee of Ministers, 115
European Forum for Mediation and Restorative Justice, 115
European Union, 12

F

"F". *See* Forgiveness
Facilitator's role, 239–241, 252. *See also* Mediator presence; Mediator qualifications and qualities
  alternative procedures, 260–261
  bringing each to the other, concept of, 257–258
  determinants of, 239–240
  during dialogue, 258–259
  during follow-up, 259–260
  humanistic/transformative mediation. *See* Humanistic/transformative mediation
  with offenders, 254–256
  self-care significance, 261–262
  settlement-driven and dialogue-driven mediation, differences between, 241–244
  with victims, 253–254
  in Victim-Offender Dialogue (VOD), 227–229
Fairness perceptions, of Victim-Offender Mediation (VOM), 131
Family caucus, 150, 151, 152
Family group conferencing (FGC), 19, 20, 23, 38, 57, 59, 85–86, 143
  under domestic violence program, 307–308
  Family Group Decision Making (FGDM) model. *See* Family Group Decision Making (FGDM) model
  New Zealand style model. *See* New Zealand style model
  and Victim-Offender Mediation (VOM), 112
  Wagga Wagga model. *See* Wagga Wagga model
Family Group Conferencing: New Directions in Community-Centered Child and Family Practice (2000), 38
Family Group Decision Making (FGDM) model, 96
  in New Zealand, 166
  procedures for implementation and facilitation, 168–169, 170
  process of, 170
  research findings, 169, 171
  summary, 171–172
  types of, 168
Family Services in Somerset, New Jersey, 309
Farewell circle, 203

Follow-up, 123, 127–128
   facilitator's role during, 259–260
   stages for dialogue process, 101
Forensic cases, 168
Forgiveness, 74–75, 230
   as bilateral process, 233
   defining in restorative justice, 231–233
   facilitator's perspective, 233
   offender's perspective, 233
   to Victim-Offender Dialogue (VOD), 231
   victim's perspective, 232–233
Foundational framework
   harm as organizing principle, 89–91
   inclusivity, 92–94
   nondirective facilitation, 95–96
   personal accountability, in response to harm, 91–92
   voluntarism, 94–95
Fraser Region Community Justice Initiatives Association (FRCJIA), 212, 235
Funds, securing, 119

G

Galaway, Burt, 38
Genesee County, New York, 25
Georgia Council for Restorative Justice, 315
Germany, 12, 115, 128
Geske, Janine, 304
Globalization
   colonial legacies, 286–287
   community concept, variations in, 283–284
   cultural considerations, 283
   indigeneity and restorative justice, 282–287
   of restorative justice, 281
   socially stratified cultures, 284–285
Goering, E., 121–122
"Good Intentions", 280

Government of Canada, in 2003, 157–158
Greensboro: Closer to the Truth, 279
Group conferencing. *See* Family group conferencing (FGC)
Gustafson, David, 293

H

The Handbook of Victim-Offender Mediation: An Essential Guide for Practice and Research, 37
Harm as organizing principle, 89–91
"Harmed parties", 295
Harmony and balance, 75–76
Hate Crime Prevent Act, 275–276
Hate crimes, 275–279
Hawaii, 46
Healing circles, 23, 50, 201, 202, 313
Henry I, William the Conqueror's son, 4–5
Hermeneutic phenomenological approach, 70
Hmong peacemaking circles, 14
Ho, Karen, 216
Ho'oponopono process, 46
Holistic response, 48–49
Hollow Water First Nation community, 6, 23, 204
Home Office, in England, 115
Hudson, Joe, 38
Human connection, centrality of, 52–53
Human relationships, importance of, 51–54
Humanistic/transformative mediation, 21–22. *See also* Dialogue-driven and settlement-driven mediation
   mediator presence, 245–247
   mediator qualifications and qualities, 247–252
   and problem-solving mediation, 243–244

I

Inclusivity, concept of, 92–94
Indigeneity and restorative justice, 282–287
Indigenous peoples, 6, 43, 46, 182, 282
Inequities, by criminal justice system, 44–45, 265
Information sharing, in New Zealand FGC, 150, 152
In-prison programs, 55, 300, 301
Intake phase. *See* Referral, phase
Integrity, social work value of
   trustworthiness, 54–55
   truth telling, 55–56
Integrity board, 54, 295, 296
Intention-to-Charge Conferences, 147
Interethnic conflict, 266, 279–281
The International Institute for Restorative Practices in Bethlehem, Pennsylvania, 57
Intervention, restorative justice as, 81–107
Intuitive decision making, respect for, 250–251
Irish Republican Army (IRA), 15
Israel, 15, 279, 280
Issacs, William, 83

J

The Jerry Lee Program on Randomized Controlled Experiments in Restorative Justice, 58
Jewish community, 15
Judeo-Christian Bible, 6, 69
Judicial officer, 295

K

Kansas Department of Corrections, 145
Kitchener, Ontario, 10, 113, 115
Ku Klux Klan, 279

L

Language, density of, 270–271
Legislative statutes for Victim-Offender Mediation (VOM), in United States, 116–118
Lincoln Center Elementary School, 206

M

Making amends, 24, 46, 100
Making righting a wrong, 75, 127
Man Alive Violence Intervention and Prevention Curriculum, 313
Management information system
   in Victim-Offender Mediation (VOM) program design, 121
Maori, in New Zealand, 6, 16, 46, 85, 146–147
Marquette University Law School Restorative Justice Initiative, 304
Martinson report, 36
Maximalist model, in restorative justice, 317
McCold, Paul, 317
McElra, Fred, 147
McVeigh, Timothy, 315
Mediation, humanistic. *See* Humanistic/transformative mediation
"Mediation in Penal Matters", 115
Mediation phase, 123, 125–127
Mediator presence, 245
   being centered, 246
   being congruent, 247
   being connected to values, beliefs, and highest purpose, 246–247
   connecting with humanity of participants, 247
Mediator qualifications and qualities, 247
   being nondirective results, 251
   capacity for intensity and deep listening, 250
   confidentiality and discretion, 249–250

intuitive decision making, respect for, 250–251
knowing what not to do, 252
process understanding, 251
tolerance for uncertainty, 250
victim-centered and offender sensitive, ability to remain, 249
willingness to listen to all sides, 248
Mediator's role, 128. *See also* Facilitator's role
Mennonite Central Committee, 10
Minnesota Circle Sentencing (MCS), 311–313
Minnesota Department of Corrections (MDOC), 56, 303
Minnesota v. Pearson, 2002, 118
Minnesota, St. Paul, 14, 16
Mixed gender culture circle, 311
Mock scenarios, 229
Moral motivations, 303
Motivators for change
 positive energy flow, 104–106
 process orientation, 101–102
 respectful interaction, 103–104
 safety establishment, 102–103
Multicultural implications of practice, 267
 body movements, 269
 density of language, 270–271
 paralanguage, 269–270
 racism impact, on perceptions, 271–274
Mutual Responsibility Conference Models, 297

N

NASW (National Association of Social Workers) News, in 2005, 38
NASW Code of Ethics, 40
National Conference of Charities and Corrections, 36
National Organization for Victim Assistance (NOVA), 11
National Restorative Justice Training Institute, 37

Navajo peacemaker courts, 5
New South Wales Government, 157
New Zealand, 6, 16, 23–24, 46, 47, 57, 85, 307
 family group decision making. *See* Family Group Decision Making (FGDM) model
 style model. *See* New Zealand style model
New Zealand Ministry of Justice, 137
New Zealand style model
 Children, Young Persons, and Their Families Act of 1989, 147–148
 conference, 152–153
 family group conference, 146, 154–155
 preparation, 151–152
 principles and goals, 148–149
 procedures for conducting, 149–155
 process of, 150
 research findings, 153–154
 summary, 155, 156
Newfoundland and Labrador FGDM project, 171
Nondirective facilitation, 82, 95–96, 251
North Carolina Family Group Conferencing Project, 307
Norway, 115
"Nuisance party", 297

O

O'Connell, Terry, 157
Offender accountability, 86, 313
Offenders, facilitator's role with, 254–256
Office of Juvenile Justice and Delinquency Prevention (OJJDP), 78
Office of Student Conflict Resolution (OSCR), 298–299
Ohio, 14, 215, 221, 223
Orange County, California, 13
Organizational circles, 202
OSCR Spectrum Model program, 299
"Other", restorative justice dialogue type, 20

P

Palestinian community, 15
Panchayat, 285
Paralanguage, 269–270
Parents Circle-Families Forum, 61, 280
Participation rates and reasons, in Victim-Offender Mediation (VOM), 129
    fairness, 131
    participant satisfaction, 130
Peacemaking circles, 17, 19, 38, 86–87. *See also* Circles
    balance and harmony, 75
Peacemaking Circles: From Crime to Community, 183
Penal mediation, 12
Pennell, J., 307
Pennsylvania, 14, 57, 117, 162
Personal accountability, in response to harm, 91–92, 127
Person-in-environment perspective, 49
Planning and preparation
    circle process requirement, 195–196
Plans, in New Zealand FGC process, 150, 153
Police-led conferencing, 157, 162, 163
Positive energy creation, 104–106
Possible witnesses, 44
Pranis, K., 99, 183
Preparation
    for dialogue, 97–98
    for mediation phase, 123, 124–125
    New Zealand style model, 151–152
    phase, in facilitator's role, 257
    and planning, in circle process, 195–196
    stage, in Victim-Offender Dialogue (VOD) procedure, 221–223
PreSentence Circle, 312
Prigogine, Ilya, 319
Prison Fellowship, 303
Problem-solving and humanistic/transformative mediation, 243–244

Process orientation, concept of, 101–102
Project Greenlight, in New York City, 145
Project Turnaround, 154–155
Purist model, in restorative justice, 317

Q

Quakers, 67, 93
Quantum change, 72
Queensland Department of Justice conferencing program, 164

R

Racism impact, on perceptions, 271–274, 287
Ramat Efal, 280
Recidivism, 23, 132–133, 146
Referral(s), 95, 199, 307, 311
    for family group conferencing, 85
    phase, 122, 123, 124
    sources of, 119–120, 137, 207
Rehabilitation, 36
Reintegrative shaming, 72, 158, 161
Reintegrative Shaming Experiment. *See* RISE (Reintegrative Shaming Experiment)
Relationship building, between victim and offender, 53–54
Religiosity, spirituality and, 69–70
Remorse, expressing, 56, 73, 99, 100, 126, 161, 304. *See also* Apologies
Repair of harm circles, 19
Repairing harm, 3–4, 126, 127
    and restitution issues, 131–132
Reparation, 22–23, 100, 131–132, 260, 288, 296, 297, 299
Repentance, 73–74
Research findings
    in Family Group Decision Making (FGDM) model, 169, 171
    in New Zealand style model, 153–154
    in Wagga Wagga model, 164–166
Residence Education and Housing, 298

Resolve to Stop the Violence Project (RSVP) program, 313
Respectful interaction, 103–104
Respectful process, between victim and offender, 48
"Respondents", 295
Restitution, in FGC, 165. *See also* Reparation
Restorative Community Justice: A Call to Action, 11
Restorative group conferencing. *See* Family group conferencing (FGC)
Restorative justice. *See also* Circles; Dimensions of culture; Emerging areas of practice; Facilitator's role; Family group conferencing (FGC); Social work core values; Spirituality; Victim-Offender Dialogue (VOD); Victim-Offender Mediation (VOM)
  antecedents to, 4–6
  assessing restorativeness, by type of practice, 87–88
  chaos theory and, 292, 293, 319–322
  components of, 88–106
  creating context for change during dialogue, 101–106
  and criminal justice, 8
  definition of, 6–10
  dialogue, meaning of, 83–84. *See also* Restorative justice dialogue
  family group conferencing, 85–86
  foundational framework, 88–96
  history and development of, 10–13
  as intervention, 81–107
  opportunities for expanding vision, 24–27
  overview of, 3–13
  peacemaking circles, 86–87
  in practice, 13–18, 59–62
  program examples, 13–15
  questions for future, 27–29
  and retributive justice, 7, 8
  as social movement, 1–29
  stages for dialogue process, 96–101
  systemic change examples, 15–18
  Victim-Offender Mediation (VOM), 84–85
"Restorative Justice: A Model of Healing", 38
Restorative Justice Across the East and the West (2008), 38
Restorative Justice Approaches to Elder Abuse Project in Ontario, Canada, 203
Restorative justice circles, 19
Restorative justice dialogue, 18
  description of, 19–21
  evidence-based practice, 22–24
  humanistic mediation, 21–22
  types of, 19–21
Restorative Justice: International Perspectives (1998), 38
Restorativeness, by type of practice, 87–88
Restoring Peace model, 301, 302
Restoring Peace: Using Lessons From Prison to Mend Broken Relationships, 301
Retributive justice, 7
  and restorative justice, 8
"The reunification of human culture", 319
Reverence, defined, 69
Righting a wrong, making, 75, 127
RISE (Reintegrative Shaming Experiment), 157
Rituals, 74, 76–77, 188–189
Roca, in Boston, 60, 97, 183, 188, 202
Rogers, Carl, 245
Royal Canadian Mounted Police (RCMP), in 1997, 157

S

Safety, establishment of, 98, 102–103
Safety planning model, 307
Saleeby, Dennis, 245
Same sex groups, 310
San Francisco Sheriff's Department, 313
Saratoga County District Attorney's office, 296

Satir, Virginia, 55, 245
Satisfaction, with Victim-Offender Mediation (VOM), 130
Schrage, Jennifer Meyer, 298
Schwartz, William, 245
Secular in-prison restorative justice programs, 303–304
"Seed planting", 17–18
Self-care significance, facilitator's role, 261–262
Self-determination, 50–51
Self-respect, 48
Sentencing Act (2002), 47
Sentencing circles, 19, 60, 182, 183, 198–201. *See also* Circles
  balance and harmony, 76
Servant leadership, 42–43
Services, in restorative justice, 40
  servant leadership, 42–43
  sharing of authority, 42
  voluntarism, 41–42
Settlement-driven and dialogue-driven mediation, 241–244
Severe violence crimes
  Victim-Offender Dialogue (VOD). *See* Victim-Offender Dialogue (VOD)
Seward Montessori Elementary School, 206
Shakopee Women's Center, 303
Shakopee Women's Prison in Minnesota, 304
Shalom community, 6
Shame, 72, 160, 161
Sharing
  of authority, in social work, 42
  of information, in New Zealand FGC, 150, 152
Shepard, Matthew, 275
Shuttle mediation process, 19, 112, 116, 299
Skidmore College, 26, 54, 295–296
Small groups model, 301–302
Social Compact, 312

Social justice
  challenging inequities, 44–45
  empowerment, 45–47
  mediation, 299
  in social work value, 43
Social movement, restorative justice as, 1–29
Social Work Abstracts (2006), 38
Social work core values
  competence, 56–59
  and criminal justice system, 36–39
  dignity and worth of person, 47–51
  human relationships, importance of, 51–54
  integrity, 54–56
  movement grounded in, 35
  and restorative justice principles in practice, 59–62
  restorative values and social work practice, 39–59
  services, in restorative justice, 40–43
  social justice, 43–47
  trustworthiness, 54–55
  truth telling, 55–56
Social worker, 149
Socially stratified cultures, 284–285
South Africa, 15, 279
South African Truth and Reconciliation Commission (TRC), 279
South Saint Paul Restorative Justice Council, 41, 202
"Spectrum of Resolution Options" menu, 298
Spirituality
  challenges, 68
  common human bond, 73
  components of, 71–77
  connectedness/belonging, 72–73
  defined, 69
  forgiveness, 74–75
  harmony and balance, 75–76
  making right a wrong, 75
  and religiosity, 69–70

repentance, 73–74
and restorative justice, 68–69
rituals, 76–77
study methodology, 70
transformation, 71–72
unexplained spirit/supernatural, 77
Sponsors, 310
St. Paul, Minnesota, 14, 16, 205
Stakeholders, 7, 20, 43, 45, 119
Statutory authority, for Victim-Offender Mediation (VOM), 116, 117
"Stay of adjudication", 312
Stewart, Barry, 183
Storytelling, as personal truth, 99–100
Strengths perspective, in social work, 49–50
Stuart, Barry, 179
Student misconduct, in higher education, 293–300
  Skidmore College, 295–296
  The University of Colorado, in Boulder, 296–298, 300
  The University of Michigan, 298–300
Supernatural/spirit, unexplained, 77
Support circles, 202
Surrogate dialogue programs in prisons, 300
  Bridges to Life (BTL), 301–303
  secular programs, 303–304
Survivor Restorative Advisory Committee, 313
"Sycamore Tree" project, 303

T

Talking circles, 183, 202
Talking piece, 19–20, 86, 190–192
Te Whanau Awhina project, 154–155
Texas, 14, 55, 120, 136, 169, 171, 212, 215, 220, 234, 301
Thames Valley, in England, 157, 163, 164
Timor Leste, 56
Training, in restorative justice dialogues, 56–57

Transformation, in spirituality, 71–72
Tribal Justice Exchange in Syracuse, New York, 26
Trustworthiness, 54–55
Truth and Reconciliation Commission (TRC)
  in South Africa, 15, 279
  in Timor Leste, 56
Truth telling, 55–56
Tubman Family Alliance, in Minneapolis, 311, 312

U

"UN Basic Principles on the Use of Restorative Justice Programs in Criminal Matters", 12
UN Economic and Social Council, 281
UN Handbook on Restorative Justice Programmes, 281
United Kingdom, 16, 57, 115–116, 131, 168
United Nations, 12, 281
United Nations Congress on Crime Prevention, 12
United States, 37, 44, 118, 161, 214, 303
The University of Colorado, in Boulder, 26, 296–298, 300
The University of Michigan, 298–300
The University of Minnesota, 37, 57

V

Values and principles, of circle process, 185–187
van Wormer, 37, 38
Vandalism, 122
Vermont Reparation Board program, 23
Victim-centered process, 4, 7
Victim-centered restorative justice, 249
Victim-Offender Conference (VOC), 297. *See also* Victim-Offender Mediation (VOM)

Victim-Offender Dialogue (VOD), 59, 61, 97, 213. *See also* Victim-Offender Mediation (VOM)
  characteristics of, 216–218
  death row cases, 229–230
  facilitator role, 227–229
  follow-up, 226–227
  forgiveness question. *See* Forgiveness
  history and development, 214–216
  meeting, 223–226
  preparation, 221–223
  procedure, 220–227
  readiness, foundation for, 221
  reasons for meeting, 218–220
  research on, 234–235
  in severe violence crimes, 211
Victim-Offender Mediation (VOM), 10–11, 12, 13, 15, 16, 19, 20, 38, 84–85, 111–112, 213. *See also* Victim-Offender Dialogue (VOD)
  community support development, 119
  cost, 133–134
  development of, in Europe, 115–116
  dimensions of, effectiveness, 128–136
  follow-up phase, 123, 127–128
  history and development, 113–118
  legislative statutes, in United States, 116–118
  mediation phase, 123, 125–127
  mediator's role, 128
  ongoing concerns, 136–137
  participation rates and reasons, 129–131
  preparation for mediation phase, 123, 124–125
  primary and secondary goals, 118–119
  procedure and stages, 122–128
  process studies, 134–136
  procuring funding, 119
  program design, 120–122
  program implementation, 118–122
  recidivism, 132–133
  referral/intake phase, 122, 123, 124
  referrals sources, 119–120
  research developments in, 134–136
  restitution and repair of damage issues, 131–132
  statutory authority for, 116–117
  Victim Satisfaction with Offender Dialogue Scale (VSODS), 134
Victim-Offender Reconciliation Programs (VORPs), 10, 11, 37, 113. *See also* Victim-Offender Mediation (VOM)
Victim Outreach Specialist (VOS), 315
Victim restoration, 313
Victim Satisfaction with Offender Dialogue Scale (VSODS), development of, 134, 260
Victim survivors, needs of, 314, 315
Victims, facilitator's role with, 253–254
Victims Services Division of the Texas Department of Criminal Justice (TDCJ), 215
VOCARE (Victims, Offenders, Community, A Restorative Experience) Project, 303
Voluntarism, 41–42, 57, 94–95

W

Wagga Wagga Juvenile Cautioning Process, 155
Wagga Wagga model
  family group conference, 95–96, 155, 157–158
  procedures for conducting, 158, 159
  process of, 159
  research findings, 164–166
  role of authority in, 162–164
  summary, 166, 167
  theoretical and explanatory framework, 158, 160–161
Walgrave, L., 317

Washington County Court
    Services, 16, 17
Washington State Reformatory, 303–304
West African nation of Liberia, 15
Wilson, Jon, 216, 249
Wisconsin Supreme Court Justice, 14

Y

Young offenders, family group
    conferencing for, 146, 155
Young Offenders Act, in 1998, 157
Youth conferences, in United
    Kingdom, 57

Youth Court
    magistrate, 158
    in New Zealand, 147
Youth Criminal Justice Act, 157–158
Youth justice
    coordinators, 149
    in New Zealand, 149
Youth Justice Board for England and
    Wales, 47

Z

Zehr, Howard, 37, 148, 315